Walter Oakeshott

Take these two lives, active and contemplative, sithen God hath
sent thee both, and use them both, the one with the other. By
that one life thou shalt bring forth fruit of many good deeds in
help of thine even-Christians; and that is by active life. And by
that other thou shalt be made fair, clean and bright in behold-
ing the sovereign brightness that is God.

WALTER HILTON (d. 1396), *Epistle of the Mixed Life*, ch.9

Walter Oakeshott

A Diversity of Gifts

JOHN DANCY

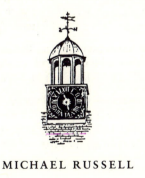

MICHAEL RUSSELL

For Jasper

ΔΙΑΔΟΧΩΙ ΣΥΓΓΡΑΦΕΥΣ

First published in Great Britain 1995
by Michael Russell (Publishing) Ltd
Wilby Hall, Wilby, Norwich NR16 2JP

Typeset in Sabon by The Typesetting Bureau
Allen House, East Borough, Wimborne, Dorset
Printed and bound in Great Britain
by Biddles Ltd, Guildford and King's Lynn

Indexed by the author

ISBN 0 85955 219 5

Contents

List of Illustrations

1 A chariot team of four horses, from a fifth-century Greek vase contemporary with Euripides' *Hippolytus*. This rare drawing by WFO was made as a programme cover for the Balliol Players' production of the *Hippolytus* in 1926, then inscribed and presented to Philip Mason, by whose courtesy it is reproduced. Photograph by Mark Mason.

2 Walter and Noel outside the church of St Michael and All Angels, Aston Tirrold, after their wedding on 11 April 1928.

3 WFO as High Master of St Paul's School. Presentation portrait, on his leaving in 1946, by William Dring, RA; reproduced by permission of the present High Master.

4 Two illuminated initials from the Winchester Bible (reproduced at 80% of actual size), the work of two of the artists distinguished by WFO. The 'V' to the book of Jeremiah, by the Leaping Figures Master, shows the call of the prophet: the artist's style conveys the tiptoe excitement and apprehension on the part of the young man (Jeremiah, 1, 6). The 'R' to the Prayer of Jeremiah (ch. 5 of the book of Lamentations), by the Morgan Master, shows the prophet later in life, grey-bearded and sombre, appealing to the God ('a very Byzantine Pantocrator' – WFO) by whom he feels abandoned. Photographs by Miki Slingsby, copyright the Dean and Chapter of Winchester Cathedral.

5a Bust of the Virgin Mary in mosaic made c. 705 for the old basilica of St Peter, Rome. It was removed in 1609 to Orte Cathedral, S. Italy, when the inscription and the outer gold background were added. WFO tracked it down there in 1965, and wrote of it in *The Mosaics of Rome* that 'it has a grace and delicacy of touch which is outstanding'.

5b Bust of the Virgin and Child in stained glass, made by Thomas of

Preface

When Walter Oakeshott's children asked me in 1992 to write their father's life, I little knew what I was undertaking. The work has proved exceptionally rewarding, for two reasons.

First, I have learned a great deal more about this man who was already to me both a hero and an enigma. I now see that his range of interests and achievements was even wider than I had imagined. Yet what I have learned, in that and other ways, has not resolved the enigma, only clarified the terms in which it has to be stated. This book therefore poses more questions than it solves.

Secondly, the sources available are of high quality. Most notably his family has given me access to a remarkable collection of letters, particularly some 1,300 exchanged between him and his wife Noel from their engagement in 1926 to her death fifty years later. The early ones, up to 1938, are unusually revealing on both sides; and many of Walter's, from all periods, are sheer delight. His scholarly writings could be heavy. His letters, to family and others, sparkle like his conversation. I have drawn upon them extensively, preferring wherever possible to tell his story in his own words.

He also left a good number of occasional pieces. Though some of those are published, most are not. The best of them are addresses, whether lectures or sermons, given to a select audience to whom he could speak in some sense as friends. Then about 1970 he began to note down fragments of autobiography. Those which concern his public career he entrusted for safe keeping to colleagues or to bodies such as the Pilgrim Trust. There is also extant, in family hands, a larger and more systematic narrative entitled 'Odyssey in a Cockleshell', whose chapters mainly record his discoveries in art and literature. (p. 321) Many of these pieces were written at a time when his memory for detail, especially dates, was distinctly unreliable, and therefore have to be handled with care.

Apart from his own writings and those of his family, I have been able to draw on a variety of sources. These fall into three main categories. First are the archives of the various educational institutions for which he worked during most of his life. Second is the collection known as the Walter Oakeshott Papers, held in the Getty Center for the History of Art and the Humanities, Santa Monica, California. Most of the Getty material concerns his scholarly work, but there is a good deal else as well, including four manuscript notebooks of sermons and the typescript of his unpublished book 'History and the Gospels' (p. 260). My third kind of source is the testimony, whether written or oral, of friends and colleagues who knew him at various stages of his life.

These sources I have used in somewhat cavalier fashion. In quoting from either his own works or other evidence, I have identified the source only where it might affect either the reliability of the quotation or the interpretation to be put upon it. For this book does not purport to be a work of scholarship in the strict sense. By the same token I provide no bibliography of the books and other secondary sources I have used. In each case I aim to give just enough information for the curious to pursue the matter further.

My last source is my own memory. I first met Walter Oakeshott as a schoolboy, at Winchester in 1938. We classed him, in the cant of those days, as 'a worshipful man'. Then, having been invited during the war by my old headmaster Spencer Leeson to go back on the staff, I learned in 1946 that he was himself leaving for a parish. I wrote to say that I was no longer sure I wanted to take up the invitation, 'unless by any chance it is Mr Oakeshott who succeeds you'. It was, and I went. For five years I served under him, and quickly came to admire and love him.

I have drawn on my own memories of that period, anonymously except for this one. In 1955, after he and I had both left the staff, I went back to visit the school and was standing by the headmaster's notice board when a boy I knew came up. I asked him how the new headmaster compared with the old one. 'Ah well.' he said wistfully, 'Mr Oakeshott – we would have followed him to the ends of the earth. But,' he added, loyalty taking over, 'Mr Lee is a very good headmaster too. He's done a lot for the school.' I asked him what sort of thing. 'Oh,' said the boy, looking round for inspiration and eventually finding it, 'Oh, I know: he's replaced the 50 watt bulb over this notice board by a 100 watt bulb.' Some years later, when I thought it was safe to do so, I told Walter that story. He looked away in silent embarrassment, and I knew I had offended.

Nevertheless we kept in fairly close touch. I was with him in 1959 on one of his Hellenic Cruises, and went to see him from time to time at Lincoln and Eynsham. He lent my wife and me the Bell House in 1951, and similarly offered us the flat in Rome, though we could not accept. On two occasions after Noel's death he came to stay with us.

By chance, I find that I have also known most of the people mentioned in this book. Of those I did not know, the greatest loss is his sister Maggie. But I would have liked also to have known Vere Hodge, Maurice Tyson, Harold Cox, Hugh Keen and Folliott Sandford. Without their testimony my account may well lack an important dimension for each phase of his life.

I have one other serious handicap in writing this book. My knowledge of the medieval world and its art is slight: what little I know is caught from him. I have therefore relied heavily upon his friends and ex-pupils such as Professors Charles Mitchell and Michael Kauffmann, and Dr Maurice Keen of Balliol. Mitchell explained to me the importance of Saxl. Kauffmann and Keen independently adduced the notion of 'the mixed life', and Keen supplied the quotation I have used as an epigraph. Keen has also, among much other help and encouragement, let me see in draft the admirable appreciation of Oakeshott which he wrote, with Jonathan Alexander, for the *Proceedings of the British Academy*, 84, 1994, 431ff. In that same field – but not in that field alone – I am much in the debt of Jasper Gaunt, Walter's grandson. His knowledge is extensive, not only of his grandfather's writings on the Winchester Bible but also of various tangential matters: Beazley's work on Greek vases, Walter's collection of books and works of art, and Noel's scholarship. All this he has put at my disposal, together with his list of Walter's published works.

For the rest, my first debt is to Walter's children. Helena, Evelyn, Robert and Rose have compounded the honour of their original invitation by providing me with all the documents they could lay hands on, by suggesting lines of inquiry, and by correcting the facts and emphases of my drafts. They have also generously met all my expenses. With family belong Walter's two earliest girl friends, both happily alive: Hilda Duckett and Cecilia Russell-Smith (*née* Streeten). Each of them is blessed with an evergreen memory, and with a charm which renders a part of his life immediately intelligible.

A number of other people have not only given important information or advice but also been kind enough to vet relevant sections of

my draft: Dr Arnold Taylor (ch. 3); Mr Alan Cook, Dr Geoffrey
Woodhead and Mr Hugh Arnold (ch. 5); Dr John Harvey and Mr
John Gammell (ch. 6); the Revd Dr Vivian Green and Dr Donald
Whitton (ch. 7, Lincoln); Mrs Rosalind Brain and Mr Michael Brock
(ch. 7, Oxford); Mr Myles Glover (the Skinners' Company). Others
who are not much quoted in the text but have given valuable help of
various kinds are Miss Irene Allen, Mr John Allport, Dr Christopher
de Hamel, Mr David Kemp, Mrs Janet Lynch (*née* Roseveare), Mrs
Jean Mitchell, Mrs Phyllis Owen (*née* Alcock), Sir Hans Singer, Lady
Stubbs, Mrs Helen Wright.

To various public bodies are due warm thanks: formally, for
giving me largely unfettered access to their archives; personally, to
their agents for helping me find my way about. I list them in rough
chronological order of Oakeshott's life: the Skinners' Company and
Tonbridge School, with Mr John Parsons, Clerk to the Governors;
the Master and Fellows of Balliol College, with Dr John Jones,
Archivist, and Dr Penny Bullock, Librarian: the Warden and Fellows
of Winchester College, with Dr Roger Custance, Archivist, and Mr
David Vellacott, formerly Bursar; the Trustees of the Pilgrim Trust,
with the Hon. Alastair Hoyer Millar, Secretary; the Mercers' Com-
pany, with Mrs Anne Sutton, Archivist, and St Paul's School, with
Mr Christopher Dean, Archivist; the Director of the Warburg In-
stitute, with Dr Anne-Marie Meyer; Messrs Faber, with Mr John
Bodley; the Headmasters' Conference; Mrs Fiona Piddock, Librarian
of Lincoln College; the University of Oxford, with Dr A. J. Dorey,
Registrar, and Mr Simon Bailey, Archivist; the Oxford University
Press, with Mr Peter Foden, Archivist; the Dean and Chapter of
Winchester Cathedral, with Mr John Hardacre, Librarian.

Collectively, all these people, together with others too numerous to
mention, have given the kind and the amount of help a biographer
dreams of. Its benefits are visible on every page. There are also three
others to whom the book as a whole owes a special debt. My wife
Angela not only brought the dedication of an opsimath to the use
of the word-processor, but also, as an enemy of gush, curbed my
worst excesses of style. Anthony Sheil, out of affection for Walter and
Robert, gave professional advice on format and publication. But it is
above all to Philip Mason that the book owes its final tone and shape.
To his judgement of tone he brought his knowledge of Walter from
their Balliol days together. To his advice on shape he brought his own
experience as an acclaimed biographer (under the name of Philip

Woodruff). He gave this advice over three years in spite of growing blindness. I have tried always to take it. Where I have failed, as with my other sources and helpers, the fault is mine.

Mousehole, 1995   J.C.D.

Prologue

If you go into the British Museum and turn right, you shortly find yourself in a large exhibition room which displays the treasures of the British Library. The nearest show-cases contain the outstanding manuscripts of English literature from its beginnings. Of the earliest twelve of these, two were 'discovered' in this century by one man – and he was not a professional scholar but a schoolmaster. Walter Oakeshott was thirty-one, on the staff of Winchester College, when he recognized a medieval manuscript in the school's possession as a text (in fact the *only* existing manuscript text) of the *Morte d'Arthur* by 'Sir Thomas Malleore, Knyght prisoner'. He was forty-nine, and himself Headmaster, when he recognized a manuscript notebook in his own possession as being in the hand of Sir Walter Raleigh. It contained the notes which Raleigh made, when imprisoned in the Tower of London, as another knight prisoner, in preparation for his *History of the World*; and also a hitherto unknown poem of Raleigh's to Queen Elizabeth.

Even apart from this unique 'double', Oakeshott's career was remarkable enough. His public reputation – and his bread and butter – derived from the posts he held as High Master of St Paul's School, Headmaster of Winchester College, Rector of Lincoln College, Oxford, and Vice-Chancellor of Oxford University. These posts constituted the central stem of his career. But two branches sprang off that stem, one on each side. One of them (that on the left, one might say) led off into public affairs, including politics, which nearly claimed him in the first half of his life. The right-hand branch led off into scholarship, especially medieval art; and it did claim him in the second.

But for the life of one who was knighted 'for services to medieval literature', a more appropriate model is provided by a distinction commonly made in his beloved Middle Ages. Some men, on that analysis, are called to the active life, some to the contemplative life, But there was a third approved vocation, to the 'mixed' life, part active and part contemplative. This mixed life was especially suited to those 'in care and gouvernaunce of others or in temporal soverynte'. Admittedly the contemplation which writers like Walter Hilton had in mind was religious. But in Oakeshott's case, whatever his religious views – and they varied during his life – his love of beauty in art and poetry was so intense that the language of spiritual devotion is not inappropriate. Moreover, being himself inspired by beauty, he was able in turn to inspire the love of it in his pupils.

Remarkable as Oakeshott's career was, to anyone who knew him it is nothing like as fascinating as his personality. 'A most elusive man, and the most elusive of Vice-Chancellors' was the verdict of his senior university official at Oxford.[1] At every turn of view the colour of the shot silk[2] alters, and contradictions come to light. Many of the contradictions arose from the tensions inherent in the mixed life: between worldliness and unworldliness, between the public and the private man. Others may be explained by a remark he made of himself at the age of about sixty: 'I have felt like a different person in every different stage of my life.'[3]

Highly ambitious, he still had all the qualities of the gentle scholar: he never pushed, shouted or intrigued, he hated the limelight, and could not take rows – 'literally could not breathe'.[4] He knew all the right people and many 'important' ones, but lacked all self-importance. An effective head of major educational institutions, he was bored by administration, disliked making decisions, and was not interested in 'education'. Brilliant teacher and inspirer of sixth-formers, he rejected the chance to teach undergraduates, and wrote nothing about teaching. Impressive preacher, and scholar of the text of the Bible as well as its decoration, he claimed to have been a 'lifelong agnostic'. In his main field of study he could afford to trust his eye and his flair; but his books lack the normal scholarly complement of notes, indices and bibliography. Always anxious about money, he was generous with expensive presents. Beneath his genuine reserve and apparent remoteness there bubbled extravagant enthusiasms. Even in his marriage contradiction appears: his wife was a scholar in a closely related field, yet they were separated by 'contrary imaginations': he romantic, she classical. Successful, loved, and regarded by many as saintly, he was given to frequent bouts of anxiety and self-doubt. These ingredients, seasoned as they were with wit and topped with liberal dollops of charm, combined to produce a flavour of rare subtlety. How did it come about?

I

Childhood and Schooling

Walter Fraser Oakeshott was born in South Africa on 11 November 1903. His father and grandfather, like the men in the five generations before them, were doctors. The exigencies of medical practice account both for Walter's birth abroad and for his return to England.

Dr John, his grandfather, was born in 1815, and had his first job as a ship's surgeon in the China Seas before Hong Kong was thought of. When he had made enough to retire from the sea, he joined a practice in Highgate. There he was well respected in his profession and also served for twenty-one years on the Managing Committee of the Highgate Literary and Scientific Institution. Alas, in 1879 Dr John was knocked down and killed while crossing Northumberland Avenue.[1]

For his funeral 'the shops in the village [of Highgate] were closed, and the greatest sympathy was expressed by all classes'. The Institution paid him a handsome tribute. 'His kindly unpretending manner, unselfishness, and goodness of heart, had endeared him to a large circle of friends. It is well known that scarcely a week of his life passed without some unspoken act of professional generosity or disinterested kindness.' Such sentiments were common in those days. But if one may reason *a posteritate*, they may well have been justified.

Dr John's friends and admirers paid him two other tributes. First, they got a street in Highgate renamed after him – Oakeshott Avenue.[2] Secondly thay took a practical measure. In view of 'the melancholy circumstances under which his life was so sadly and suddenly terminated', they set up an Oakeshott Testimonial Fund. The Fund was managed by a committee of twenty-eight, with two MPs as treasurers. Its purpose was to help his widow who was left in financial straits. Her seven eldest children, all girls, were mostly off her hands, but the two boys were still at school. The elder of them, Walter, was desperate to follow the family profession. On leaving school he took a job in the Survey Office to keep himself while he studied medicine at St Bartholomew's Hospital, where he became a gold medallist.

But even then he could not afford to buy into a practice in England. After three months in 1889 as a *locum tenens* in Tonbridge, he was offered a post at Lydenburg, a small country town in the Transvaal. He was to be employed by the Lisbon Berlyn Mining Company at a salary of £200 p.a. all found, rising to £300 p.a. after two years.

His responsibilities to the Company were not confined to health. He was also expected 'to advise the management on chemical matters, and take photographs of distant workings'. Before his arrival the nearest doctor was a week's journey away, so the Company had a surgery built under his direction. From that base Dr Walter soon established himself in civic life. He was active in the Lydenburg (social) Club, where British and Afrikaners mixed on friendly terms and the minutes were recorded in both languages.[3] As a committee member he waged a long and ultimately successful campaign to lift the ban on Sunday billiards. Among the other members he was delighted to find a public librarian 'who used to be at the Bodleian – it was a great break to get hold of people who could talk'.

When the Boer War broke out, Lydenburg was for a time in the front line, and Dr Walter was appointed Acting District Surgeon. In September 1901 British troops entered the town. The Boers commandeered all the cattle, including three cows of his, and withdrew into laager in the hills. From there they sent a message the following month asking him to come out and treat a case of strangulated hernia. With the permission of the British authorities he went out and brought the patient back to hospital – three days each way by bullock-cart. In December 1901 the *Pall Mall Gazette* sent a reporter to interview him and 'discover the truth' about the war. The article describes him as one who 'knows the Boers well and, though his country's friend, has many friends among them'; and the description is borne out by his surprisingly even-handed answers to the reporter's questions.

A year or two earlier he had proposed marriage to Kathleen Fraser, a local girl of Scottish-American stock, daughter of a colleague in the Mining Company. Since he was now well into his thirties they lost no time in starting a family. Four children were born in quick succession, of whom young Walter, born on 11 November 1903, was the third. Then, sadly, history repeated itself. In July 1905, when Dr Walter was only forty-one, he caught pneumonia on a visit to a patient and died. By the time of his death he had risen to be Mayor, and on the day of his funeral, as of his father's, 'all the stores in town were closed'. He too had left a widow with children but no money. Moreover the Frasers were not in a position to offer Kathleen the help she needed.

Meanwhile, however, the fortunes of the Oakeshotts in England had taken a turn for the better. Two of Dr Walter's sisters had married well but had no children of their own. Collectively they offered to look after the young family. So for England they set off. Young Walter was just old enough, at three and a half, to remember the 100-mile journey to the railhead by bullock-cart. 'Technologically', he said rather wistfully at the end of his life in recalling the journey, 'I belong to the age of Abraham.' He only went back to South Africa once, but it exercised a permanent hold upon his imagination.

By the generosity of her sisters-in-law, Kathleen was enabled to rent a house in Pirbright in Surrey as a home base. The children, who knew her as Moogie, were as devoted to her as she to them. But all she could provide was love and the bare necessities of living. Food was plain. Clothes, even shoes, were handed down; Walter's bad feet in later life were sometimes attributed to wearing his brother Jack's shoes. Pocket money was meagre.

Everything else came from 'the aunts'. The aunts invited them to stay, with parties at Christmas; and they paid for summer holidays at Brodick on the Isle of Arran. They also met the cost of education, Auntie Harriet for Jack and Auntie Jess for Walter. This meant boarding school from the age of eight: in Walter's case, Westerleigh in Sussex followed by Tonbridge in Kent.

The financial circumstances of his childhood left a permanent mark on Walter. Poverty, though relative, fuelled a burning ambition, tempered by a lifelong anxiety about money. Gratitude prompted him to family generosity in turn, first to his mother, who shared his dislike of being a poor relation, then to his favourite sister Maggie. When brother Jack became a general, Walter offered what he could, to put him up for the Athenaeum. But Jack wanted no charity. Walter too had resented the charity – and felt all the guiltier for that.

He never published anything about his youth, except for his schooldays at Tonbridge. But his letters and other unpublished writings, mostly from later in his life, contain some illuminating vignettes: incidents remembered for their significance and perhaps influence. For example, 'Auntie Harrie[t] used to have Shakespearean readings in her house once a week, in Blackheath, with sherry and cake provided for refreshment.' Walter recalled especially 'Wolsey's great speech from *Henry VIII* on ambition'. It is true that he did not himself follow Wolsey's general advice to Cromwell to 'fling away ambition'. But specific items he did accept: 'Love thyself last'; and 'still in thy right hand carry gentle peace, to silence envious tongues'. Therein resides one of the central paradoxes of his character.

But the city was not his natural habitat. Pirbright was homely because 'a car was such an unusual sight that if we heard one was likely to be about, the whole village turned out to watch. As like as not we were disappointed, and it broke down before trundling into sight.' In the spring of 1913 Moogie took the children for a few days' holiday on the Sussex coast. The scrapbook he made of the holiday shows the serious side of him – postcards of churches visited and scraps of Tennyson copied out – but in the snapshots of playing on the beach it is the impishness of his smile that catches the eye.

Of his time at Westerleigh he recorded little beyond a rather idealistic description of Latin lessons, possibly designed to counterbalance Chuchill's famous mockery of learning Latin at Harrow.

My mother, who had never been to a school, in the remote African township where she was born, had imbued me with the idea that Latin was the way through to a wonderland, a sort of visionary experience. My own elementary Latin had been learned from the village curate, *à deux*. . . . 'A table, O table, of a table etc' – what did it all mean? I had of course not the remotest idea. But I was intensely aware that the fringe of a curtain was being lifted, a curtain which led to a whole other world of experience. One day I would see far back beyond all those tables etc into the dim past. I would meet Alexander and Ulysses almost face to face (for Church's *Stories from the Odyssey* were already my most important experience).

He was also struck by a poem written by a boy in his form when war broke out in 1914:

> The war / is sore.
> Men die / women cry.

'It just about sums it up,' he commented. But otherwise the Great War left surprisingly little trace in his thinking, though the armistice fell on his fifteenth birthday. Much as he loved romance, there was none in that war. Poetry too he loved. Perhaps he was just too young for the poetry – and the pity – of war.

He knew, at Westerleigh, what he had to do: get the best scholarship he could to his next school. In June 1916 the examiners of Westminster School placed him 23rd out of 55, and gave him 1% for his Greek Prose. A year later he won the top scholarship to Tonbridge, worth £100 out of fees of £120 p.a. He was grateful to Westerleigh, and in 1957 went back to preach at the school's centenary service – the last sermon of his life.

At Tonbridge he went into Judde House. The higher command he found in the hands of two formidable men. First

> there was the revered but unaccountable figure of the Headmaster, Charles Lowry, on a pedestal that dissociated him from anyone else in the *régime*; benign, and normally gentle in every sense of that word, though there were from time to time formidable outbursts of rage which appeared to render him speechless for several moments. We had, and still have, no idea whether they were genuine or simulated. But one took them seriously.
>
> Then there was Walter Gordon, with his sleek grey hair, a powerful figure; grey-suited, except when he was applying for headmasterships when he wore a black morning coat; and with a system of computerising Latin and Greek that gave our proses the right phrase in the right place. He brought it off, even with those of us who were incapable of any real understanding of the languages concerned. And paradoxically, he had also that meticulously fine scholarly handwriting, which we copied *longo intervallo*. He it was who drilled us into university awards, by methods summarised in the well-known story of the unexpected visitor to the Upper VI room who, as he entered, heard Gordon exclaim 'Come on now; get down a note about the Holy Ghost'.

Gordon was not only form master of the Classical Upper Sixth but housemaster of Judde House. He left Tonbridge in 1922 to be headmaster of Wrekin College, which his commanding personality and stern Tonbridge methods soon 'made into a public school'. He also took with him his nickname of 'Swine' and his passion for handwriting. This training in calligraphy was crucial to the young Oakeshott.

Not that he adopted 'swinescript' permanently as others did – legend tells of two Old Tonbridgians in the Indian Civil Service recognizing each other by it halfway across India. He soon modified it to suit himself, though he could always pen an exquisite hand when he wanted to*, and set out a handsome page, justified at both margins. More importantly it did something to fill the gap in his education left by the absence of any art teaching at the school. The foundation of Oakeshott's later scholarship was a close attention to minute visual detail. The ground was watered by Beazley but the seed had been sown by Gordon.

But more immediately important than scholarship was happiness. Happiness, for a young boy in a boarding-school, depends much less upon the masters than upon the boys. 'I hated my early days at school,' he wrote in his forties. The war was 'an age of barbarism in almost all schools', and Tonbridge in 1917 was no exception.

> No terrors will ever be as paralysing as those of the new boy at school, conscious of having erred, and in doubt whether retribution will come , and what form it will take. . . .
>
> Big Study, with ten Novis [new boys] in it, was the grimmest room I ever lived in. I can still smell the dust which was kicked up endlessly; hear the clatter as we skidded round the corner when there was a shout of 'Boy'; and relive the moments waiting outside for one's turn when a beating was in progress. The dark passages and the grit on the floors and the fear of contact with other people became a sort of obsession.

Naturally shy, he preferred books to ball-games, and privacy, that rarest of commodities in a boarding-school, to the hurly-burly of the changing-room. To cap it all, the food was utterly inadequate. 'We ate ravenously whatever we could get; we cadged shamelessly from the fortunate; we robbed orchards; we collected sweet chestnuts and roasted them over the gas light in Big Study.'

For himself, he was tough enough to survive. But he kept his unhappiness from his mother. 'I always longed to keep apart the two worlds of home and school, and resented any intrusion of the one upon the other.'[4] For 'the fourteen-year old is often at a stage when he is beginning to be especially shy of his own parents. . . . His moodiness evokes a solicitude which is exactly what he wants to avoid.'

*He himself said of Raleigh that 'he could write finely, though most of what survives is careless scribble'.

Gradually however school work began to play a serious part in his life, since it began to be a real experience.

In so far as time is spent at school simply in the amassing of facts, this is only the preliminary to education. ... When, on the other hand, a boy first notices that if he listens to himself playing the 'Harmonious Blacksmith' he can make his playing into something which is no longer automatic but exciting, then a new stage has been reached; ... when he is first aware that the lines of Vergil which he is reading are not only a matter for translation into English. ... but are also charged with an additional content, indefinable, but enormously important, then he has gone on to a new experience.

This he called 'a much more emotional stage, more romantic: the stage when the interest in the sweep of history, not simply in its detail, begins: often a stage of moodiness and dissatisfaction'. 'Romantic' of course in his vocabulary was always warmly toned. 'It is desirable that we should all fall at one time or another under the enchanter's spell. ... If I have to choose between the half-baked and the hard-boiled, give me the half-baked every time.'

Growing maturity thus helped him to leave behind the 'bemused hobbledehoys' of the middle school. Academic success seemed to come easily. Younger boys remember him in the Classical Sixth, reclining lazily in his chair, with his legs crossed, 'as if he already knew everything'.[5] But when he himself looked back on those days his words were 'I doubt whether any moment in my life has ever been so important to me as were moments of failure or success at school.' Typical of him is the order 'failure or success' – and each of them in his own eyes, not in the esteem of others.

For with all his spectacular achievements at school, he never put on side. On the contrary he was determined to see that his successors were happier than he had been. Inevitably it is only his younger contemporaries who are still alive. What they recall is his kindness to the new boys and the help he gave the juniors with their work. They remember especially that he always found some way to avoid wielding the cane himself. He also avoided ball-games, although they were supposed to be compulsory, and were in any case the usual source of schoolboy popularity. Yet he was physically tough when he had to be. Even his impracticality was legendary: he once tried to boil an egg in a tablespoon held over a gas-jet. And there was plenty of fun. He himself told the story, in a way that let one guess his own part in it, of the short-sighted master who would always rise to the bait of a dummy concealed behind the blackboard with the words 'Come out from there; I know your name. What is it?' Of such stuff are schoolboy heroes made.

For five years from 1920 onwards Oakeshott had an extraneous source of happiness: long and carefree summer holidays on the Isle of Arran. There he was the guest of some cousins on his mother's side, the Ducketts. Mr Duckett was a successful Glasgow businessman who used to rent a holiday house at Brodick during August and September every year. He himself then commuted by ferry to Glasgow, leaving his wife and two daughters to enjoy themselves. Between 1920 and 1925 they invited Walter and his two sisters (brother Jack being now at Woolwich) to join them for as long as they could.

Walter was nearly seventeen when these house parties started, and he went every year until his last at Balliol. For much of the time he found himself in a congenial position as the only man among five women and the moving spirit in their various activities. When they paired off, Walter's pair was always little Hilda, the youngest of the Duckett daughters, five and a half years his junior. He was strong and fit – no trouble in those days with asthma or feet or exposure to the sun. She was a tomboy, with a special love of swimming. When she did the long swim round the headland to the next bay, he typically took a boat and rowed round as her escort.

More attractive to him than swimming was walking. Arran was a walker's paradise in those days. Even the roads beckoned, with no cars allowed on the island except the Duchess of Atholl's. Better still were the fells: mile upon mile of rough country, rising to Goat Fell at 2,700 feet six miles away. They never forgot 'rushing up Goat Fell at midnight', with Hilda in bare feet, in order to see the sun rise – only to be defeated by a curtain of mist at dawn.

There were other games, where Walter's imagination came to the fore. In charades Hilda recalls her mother's consternation when he came in balancing an expensive vase on his head, as 'Agag walking delicately'. When one of the girls had a Brownie camera, he thought up dramatic sequences for filming. One was a pirate drama which included walking the plank. The only plank they could find lay across a culvert by a roadside. Walter, blindfolded, started to walk across, and the camerawoman was all set, when the driver of a passing bus saw the alarming sight and stopped to offer rescue.

By the time of his last holiday there in 1925, Walter was twenty-one and in love with Hilda. She, at a rather immature fifteen, was too young to be in love. But she was devoted to him, and simply assumed that when she was grown up they would get married. In the event each of them married someone else. But he never forgot her. They wrote to each other for fifty years, and he kept her letters. Yet she never met any of his children, nor he hers. She occupied another of his private compartments, an innocent symbol of youth and vigour and uncomplicated love.

Back at Tonbridge there were warm friendships also. Three of them stand out as long-lasting. An exact contemporary was H. C. A. (Tom) Gaunt, who sat second to him in the Classical Sixth. Gaunt later became Headmaster of Malvern, but left there in 1954 when Oakeshott asked him to go to Winchester as head of a new English Department. Friendship became family in 1964 when Gaunt's son David married Oakeshott's daughter Rose.

Closer than Gaunt was the form-master of the Classical Lower Sixth, Vere Hodge. In 1975 Oakeshott wrote an introduction to a posthumous collection of his cricketing verse. From it I take a paragraph more for what it tells of the author than of his subject. It has the charm of style which Oakeshott could not afford in his scholarly works – and the long semi-colon'd sentences which he could. It also reveals much of how he himself saw the role of schoolmaster and aspired to fill it.

Lastly there was Vere Hodge, 'Vera' to the school, inevitably, but Hugo to most of us in later life: slight, neatly built, though with the loose-limbed gait of a slow bowler; conventional only because he was steeped in those traditional values that survive because they have survival value, and which he knew from his own experience of them to be good: a scholar whose interests in the subtleties of the classics were profound, who had a marvellous gift of communicating his sense of poetry, in any language, when he read it to us; familiar with the literatures of France, Spain, and Italy; a traveller who would interrupt Pliny to tell us about his beloved Naples, or Pompeii, or Thucydides to tell us about Syracuse, but who was nevertheless rigorous in his insistence that work set must be done punctually and thoroughly; a cricketer, who had often enough taken wickets enough to know that of all forms of human experience, this was one of the most satisfying. How little the modern slick categories in which the bachelor schoolmaster is classified fit him. Obsessed with the charm (and how charming it is) of the 'growing boy'? But his interests ranged through the cultures of Europe. He could be spellbound by the sound of a single word in a phrase of poetry, but to call him 'obsessed with words' is surely equally nonsensical. Obsessed perhaps by the importance of precise scholarship? But no one knew better how to see beyond it, to the vistas of experience to which it could open the way. Gay and serious by turns; a man who loved company and yet had an inner life, of which in some subtle way we were aware, that made him in a sense self-sufficient; his obsession, if he had one – and in the later years of his life it might perhaps have been called that – Tonbridge School.

Among Vere Hodge's passions were early printed books. Oakeshott never forgot

being shown as a schoolboy a copy of the Jensen *Pliny* of 1472. I can see him taking it down with infinite care; reaching back beyond the spine to lever it out by the foredge, and drawing attention to its points. 'The type – with that untheatrical grace. The blackness of the ink – amazing. The paper as good today as the day it was printed. But look,' he said, drawing a finger slowly and lovingly down the broad blank edge of the page, 'LOOK AT THOSE MARGINS'.

Thus was the teacher's passion communicated to the pupil.

Many people thought Vere Hodge stiff and difficult. But he loved Walter and Walter loved him. In 1931 when Walter came back to Kent to join the staff of the Education Authority, Hugo wrote to him quoting Dante in order to compare his arrival to a visitation of angels. They often went on walking holidays together, in the Dolomites and elsewhere, and Walter finally became his literary executor.

Closer even than Hugo was Cecilia Streeten. Cecilia's brother Francis was a day-boy contemporary, and their father was a keen member of the Skinners' Company which runs Tonbridge. Living nearby, he regularly invited senior boys out to dinner. They were allowed half a pint of Worthington's Elephant Ale and one glass of port with the dessert, the latter being their 'introduction to the world and the flesh'. His eldest daughter Cecilia, who often acted as hostess, still remembers the day in 1926 when she was twelve and her father introduced the seventeen-year old boy; 'This is Oakeshott.' She fell for him immediately. That Christmas the Streetens gave a dance, and he came to stay. Having said he didn't dance, he was persuaded by her to try. At the end of the evening he cooed 'I think I do rather like dancing after all.' The liking proved ephemeral, but his warm attachment to Cecilia was not.

Another frequent visitor in the Streetens' house was a future theologian of distinction, the Revd Charles Raven. Raven was a young don at Cambridge when war broke out, but like many such was encouraged to go and teach school for the duration. He was on the Tonbridge staff from 1915 to 1918 (except for a short period at the front, where he was gassed), prepared both boys for confirmation and won their confidence. Young Streeten invited him home, to the annoyance of his father, who did not like a cleric to wear a red tie.

Oakeshott found Raven 'one of the most exciting teachers that have ever been', and remembered especially reading Keats with him. He was also for a while much influenced by Raven's modernist Christianity. In *What Think Ye of Christ?* (1916) Raven had written, 'I discovered (as an undergraduate) that utter sincerity was the only method, that catchwords were useless. ... The personality of Jesus came to mean more and more, while the metaphysics of the creed meant less and less.' For many years Oakeshott might have echoed that formulation, and Raven was a welcome preacher at both the schools over which he presided.

In November 1920, the month of his seventeenth birthday, he made an early attempt at a scholarship to Balliol, offering English literature as an optional paper. Ideally he would get a £100 scholarship, to go up in 1921 and read classics followed by law with a view to a career at the Bar. But his compositions (translations into Latin and Greek) were not good enough for a Balliol scholar, and he was awarded only a Domus Exhibition of £80. This was a blow, both to confidence and to finance, and the question arose whether he should not after all stay at school another year, hoping to improve his performance and go up in 1922.

Many letters[6] were now exchanged between Cyril Bailey, classics don at Balliol, and a Tonbridge master who emerges as yet another important influence on Oakeshott. D. C. Somervell was the author of an excellent school *History of England* and was later to abridge Toynbee's *Study of History* in one volume. In his catalogue of the staff who collectively acted *in loco parentis* to him, Oakeshott said:

> In the more general subjects we all owed a great debt to David Somervell: lanky, untidy, his body so long that there seemed to be twice as many buttons needed to reach down the front of his jacket as were required for anyone else. In those days he was a most stimulating teacher, delighting in the destruction of conventional notions, of which, at Tonbridge at that time, we had more than our fair share.

Somervell became a friend, if not as long-lasting as Vere Hodge, and ten years later Oakeshott acknowledged his debt in the introduction to his first book, *Commerce and Society*. 'It has been humiliating for me invariably to discover, on the rare occasions when I thought I had hit on a neat phrase, that it was a recollection from him. He may disagree with some things that he finds in this book but he cannot disclaim ultimate reponsibility for it.'

Somervell now took it upon himself to sort matters out with Balliol on Oakeshott's behalf. His letters are a model of diplomacy. On 21 March 1921 he wrote:

> I am very fond of and much interested in O. who is one of the half dozen or so best boys (I am thinking of character more than of intellect) that it has ever been my privelege [sic] to teach. ... I will talk it over with Gordon. Gordon I know wants to keep him, partly to be head of his house. Lowry also wants to keep him. In fact we schoolmasters always want to hang on to our best as long as we can, and we do not always distinguish between the interests of the school and the interests of the boy. ...I am a little afraid of his getting bored in his last year here. We are a good school in some ways and Gordon an excellent sixth-form master of a rather genial, driving schoolmasterly type; but, as compared with some of the leading schools[7] we are rather a crude and childish community. Of course if he stayed I'd do my best to get him a fairly free rein, but 'free rein' is not the characteristic of this place so far as my short experience goes. ... But then, I am given to understand, I always was a bit of a Bolshevik.

Bailey, replying on 7 April, came to the same conclusion for different reasons. Having consulted his colleagues, he proposed that Oakeshott should stay at school. 'The main thing is to get his work more accurate, and that can be done at school better than here.' One way for him to do so was to widen his reading in classics, and that he set about doing. In October he wrote to Bailey in his best script listing what he had now read: the *Agamemnon* of Aeschylus, three plays of Euripides, two each of Sophocles and Aristophanes, eight books of Homer and half the *Aeneid*. He commented 'I feel myself that there are enormous gaps in it', but did not take all the blame: 'I have sounded the Headmaster on the subject of private study, and he did not at the moment seem particularly accomodating [*sic*].' Nevertheless 'personally I feel that whatever happens the extra year at school will prove to have been valuable.'

Somervell then wrote to Bailey recommending a widening of the boy's *general* reading, including some work under himself, since 'there is now no competition for him in classics and he is not receiving much separate attention'. But that would require a tactful letter from Bailey to Lowry. Bailey wrote it, adding to Lowry that 'he ought ultimately to develop into a very good scholar.' Lowry, unaware, agreed to the proposal but justified himself by saying that 'Oakeshott has developed wonderfully as a man in this last half year.'

In the event he did not succeed in converting his exhibition into a scholarship – he would never make a 'composer' – but in other ways the further year at school did prove beneficial. He needed the extra maturity for post-war Balliol, and he profited greatly from Somervell's course of 'general reading'. His range of interests now extended beyond the classics and English literature into English history and, more surprisingly, into economics.

The only serious lacuna was paradoxically in what was to be the field of his main scholarly achievement. But the ground was tilled and a few seeds sown. As well as practical training in calligraphy, he was given a gentle introduction to aesthetic theory in the writings of Lascelles Abercrombie. More important to him was music. In his third year appeared a new Director of Music, Tommy Wood, who opened 'a new world of concert and choral and chamber music'. For the choir Wood wrote his own motets and introduced new hymns and carols. Oakeshott always remembered 'the revelation' brought by the tunes for 'Let all mortal flesh keep silence' and 'The noble stem of Jesse'. He himself sang bass in the choir and won the choir prize in his last term. At the end of it he had this perceptive report from Wood: 'He has always taken the greatest interest in his music, and has brought to it that intelligence and artistic insight one would expect of him.'

One other long-term interest goes back to his schooldays: the drama. The master who produced the school plays knew Clemence Dane, and she used to come down for rehearsals. 'Don't you know how to KISS, boy? Let me show you !' The young Oakeshott's range was of course limited. His Mark Antony in his final year in the school earned this back-handed criticism from *The Tonbridgian*: 'Oakeshott spoke his words well, but in his first big scene he failed to convince, by cleansing Antony of most of his brutishness and villainy.' All his life he was short on brutishness.

End of year examinations for the Upper Sixth were conducted by a mixed team of scholars, mostly from Oxford. Prizes were awarded to the best performers in each of the three main subjects: classics, mathematics and science. By the provisions of Sir Andrew Judde, the Founder, in 1564, the prizes consisted of three pens. The boy placed first won a (wholly) gilt pen: the second prize was 'parcel gilt' ('parcel' = partial): the third was plain silver. No boy could win the same pen twice for the same subject. Oakeshott had won the parcel gilt in 1920 and the gilt in 1921; so in 1922 he had to be content with the silver. The Chairman of the Examiners that year was Geoffrey Faber, Fellow of All Souls. Perhaps by way of consolation he invited Oakeshott to dinner in All Souls on his first night in Oxford; and he reappears in the story more than once.

Prizes were awarded on Skinners' Day – 29 July 1922. Proceedings traditionally began before breakfast in the school's open-air swimming pool, where custom required the head boy to dive off the top board. Oakeshott had never been seen up there, and the school watched agog. He climbed the steps, paused – and belly-flopped. When he came up his whole front was scarlet, but with characteristic stoicism he gave no sign of the pain.

The more formal proceedings opened with the Oratio Congratulatoria, spoken in Latin by Oakeshott as head boy and responded to by Faber. In the prize-giving which followed Oakeshott swept the board. The award of the silver pen for classics served, as the Master of the Skinners' Company put it, to 'complete his collection'. He also won the prizes for Latin Prose, Greek Prose, English Literature and Reading. Less romantic but more valuable was the Judde Leaving Exhibition of £75 p.a. for classics. When he went up to receive them there was an astonishing scene. In a show of affection and admiration to which no one can remember a parallel, the whole school stood to cheer its humane and unassuming hero.

That evening he took Cecilia punting on the Medway. Her starry eyes, which had judged him 'splendidly stern' as Antony, now observed that 'he punted beautifully'. And perhaps it was that memory of the day which lingered with him longest. All his life position left him unmoved and plaudits embarrassed. That was one advantage which he had over many contemporaries in going up to Balliol: no problem, for him, in the metempsychosis from big fish in small pool to small in big.

2

Balliol

1922 – 1926

Just as the ancient Athenians could call Athens 'the Hellas of Hellas' so Balliol men could regard Balliol as 'the Oxford of Oxford'. But it was the quintessence, not the type, for in one important respect it differed. The Balliol tradition, which in the 1920s was still strong after half a century, was shared by New College but few others.

It was a tradition[1] compounded of intellectual earnestness, broad church Anglicanism, and social concern leading to social and political action. It was idealist, both in the philosophical and in the common sense of the word. Man was a child of God, capable of rising to communion with God, or (its secular equivalent) to self-realization. He could achieve that through the highest development of his intellectual, moral and spiritual faculties – again the members of that trinity were so closely related as to be almost identical, with the aesthetic following a little way behind. But this development was impeded by the evils of ignorance, disease and poverty: essentially social evils, for man in the idealist tradition finds himself only in society. It was therefore incumbent upon 'those to whom much is given' to devote their lives to the defeat of those evils – indeed to their total eradication, for nothing was impossible to those working with God's plan for humanity.

For that purpose high-mindedness was not enough. Action was needed, and that action must be political. The politics therefore had inevitably a radical thrust: many of the Balliol idealists, from Scott Holland and Gore to William Temple and Tawney, were Christian socialists; Asquith, Grey and Beveridge were Liberals; and even Conservatives like Curzon, Macmillan and (later) Heath were one-nation Tories.

But for every Balliol man who went into politics, two or three went into education, an activity which was clearly central to idealist thinking. For nearly a century they were at the forefront of educational reform at all levels. In the ninetenth century Frederick Temple, Acland and Matthew Arnold had worked to establish a public system of schooling; in the twentieth, Tawney and Ernest Barker did the same for 'secondary education for all'. In higher education Balliol men were active in the founding of the great civic universities. Lindsay's Keele (1949) was a late but pedigree flower, and even Sussex (1959) was known as 'Balliol by the Sea'. Even more typical was the development of university extension lectures. This led on the one hand to the Workers' Educational Association, of which Tawney was a founder and Temple the first president, and on the other to educational settlements. The settlements ranged from Toynbee Hall* in Whitechapel (founded in 1885, named after Arnold Toynbee, father of the historian, both Balliol men) to Maes yr Haf, founded by Lindsay in the Rhondda in 1927.

Within Oxford itself, the best known 'Balliol' invention was Modern Greats or PPE (politics, philosophy and economics), a course specially designed to prepare men for a life of civic leadership in the modern world. Heath was the first of them to read PPE; all the others had read (classical) Greats. Three of those others were to figure often in Oakeshott's life: Temple, one of his two heroes; Beveridge and Lindsay, whom he found less congenial.

The philosophical creator of this idealism was of course Plato. In the *Republic* Plato had set out the analogy between the just (i.e. well-ordered) man and the just city. Just as reason should govern the individual, so the city should be governed by philosopher-kings, carefully chosen and educated for the task. In the *Phaedo* Socrates discourses on the immortality of the soul while awaiting death by hemlock – an inspiring story which Toynbee tried to show had influenced the gospel narratives of the Passion. The *Symposium* introduces the myth of the 'ascent of the soul': rising up from the love of beautiful objects through the love of beautiful people to the love of Beauty itself in the absolute, and so to communion with the divine.

It is easy to see how the Platonism could be grafted on to Christian theology. So it had been by Hegel and Coleridge; so it was by the two most influential Balliol men of all, the philosopher T. H. Green (1836–82) and Benjamin Jowett (1817–93, Master 1870–93); so it was by many of their followers. On the other hand it could stand on its own, as a kind of mystical theism: in Arnold's terms, one could have

* Tawney lived there for a time, as did his brother-in-law Beveridge, who even gave a class in Greek.

the Hellenism without the Hebraism. In this, as in other ways, Plato is so wide-ranging – even so unsystematic – a thinker that one can take what one wants from him; but also so poetic a writer that, once carefully read, he is never forgotten.

Oakeshott entered this Balliol at a very good time. There had been a few years after the war when an extravagant irresponsibility had dominated undergraduate life – a natural reaction from the horrors of the recent past. By 1922 things were settling down to a reasonable mix of play and work – initially in that order. 'Coming up to Oxford was absolutely marvellous,'said Oakeshott in an interview in 1971. Balliol offered 'a particular kind of freedom, partly because one had led an enormously restricted life at school'. But 'I don't remember anyone having a girl-friend at Oxford at that time. Life was extremely satisfying without it.'

The friends were men. Oakeshott's immediate contemporaries were an able bunch. They included Henry Brooke, H. A. Hodges, Roger Mynors and Jack Westrup, who read classics, and Robert Birley, who did not. All these friends stayed with him and reappear in his later life. So did two classicists senior to him, Hugh Keen and Ken Johnstone; and a historian his junior, Philip Mason.

But work had to be done. Balliol men in general came up expecting to work hard, and to succeed both at Oxford and later. For classicists the course consisted, as it still consists, of two parts. Moderations (Mods) involves the study of the ancient languages and literature and takes five terms; Greats, which takes seven, involves ancient history and both ancient and modern philosophy. There are also certain special subjects that can be offered additionally with each.

The Balliol Mods tutor was Cyril Bailey, a Lucretius scholar. Oakeshott later described his lectures as 'surely among the best things the Mods course has ever offered'. He added that 'one saw him constantly wrestling with [Lucretius's] description of scientific phenomena' – the earliest evidence of his own lifelong interest in the history of science. An undergraduate would also go once a week for an individual tutorial, going though a 'composition' or reading an essay on a classical or general subject. When Oakeshott came to sum up Bailey's teaching as a whole, he wrote in a posthumous appreciation: 'There was a reckless generosity in his sharing of his feelings with his pupils. It was as if his spiritual life was being lived in public for our benefit. ... For most of us it was one of the formative influences of our undergraduate days.'

The typically Balliol epithet 'spiritual' begins to reveal the nature of that influence. Not that Bailey's Anglicanism affected Oakeshott. 'I never went inside College Chapel during the whole of my time in Balliol, and very few of one's friends did.' But Bailey and his wife Gemma held open house, and Oakeshott and many of his friends became frequent visitors there. One joint enthusiasm was music. The Baileys were devoted members of the Bach Choir, and on Sunday mornings held a regular practice at their house of the music currently under rehearsal.

In the vacations the Baileys would take a small group of under-graduates on reading parties, 'to work intermittently, feed royally, walk earnestly and talk endlessly'. The countryside was a joy in itself. Oakeshott was used to hill walking, but the flora and fauna were new to him. He carried away lasting memories: the sands near Bam-borough Head 'where *geranium sanguineum* was to be found in its beady brilliance'; a favourite place in Shropshire 'under the shadow of Caer Caradoc, where the flavour of the bacon was legendary and the lanes at night in summer were starred with glow-worms'; and talking with Gemma about 'the swooping flight of the woodpecker, and the strange liquidity of its voice in early summer'. Flowers be-came a lifelong interest with him, but birds – and indeed all animals – were a blank.*

When Bailey died in 1958 Oakeshott wrote an appreciation of him for the British Academy. As with Vere Hodge, some of the traits noted in the tutor apply no less to the pupil. One is that

> he used to speak in characteristically depreciating terms about his scholarship. There was indeed something in his disposition which made him always refer to himself as wholly inadequate to the task he had in hand or had accomplished. It may be guessed that it originated in part during his childhood, in an intense desire to excel in athletic pursuits.

Again

Bailey delighted in contacts with all the great. He used to discuss

---

* Except in art. He took a great dislike to a Roman sculpture of a dog looking for fleas, and observed in a letter that 'the classical Greeks and Romans did not under-stand animals' other than lions. Contrast 'the superb Egyptian bronzes of cats. The Egyptians understood what they are about, those bronze cats: independence; pride; they're looking for other CATS, not fleas!'

these contacts with an air not so much of pride as of unmerited privilege, as one who could not imagine why they had happened to him in particular. But there was also a simplicity about him which made his friendship with those who had little or no academic training, or with children, easy and sincere.

All this comes so close to a description of himself that one suspects either influence or unconscious autobiography.

Another interest of Bailey's was drama. He had produced regular Greek plays in translation for the OUDS before the war, and in the summer of 1923 he restarted the tradition with the *Rhesus* in New College gardens, with Bobby Longden in the lead. Oakeshott admired the production, but he was thinking ahead to another production in the coming vacation. That was to be the first post-war tour of the Balliol Players,[2] master-minded by Kenneth Johnstone.

To take Greek culture to the people was of course plumb in line with the kind of idealism described above. Later in life Oakeshott looked back ironically. Johnstone 'kidded us all into believing that if we could act Greek plays to the masses, the masses would be deeply moved'. But they also 'had great fun'. For what could be more delightful than to go with friends to beautiful places in England in late June? So the cast and their supporters set to work with zest. Two plays were to be taken to the West Midlands: the *Merry Wives of Windsor* and the *Oresteia*. The latter was an abridged version of Aeschylus's trilogy run into one, in a new translation by R. C. Trevelyan which preserved the choric rhythms of the Greek. Johnstone had seen it the previous year in Cambridge and longed to produce it himself. Music for it was composed at great speed by Westrup, and the company set off.

The props were transported by lorry, but the players all but one travelled by bicycle. The one went ahead on a motor-cycle every morning with a trumpet to summon the citizenry at each new venue to a performance later in the day. It quickly became apparent that the length of notice was hopelessly inadequate. At Edgbaston, for example, an indoor hall had been hired for a matinée of the *Wives*. By the time of the performance only three seats had been taken – by three of the Oakeshott aunts. That tour made a loss: next year's had to be better planned.

But before that there was serious work to be done for Mods: not just sixth-form work raised to a higher level but something entirely new. For Bailey had recommended the special subject of Greek Art, taught by a former pupil of his. J. D. Beazley, who was the University Lecturer in Greek Vases, has claims to be regarded as the greatest English classical scholar of the century. But his particular forte was a technique he had perfected for the attribution of vases to painters.[3] The technique rested upon a minute study of the kinds of detail for which an artist over time develops an almost unconscious formula: physical features, such as eyes, ears and hands; drapery; and decorative motifs, especially round the borders of the 'picture'. Oakeshott's preface to his *magnum opus*, *The Two Winchester Bibles* (1981), says of Beazley: 'His is the inspiration behind the book.'

When it came to sitting Mods, in March 1924, Oakeshott and his friends faced the examiners with some equanimity. They had been extremely well prepared by Bailey and they had worked hard, more perhaps in the vacation than during the term. Virtue or talent were rewarded, and all but one got Firsts.

With Mods now behind him, Oakeshott threw himself into planning the 1924 tour. The college authorities took a cautious view of the enterprise, resolving on 21 May 'that the "Balliol Players" be not allowed to begin rehearsals till the last fortnight of term'. They clearly shared the view of a contemporary Cambridge don, that 'two things ruin an undergraduate's work: amateur dramatics , and a virtuous attachment'. The Players had no qualms about their work, but they could not afford another loss.

This time they took only the *Oresteia*, and chose a new itinerary in Wessex, with dramatic outdoor settings, including Wells (the Bishop's Palace), Glastonbury, Corfe Castle and Old Sarum. Johnstone produced again, but Oakeshott was business manager (as well as playing Orestes) and, according to the official history, 'to his untiring labour of organization the success of the tour was chiefly due'. Later in his life he was often criticized for poor organization; now for the first time he showed what he could do when he was minded to.

The first problem was publicity. One of the cast took two roundels of Greek vases of the period and reproduced them strikingly, one for the posters and one for the cover of a programme handsomely designed by Oakeshott. He wrote a personal letter in his own hand to all the schools and all the big houses of the various neighbourhoods, and 'contrived to make an enormous number of people feel they were personal friends and supporters'. Nearer the time he distributed posters, handbills and programmes to local agents, usually a book-shop or a stationer. They in turn hired chairs and set them out, and reserved a hall in case of rain.

The success of the operation was evident. At Old Sarum, wrote the local paper, 'a special service of buses was run from Salisbury and every vehicle was packed'; all the seats were taken and the overflow sat on the grass or stood. But the greatest success was Corfe Castle, where 700 people came from near and far.

In a talk of 1972 at the British School at Athens, Oakeshott recalled that performance, among

> those monolithic masses of rubble, huge irregular forms tumbled on their sides by an explosion that reduced them to ruin, 300 years ago. It was a summer evening. A beacon had been lit, away on the ridge above. The watchmen waved the eyes of the audience towards where, incredibly, it had burst into flame. As the evening darkened, the tragedy unfolded; till at last in the trial scene, the sky was a vast indigo backcloth, sparkling with stars. Athena counted the votes. Orestes was acquitted. And then the Leader of the Furies, Anthony Asquith, a tiny figure in an agony of rage and frustrated violence, flung his arms up towards the sky: 'Hear my fury, O mother night!' Then came the dialogue with Athena; gradually swayed by the powers of Persuasion, the leader of the Furies turned from curses to blessings; and at last there came, winding up the steep slope from below, the processional escort with its flickering torches, to lead the kindly Goddesses to their home. I recall this because it has I believe entered more deeply into one's being than any other remembered aesthetic experience.

The tour made a profit of about £40 for the company and paid unexpected dividends to Oakeshott. He had written on 15 June to Thomas Hardy inviting him to the performance on 1 July in the amphitheatre at Dorchester, but offering as an alternative to bring the play to his garden at Max Gate. Hardy, who was a warm admirer of Greek tragedy, replied in most courteous terms.

> It is doubtful if (on account of rheumatism etc) I shall be able to go to Maumbury Rings. But then there is the question of giving the players the labour of doing the thing twice over in one day, for which the tea my wife would be glad to invite you to would

prove but a poor recompense. So that it seems rather selfish to say that I should be delighted to have you do it here.

For the performance there was one problem: the effect of the torches would be lost in the bright afternoon sun. So with Hardy's agreement and to his delight the elders carried tall spikes of a giant spiraea picked from one of his herbaceous borders, Over tea afterwards, the cast met the only other members of the audience, the Granville Barkers and Sydney Cockerell. Cockerell, the distinguished connoisseur and collector, became a lifelong friend of Oakeshott; and he always remembered the contrast: 'Hardy, small, bright-eyed, quiet, and utterly unassuming; S. C. equally small, but possessive and masterful.'

The final performance of the tour, on 10 July 1924, was in the Headmaster's garden at Winchester College. The *Hampshire Chronicle,* in a report doubtless written by a member of the school staff, records that 'the part of Orestes was played with unusual distinction and dramatic force, and with oratory perfect in cadence and enunciation'. The audience will have included the headmaster, A. T. P. Williams, and a young classics master, Spencer Leeson. Within a decade each of them had offered Orestes a post on his staff.

But by July 1924 there had already begun the long and arduous run up to Greats which was to occupy the next two years. It is certain that Oakeshott was more of a historian than a philosopher. As tutors in philosophy he had John Macmurray and Charles Morris, a young Tonbridgian who had already examined him for the Judde Exhibition in 1922. But the subject was not for him. A letter of 1927 records that he 'found aesthetics the one possible thing of that kind' i.e. presumably philosophy 'to grasp even dimly at school ' – an imprecise formulation which however leaves a clear negative impression. Ancient history was altogether more attractive. He mastered the central core of it thoroughly but also had time for the fringes. In addition to art, archaeology was already an interest, stimulated by current excavations at Windmill Hill and the beginnings of air photography, and he encouraged his friends to read H. J. Massingham's *Downland Man*

Friendship groups at Balliol were formed not so much laterally by age as vertically by interest. The two best known groups were the hearties and the aesthetes. Oakeshott was never a candidate for the former. He did row for the College in each of his four years, reaching

the First VIII in 1924, but the Boat Club he found 'singularly philistine'. Nor was he attracted to Cyril Connolly's gay band of aesthetes,
in spite of their links with the stage. It was the Balliol Players who
were for him 'the closest association of all'.

But there were other smaller, private and more frivolous groups,
many of them also with a dramatic component. Their members
would meet every so often to eat and drink, both quite moderately
(once at Balliol Oakeshott drank too much, and vowed never again),
and to read plays or themselves play grown-up charades or practical
jokes. One such group was the Heptarchy. Each of its seven members
was allotted a medieval kingdom of Britain with a sumptuous cos-
tume. At meetings of the Heptarchy the kings competed among
themselves over a huge map of Britain: contests, either diplomatic or
military, were conducted according to complicated rules. Oakeshott
was King of Mercia and 'looked very fine in an apple-green jerkin
with a silver gallias on his chest, a bronze kilt and a dark green cape'.

Other members of the Heptarchy were Birley, Keen and (from
1924) Philip Mason, a future historian (as Philip Woodruff) of British
India. Mason is the only surviving source for the figure Oakeshott cut
at Balliol.[4] He was always rather slight of build (he weighed 10st 4lb
at that time) though not as slight then as later; not exactly handsome
but, with golden brown hair, almost pretty. His clothes were distinctive without the extravagance of the aesthetes. For walking etc he had
a suit of plus fours, but in college he wore trousers of an unusually
light grey, with light-coloured ties and shirts, and 'looked springlike'.

For stereoscopic vision there may be added Cecilia's description of
him as a young man, even though she never saw him in Balliol. The
feminine eye was critical of his clothes: 'he was never very dressy, and
did not look right in casual clothes'. Out of doors he usually wore a
hat, first for protection against the sun, later, after his hair began to
thin, to stop the wind blowing it about. Spectacles he wore to correct
his long-sightedness. When he took them off for reading or talking,
he would tilt his head back – hence the characteristic pose of his
portraits. Another characteristic, the quizzical lift of the eyebrows, he
had acquired by dint of much practice from her father.*

But all alike – men and women, contemporaries no less than older
and younger people – were captivated, chiefly by his charm and
gentleness: he was never heard to speak a malicious word. His friends

* But in spite of practice he never could raise one without the other.

knew he meant to teach, and were confident that in that profession his qualities would make their mark. Equally suited to teaching were his governing interests and ideals, Mason is sure that 'the key to everything was his deep conviction of the essential beauty of the good – in a Platonic sense'.

Of all his friends the one who had the most lasting influence upon him was Roger Mynors, future Fellow of Balliol and Corpus Professor of Latin. Mynors had been at Eton under M. R. James and had already learned from him how to read a manuscript or an old book and extract all its secrets; not just to decipher the text but to divine its date and country of origin and something of its subsequent history. Oakeshott now 'at one remove watched that unerring, unhurrying assessment'. Blackwell's being only just down the road from Balliol, they found how much could be bought, in those days, almost for a song. In 1924 Mynors gave him the 1514 folio edition of Martial. In the same year, he himself bought a fine old edition of Rabelais and had it specially bound in dark green leather as a twenty-first birthday present for another friend, André Nairac[5] – 'wildly expensive', says Mason, 'for his means at the time.' And when he won the James Hall Prize, a college award worth £15, with an essay on the Weimar Republic,[6] he spent it all on 'old books', as his sister Maggie commented in down-to-earth disgust. He had, in his own words, 'caught the disease'.

The amount of time being spent by undergraduates on drama was by now causing anxiety not only in Balliol. In October 1924 the Vice-Chancellor wrote a letter to all colleges 'with regard to college dramatic societies', and the Fellows of Balliol set up a committee to consider what reply to send. Nothing further is recorded in the minute book; but in June 1925 there was no tour by the Balliol Players; in December Oakeshott was forbidden to take a part (though he did prompt) in a performance of a medieval Nativity play in College Hall; and in 1926 he was also refused permission to produce for the revived Balliol Players' tour. The path was cleared for his final run up to Greats in early June 1926.

Then on 3 May the General Strike was called. What had looked like a containable stoppage suddenly exploded. Intransigence was being shown by both government and miners; there were fears of civil war; and alarm bells rang all over the country. In Oxford the university took no position: it was left to colleges and individuals. In Balliol many undergraduates went out as strike-breakers, feeling big and getting paid. But the Master was now Sandy Lindsay.* As a socialist, his sympathies were doubtless on the side of the miners, but as a Christian he responded to the national call by the churches to work for peace. He himself set up and chaired the Oxford Conciliation Committee, but his connexions and influence extended well beyond Oxford.

Oakeshott's social conscience had hitherto been a little dormant. He had, for example, stood aside from the Balliol Boys' Club, supported though it was, in their different ways, by Cyril Bailey and by friends like Brooke and Mason. Looking back in 1971, he could dismiss 'this very unsophisticated idealism that one did get from a few dons'. In retrospect it seemed 'wildly impractical'. But in 1926 there were various signs on the other side. 'We all of us read Hammond and Tawney: they were very formative books for our generation.' Moreover he himself had recently decided to go, for his first teaching post, to a new secondary school opening in Wandsworth.

The Strike was a crisis point for idealists and hedonists alike.

> We [had] all enjoyed ourselves enormously but on a very super-ficial level. The General Strike suddenly and vividly brought one up against reality. My most powerful recollection of it is being in one of the streets of the East End when the tanks came in. *Any* of us for twopence halfpenny would have thrown themselves in front of the tanks just to make a demonstration, because we felt so powerfully about it.

But his forte did not lie in demonstrations. Instead, he resolved to work for reconciliation by appealing to 'the sacred authority of persuasive reason': that after all, as he wrote later, was the final message of the *Oresteia*. So he conceived the idea of producing a national 'newspaper' devoted to that cause and, with the backing of some 20 friends, set about it with astonishing speed, imagination and persuasiveness.

The friends included John Hicks, later Professor of Economics at Oxford and Nobel prizewinner, as co-editor; and a Rhodes Scholar named McVeagh, who had had experience of undergraduate journalism at Harvard and became business manager. Together they

---

*Oakeshott was initially impressed by Lindsay. 'His lectures over-ran deliberately the borderlands between politics, philosophy and economics, with what sometimes seemed a reckless abandon, but was undoubtedly an abandon very exciting to the undergraduates of the 1920s', who 'filled College Hall' to hear them.

secured Lindsay's backing.[7] Lindsay helped them to square both the
Government censor and the TUC. The TUC agreed, so long as the
paper was cyclostyled, not printed. Working capital of £500 was
provided by sister Maggie's employer, who had been something of a
father figure to both of them: this covered the purchase of paper and
the hire of two Gestetners. An office off the Strand was borrowed
from a church organization. Charles Morris lent them his car. Now
all they needed was copy.

Most of the first issue of the *British Independent*[8] was derived from
interviews which Oakeshott and others had secured with prominent
people: Ramsay MacDonald, leader of the Labour opposition; Lord
Grey of Fallodon; Winnington-Ingram, Bishop of London, St Loe
Strachey, editor of the *Spectator*. Dated Tuesday 11 May, 'printed and
published by W. F. Oakeshott and J. R. Hicks, price 2d', it opened with
'an abridgement authorized by Lord Grey himself of the speech broadcast by him on Sunday night'. The top billing for Grey was justified
by an editorial note that 'Viscount Grey's opinion is perhaps more
respected* by the country than that of any other statesman of our time'
– he was, after all, a Balliol man. Then came an appeal by the
Archbishop of Canterbury (another Balliol man) reprinted from *The
Times* of Saturday, with an editorial note underlining his recommendation that concessions should be made by both sides *'simultaneously
and concurrently'*. Third was a message from Ramsay MacDonald: 'I
welcome most heartily your efforts for conciliation.'

The editorial set out

'to explain the appearance of this paper. . . . Each party to the
dispute has its platform; but we feel confident that there exists
in the country a large and growing body of opinion which is
convinced that . . . the language of conflict is only calculated to
embiter [*sic*] the relations between men who will later have to
cooperate in restoring the fortunes of their common country,
which is ours. . . . This paper is being run by a body of Oxford
undergraduates. We are in touch with several bodies which are
working for a peace truly peaceful; and that cannot be unless
regard is paid to the susceptibilities of all parties concerned'.

---

*Oakeshott's admiration for Grey went back to the events of 1913–14 when 'what
made the most powerful impression on me was the strength of one man, Edward
Grey' (from the sermon quoted on p. 155).

The content, and the semicolons, confirm the authorship of Oakeshott.

The first issue was run off late on Monday 11 May, the eighth day of the strike – no mean speed. In the early hours of Tuesday members of the team rushed copies to suburban bookstalls and city newsvendors, then stood at the stations to catch the morning commuters.

The second issue contained reports of meetings held all over the country in support of the Archbishop's Appeal and the peace movement in general. The editorial (by Hicks?) analysed some heated speeches which had immediately preceded the breakdown of negotiations, and remonstrated even-handedly. 'If every word uttered in public bound the speaker for ever, all political life would become impossible. A readiness to withdraw extreme proposals is the essence of collective bargaining.'

Sales of the second issue encouraged the laying of plans for a print-run of 20,000, to be on sale in Manchester as well as London. Then suddenly on 12 May negotiations were resumed and the strike came to an end. The following week Lindsay gave a dinner in Balliol for the conciliation workers'. At the dinner some verses about the B. I. were spoken by McVeagh. Modelled on Kipling's poem 'M. I.', they named only one member of the team:

'Here is our story – remember as an acorn we began,
But an Oakeshott up in the morning, and thousands read – and ran.'

When Oakeshott himself came to look back on it all later his comments were typically generous. In his *Commerce and Society* (1936) he noted as the most remarkable feature of the strike 'the general good humour with which it was conducted and the small amount of bitterness it left behind'. Of the undergraduate team he remembered that 'the thing depended very largely on the energy and ability' of McVeagh. 'The fact that any copy was ever produced was due to him'. Of his own contribution to the B.I. he said nothing. And when c. 1984 there was a proposal to write his life, he demurred on the ground that 'my way of doing my jobs has always been to get other people to do them and just be around'. That is true of the 'jobs'; but his were the confidence and the courage, and his the inspiration and the quiet leadership that 'got other people'.

After the B.I. there was barely a fortnight left before Greats. Gallons of midnight oil must have been burned but undergraduate high spirits were not doused. The group agreed among themselves that they would all of them somehow work into their Roman history paper the sentence: 'In the third century BC the Carthaginian clergy spoke Punic.' Otherwise nothing is recorded of the ordeal.

As soon as it was over, the Balliol Players began rehearsals. The play was Euripides' *Hippolytus*, this time in Johnstone's own translation. Oakeshott, being forbidden to produce, took the title role. Mason, who was business manager that year, learned the tricks of the trade from him, and later wrote the official report on the tour. He recalls a magnificent performance by Oakeshott, especially in the great speech against women. He shed his usual deliberateness of utterance, and spoke with a new speed and force. Oakeshott also himself drew the design for the programme cover. He followed precedent by taking from a roundel on a Greek vase a four-horse chariot-team to suit the play. He gave his original drawing to Mason (see illustration): it is one of only two printable drawings of his extant. The 1926 tour was another success, and the company vowed to meet again.

Immediately however Oakeshott went back to Tonbridge for ten days as an external examiner for Vere Hodge's form, the Classical Lower Sixth. He was glad of the honorarium of 20 guineas, and the hospitable Streetens offered him accommodation. He had kept touch with them while at Balliol, going regularly to stay for their Christmas dance. Now they provided him with a card table in the billiard room for correcting his papers. One afternoon he was working there when Cecilia met the butler in the hall with a telegram for him. She took it and ran in with it: he had got his First in Greats. Giving up work for the day, he ran down the garden with her, playing like children, and she gave him a golden dahlia to go with his golden hair. She was just on eighteen. He was twenty-three, a man setting out, after a magical interlude, upon a career in the real world.

3

Marriage and Career

1926 – 1931

The appointment to Bec came about in the way that most things happened to Oakeshott. He had been given an introduction to George Gater, Director of Education for the LCC as it then was. Gater had a new school, the first public secondary school for boys in Wandsworth, just completed and due to open in the following September. It was something of a showpiece school. The headmaster, S. R. Gibson, who stayed at Bec until his retirement in 1950, had collected a distinguished staff. Three of the original six had Firsts and went on to be headmasters: two (W. J. Langford and T. W. Mellhuish) became national figures in the teaching of their subjects. The boys were predominantly middle class. Three quarters of them came from families which could pay part or all of the fees of 4-5 guineas a term. Of Oakeshott's form of thirty, six went on to university or teacher-training, and a seventh became an admiral.[1]

Oakeshott was paid £229 p.a., including a London allowance, to teach Latin, English and history. He was also 'appointed librarian and given £100 to spend – in those days quite a princely sum'. As a teacher he is remembered chiefly for the usual boyish reasons. Alone on the staff he wore no gown over his suit. The quiet 'Oxford drawl' fascinated, especially in gentle rebukes 'Oh! you rabbit!' or (more surprisingly) 'You are a bloody little fool, aren't you?' His speech and manner were 'best described as languid'. He was 'in every way a popular and unconventional teacher – a real school character'. But there was serious work too. A boy who later became a university lecturer in physics 'can still clearly recall him reciting the declension of *puella* in a rather mincing "Oxford accent". However he fired me with an enthusiasm for Latin grammar.'[2]

Oakeshott was living at this time with his mother in a flat at the top of Prince of Wales Mansions, overlooking Battersea Park. She was a sweet woman, loved by everyone but rather crushed by life.

Walter was always extremely solicitous of her, and he now had the chance to spoil her a little. His military brother Jack had a car, which Walter used to borrow to take her out for drives. She was very nervous – not without reason, to judge by his later reputation behind the wheel – but he learned to allay her fears about speed. The car had an oil pressure gauge on the passenger's side calibrated up to 20: he told her it was the speedometer, so that they were never going more than 20 mph.

Sister Maggie was also living at home: 'an absolutely engaging creature', he wrote that year, 'with a kind of brightness and resilience that knocks me out '. To Philip Mason, a frequent visitor, she was simply the most beautiful woman he had ever known. She was also a great gossip: 'She has that delicious way of getting excited about a thing – she giggles with joy and can't tell it fast enough.' In many respects she was the opposite of Walter, who used to say 'but she's very good for me' – that is, as a corrective – and was as devoted to her as she to him. Like all the women in his family she was protective, even possessive, of him and critical of all women outside it except Cecilia.

The autumn term of 1926 had scarcely begun when plans were laid for a revival of the Balliol Players' *Hippolytus*. The nucleus of the new company was to consist of former Players who had now gone down and were available in London. They took the title of the Holywell Players, after the Balliol house where Oakeshott and Johnstone had lived in the previous two years and Mason was still living. The plan was to take the play round various halls, in London and the home counties, in November-December under the auspices of the WEA. Johnstone was to produce, with Oakeshott as Hippolytus. Players who were unavailable were replaced by newcomers, and the opportunity was taken to bring in women for the female parts.

The new Leader of the Chorus was to be Noel Moon. In so far as a woman could at that time, she had become a member of the Balliol circle. Her schooling had been unorthodox. Mayortorne under Isabel Fry[3] taught her music and Latin, dairy farming and drama, including Gilbert Murray's translations. At her father's request she had been given private lessons in Greek, and learned enough to get a place as a 'home student' at Oxford. There she lodged with D. G. Hogarth, then Keeper of Antiquities in the Ashmolean Museum, and so met a number of the classical dons, including the Baileys. She read Mods at the same time as Walter. After Mods, however, she was advised not to go on to Greats but to switch to the Diploma in Classical Archaeology under Beazley. As the best Diploma student of 1926, she had been awarded the Gilchrist Studentship at the British School at Rome, to be taken up in 1927. Meanwhile in October 1926 her first article had been published, entitled 'Greek Vases of the Red-Figured Style'.[4]

Among the undergraduates her chief link was with Hugh Keen: they sang duets together, and she was a welcome guest at his parents' home. There, before she had ever met Walter, she heard his name mentioned, and his praises sung, by Mrs Keen. In December 1925 she had taken part in the Nativity Play in Balliol Hall. Mason remembers her as Our Lady, speaking the 'Magnificat' very movingly. She was a natural recruit to the Holywell Players' *Hippolytus*.

The surprise introduction to the cast was Walter's own choice, Cecilia Streeten in the female lead as Phaedra. When rehearsals began, Cecilia came up to stay in the Battersea flat. Maggie and she became firm friends, and Walter drove her out to the various venues.

The performances went well. Walter was tired at the end of his first term's teaching but, according to a cousin of Noel's, 'was in great form on the stage'. Noel is remembered as 'looking very Etruscan'. The two of them gradually came to see more of each other. She stayed with the Keens, and Walter went there too. He took her to the Russian Ballet and (more significantly) gave her a short story of his to read. They fell in love. About 17 December 1926 he proposed marriage and she accepted. No date was fixed for the wedding, though privately they had Christmas 1927 in mind for it.

The news of the engagement was greeted by their friends with pleasure but also with surprise, and even shock. It was an unspoken assumption among the Balliol group that none of them would marry until sufficiently established in a career to support a wife. Nor were Walter and Noel an expected pair. Bailey, who wrote sending 'love and blessings' to both of them, told Mason privately that 'he always thought she would marry one of them, but hadn't expected it to be Walter'. Moreover Walter's affection for Cecilia, and hers for him, were well known. Indeed the Streetens had, on the strength of it, invited the whole cast down to Tonbridge for their usual pre-Christmas dance. On the morning of it Cecilia's father received a letter from Walter to say that he had become engaged to Noel and neither of them would be coming. Cecilia put a brave face upon it and spent the evening dancing with Johnstone. But the bottom had fallen out of her world. For her father the shock was scarcely less.

Nevertheless everyone agreed that Noel was in principle eminently marriageable. She herself was attractive, in a rather ethereal way ('something of an icon' was Mason's phrase), and 'accomplished'. Well read, she had also quite a turn of phrase on her own account. She spoke fluent French with some German, played the piano and sang rather well. Though a little prim and proper – something of 'the colonel's daughter' was already visible – she could be witty and amusing. Finally she was without question intelligent and scholarly, interested in the very subjects which Walter would make his own. For what it was worth, Noel also came of a 'good' family, connected by marriage to the fourteenth Earl Ferrers.* Her father, an eccentric Wykehamist doctor, had a London house in Montagu Square, a 'good' address, and also rented a largish farmhouse, Copse Stile, at Aston Tirrold near Reading, where he had plenty of servants.

On the other side things were not so easy. Walter in his excitement had failed to ask Noel's father for her hand. Ostensibly the Doctor took no umbrage. Noel on 20 December wrote to Walter quoting her mother to the effect that 'though he has only seen you once or twice he feels sure that he knows the person you are and that he will fully appreciate you'. But 'she says that what he really wants to ask you about, more than anything practical, is exactly what was in your mind when you decided to teach in a secondary school'. The tone, even at third hand, is unmistakable.† But underneath the snobbery lay a point of substance. Everyone agreed that they could not possibly marry on his salary at Bec.

One other hurdle was seemingly surmounted. Noel told Walter of various admirers of hers, including the author Richard Hughes.[5] He had written her some sentimental letters in 1922–3, which she kept all her life. In return Walter told her about Hilda. Innocently, she wrote to him on 21 December 'I'm awfully sorry you have felt worried about your cousin, but honestly 17 is too young. I expect I shall like her all the more because you loved her.'

The couple had only a fortnight between their engagement and her

*The Ferrerses were lineal descendants of Queen Elizabeth's Earl of Essex, a link which must have intrigued Walter later on.
†It was echoed by a royalist French cousin of Noel who expressed surprise that she was marrying a teacher: since the Revolution it had not been done for people of quality to marry into any part of the Civil Service.

departure on 3 January 1927 for four months in Italy, based at the British School at Rome. There she planned, with Beazley's support, to work on the Greek vases of southern Italy. This was a field to which she could apply his techniques with the chance of achieving something serious, and she seized it with both hands. The British School provided her with rooms, library and scholarly guidance. The Director, Bernard Ashmole, with his wife gave uncovenanted support and affection and they became lifelong friends. Italy was also a finishing school. There was the language to learn, galleries to visit, music to play and hear. There were journeys to be planned, and museum staff to be placated or charmed. She got herself with a woman friend to Naples for a fortnight and to Sicily for a few days. From Sicily she sent back to Walter a postcard of the twelfth century Pantocrator in the dome of Cefalù Cathedral – his first introduction to medieval mosaics.

During her four months in Italy they wrote to each other every day. All her letters survive, but none of his; so his doings and feelings have mostly to be inferred. Of his teaching at Bec nothing emerges. But he had enough work outside the teaching to keep him permanently tired in term-time. First, he was still heavily involved in the Holywell Players. In March 1927 they put on a production of *Tartuffe* for the local schools. But the response did not justify the effort, and he decided to withdraw from his responsibility to the company. He was also writing. A short story of his, probably the one he had shown Noel, was turned down by the *London Mercury* but the *Times Educational Supplement* took an article entitled 'Boys and Books'.

The article[6] is a rather solemn piece on the importance of reading as against 'the pictures' i.e. the cinema or, still worse, 'the comic paper'. 'Reading should, and can be, a moral experience. . . Stories of pirates, of explorers, of soldiers and sailors and missionaries, appeal directly to "the spirited element" in boys.' It is also 'a discipline which counteracts superficial brightness' – and now we hear the plaintive note of one brought sharply from the sunlight of Platonic theory into the cave of classroom reality. 'What is one to do with the type of child who, after appearing to be attending more devoutly than all the rest, puts up his hand and answers one's eager expectation of an intelligent question by asking how many marks he got for the last exercise?'

A good deal of Walter's time – and of his correspondence with

Noel – was taken up by his search for another job, so that they could marry. They discussed the pros and cons of a number of posts for which he presumably applied without success. The list included a lectureship at Manchester University and an assistant directorship of education at some place she could not decipher. The post which attracted him most was dangled before him by Spencer Leeson, the new headmaster of Merchant Taylors' School. That fitted an ambition he had already formed, to be headmaster of a public school; it also suited Noel, who much preferred London to the provinces. But Leeson was not sure of having a vacancy, and the uncertainty hung over them all the time she was in Italy.

And gradually anxieties began to build up. High on the list of them was money. Her father planned to settle £100 p.a. on her, and her mother could find another £100 or even £150 p.a. With £25 p.a. of her own, the total was greater than his salary. It was all kindly enough meant. Her income would enable him to pay his mother more. It would also provide the servants without whom he would be involved himself in domestic chores. For Noel's upbringing had totally unfitted her for the role of good wife to a poor man. Not only would she need to learn how to cook and sew and iron; she had never lit a fire, cut bread or rinsed her hair by herself. Even with her allowances, she could see that, married to Walter, she would 'not be rich any more'.

Differences of temperament were also emerging between them. She described herself variously in letters as fastidious and extravagant, 'chronically maiden-auntish', 'critical and *difficile* and hard to please', and 'essentially frivolous, except over vases and music'. The open air made no appeal to her: when they were married she 'would like a day indoors sometimes as a treat'. Her interests were limited. When he teased her about 'not being interested in AD', she admitted that she would 'never be able to feel the same affection for it; and I shall always be quite happy *not* knowing about the middle ages'. All this showed a nice wit and some self-knowledge. Walter's self-criticisms on the other hand, at least as filtered by her, are vague: he is 'a bumpkin' or 'gingerbread without the gilt'.

On one matter Noel was unfailingly generous. She had hardly left England when he became concerned about Cecilia. On 10 January she wrote 'I'm so sorry you have all this worry about Phaedra, and I don't know that I understand it very well. . . I expect you can help her if she wants you [to?], only I know that feeling that one may do more harm than good.' In February he had dinner with Cecilia, and Noel wrote 'thank you for telling me'. Cecilia found their friendship was unimpaired, but neither then nor ever afterwards did he account to her for his proposal to Noel.*

Hilda too was much on his mind. Her family asked him to join them in Arran over Easter: it was to be Hilda's last holiday there before she left school to study music in Vienna. Noel urged him to accept, but he did not. On 22 April she wrote to him even more generously. 'If you did get to feel that after all your life would go better with Hilda's, then you must be brave and tell me, my heart, and face my minding it, because I would understand and wouldn't think it at all peculiar of you to think like that.'

It seems that by this time his own anxiety and indecision was beginning to brush off on her. From mid-March onwards he had been in 'depths of misery'. She feared that he 'might get what's called a nervous breakdown' (19 March), though she consoled herself for the long run: 'Never worry about whether you'll have fits of depression when we're married... it only happens because you are tired' (2 April). In his distress he wrote privately to her father offering to withdraw from the engagement. Presumably he felt it to be unfair of him, without prospects, to keep her hanging on a string. Dr Moon reassured him. Noel, when she heard of it, accepted that 'what you did was done for my sake', but was still unnerved. Each loved the other dearly, but neither could be absolutely sure.

Her return to England in mid-May 1927 came just in time, and for a while things were easier. In June Leeson confirmed the offer of a post at Merchant Taylors' at a salary twice what Oakeshott was earning at Bec. This enabled the engagement to be announced in *The Times* of 23 June. But no date was fixed for the wedding, which remained a matter of dispute. The young couple still wanted to be married at Christmas, and were supported by both mothers. But Dr Moon, exploiting his dual role, overruled them all. His diagnosis, that Walter was 'ill in mind and spirit', was reasonable. His therapy was not. The wedding must be put off till Walter was well; in the meantime, he and Noel should see less of each other; indeed Walter should ideally go away for a long holiday, for which he would himself pay. He called in another doctor for a second opinion, which

---

* The principle held (p. 8), of keeping his worlds apart. Cecilia and Hilda never learned of each other's existence.

turned out to coincide with his own. Only later did clear evidence emerge that he had leant on his colleague. Noel's loyalty to her father only just survived the discovery. Dr Moon's behaviour was indeed less than admirable throughout the sad story. It is hard to resist the conclusion that the old tyrant's chief desire was not to lose his favourite daughter.

But Walter had at least got plenty of other things to occupy his mind during that summer. There was an old job to be wound up and a new one to be entered upon. Nor did his move from one to the other mean the drying up of his social conscience. On the contrary, during that year at Bec he had been drawn in to a new venture which proved to be a much more lasting commitment than the *British Independent*.

In 1926 a remarkable Quaker couple, the Nobles, had had a 'concern' to go to South Wales during the General Strike to relieve the distress among the miners. With money raised from Quaker sources, and the enthusiastic support of Lindsay, whom they had met at WEA conferences in Oxford, they opened an educational settlement at Maes Yr Haf in the Rhondda Valley. The settlement included workshops – e.g. for making clothes with donated materials – and also programmes of lectures and study. Lindsay encouraged Balliol men to visit the settlement: one of the first was Henry Brooke, who spent a winter there teaching philosophy. The flavour of the classes is given by the story of a group studying the *Republic* who ended up in an undertaker's warehouse, sitting on coffins. The story gave rise to a famous stage direction in a playlet by Max Beerbohm:[7] '*Exeunt* several cobblers to read the Platonic dialogues.'

Oakeshott went to Maes Yr Haf for a week at the beginning of August 1927. The experience there was an eye-opener, as his four letters to Noel show. On his way down from London by car he gave a lift to two tramps in succession. The first 'shared my lunch but didn't like it awfully. He would not have been very good at the murder game as there were discrepancies in his story.' In general he

> was not a great success. The second was a very good man. He was a ship's cook, out of work, who'd just been to Plymouth in search of a job and was tramping back. He was nearly starving. We had cups of tea and sandwiches at a shop he knew in Newport. He didn't drink beer. He was another man after we had had our meal; his face flushed and he was as gay as a bird.

Oakeshott never forgot the contrast between these two alternative responses to unemployment.

In the Rhondda Valley he was sensitive to both faces of life. 'It has extraordinary beauty, some of it. But there is a drabness and blankness about it all; and the feeling that it's played out, that the people are living on the parish, most of them, and that the owners are blustering about reopening world markets which in fact are gone for ever.' It seemed that 'there'll be always there some hideous inertia with the empty trams drearily rattling and shrieking through it. That's why they're communists, lots of them.' Communism and fascism 'exist to get things done. Unless democracy realises that it too must get things done with vigour, democracy will go under.'

For his hosts the Nobles he had much praise. They 'lead a life of incredible simplicity. The way in which they have made the people absolutely free and open with them amazes me constantly.' All, in fact, was proceeding serenely for Oakeshott when he was asked at a few hours' notice to take an English literature class. Sudden panic: all he had with him was Sophocles' *Ajax* in Greek, 'a vast history of Russia, and the report of the Coal Commission'. But afterwards he felt 'a fierce kind of excitement', which made him 'think of offering to come down at weekends next term and continue teaching the class on Saturday evenings'. For 'I've never in my life met anyone so intelligent as those miners are; one had no conception somehow of a truly thoughtful proletariat, incredibly sensible to [sic] any sort of change, and any sort of experience.' In the event he did not go back there the following term to teach. Instead he took on a course of evening lectures at the London Working Men's College on economics: feeling himself ignorant of the subject, he decided that was the best way to learn. But he was back at Maes yr Haf ten years later for a longer stay, his idealism (by youth out of Balliol) only slightly tempered by the interval.

These generous sentiments shine the more brightly against his recurrent blackness of spirit. While he was at Maes Yr Haf Noel was staying at Bridgwater in Somerset. With her father's permission she invited him to join them there for a couple of days before he went on the planned holiday abroad. His letter of 9 August 1927 shows his continuing confusion.

I don't feel it's awfully playing the game and all that, but I would absolutely love to come. . . . I don't know what will happen if I don't. You see, my darling, when I'm away from you for a long time like this, I can never, never drive out of my head the worry that I have for being so disloyal. I'm sure it's only because I knew Hilda [Duckett] so much better than I have had a chance to know you, and so much longer – I'm sure that's all it is. . . That's why I'd longed so that we might be married soon, because I thought that after that worrying would be impossible.

What he wrote about Hilda was indeed absurd. His friend Keen told him so, and his mother wrote to him explaining why.

I am perfectly sure Hilda's love for you was not of that kind at all. . . You see she was *really* only a child, and could not even understand the kind of feeling you had for her. Noel is the one you must think of when she has given you all her love. . .The more you worry the worse it makes it for everyone. Cheer up, old son, you have the dearest girl in the world – and come back to us your own cheery self.

He did go and see Noel for a couple of days and then went off abroad for a walking tour in the Italian Dolomites with James Cullen. Cullen was a Tonbridge and Balliol man, now teaching classics at Winchester, with whom he had at some earlier date climbed in Skye. In preparation for the trip he went shopping in London 'and bought a pair of bags [i.e.trousers] and a blazer – both very worthless and common articles, but we went rather unadvisedly to a rather bad shop and they were the best they had and I never dare to walk off and say that a thing won't do.'

His letters to Noel from Italy are out to entertain. The proprietress in one *pensione*, 'a damsel built on a grand scale, moves like a quinquereme that has just been unloaded' and 'had a sort of hippopotamian flirtation with James'. The Dolomites

rise up with a kind of Gothic magnificence, pinnacles massed over a gigantic square lump of mountain; and they're dead, absolutely dead, like the mountains of the moon. . . . As you get nearer to them in the evening, a terrible sort of heartless grey, they tower above you in the most awful way, so that you really know what sort of mountains the people would have been crying out to when they said 'fall on us'.

Noel as usual wrote daily. She herself is now reading the *Ajax* and comments 'We'll have to tell our children all these stories, and they'll have to be fearfully excited about Troy, for it holds such a vast share of the romance of the world. Probably though they'll be mathematicians or something queer, and then they can be given grandfather Moon's great work "M divided by Naught".' The letter ends with a recommendation to take 'a draught of the mixture', doubtless with reference to a prescription which his mother had sent him before he had left England. The women vied with each other to cosset him. At various times his mother recommended 'gargling with water to which a little Sanitas has been added'; Auntie Harrie 'Sanatogen, a real standby and mixed with milk quite palatable'; and Noel 'Bemax with your evening cocoa'.

On return from Italy he set about preparing for his first term at Merchant Taylors'. He had been hired to teach English, with classics as an expected and economic history as an unexpected adjunct. He repaired to Oxford to work, and from there wrote to Noel on 7 Sept 1927. 'I've been reading *The Defence of Poetry*. I'll make the Upper VIth do it, with perhaps Browning's essay on Shelley ... the source from which practically all modern aesthetic theory springs. At meals I read industrial history.'

On the same day Cecilia wrote to him to say that she is 'in infinite despair and plan[s] to cross the Atlantic'. He went down as before to offer help, and found she was planning to marry a Canadian. Noel sympathised. 'It does seem so awful for Mr Streeten that she should go, knowing what a blessing it would have been to them if you had married her.' Walter succeeded in reconciling him to the loss of his daughter, who sailed for Canada on 29 September. Noel then admitted that she had been 'always rather frightened of her'. In truth Cecilia was marrying on the rebound. The marriage was not a success, and in due course she resumed her old friendship with Walter. His children sometimes refer to her as 'the woman father ought to have married'.

Term at Merchant Taylors' began on 17 September 1927. Leeson had arrived there only in that January. 'His impact on it was as if to some torpid organism a powerful electric current had been applied, the charge being increased rapidly as it sprang into life.' The school was then still located in Charterhouse Square EC1, 'on a hot summer's day well within range of the smells of Smithfield'; but there was already talk of its moving out of London, which it did in 1933.

Oakeshott was one of Leeson's first three appointments, all of whom went on to be headmasters.

From the post at Merchant Taylors' (1927-30) some fifteen pupils remember him well; of these one became a lifelong friend, another served later on his staff at St Paul's. Not that all the fifteen were equally taken with him. 'Oakeshott did not impress me as a teacher' writes one 'and I am surprised that his personalitywas strong enough to rise to the achievements he attained. He did not seem to me to have the strength of personality which Spencer Leeson undoubtedly had.'[8] That judgement is echoed by another: 'his personality did not seem likely to thrust him so highly.'[9] The comparison with Leeson, often made later, was bound to lead to that initial verdict. Leeson spoke like a headmaster, in indicatives and imperatives; Oakeshott like a scholar, in subjunctives and optatives.

Others of his pupils found this very gentleness attractive. A bewildered new boy was rescued by him and correspondingly 'desolated' when Oakeshott left at the end of his first term. An insecure senior boy, a future archdeacon, writes of him as 'certainly my favourite schoolmaster – the first to give me any self-confidence as a not-very-bright boy. He was such a sensitive man and made me realise that to be sensitive "religiously" was not to be sissy.' In class Reggie Maudling always recalled having been given 12 out of 10 for Latin sentences; 10 out of 10, said Oakeshott, was only par, not the maximum. His most stringent criticism was 'you awful man', uttered reproachfully in the much imitated drawl. And perhaps the man was also proclaimed by the apparel. A bright blue shirt, worn with floppy collars and 'arty' ties, together with his fair hair, inevitably earned him the nickname of 'Little Boy Blue'. Of his sixth-form teaching two courses were to prove especially fruitful – not only for his pupils. One was 'his account with detailed maps and plans of the defeat of the Spanish Armada: *flavit deus et dissipati sunt*'. Another was the study of Tennyson for the Higher School Certificate. When it came to the *Morte d'Arthur*, he read them the Malory account for comparison. 'We all agreed enthusiastically that Malory was better suited to the subject.' After the examination, according to another member of the class,[10] 'the examiner wrote to the school that they had been impressed by the thorough knowledge of the poems shown by the candidates, but thought it a pity that *not one* of them appeared to have found there was anything to admire in any poem of Tennyson's.'

Whilst Walter was working out his teaching, Noel was pursuing her research. She did so with the same single-mindedness which he was to show later in his own scholarship. With Beazley's warm encouragement, she spent much time in the Ashmolean Museum in Oxford and at the Hellenic Society in London. Being able, unlike Walter, to read both German and Italian, she missed no tricks. When she showed her draft to Beazley in November, he congratulated her, and she sent it off for publication in the *Papers of the British School at Rome* under the title 'Some Early Italian Vase-Painters'. In it she not only identified a number of Greek artists working in Southern Italy round about 400 BC, and gave them the names by which they are still known, but also discussed their style, located their workshops and established a chronology. It was an article of fundamental importance. Other scholars, especially A. D. Trendall, built upon it, not always with due acknowledgement. She herself never managed to follow it up as she would have liked, but it remained a major interest all her life.

By November 1927 Dr Moon had so far relented as to agree that the wedding should take place in April 1928. But he continued to insist that they should not see too much of each other. By now Noel at least had come to see that 'three quarters of the trouble is that our engagement has been so long'. But they still respected his wishes; and so, while she set about learning from his mother how to cook the simple meals he liked, his anxieties returned.

Behind his worry about money lay another about the life-style of the two families. In November he told Noel that he 'did not care for the aristocracy'. He felt he had been criticized at Staunton Harold, the seat of the Ferrerses, for not following the right order of precedence in handing round the chocolates after dinner. She told him he had misinterpreted the incident, but defended 'the aristocracy', and admitted to a difference between the two of them. 'I believe in the conventions concerning them, simply because it's instinctive in me to do so, just as it's instinctive in you to rebel against them.' It was a good point: there was always this rebellious streak in Walter, though he suppressed it for most of his life. But she did not help matters by writing to him on 1 December, when they were considering where to live after the wedding: 'I believe it would worry mother desperately if we took up residence in a mews or something of that kind.'

Around the turn of the year 1927/8 the clouds began to gather again – if, indeed, they had ever lifted. Among Walter's anxieties was one which has not been mentioned hitherto. It may have been present all along; it must have increased as the wedding approached. Like almost all young people in those days, they were both sexually inexperienced. Cecilia recalls that Walter had never held her hand, let alone kissed her. With Walter's deep sense of inadequacy and Noel's fastidiousness, the wedding night must have been an alarming prospect.

For all these reasons the pressure on him built up to the point where it was agreed that he should see a psychiatrist, Dr William Brown. The consultation was arranged through Dr Moon, and the verdict, delivered on 17 January, did not displease him: Walter needed a long absence from Noel, preferably travelling round the world. Since it was term-time, the separation had to be begun by Noel. She went to Paris for a long stay with French cousins. Five weeks later, the Lord looked down from heaven. Walter was found to be suffering from a chronic appendicitis, and prepared to enter St George's Hospital for an operation. He would be off work for the last six weeks of term, his teaching taken over by Noel's brother Penderel, who had recently won a Prize Fellowship at All Souls.

The diagnosis was greeted by an enormous sigh of relief all round. The trouble, having been located, could be cured. And the optimism was not unreasonable. It was true that there had not hitherto been any physical manifestations of his mental illness. But his subsequent bouts of ill health, throughout his working life, generally had nervous correlates: on the one hand asthma and eczema, shortness of breath and insomnia; on the other hand anxiety and depression.

Only Dr Moon still dragged his feet. After the diagnosis was made, he allowed Walter just one letter to Noel in Paris. Her reply is ecstatic: 'all our troubles are over'. She now revealed to him that 'the last time I saw you was on the platform at Victoria. I felt it my duty to slip behind a pillar till you had passed. We'll never need to do that again.' She had underestimated her father. He still insisted that on her return from Paris she should not see Walter till his convalescence was over. But he finally agreed to a wedding on 11 April, and the preparations began.

Among them was one bold move. For some time – most recently in January 1928 – Noel had been urging Walter to go and see Hilda Duckett, presumably in the hope of exorcising the ghost. Now she invited her to be a bridesmaid. Hilda was currently abroad studying music, and her parents declined on her behalf without telling her.

Noel wrote to Walter that she was sorry 'there should be nobody of yours' among the bridesmaids.

The wedding took place on the Wednesday in Holy Week in the village church at Aston Tirrold. The *Oxford Chronicle* gave a full report, since Dr Moon was prospective Liberal candidate for Oxford. Noel looked ethereal in a dress of pale gold lace over corn-coloured chiffon, with a veil of Honiton lace and a bouquet of rose-coloured orchids and myrtle. Hugh Keen was best man, Jack Westrup at the organ. Their most remarkable present was a two-seater car from Penderel. Other presents included a chèque [*sic*] from Earl and Countess Ferrers and a Japanese 'famille rose' bowl and plate from Maggie. Noel gave Walter a Roman glass plate; he gave her a cross of green jade.

The official honeymoon was spent briefly on Dartmoor, but a private gift from one of Noel's uncles made possible a further holiday in Greece. From Athens it was a short trip to the monastery at Daphni. The mosaic of the Pantocrator in the dome was the first great Byzantine work of art he had ever seen, and its image remained vivid all his life: 'the All-ruler contemplating his world and not finding it good like the Creator of Genesis; rather moved to the depth by its anxieties and sorrows.' Travel further afield in Greece was primitive in 1928 and, for the young bride, often a severe test. To get from Athens to Delphi they went by train to Lebedeia near Thebes, then twenty miles on foot by mountain and moorland paths to Hosios Loukas. There they spent a night in the monastery. A year later he described that visit in an anonymous article for *The Times*. In it he was already comparing the mosaic of the Pantocrator in the dome there with the corresponding figures at Daphni and Cefalù.

At the 'cross-roads' between Osios Loukas and Delphi, the place where Oedipus killed his father, an old man was sitting alone breaking stones for the new road. Typically Greek, he invited them to share his coffee and inquired all about them. They loved it. Pressing on, they managed to hire a mule for the last few miles and so clattered down the hill at last into Delphi. Astonishingly they remember no other travellers there at all. Mycenae too was unforgettable, especially the beehive tomb known as the 'Treasury of Atreus'. Their guide had pulled up an armful of heather on the way. Inside the tomb, in the darkness, he threw it down and put a match to it. It blazed up and the light flickered over the vault far above, 'as if we were witnessing the last glow of a funeral pyre'.

From Greece they returned to live in the flat in Battersea. His mother and Maggie moved out to stay with various relatives until permanent arrangements could be made, and left the flat to the newly-weds. Unfortunately the hope that marriage would restore his health was not realized. Even the physical symptoms lingered on. Three months after the wedding, he was writing to Noel 'I've got more ulcers and things which make eating exceedingly unpleasant', and still in September 1928 he was feeling very queasy and sick.

Noel herself was away for the first three weeks in that July, staying with family and friends. He wrote to her about his work at school and about their shared interests. For example, on two successive weekends he drove down to join the Balliol Players on tour with Euripides' *Orestes* at Corfe Castle and Salisbury. When at home alone he tried to play the piano, 'not having touched a note for ages'. But for whatever reasons – which might include her absence – his anxieties returned.

Their correspondence during those weeks survives on both sides. Two exchanges in it are especially revealing. One started with his sending her a book by Chesterton. She wrote that she 'didn't find it palatable', and added: 'I have a desire to tell you this and yet I'm afraid you'll groan and muse on our incompatibility of temperament and divergent tastes. I pray that you won't.' But he did.

I felt as soon as I had given it you that you wouldn't like it probably. Although I don't of course write with the brilliance of Chesterton or anything like that, what I'm driving at when I write is the same thing which turns your stomach in all these people [a category that includes Clemence Dane!]. They're journalists, and I am at heart – I suppose that's it. That's why I never write letters to you like I can to some people – because I know they'd make your tummy revolve just a little. I don't think I've ever been frenzied with excitement when I've written to you – I just didn't dare, or didn't feel like it because I knew it wasn't your sort of thing.

All this is partly why this queer sort of inhibition has come over me lately, you know. We've just got to face it. I knew all about it ages before we were married, of course; from the very beginning. It's just fearfully odd that we're so absolutely different on those kinds of things. Sometimes we'll be able to have a chirp together in the valley that lies between us, because of course we aren't absolutely separated – it would be foolish to pretend that. But for the most part we'll just each be wandering on our own hill, and we won't be able to cope with the other at all. I've always known how it would be, my darling, and you mustn't think I haven't; and if ever I do write anything, you'll just have not to read it, or to read it and be quietly sick and then chirp up and we'll think about other things like how good it is to mooch about on the downs; and we won't fuss about anything.

Noel's reply was sensible. Specifically, 'GKC didn't make me feel seeek [*sic*]. I just got bored after a bit.' Generally, 'It must be rare for two people to touch at all points. I know you feel we touch at fewer than the average, but where we do it's pretty satisfactory.'

Their letters exemplify his point. Like Chesterton, he did aim in his writings, and in the best of his teaching, to move people. Owlish-looking, he wished to win, to woo. Throughout his life he expressed his enthusiasms far more openly, even extravagantly, than the reserved and critical Noel. Nothing to him was ever 'pretty satisfactory'. Time and again experiences are 'perhaps the most exciting thing that has ever happened to me', and objects 'in many ways the most beautiful thing I have ever seen'. He had to learn over many years the austere style of professional scholarship which came naturally to her. They were indeed opposed in temperament as romantic to classical. There were plenty of chirps; but the valley remained deep, until her last illness.

The second exchange centred round the difficulties each of them had in getting on with the other's family. She had been with him to stay at the Ducketts (in Hilda's absence). This, she said, was 'absolutely the way of life you like'; but it had not been a success. He too finds that, though he *likes* her family, he is 'not made in the way that can get on with them very well'. For example, 'I just can't stand the pace they live at as far as general intelligence goes.' The last phrase may refer to Dr Moon's affected style of speech, of which Noel once gave an example: he hoped 'to make a *treffend* observation, *qua* sniffer of the *Zeitgeist*'.

Noel's comments are, as before, sensible. 'It will probably be best if we don't stay with any relations much until we are more of a unit. You'll probably understand what I mean. Things will be much easier then. We haven't settled down with each other yet, so naturally it's hard.' Walter agreed. He on his side offers to 'give up some things, the Ducketts for example'. He will also try to ensure that, when he does meet her relations, there are no rows, 'because I absolutely loathe them; they make me feel physically sick anyhow and generally awful'. That was certainly true: all his life he went to extreme lengths to avoid a row.

Family differences are part of the small change of married life. In this case they were exacerbated by the fact that the Oakeshott women were possessive of their favourite male, while Noel retreated rather often into the bosom of a large and demanding clan who would have liked to absorb Walter. But his anxieties – for by now they were much more his than hers – are another matter. Some of them were rational enough e.g. the worry about money. Others represent an acute phase of a lifelong trait of character: his sense of unworthiness. But the moods of black despair were more severe and lasted longer than ever again in his life, even when he was Headmaster of Winchester. Why should this have been ?

The explanation that leaps to mind is the Freudian one: the frustrations of a long engagement were not yet assuaged. But a strange passage written when he was thirty five may throw some further light. In it he writes of the young unemployed, i.e. 18-24-year-olds. 'These men are at an age when many men are in some degree abnormal, acting on a violent impulse, subject to exaggerated excitement and exaggerated depression, trying to discover what their own position ought to be in the community in which they live and trying to get others to accept it.' The fit is not exact but some of it looks autobiographical. If so, his own interpretation is that his moods were growing pains. Either way, his own sufferings help to account for the acute sensitivity he showed all his life to the needs, and the tribulations, of the young.

However, as he said, he 'got better at school'. And MTS offered plenty to do outside the classroom. Not surprisingly, his most striking contribution to the intellectual life of the school lay in drama. He gathered a group of sixth-formers which met in Leeson's study to read plays and give short papers. From time to time he took them out to West End plays: *King Lear* at the Old Vic, followed by scrambled eggs, pork pie, and strawberries and cream at the flat in Battersea; or a dinner at Beguinot's restaurant before Clemence Dane's *A Bill of Divorcement*, through which he himself 'wept callow tears'.

In March 1929 Oakeshott was encouraged by Leeson to produce *Macbeth* as the first ever full-length play on Speech Day. Conditions were less than ideal. The Great Hall in Charterhouse Square, an enormous 1875 neo-Gothic building with a high roof, had no stage, only a small improvised platform for the speeches. Most of the costumes were lent by the Holywell Players, but it proved impossible to hold a complete dress rehearsal at all. The producer was however warmly praised in *The Taylorian*: G. H. Stainforth, a future Master of Wellington, wrote that 'the swiftness with which scene followed scene was most refreshing in comparison with the performance in London some years ago'. He also found 'the scenery and lighting extraordinarily effective', and hoped this would be the first of many such productions. It was, though only one more was Oakeshott's.

As well as drama he was drawn into two other school societies, both characteristically presided over by Leeson. In the Debating Society he seconded a motion that 'the school training in science tends to stifle romance'.

> He feared the test-tube, [according to *The Taylorian*] not only because it might explode but also because it revealed to him that he was made up of molecules, and this destroyed the romance of himself. The unknown was the romantic; hence his motor-car was an infinite romance to him, for he knew nothing of the mysterious sparking and plugging of the sparking plugs.

The motion was deservedly lost 44–19.

Oakeshott's association with the Archaeological Society was more lasting. At its AGM on 10 July 1928 he was elected a Vice-President, which he described to Noel as 'a minor throb'. Later that month there was an expedition to Silchester near Reading. Transport was provided by six cars, including his and Leeson's. An incident on the journey was noted in *The Taylorian* and remembered ever afterwards by the boys in his car. A banana skin thrown from a car going in the opposite direction landed on the driver's lap. His only reaction was the comment 'Oh, how perfectly dastardly!'

A second innovation of Oakeshott's at MTS involved his friend William Temple, now Archbishop of York. He had first met Temple at Oxford through Cyril Bailey, their common Balliol tutor, and had kept in touch since. When his First, and later his forthcoming marriage, were announced in *The Times* there had been a handwritten note the next day. In July 1928 Temple had sent him a copy of his Scott Holland lectures entitled *Christianity and the State*. Later in the year Oakeshott sent him in return a 10,000-word essay on

Nationalism. He had had the typescript specially bound, and inscribed the fly-leaf 'To William Temple, the kindest and wisest friend, from Walter Oakeshott'.

In it he distinguishes nationalism from nationality. Nationality is good. 'It will always be a thrill to hear a Frenchman shout *Liberté* in Paris, even if it is only the name of a newspaper.' Nationalism is however too easily corrupted into absolutism. Bolshevism in Russia and *'Fascismo'* in Italy have already taken that road. Germany is teetering on the brink. The victorious Allies conspired to hamstring the Weimar Republic in what may prove 'the most tremendous blunder in history'. But it is 'too early yet to say' which way Germany will go. The only hope for the future lies in an internationalism which will happily lie down with nationality, though not with nationalism.

Temple was enthusiastic. If Oakeshott can find a publisher, he will be happy to write a foreword to it now. Better however would be '*not to publish it as it is, but to work it up into something a good deal bigger to be published later. ... I cannot help feeling that it is the outline of a really important book.*' Unfortunately there is no record of any follow-up.

Nevertheless he kept close touch with Temple. Much later in life he recalled that during those years Temple 'used to ask me to dine with him in Lambeth Palace, where he had a flat, and occasionally he visited us in Battersea'. So it was natural that he should ask Temple to inaugurate his planned series of lectures on classical subjects. Parties were invited from all the London secondary schools, and the plan was for each school to offer a venue in turn. Merchant Taylors' was host for the inaugural lecture in November 1929.

Temple responded with a rousing display of Balliol Hellenism. 'Latin literature at its best – even Vergil – is but an imitation of Greek models. ... With the Greeks (sc. unlike the Romans) thought counts more than deeds. ... In tragedy', reported *The Taylorian* 'he placed the *Agamemnon* of Aeschylus first and foremost.' All good fighting stuff, and Oakeshott would have agreed with it.

Some six years later that connexion with Temple – one of Oakeshott's two chief heroes – was to prove crucial to his career. For the moment however he was keeping his options open. In January 1929 he went to Charterhouse to one of those select gatherings of 'dons and beaks' which attracted the ambitious, at least among the latter. There were 'about 50 people jabbering education', including 'various great men whom I really don't know at all'. It was doubtless

Cyril Bailey who got him invited and 'made quite the best speech of the conference'. His health was still troubling him: a boil on his arm, like a previous one on his leg, had to be lanced by the doctor when he got back home.

But his varied activities continued unabated. At the end of May 1929 there was a General Election. Noel went to stay in Oxford to help her father in his campaign, and his letters to her record how he spent three successive evenings. On the first he gave a two-hour session at the Working Men's College. The next two he devoted to electioneering in Battersea. The sitting member was the Communist Saklatvala. Oakeshott cared neither for his politics nor for him – 'a dirty little man' – and was working for Labour which offered the only hope of ousting him. His second evening he spent driving 'old Sanders', the Labour candidate, round from meeting to meeting.

The third evening was to be a big occasion. Sanders having been secretary of the Fabian Society, Sidney Webb had agreed to speak. But his time of arrival was uncertain, and Oakeshott was put up as a time-filler 'to gasbag wildly about the Government's foreign policy'. It turned out to be 'a fearfully frantic evening'. Webb was late, and Oakeshott was flustered. For once he wrote disparagingly about everybody present. Webb, 'poor little man, did get treated badly, chiefly because he was completely inaudible at the back'. The Chairman 'was offensive beyond words'. Even Sanders is 'not a great man, but I very much hope he gets in'. Sanders, to his own surprise, did; Dr Moon did not. As to Oakeshott, if he had ever had any party political ambitions, they were never heard of again.

But his ambition of the time seems in retrospect scarcely less strange: it was for a career in educational administration. At that time the Kent Office under Salter Davies had a good reputation. Philip Morris, brother of his old philosophy tutor at Balliol, was head of the Elementary Department there. Through Gater and others a post was found for him as a trainee clerk at Maidstone, to start in March 1930. But Leeson offered, if he should wish to return to teaching after all, to try to keep a place open for him at Merchant Taylors'.

Before he left MTS he had his most notable triumph still to come: the school play of 1930. His *Oresteia* was based upon that of the Balliol Players in 1924, with Trevelyan's translation abridged and set to Westrup's music. But the chosen day being 6 March, the play had to be given indoors. Some improvements could be made over the previous year's *Macbeth* by turning the bench seating round to give a better stage at the rear of the Great Hall. But much was inevitably lost by the transfer indoors – Agamemnon, for instance, had to dismount from his chariot in the courtyard outside. Nevertheless Oakeshott insisted on retaining the naphtha-flaming torchlight procession at the end of the trilogy. Boys were stationed with buckets at each exit door of the Hall, with another in the courtyard by a hydrant; nevertheless fingers were kept crossed. One small compensation for the indoor setting was the opportunity, boldly seized, of bringing in the organ; and though some were heard to deplore 'a shocking anachronism', most felt it successfully underscored the deep religious element in the drama.

For the programme Oakeshott made only two changes from the one he had designed for the Balliol Players. First, he re-wrote the synopsis for a school audience – by chance his draft survives, literally on the back of an envelope received a few months earlier. Second, he omitted any name of a producer.

The seven survivors of a long-lived cast remember the rehearsals vividly. The Lent term of 1930 began with a talk on the *Oresteia* by Leeson. After auditions (speaking and singing), rehearsals began on 10 February with every member of the cast being given his part especially written out in handsome longhand by Oakeshott. From then on the play dominated their lives. Walter was meticulous in his attention to detail but never finicky or impatient. Noel was wardrobe mistress. Many of the costumes came from her family home, and the cast went to the Battersea flat to be fitted. At one of these fittings Charles Mitchell (Orestes) observed Walter laying a hand on Noel's shoulder, as she knelt down with a mouthful of pins to adjust a chiton for a boy, with a tenderness he has never forgotten. If one may judge from a single observation, their marriage was now well established. Helena was born in the following year.

The performance on the night was memorable in the best sense. There were no hitches, and the flamboyant procession passed off without danger. But the Court of the Merchant Taylors' Company, who had attended carrying their traditional apotropaic posies, had been sufficiently alarmed to forbid any more naked flames in the Great Hall. Fourteen years later, Hitler burned it down for them.

Stainforth, reviewing the production for *The Taylorian* 'could not have wished for a more impressive finale'. Of the players he singled out Mitchell in Oakeshott's own part of Orestes as 'responsible in no small degree for the success of the entertainment'. A more significant verdict was delivered by the man who took over as the school's chief producer a few years later: 'It was amazing how the majesty and power of this great classic came over to an audience largely ignorant of the historical and religious background.' More recently still a semi-official history of *Drama at Merchant Taylors' School*[11] says of Oakeshott that 'he, if anyone, was the creator of drama at Merchant Taylors'. He did it with some canvas-covered frames and a few lights – the rest of his resources were human.' Oakeshott himself would certainly have wished to add to the credits the name of Aeschylus.

Afterwards he made each of his principals a present of a book. A. J. Taylor received a copy of an address to Greats men by A. J. Toynbee of Balliol, and others one of (OMT) Gilbert Murray's translations. And still now when the octogenarian survivors meet, they will greet each other with the words of the final chorus in Westrup's setting: 'Joy to you' and ' Joy to you also'.

On 29 March it was the turn of the school to make a presentation to the young master with the unimpressive personality. He had asked for a set of the *New Cambridge Shakespeare*, but the sum subscribed was too large even for the leather-bound edition; so they gave him a book-table as well. Replying to a speech by the Head Monitor he referred to his move into educational administration.

> He himself had learned so much during his teaching career that he felt it would be good for everyone to become a schoolmaster for a period before going in for some other career. ... The elementary and state-aided secondary schools were, in educating the mass of the people, doing some of the most important work in the country.

Leeson's estimate of Oakeshott's eight terms at MTS can be derived from a reference he wrote for him in 1938 for the High Mastership of St Paul's. On the one hand his health was not good, and 'he used to show want of clutch and grip in dealing with practical questions'. But 'he took his part in the rugger and cricket supervision and produced our school plays for several years.' More positively, Leeson was confident that 'his influence would encourage just that width and breadth of culture that the London boy with his sometimes narrow background and materialistic aims needs most'; and his 'quality of character could not fail to leave its mark, as it did at Merchant Taylors' '.

For the new job, based in Maidstone, the Oakeshotts rented a house nearby at East Farleigh, just up the Medway on the Pilgrims' Way. A year before, in a low moment, he had written: 'I feel I want to retire to a country village and live the life of a monk or a scholar', but then immediately corrected himself: 'it's wicked really to feel like that'. Apart from other pressures of city life, one in particular weighed upon him: the noise of the traffic aggravated his insomnia. So it was a relief to escape from London. Moreover now for the first time in his life he had a largish garden of his own, and he clearly took delight (and exercise) in planning and planting, mowing and picking. His letters speak with joy of the fruit and the flowers: in May he had been round greeting the new roses, in July he finds the American pillar 'the loveliest rose in the world'.

It may indeed be that this was a necessary fallow period of his life. The work was not as emotionally demanding as teaching, he had his evenings and weekends, and he was no longer driving himself to the limits of his constitution. It was the right time for founding a family. True there were still problems of money and health; but with their own relationship on an easier footing, these problems could be faced.

In June 1930 Noel went into a London nursing home for an operation which kept her there for a fortnight. Walter travelled up to see her every day when he could and wrote when he could not. She then went for a month's convalescence, first at Staunton Harold, the seat of the Ferrerses, then at Aston Tirrold. In August they were together again. Their first child Helena was born on 19 May 1931. From then on for twenty five years Noel was launched on what, perhaps unexpectedly, proved to be her most successful and rewarding career, as a mother.

Walter's career meanwhile was in an office. Having started in April 1930 as a temporary clerk at a salary of £300 p.a., he was upgraded after a while to the rank of 'officer in training with the Elementary Education Department'.[12] But Morris, as head of the department, was paid only £700 p.a., so Oakeshott's salary still must have represented quite a drop from Merchant Taylors'.

Initially he found a challenge even in the office work. In June he wrote to Noel 'Today I drew up a sort of scheme of procedure which I suppose will go all round the office but which I'm quite sure no one will look at. I'm getting rather bitten with the whole thing, all the same, and I think I see several ways in which the old schedule can be improved.'

More appropriately he was given a responsibility for the provision of books in the county, and of one in particular. Kent and Leicestershire, always two go-ahead authorities, were jointly producing an abridged version of the Bible. Someone had the bright idea of asking Oakeshott to draw the maps for it. They made a small but suitable legacy from him to the county.

But what he enjoyed most were the days out of the office. He loved the gentle countryside of Kent, he often had the agreeable company of Philip Morris or James Cullen (who had a temporary term in the office in the summer of 1931), and he felt at home in the schools. He had 'a most terrific day' in Folkestone, where he saw a first-class young history teacher at work, followed by 'an excellent demonstration lesson on the role of the gramophone in schools'. And he 'learned to admire, perhaps above everything else, the selfless devotion of teachers in these small village schools.' His own personal anthology was to include a 1928 poem by Stephen Spender entitled 'An Elementary Classroom in a Slum'. The poem contrasts the foggy windows of the classroom with the map of the world on the wall, and appeals to 'governor, teacher, inspector, visitor' to see that 'this map becomes their window', and 'to let their tongues run naked into books'. In his anthology he gives the poem the epigraph 'And who is my neighbour?'

Early in 1931 it became clear to him that what he really wanted to do after all was to teach, so he wrote to Leeson. Leeson could not find room for him at Merchant Taylors' but knew of a vacancy at Winchester. On 31 August, his last day in the Kent office, he attended a meeting of the Advisory Committee for Teachers. That September, when he was still only twenty-eight, there began the most exciting and fruitful period of his life.

4

Winchester

1931 – 1938

The seven years at Winchester 1931-8 were fat as fat: replete with
promise and achievement, with varied excitements but also with con-
tinuous hard slog. During that period he wrote a book on economic
history, and the bulk of one on unemployment which has become a
classic; he made a discovery of major importance in English literature, and wrote the first accounts of it; and he began an original study
of the Winchester Bible which was to become the main work of his
scholarly life.

It was a time also when old career options closed and new ones
opened with bewildering speed. At the start he had abandoned educational administration for teaching. By the end he was still determined
on teaching. But on the way he had considered and rejected – or
perhaps been rejected by – at least three other careers, including the
one he was eventually to follow. All this required decisions, which
never came easily to him.

The magnitude and the quality of his achievements during that
period are so remarkable that one is bound to wonder how he did
it. Certainly his health was better than it had been at Merchant
Taylors': we have Leeson's testimony for that (p. 87), corroborated
negatively by his own letters to Noel in 1936–7. But his constitution
was never robust – insomnia was a permanent problem – and if, as he
said at the end of his life, he had been 'always tired' at Balliol, how
much more so now.

In the holidays, when he took them, he continued to keep himself intermittently fit by rough walking, including at least once in
the Dolomites with Vere Hodge. In term time his exercise, apart
from a constitutional walk, seems to have been confined to rowing.
He joined a 'dons' IV' with A. T. P. Williams (the headmaster), the
bishop's chaplain and a young colleague Harold Walker, but said that
'the few outings left me utterly exhausted'. He also coached a boys'

IV, one of whom remembers him as 'an inspired and enthusiastic coach'. When they unexpectedly won the cup, they broke with precedent by having him occupy the centre of their victorious photograph. But from ball games providence in the shape of the headmaster kept him pure and free – perhaps indeed because of his known other commitments.

For as well as his work he had also a growing family to think of. In addition to Helena, there were now, from 26 July 1933, twin boys as well, known immediately as Castor and Pollux.* The birth of the twins had been difficult, and for their first few years they were a great drain on the health and energy of their mother. The school house provided in Canon Street was less than ideal. The street was then considered not really suitable for a master, and Williams in offering it had hinted delicately at the possibility of bugs behind the panelling. It was also too small for resident staff (cook and nurse), even if they could be afforded. Other staff wives observed that 'the Canon St house was cleaned only once a month when for about three days the family all ate cold beef as Noel concentrated the [domestic] help she had on house-cleaning'.

She therefore took to migrating when she could to Copse Stile in Aston Tirrold. 'I cannot tell you how lovely this place is,' she wrote from it in 1938. 'As long as there is this place to come to sometimes, nothing else matters.' And everything there was laid on. The household, headed by her devoted father, contained an unmarried sister and also her own formidable old nanny.[1] The servants included a gardener/chauffeur and a supply of domestics which was reasonably adequate, though Noel once exclaimed in a letter that 'it's very fussing not having a between-maid.' There she could lead the life she was brought up to. The children also soon came to regard Copse Stile as home. It offered room to run and play, with a stretch of moat and tadpoles. It also provided stability by contrast with the nomadic existence of a public school master, whose career required him to occupy six different houses within fifteen years.

These absences of the family, though distressing in many ways, did allow Walter more time for work. But problems of organization arose, especially in a school which could offer no central feeding for staff or boys. Most of the time he fended for himself, frugally except when he entertained boys to tea – 'with a *third* boiled egg if

---

* Castor became corrupted to 'Cargie'; Pollux did not survive.

you wanted it!' Married colleagues in that hospitable community often invited him to supper. Then after a while he was asked to become a house tutor in Hopper's, where he not only received a small honorarium but could take lunch free with the boys.

The housemaster of Hopper's, Malcolm Robertson, was a giant of the old school, devoted to his boys and resistant to change. Seeing the quality in Oakeshott, he overlooked his 'leftist' leanings, and even used to lend him his own car for transporting rare books, Oakeshott having sold the AC for economy when Helena was born. Like many such barons, Robertson was suspicious of headmasters. He waged a long guerrilla war against Leeson and, when Oakeshott came back to succeed him, directed a few shafts at him too from the retirement benches. But for the moment he was a powerful supporter.

Not that Oakeshott was interested in the politics of the Masters' Common Room. His concern, then as always, was for the boys. One member of the house was the future Lord Whitelaw, who discerned in his gentle house tutor 'a very considerable person'. A less orthodox boy whom he took under his wing was Patrick Duncan, who came in late and lame (two handicaps in the schoolboy world) from South Africa where his father was Governor General. Oakeshott gave him the support an outsider needed, including private coaching in Latin. On finishing his education Duncan went back to South Africa to help lead the fight against apartheid. Oakeshott maintained affectionate and admiring touch with him throughout his life.

But it was teaching above all that he had come to do. By the Winchester tradition a young master ('don') would be given some sixth form work with specialists in his own subject, together with a general responsibility (for some 10–12 periods a week) as a form master in the main school. At all levels Oakeshott's teaching was marked by an imaginative care which showed itself both in his concern for individual boys and in the choice of teaching materials. With slower boys he was patient and encouraging; the quicker ones found their eyes being opened ever wider. The classical sixth, for example, who were not aware how much their minds needed broadening, were surprised one day to be presented with Psalm 121 in Coverdale's version, and given two hours in which to write about it on the lines of I. A. Richards's *Practical Criticism*. One of that class admits that his whole thinking was changed by that challenge.

More important, both to him and to them, was the work he did with the specialist historians. For in 1933 he discovered in the

Fellows' Library an exceptional resource potentially available to teachers of early modern history at Winchester. This was an astonishingly rich collection of maps of the world between about 1400 and 1600. Three of them covered the whole transition from the medieval to the modern world. The Founder's Map, a manuscript bequeathed by William of Wykeham to his school in 1404, still has Jerusalem as the centre of the world and 'Paradise' at the top – not really a map at all but a notional design. The Ulm Ptolemy c. 1490, a very early printed edition of the greatest geographer of antiquity, tangibly demonstrated the new rebirth of science, on whose basis many of the first navigators set out to explore the world. Third was Mercator's famous atlas of c. 1570 which incorporated, albeit rather belatedly, the results of their explorations and is thus the first of the true modern atlases.

Oakeshott was carried away by the excitement of these maps. He was shy of speaking about it to adults, but he began collecting them himself and he made full use of them in his teaching. Fondled and interpreted by him, they could thrill boys of all ages. For the sixth forms they illuminated the history of science and religion, exploration and empire. For his junior forms they deepened the stories of the famous explorers and adventurers. For anyone susceptible they could provide a first heady taste of scholarship as discovery, coupled with the joy of access to fine objects.

His junior form was a kind of 'science Fifth', boys who intended to specialize in science later. The ability range was wider down there, but Williams noted his painstaking success, 'not least with the slower of them'. One such, who left in 1934 after a year with Oakeshott to join the Army, was Archie John Wavell. Son of a more eminent father, who had been a scholar of Winchester in the previous century, Archie John, so called to distinguish him, was nevertheless a man of very considerable talents. No scholar in the academic sense, he learned from Oakeshott a love of English poetry, especially Hopkins and Eliot, and an interest in textual criticism. No militarist, he spoke in the school Debating Society against 'tradition'. At school he was often in hot water. His most famous exploit was a round of golf at Hockley, played between midnight and 3 a.m. in 99, when he 'just won an exciting bet by one stroke'. It was an early exercise in command, since it required a team of supporters 'trained to locate the fall of a shot by sound first, roughly, and then to pin-point it by torchlight afterwards'.

On that occasion Wavell got away with it. On others he did not, and powerful allies were needed. 'I in my small way', wrote Oakeshott, 'and Williams, the Headmaster, in a much bigger way, spent a considerable amount of time playing down his misdeeds to our colleagues. . . . Williams succeeded, by that masterly technique of kindly inactivity, which in later years I tried to copy so much less successfully, in bringing everything off the boil.' Wavell became a family friend of the Oakeshotts. He must also have made it up with his housemaster, the mountaineer R. L. G. Irving, for we find the two of them in 1946 trying to get Oakeshott to join them for a climbing weekend in North Wales.

As form master of his 'science Fifth', Oakeshott had to teach not only English but Latin, divinity and history. The syllabus was flexible enough to allow a man to teach what interested him, so that under history he could include economics or scientific ideas. There was also a general essay on a set subject each week, which offered unlimited scope for broadening. Entirely typical of him was the occasion when he asked his form to write about the Greek vases in the school museum, and offered prizes, paid for out of his own pocket, of tickets to the current Winchester Guildhall concert – not to 'the winner' but to anyone who reached a reasonable standard.

Greek vases appropriately enough provided the first in a long series of discoveries that punctuated Oakeshott's life. One day in 1934 or so, the art master Dick Gleadowe, himself a classical scholar, found in clearing out his art-room a packing case containing a number of fragments of Roman glass.[2] He asked Oakeshott to look at them in case they were of any value. They were not. But under them could be seen sheets of a newspaper printed early in the century. They were lying quite flat, which suggested there might be something else below them again There was: an Attic black-figure cup, in fragments. Walter was excited; Noel, even more so, took them to Beazley. Beazley turned them over meditatively, then looked up. 'Very nice,' he said, 'the Theseus painter.' 'His choice of adjectives', wrote Oakeshott later, 'was always precise. "Very nice" did not mean a magnificent vase; but a nice vase for a school collection to have.'[3] As always, Oakeshott was fortunate; but fortune, in such matters, favours the careful observer.

But Winchester College, however absorbing could not monopolize his educational interests. He took on the duties of secretary to the Governors of King Alfred's, then the Diocesan Training College, of

which Williams was chairman. Nor could the past, however fascinating, divert him from contemporary affairs; indeed one function of the
study of the past was precisely to illuminate the present. Hence his
first book, *Commerce and Society*.

The book seems to have been conceived out of his lectures to the
Working Men's College 1926–9. It was begun while he was with
Kent and continued during the holidays in his first three years at
Winchester. Some of the text was read in manuscript by a colleague,
Ernest Sabben-Clare, who spent the calendar year 1933–4 on the staff
before entering the Colonial Service. To him in gratitude Oakeshott
gave a leather-bound first edition of Mungo Park's *Travels*.

Oakeshott offered his book in 1935 to the Oxford University
Press, under the title 'World Economic History'. Tom Norrington, a
Wykehamist who was working for the Press, recommended it to his
superiors in July 'on the grounds that it is a service to teachers, the
author is a coming man, and there should be a large enough demand
at least to avoid loss'. It was accepted with a change of title. In
December, when proofs were already being read by Williams, Norrington realized that 'nothing has been formally agreed about terms'.
Published in 1936, the book was almost sold out by 1946. Norrington
then wrote to say that 'this very good book has never had the sale it
deserves'. But he did not propose a reprint, since 'it does not fit any
course currently followed at school or university'.

Oakeshott's avowed purpose in writing *Commerce and Society*
was to help economics 'play a larger part in the curriculum of
schools'. But since 'the "dismal science" is not only superficially
dismal but has also an increasing tendency to avoid human issues and
concentrate upon abstractions', his book would be 'an attempt to
sketch the history of commerce as a part of the history of western
society'. It was clearly an ambitious undertaking for a young man
who had not been trained in either economics or modern history.

Reviews nevertheless were generally favourable.[4] The *TLS* called it
'a courageous attempt' which 'goes some way towards fulfilling
its ambitious purpose'. The reviewer raised an academic eyebrow
at the 'conversational character of his style', but commended his
avoidance of over-simplification and over-schematization. He gave
warmest praise to the admirable illustrations with which 'his volume
is graced'. Most of these were maps either specially drawn or
simplified by the author.

To a later reader the book seems to fall into two halves. The first is a lively history of trade, empire and seamanship, themes which he was to take up again in *Founded upon the Seas*. The second is indeed more dismal: a standard economic history with special attention to banking. These were themes to which wisely he did not return; but he had done enough to establish some respectability as a scholar.

One or two of the asides betray his cast of mind. 'We know too much about the finite to be able to conceive the infinite.' 'Since the days when Ulysses gave Polyphemus wine to drink, civilized traders have realized how powerful an inducement alcohol may prove with native races.' There is an occasional whiff of snobbery: 'the bourgeoisie, interested (as always) in making money and (as always) with no idea how to spend it'. But the fairer tone predominates. 'Battles may be won on playing fields, but wars are not. The Napoleonic wars were won in the workshops of the Midlands and North and in the counting-houses of London.'

More interesting, in view of his next assignment, are some comments on unemployment. 'There are now millions of unemployed in every great country of the world. The immediate cause is not that it is too difficult to produce both the necessities and the comforts of life, but that it is too easy.' But (the book's last words) 'over-production is evidently a misnomer. Production is not excessive but misdirected. It is not, in fact, directed at all.'

In a speech in the school Debating Society at about the same time (December 1933) he was more explicit. The motion was 'That this house would welcome a dictator in Britain': Wavell proposed, and he seconded. 'We must not forget the conditions of misery amongst the unemployed, which democracy has in no way succeeded in improving. ... The exploitation of the poor by the rich must be broken. Only a dictatorship can do these things.' To that extent he is cautiously interested in what is going on in Germany. Many 'would claim that, if the National Socialism of Germany represents an attempt to control economics in the interests of society, it is a valuable political experiment, though they would question whether the repressive methods which it adopts are necessary for the purpose.' The judgement of Nazi Germany may have been naive in supposing that the two aspects of Hitler's policy could be disjoined. But more interesting is the early sign of liberal opinion in favour of 'a consciously integrated organic state'.

Commerce and Society was far from finished in 1932 when Williams asked Oakeshott to take on the job of School Librarian. The job carried with it an allowance of £50 p.a. which made a welcome addition to his salary of c. £550. The moment was critical. The library was about to be transferred from a mid-Victorian building to the fourteenth-century brewery where it now is. The move entailed an enormous amount of planning: arrangement of shelving and furniture, and re-arrangement and re-cataloguing of books.

All of this, in Williams' judgement, he 'carried through with enthusiasm and success'. His own letters to Noel, written at the end of each day's work during the Christmas holidays 1933–4, give something of the feel of the operation.

> I'm sitting in the library now – the lights aren't in yet, but there are the temporary lights that we work by strung about the ceiling – even so they give oddly little light except just in the patch one's sitting in, and one's surrounded by warm blackness all around. [Again]: I've had another day in the Library and in the bindery, packing up some of the books that got damaged in transit. You can't tell how lonely it is in that museum [where the bindery was] at night, with wind swirling through every keyhole and doors rattling – an absolutely bloodcurdling experience.

Typically, he also started a bookbinding class among the boys and ran it for some years. One of these, a future director of a polytechnic,[5] recalls his 'extremely gentlemanly attitude to a problematic group of chaps'.

But there were other spin-offs from the operation, as exciting as they were unforeseen. The new library building was large enough to include a strongroom. This would eventually house the magnificent collection of old and valuable books (and a few manuscripts) which constituted the Fellows' Library. That collection had always been kept distinct from the school library and, though nominally accessible to the public, had been jealously guarded by a succession of Fellows' Librarians. Oakeshott, as school librarian, now had to be involved in its move to the Brewery. What he saw there made his mouth water, both as bibliophile and as teacher. Having won the confidence of the Fellows' Librarian, he was actually allowed in February 1933 to take out some of the maps for classroom use.

Late in 1933 or early in 1934 he was even lent the key to the safe which housed the manuscripts, let into the wall of the Warden's bedroom. In it he found about twenty-five volumes, including a small group of Middle English items. One of these was a very fat book, rebound in the eighteenth century. Opening it, he noticed that the proper names, which were of Arthurian knights, were written in red, a most laborious process. The manuscript had lost sections both at beginning and end, so the title and author's name were both missing. 'Not being versed in the Arthurian legends,' he wrote much later,' I passed on without delay to the next book, till my time was up, and I reluctantly clanged the trellis to, and locked it; with nothing in particular in my head but a vague sense of excitement.'

But the manuscripts could wait. The immediate task was to deal with the printed books. That meant not just moving them: he wanted the school – and not only the school – to share his pleasure in them. For he believed 'most strongly that exhibitions of old books, maps, prints etc can be of first-rate educational value'. To that end he had 'pressed hard for there to be showcases in the new library'. In these specially built showcases he now mounted a series of six splendid exhibitions in Brewery, displaying altogether more than 100 books from the Fellows' Library, with even more borrowed from outside.

The first, over Easter 1934, was planned in cooperation with Sir Frederick Kenyon, then Fellows' Librarian. Kenyon, himself a noted textual scholar, had been Director of the British Museum. In that capacity he had recently bought *Codex Sinaiticus*, the most notable of all manuscripts of the Bible, for a million pounds which he now had to raise. The exhibition in Brewery, of some seventy fine bibles, was part of the fund-raising programme.

A few weeks later Kenyon asked Oakeshott to arrange an exhibition of modern printing, in connexion with the centenary of William Morris's birth, for the Friends of the National Libraries. The Fellows' Library, from which the books were to come, has no Caxton, but it does have a book printed with Caxton's mark by his successor, Wynkyn de Worde. In order to write a sensible label for that book, Oakeshott looked up the article on early printing in the *Cambridge History of English Literature*. The article contained a reference to Malory. 'The compilation of the *Morte D'Arthur* was finished in 1469, but of the compiler little is known save the name. No manuscript of the work is known, and though Caxton certainly revised it, exactly to what extent has never been settled.'

My heart lost a beat; King Arthur and his knights – those names all in red: could the manuscript in the safe be Malory? I bought the Everyman text of Malory, in two volumes, at the school bookshop. It is an almost word-for-word reprint, though with the spelling modernised. I again asked the man in charge of the Fellows' Library if I might borrow the key to make a check. Five minutes was enough to know that our text was a pre-Caxton manuscript.[6]

There was no opportunity before the opening of the exhibition to consult Kenyon. Oakeshott therefore took it upon himself to put both items side by side in the same showcase: the late Caxton, 'a fine copy of a very fine book', and next to it the manuscript 'with a card saying that it was believed to be the only pre-Caxton text of Malory in existence'. The party of visitors was led by Professor H. D. Ziman, who happened also to be literary editor of the *Daily Telegraph*. The next issue of the *Telegraph* (25 June) reported 'what appears to be a remarkable discovery'.

Four days later Oakeshott was presiding over a small luncheon party in Canon Street. It was the first day of what he called 'Winchester's great pagan festival', the cricket match against Eton, being played that year at Winchester. In the middle of lunch the front doorbell rang imperiously.

> It was manifestly a scholar. He introduced himself as Eugene Vinaver, and explained (truly enough, as it soon turned out) that he was the authority on Malory's text. He had nearly completed for the Oxford University Press an edition collating all known sources, and claimed the right to edit the manuscript, if indeed it was what it was said to be: he must see it at once. I left the salmon and the strawberries and took him over to the [new] library, explaining on the way that I was not the responsible librarian, and that I could not open the showcase without Kenyon's permission. . . . The more urgent his demands became, the more adamant was I; and down we went, on the chilliest of terms, to look at it through the glass.

Vinaver confirmed the attribution but 'went away believing that I was being deliberately difficult'.

It was now for the Warden and Fellows to decide who should be invited to edit the manuscript. Kenyon, who had himself identified the only manuscript of Aristotle's *Constitution of Athens*, believed strongly in what he called 'discoverer's rights', and pressed Oakeshott to edit it himself. But to do so, he could see, would mean a complete change of career, from schoolmaster to scholar, and even then it would take him ten years to get to the point at which Vinaver started. The Warden and Fellows decided that the manuscript should remain at Winchester long enough for Oakeshott to write it up in *The Times* and the *Times Literary Supplement* but should then be deposited at Manchester University, where Vinaver could use it as the basis for an edition to replace his now outdated draft.

Oakeshott's relations with Vinaver were to undergo a number of vicissitudes until much later when he was able to propose him for an Honorary Fellowship at Lincoln, and they became firm friends. Later also Oakeshott learned (from Archie John Wavell) that there was all the time another scholar who would have liked to edit it: T. E. Lawrence. If Lawrence had been asked to take it on, 'that might have given a meaning to a life so manifestly then in process of being destroyed – by frustration'.

The two articles in *The Times* (25 August) and the *TLS* (27 September) were written in six weeks over the summer holidays. They give an account of the finding of the manuscript but they also take up three points of scholarship. First was the identity of the author. Although the final colophon of the whole work was missing, others were extant at the end of component books. Several of them confirmed Malory's name, and the one at the end of Book IV added a poignant detail: 'this was drawyn by a knyght prisoner, Sir Thomas Malleore, that God sende him good recover'. This confirmed a hypothesis already put forward among others by a noted American Malory scholar, G. L. Kittredge. Oakeshott sent him a photocopy of it, and was delighted with the reply dated 28 September: 'Nothing that has crossed my path of late has stirred me so deeply. This colophon, with its spelling of Malory's name and its "prisoner", is like a voice from the great deeps.'

The second point of scholarly interest was the relation between the Winchester ms. (W), the Caxton edition (C) and the putative original ms. of the author (M). Having reviewed some of the more surprising discrepancies between W and C, he showed that sometimes W and sometimes C agreed better with Malory's French originals and there- fore must be closer to M. For example, where C had printed *ryver and hyghe mntayn* W read *ryver and an mortays*. Since the French version of the *Quest* which Malory had used gave *l'ave grant que on apeloit Marcoise* Oakeshott could be sure that the *hyghe* of C was a mistake for *hyght* meaning '(was) called', and that W's *mortays* was a more accurate representation of M's original manuscript than C's guess. The conclusion was that W and C were independent of each other and that neither could claim priority.[7] Vinaver accepted that.

The third point was of a different kind. He adumbrated in his *Times* article a view which he came back to amplify at the end of his life. In Book V the original of Caxton's text is not French but English, a long alliterative poem which he 'edited' even more boldly than usual. Not only did he cut it by half, but he handled it in a way which revealed an entirely different – and shallower – conception of tragedy from that visible in W's treatment of it. Here Oakeshott did not hesitate to claim both primacy and superiority for his Winchester manuscript.

Meanwhile in the summer and autumn of 1934

Malory became very much a part of what my Division 'learnt': the Minster, where the knights went for service that Whitsunday; and the 'meadow beside Wynchester' where they jousted ere they departed. It was easy for those who lived with those same surroundings, which Malory had surely himself seen, to people that piece of land with those knightly figures – though they had never existed. After all, the myth of chivalry, like all the great myths, embodies a profound truth about human values.

In the following year, 1935, fortune prepared another excitement for him – though this time it had a fifteen-year time-fuse. Once again it started with maps. A Sotheby's catalogue included mention of a 'commonplace book', containing a 'geographical dictionary of Egypt, Palestine and other adjacent regions, c. 1600, and containing some manuscript maps'. Oakeshott got in touch with his friend the bookseller Clifford Maggs, 'who used to lend wonderful books for our exhibitions in the College library'. Maggs, having looked at it, reported that one or two of the maps were rather good but for the rest there was nothing much. 'If we were lucky I ought to get it for a few pounds.' He did get it for £4.15s.

Looking through it at home, Oakeshott found the contents distinctly interesting. True, the entries in the geographical dictionary turned out to be derived largely from the Old Testament, text and commentaries. Most of the maps too were copied from books on the Bible. But there was also a list of the compiler's library, some 500 or so items, which gave special pleasure because of the original owner's interests over-lapping extensively that of its new possessor. [Also] there was, as is not infrequently found in books of the period, a set of verses on one of the fly-leaves, in a crabbed hand more difficult to read than that of most of the book. Altogether an excellent £5 worth, which, when I first acquired it, I handled frequently; poring over it and pondering.

But he 'did not read it through systematically', and after a while he put it on one side. There was too much else to do, including always teaching.

For Oakeshott was, and wished to remain, primarily a teacher. But just as teaching could use scholarship, so it could embrace a headmastership. And so we find him keeping contacts burnished. He became Secretary of the UU[8] in 1935, and is still vividly remem-bered by a surviving member, for his 'brilliant mind, full of excit-ing ideas and knowledge, combined with a gentleness and sensitivity which prevented him from being overpowering: he always seemed winningly concerned to listen to other people's half-baked ideas as well as to share his own infinitely richer store' – again the qualities of the teacher.

In addition to all these interests and excitements he still felt the draw of public affairs. In December 1934 we find him reluctantly taking the chair at a League of Nations meeting. In June 1936 he drafted a long letter to *The Times* (not published, perhaps never sent), arguing that Britain should give a lead in putting her colonial empire under League of Nations trusteeship. Nor was this cause merely cerebral. At the end of his life he told Helena that he would have gone to fight in Spain in 1936 if he had had the guts and not had a wife and a young family and an important new commitment in England: 'certainly those I knew who *did* so, were some of the best people I knew.'

That new commitment was the unemployment inquiry of 1936–8 financed by the Pilgrim Trust. His involvement in it was chiefly due to William Temple. Temple had kept contact since the move to Winchester in 1931. His own concern was already then focused on unemployment, and early in 1933 he had called together a committee of people who shared this concern. In March 1934 he wrote to *The*

Times arguing that, if there were to be any surplus in the national budget for the following year, the unemployed had first claim upon it. He urged those who agreed with him to write to their MPs pressing that restoration of the cuts in unemployment benefit should take precedence over any form of tax remission. Neville Chamberlain, as Chancellor of the Exchequer, much resented this 'interference'.

Among many other people concerned about unemployment were Lindsay and Thomas Jones. In 1933 the Ministry of Labour asked the National Council of Social Service to coordinate all its work for the unemployed; the NCSS thereupon set up an Unemployment Committee with Lindsay as chairman. Thomas Jones (TJ), who had been Deputy Secretary to the Cabinet under both Lloyd George and Baldwin, was also an old Oxford friend of Lindsay: as a Welshman he had been involved with him in Maes yr Haf from the start and had personally raised £400 p.a. for it for some years. When he retired from the Civil Service in 1930 he became the first Secretary to the Pilgrim Trust. His own experience and contacts, coupled with the resources of the Trust, made him with Temple the most influential person in the field.

When Edward Harkness founded the Pilgrim Trust in 1930, he 'desired that the gift should be used for some of the country's more urgent needs and in promoting her future well-being'. In 1931 and 1932 it had made substantial grants towards developing educational and social work in the areas most distressed by the slump. Now in 1935 Temple, with TJ's support, asked the Trustees to finance what he called 'a thorough investigation of the work that could be done by voluntary societies for the unemployed, an investigation which must inevitably involve an inquiry into the effects of unemployment and the real needs of unemployed men'. That somewhat curious formulation papers over the gap between two objectives which had to be held in balance throughout the project. The Trustees were especially concerned with the more limited objective which Temple placed first, 'in order to aid them in a wise allocation of their funds, in so far as these were used to finance pioneer enterprises'. Temple's committee had been concerned rather with the wider picture, but the formulation was tactical. In July 1935 the Trustees voted £4,000 for the inquiry.

The steering committee for the project covered this twofold aim. TJ and one other Trustee held a watching brief for the Trust, but most of the members came from Temple's own 1933 committee; as well as Lindsay they included the great Bishop George Bell of

Chichester, Sir Walter Moberly, Dr J. H. Oldham and its powerful woman secretary, Eleanora Iredale. Temple chaired the steering committee and Miss Iredale continued as secretary. Among others named by Temple as having helped the project in one way or another were Sir William Beveridge, Henry Brooke, Professor Carr-Saunders (who had helped Oakeshott with the writing of *Commerce and Society*), William Noble of Maes yr Haf and R. H. Tawney.

To conduct the research a team of three was sought. Temple's letter to Oakeshott of 21 April 1936 says 'We shall hope to secure an expert on sociological (forgive the hybrid – I see no way around it) research, and we have invited Mr Owen of PEP (Political and Economic Planning) to take this share.' Owen accepted, became the doyen of the team, and planned the whole strategy of the project with the advice of Beveridge.

Oakeshott evidently did not accept immediately. That letter of Temple's sets out to meet his hesitation, which must have concerned the twofold purpose of the project. His own committee, says Temple, was concerned all along with 'the human, as distinct from the economic, effects of unemployment'. They

> will (I trust) use the Report as an instrument for creating a new moral consciousness and a new body of sane thought with reference to this whole problem. Frankly I should not either be on the [Steering] Committee myself or suggest that you should take a year off from your work if the only aim were to advise the Pilgrim Trustees.

Temple goes on to offer 'a salary of £750 for that year, with travelling and other expenses up to a maximum of £250'. As to Oakeshott's contribution to the team,

> what we believe you could give us is a fresh impression made on a mind with a fully human (Christian) outlook by the facts themselves and the ideas of the pioneers in the field.
>
> I want to close by saying how eagerly I personally hope you will agree and find that you can come. The more I have thought over this suggestion, which at first rather surprised me, the more I am convinced that you can do supremely well just what we want. Also we shall sometimes meet!

Yours affect^{ly}

WILLIAM EBOR:

Oakeshott, of course, could not refuse such an invitation from Temple. But the letter had a second target. Leeson had by now succeeded Williams as headmaster of Winchester and had to approve a secondment. When first approached he 'disagreed profoundly with the proposal. He anticipated us producing a report heavily tainted with a mixture of socialism and "sob-stuff". But Temple's letter convinced him.' Tactfully Temple's introduction to the eventual report says that Oakeshott was 'on the initiative of the headmaster, Mr Leeson, given leave for a year, subsequently extended to four terms'.

The third member of the team was a young refugee research student of Maynard Keynes, Hans Singer. Singer was hired as a statistician, to add the steel reinforcement if the report was to go beyond the best existing work in the field, Bakke's otherwise 'brilliant study' *The Unemployed Man* (1932). But there was more to him than that. Oakeshott later described him as 'not only a fine professional but also one of the most humane chaps I knew'.[9] By acting as a bridge between the radical sociologist Owen and the Balliol humanist Oakeshott, Singer was able to convert a potential weakness of the team into a broad strength.

There was one other reef upon which the whole enterprise might have foundered. The subject of unemployment was inescapably political, as even Leeson's reaction showed, and the political ice was thin in many places. Chamberlain had already declared his hand in 1934. In 1935 the Unemployment Assistance Board (of which TJ was a member) had tried to make a further cut in benefits, but a national outcry had forced its retreat, with much loss of face to the Board and to the Government. The cooperation of the UAB was now essential to the project, and had to be secured without infringing scholarly independence. Agreement was reached that the files of the Board would be open to the researchers, but that any recommendations which they wished to make would be passed on privately and discussed before the drafting of the eventual report. The agreement worked well. Sir Walter Eady, as Chairman of the Board, was invited to some meetings of the Steering Committee, where he gave valuable help and made no attempt to influence the drafting. Similarly TJ, though 'he constantly impressed upon us the need to avoid politics', did not 'question a single detail in the proofs on the ground that it was too political'.

The strategy of the inquiry was as follows. First, 'Beveridge suggested that the crux of the matter was long unemployment', defined as being out of work for more than a year. Such men suffered and exemplified the effects of unemployment in the most extreme form. Moreover these effects might eventually make them unemployable, i.e. long unemployment could become self-perpetuating. Indeed the statistics showed that, when recovery came in 1932 at the end of the Great Depression, the number of such men did not drop proportionately. In 1929, before it started, they formed just six per cent of the total unemployed; in August 1937 they formed twenty-seven per cent. In raw figures that percentage meant 265,000 men and women or, with their families, 700,000 people.

Next the project distinguished between two contextual types of unemployment. One type was structural (called by them 'industrial'), where the dominant industry of the area has been hit by technological and other changes. The other was marginal (called by them 'residual'), where the area itself is relatively prosperous and there is no one main cause of unemployment. To fit these categories they chose six communities for close study. Four were structural: Liverpool (shipping), Blackburn (cotton), Durham and South Wales (coal). Two were marginal: Leicester and Deptford. The six were also carefully selected to be representative, when taken together, of the whole of England and Wales.

In each of them names were drawn at random from the files of the UAB of people to be interviewed – a total of about 1,000 people. No questionnaires were sent out, and everybody was seen by one of the team in their own home, not e.g. in an unemployed club. In each town all three members of the team took part in the interviewing. After every interview a standard record card was filled in. One side of it contained quantifiable objective data, which was subsequently punched on to Hollerith cards kept at the LSE. The other side recorded more personal judgements such as appearance, health, intelligence, the domestic standards of the household, the 'atmosphere' of the family and attitudes to future employment.

Somewhat to their surprise, the members of the team were generally welcomed. Oakeshott was at first diffident, feeling himself rather 'smooth'. But being by nature unfailingly courteous and never patronizing, he had no problems (Singer). 'The majority of men, and their wives also, talked readily. They often said that they had never had such an opportunity for "telling someone about it all", and each one of us is the richer by some personal friendships as a result.' Altogether they achieved about 750 effective interviews with men, of which Oakeshott did more than half, and 150 with women.

The visits took up some eight months. The routine was to spend the morning and afternoon in visits, to meet together briefly for lunch and then for a longer discussion and review in the evening. It was a good day in which anyone managed more than four to five families. They normally stayed in youth hostel type of accommodation, where Miss Iredale often joined them, as being almost a fourth member of the team. There they compared news and views, 'spreading the cards out on the floor; playing patience with them; and trying to discern patterns in the comments recorded'. Singer, whose command of idiomatic English was still uncertain, recalls Oakeshott's 'wonderful way of putting you at your ease'. If Singer quoted something a man had said and asked what it meant, Oakeshott would say gently 'Let's see – that's a very interesting question. . . . I wonder if he might have meant . . .' Once Singer had to ask why, when men referred to the Means Test people, they always called them buggers: what were 'buggers'? Miss Iredale blanched; Oakeshott explained later.

Oakeshott's diplomatic skills were required for more important issues. The redoubtable Miss Iredale, though respected for her drive and concern, set them all by the ears. Even Oakeshott, who could always charm her when necessary, referred to her in letters home as 'the harpy'. But the chief antagonism was between her and Owen. Owen, who came from a humble background, suspected an 'establishment' ring between her and Temple, with Oakeshott as an honorary member.[10] Tensions relaxed a little when he left the team in May 1937 for a Chair at Glasgow University. Later he became assistant to the first Secretary General of the United Nations, where he recruited Singer to join him. When international tempers ran high there, they would say to each other 'If only we had Walter here to keep the peace.' But Walter's letters to Noel give the credit to Singer, who 'is a saint'.

The interviews with the unemployed, though the most interesting, rewarding and, in the long run, important part of the work, were not the whole of it. The particular concern of the Pilgrim Trust had to be satisfied by a sample survey of the schemes set up by the various voluntary agencies to help the unemployed. This survey occupied forty per cent of the final report. Oakeshott was also concerned about another plank of government policy which features less prominently in the report. To mitigate the effects of structural unemployment in the 'Special Areas', schemes of transference-and-training were set up to encourage men without family responsibilities to move to less stricken regions. These schemes had a mixed reception and were of uncertain benefit. He decided to offer *The Times* a critical article about the schemes.

The article was published, unsigned, in November 1936 under the title 'Transference and the Special Areas.' In a letter to Noel he summarized it as follows.

> It's a very plain and straightforward statement of facts. The only 'idea' behind it is the necessity of regarding social factors as one regards economic factors – not to judge a policy solely on its economic results, but to see that it has social implications and take them into consideration. Not very original (incidentally it's the one idea behind *Commerce and Society**) but it's curious how blind people are to it.

The magnitude of the project's task, coupled with the loss of Owen, was such as to make it clear before the end of 1937 that it could not be completed within the academic year 1937/8. The burden of writing the report would now fall chiefly on Oakeshott. A fourth term's secondment was therefore sought and obtained for him. For that term the team was based on London, from where Oakeshott could get home on some weekends. But during the year 'in the field' the volume of work and Miss Iredale's whip kept him almost continuously on the job except for one four-week holiday, and he had to keep in touch with the family by letter. There survive almost all his and Noel's letters for that year, and they enable us to follow their personal story.

When they had to vacate 56 Canon Street in August 1936, Noel had moved her base to Copse Stile. Most of her letters are on domestic matters: the children's ailments and her own; the doings of her extended family; the difficulty of finding resident servants; and (later in the period) the problem of where they will live when the secondment is over. She encloses '£1 to buy yourself a hat. Do please get a decent one that will look nice and last.' She tells him of her reading: she has started a commentary on St John's Gospel and also 'the [C. H.] Dodd book' he had sent her. She sympathizes with him over the personal friction within the team: 'thank heaven for Singer or you

---

*He was correcting the proofs of his book at the time.

would be in rum company.' But as to the project itself 'I wish I could enter into it more'.

More happily, she was able to pursue her own work on Greek vases. Trendall's *magnum opus, Paestan Pottery,* was published at the end of 1936. She had helped him with the publication and now was asked to review it for the *Journal of Hellenic Studies.* That meant trips to the Ashmolean and visits to Beazley and Bailey in Oxford. In February 1937, when Walter was in Liverpool, she asked him to 'noze out' (*sic*) a South Italian vase in the City Museum, and check its colours for her. He did so, and wrote her a long letter, illustrated by drawings, about that vase and another dozen of possible interest to her.

Trendall's book she described to Walter as 'incredible stodge', but she managed a polite review. In the course of it she made a revealing criticism.

Mr T's penetrating observation of detail leads him occasionally to infer too much and, in explaining links between one vase and another or the direct influence of one painter on another, to imply greater contacts between painters and a greater degree of organization between the fabrics [i.e. centres of manufactory] than can be proved.

This was exactly the criticism made later of some of Walter's own attributions, and illustrates the 'valley' between them described in his letter of June 1928 (p. 47).

In May 1937, even more happily, she had three weeks in Southern Italy. A Winchester colleague's wife took the children off her hands. She was able to revisit the British School at Rome and to see most of the important museums to the south. For some of them she had Trendall's company, with Maggie as chaperone.[11] A rare note of exultation enters her letters as she describes the countryside and some of the places she saw; and she did not fail to include some reciprocal comments for him on the Romanesque architecture of the region. He similarly had been telling her of his happy escapes to see the glass of York Minster and a manuscript in the library of Durham Cathedral, which 'makes Winchester [Cathedral] seem very small beer indeed'.

It might have been thought that during the academic year 1936–7 they both had enough to occupy them: he with the unemployment inquiry, she with the children and her vases. On the contrary, it was a period of feverish activity by both of them in the matter of his career. When he asked for a year's secondment in the spring of 1936, the expectation on all sides had been that he would return to Winchester, at least for a few years. But various factors combined to unsettle first him and then her. As often with his recurrent periods of unsettlement, it is uncertain how rational his anxieties were. What is certain is that on this occasion she shared them.

The fundamental problem was his relationship with Leeson. Leeson had all along expressed doubts about the value of the unemployment inquiry. He had also in Oakeshott's absence taken over his teaching with the classical sixth, and was likely to hang on to it. When Oakeshott had been to talk about his further career, he had urged him to return and do a proper stint at Winchester before looking e.g. for headmasterships. Oakeshott persuaded himself that Leeson really wanted to anchor him at Winchester for life, and that therefore paradoxically if he wanted to get out at all he must get out now while Leeson could not block him. His hopes of preferment rested on Cyril Bailey and on Leeson's predecessor Williams, now also at Oxford as Dean of Christ Church.

In October 1936 he learned that Westminster was looking for a new headmaster. It was a school which much attracted him and, since Williams was one of the governors, he sounded him out privately. The next thing he knew was that he was called to a preliminary interview, without having cleared it with Leeson. This meant he had to own up now; and even though nothing came of the interview, relations with Leeson were not helped.

In February 1937 he saw an advertisement for the Directorship of the Oxford University Department of Education. Inquiries revealed that among the electors were both Williams and Bailey. He did not particularly want the job, but 'I do not honestly see very much future for me at Winchester, with Leeson feeling as he does about me'. His Oxford friends were not encouraging – the appointment would probably go to an experienced headmaster – but he inclined to put in, and this time remembered to ask Leeson for his support.

Leeson's reply of 23 February echoes the demurrer, then goes on.

About your future in general – I know you have felt restless. In a way your conscience will not leave you alone, and that is one of the reasons why you are such a valuable man on any staff. It seems wrong, I expect, to return to Winchester after the wildernesses you have been through this year. But – in this and what follows I am going to be very frank – your restlessness may have its dangers; a close friend of both of us said to me the other day 'Why is Walter such a fidget? MTS, Kent, Pilgrim Trust – why doesn't he settle down at Winchester for another six years or so, and then choose his line and go for it?' I felt there was something in this.

I do not think you could do with a big Headmastership – the administrative burden would worry you and might weigh you down. A small Headmastership possibly – it would depend on the place – I do not feel sure.

After emphasizing that his 'real strength lies in direct personal contact with senior boys or university students', Leeson lists the considerable amount of sixth form teaching still available to him and signs off 'Yours affectionately'.

Sending this letter to Noel on 1 March, Walter described it as 'pretty shattering'. Her own comments are extravagantly loyal. 'I *never* heard such damned cheek in my *whole* life. . . . Under all his politeness I believe he's furious. We shall have to try and clear out now if we can. He will probably do you down.' Walter replied tactfully, and went to see him; but their talk, as he reported it back to Noel, brought him closer to her view of the situation.

Leeson had repeated in that talk the mistake of disparaging both the unemployment inquiry – 'it is an impertinence to try to find out anything about the workings of official organizations like the UAB' – and the people behind it:

> my association with the Archbishop, the Bishop of Chichester and so on has already done me grave harm in the eyes of many people. . . . He advises me candidly to leave the sinking ship as soon as possible, and to thank goodness that they would not write a report for which I was partly responsible, and come back to Winchester in September. The way he put all this made my blood pretty well boil.

That apart, Leeson was fair. If Oakeshott really wished, he would support him for the Oxford post and/or extend his leave of absence for one term. He would also 'let me go in for headmasterships, just to see what happens, which means of course that I won't get them since he can torpedo any job by saying I'm not fit for it'.

In his anxiety he wrote from Lancashire to Bailey for advice; and

Noel, being close, followed up his letter by a visit – Bailey, after all, had been her tutor too. Bailey told her what he thought. Then after some days' reflection, and discussion with Williams, he wrote himself in almost identical terms. First, Oakeshott should 'go through with your present job to the end, even it it does mean asking for an extra term. . . . That does imply that you should go back to Winchester for a while longer. *But not for keeps. . . .*' As to the future,

> I am not sure that the HMship of a big Public School of the normal type would be the happiest job for you or the job which would use the best of you. That sort of HM is apt to get swallowed up in organisation, to be able to do little teaching and to be bound by the tradition or greatly hampered by it. I believe that a school more of the secondary [grammar] type would give you much more scope. . . . Far more interesting problems about the combining of day boys and boarders, and a free hand to try experiments.
>
> What puzzles me is what you say about Leeson. I cannot believe – nor can the Dean [Williams] – that he has any 'down' on you. He has so often spoken of you to me with great affection and admiration. . . . I think it possible, Walter, that he feels, as I have sometimes, that you are a bit 'restless' by nature. But that he has lost his belief in you as a teacher and as a person and in your mind and spirit I cannot for a moment believe, and I do think you may have exaggerated a temporary irritation into a permanent attitude. . . . Anyhow you know you have my love and sympathy in a difficult time.

There was a double irony about this wise advice. First, Oakeshott's 'fidgets' during the unemployment survey were much more extensive than any third party knew. His correspondence with Noel, who herself endorsed the judgement 'restless by nature', shows him also toying with work in the social field held out to him by Bishop Bell, and talking of 'burning our boats and going off to the USA or the Dominions, which I suppose would be *awful*'. Even after Bailey's letter he applied for a job at Chatham House, but then turned it down. Only after that did he follow Bailey's advice and 'settle down'. But then – the second irony – within a year he had been appointed High Master of St Paul's, an appointment supported by Leeson and Williams and, it would appear, largely engineered by Bailey.

The writing up of the report fell, after Owen's departure, mainly to Oakeshott. Singer drafted Part I, 'Facts and Figures', the important section on Liverpool, and the statistical tables in the Appendices. Miss Iredale drafted Part IV, 'Unemployment among Women'. Oakeshott edited those sections and wrote the remaining three quarters of the book – though his work was of course subject to scrutiny by the steering committee.

The punch of the book undoubtedly resides in the 150 pages which describe and analyse the nature of unemployment in 'the six towns' and its consequences. Some points in the description were not new, though they were now more securely documented. For example, unemployment was shown to be essentially a family problem: everywhere the parents went without for the sake of the children, often the wife also for the sake of the husband; everywhere the marriage was placed under stress. Again the effect of long unemployment on the individual is the same everywhere: depression, leading to despair (whether angry or resigned), and extending to the next generation, as shown by the remark of a father that his son had nothing to hope for except 'to stand behind me in the dole queue'.

But the response to unemployment might vary greatly from community to community. A casual conversation among unemployed South Wales miners might be on a point of politics or theology or logic, whereas in the Midlands or London it would be a series of monosyllables answered with a series of grunts. On the other hand there was a tendency to self-pity in South Wales which was absent in Durham where 'the quality of family life seemed even higher'. In Liverpool, which was hardest hit of all by unemployment and poverty, the team reported a response which made more impression on readers than anything in the book: that was the all-pervading passion there for football-pools, greyhounds and horses. Betting does not just give them 'something to hope for, that one day they may be able to "get out of the rut".' It also 'provides the content of social intercourse, a way of spending one's time in discussion, analysis and decision with a seeming sense of purpose and ultimate achievement.' Even 'the man who has been lucky enough to win acquires thereby a definite social standing, and his views on very different matters are heard with respect.' All this, of course, was long before television had, in Frank Field's words, 'privatized unemployment'.

The analytical section of the report identified three kinds of problem: physical, psychological and moral. The first raised and tackled the question of poverty, one of the politically sensitive issues. It was common in certain circles to doubt either the reality of poverty or its connexion with unemployment. Instead of avoiding the issue, the team met it by invoking a definition of the poverty line 'based on the BMA's minimum standards for food requirements and the standards used by various local social surveys in respect of clothes, cleaning materials, light and fuel'. On that definition, which was not challenged, they could say that seventeen per cent of their families (thirty per cent in Liverpool) were living in 'deep poverty', i.e. with incomes over ten per cent below the poverty line, and another twenty-seven per cent within ten per cent of it either way. They were also able to say that 'poverty is not only a consequence of unemployment but also a cause of it' (because of the damage it does to a man's physical and mental health), and 'it is this that makes the case against a reduction of allowances unanswerable'.

Under the heading of psychological problems they had to handle another sensitive issue, that of the alleged 'work-shy'. This too they tackled head on. They admitted that there were 'a certain number of "work-shy" men among the younger unemployed. But the number is relatively speaking not large, and tends to be exaggerated by comparison with another group . . . the men who find it more and more difficult to face repeated failure and who finally give up looking for work.' Their detailed and unemotional analysis ensured that here, as over other 'political' issues, their conclusions were not challenged.

The term 'moral problems' was used to refer chiefly to the self-respect of the unemployed. It included the maintenance of standards in the home, the notion of 'the fair wage', and a concept of financial independence which stretched beyond death. If public assistance had to be accepted during life, at least a man would not have a pauper's grave. 'A Liverpool family which had run up nearly £8 arrears of rent nevertheless kept up payments to the Burial Club. "The Means Test and the capitalists", said this man, "prevent me from having a decent life, but at least I will have a decent death".'

The report then passes to three particular issues of public policy. The first was that of wages and allowances. The general solution to the problem of poverty, they were convinced, was to be found in raising wages, not allowances. A blanket increase in allowances might even increase and perpetuate unemployment. Only one major change was needed, the introduction of family allowances for men in work: until that was done, men with large families would continue to fare better on public assistance. The second problem was that of the old who had no real prospect of getting back into regular employment. Third were the young who had found work easily enough on leaving school but were discarded as soon as they reached an age when they could expect an adult wage.[12] For neither of these categories had the report any very convincing proposals to make. The same goes for women, who form the next section. Its general trend is to suggest that married women should not go out to work, while unmarried women are better placed in domestic service than in factories. Domestic service would be much more acceptable if it was non-residential.

The final part of the report is headed 'The Social Service Movement', which in practice chiefly means the Unemployed Clubs. High praise is given to the settlement at Maes-yr-Haf with its satellite thirty to forty clubs. Other ventures are carefully assessed, some being criticized for making their members too easily content with unemployment.

One incident from the course of the project could not, alas, be included in the report. Here it is, written up by him many years later for a newspaper article entitled 'Unemployment and Violence' but apparently never published.

Maes yr Haf used to run fortnight-long 'refresher' courses in the summer, for the long unemployed, in an old Malt House near the Glamorgan coast. One such course was due to end next day. That evening, quite suddenly and apparently with absolute spontaneity, a cry arose that the forty or fifty men involved should 'march' on St Donat's Castle, now the international Atlantic College, but then the English home of the American newspaper proprietor and millionaire, W. R. Hearst, which housed his collection of armour, and his other sizeable collection, of doxies. It was some four or five miles away from the Malt House. I was only beginning to understand some things about unemployment in Wales. But I had already realised that these men had nothing material to lose. Anything, I thought, might happen.

When they reached the Castle, the gates were locked. But someone found a postern open and through that they streamed into the courtyard. I do not believe that what came next had been planned by anyone. What *did* come next was that they formed up into a solid group, and began to sing: *Jesu, lover of my soul*, not to the sentimental tune by Dykes, but to the magnificently strong Welsh tune, 'Aberystwyth'. ... Hearst (whose line was by no means the more esoteric forms of journalism) came out, almost in tears. His butler was told to cut up anything he could find, for sandwiches, and he himself wrote out a cheque for the settlement. For me, it was one of the most moving experiences I ever had.

The Pilgrim Trust report was published under the title of *Men Without Work* on 28 March 1938. On that day *The Times* gave it a leader and an article totalling 3,000 words; the *Evening News* had an illustrated report filling two-thirds of a page; and there was either a leader or an article in the *Daily Telegraph*, *News Chronicle* and *Daily Herald*. For *The Times* 'the most valuable parts of the report are those which discuss the moral and psychological problems to which long unemployment and unemployment allowances give rise. ... Men and women are seen here not as units in statistical tables but as living beings, deeply demoralized or lapsing into a still worse state of content.' Neither the *Telegraph* nor the *News Chronicle* were sympathetic: the headline in the latter was 'A City's Idle Live for the Football Pools', and in each paper half the space was given to football pools and a further quarter to burial clubs. The *Herald*, on the other hand, called the book 'an excellent and moving account, packed with revealing facts about the despair and waste which underlie our so-called prosperity'. The *Evening News* was more specific in its praise. 'This book scotches two equally foolish legends: of the "work-shy dole-chasers" and of the "hard, heartless bureaucracy". It gives instead a picture of the real conditions in this grim world which is yet a part of our world.'

Most glowing of all was the *Times Literary Supplement*.

In a field where so much sentimental and so much biased work has been turned out, it is a joy to be conscious of the play of clear, disciplined, human reason. ... Perhaps the greatest qualities of the survey are that it never allots blame unfairly, and that it pierces through to the spiritual basis of all life. ... Neither funds nor expert advice would have proved so notably fruitful without investigators of evidently first-class quality, head and shoulders above the ordinary amateur.

Oakeshott's political friends said the report had made out an unanswerable case for family allowances, but he himself played no significant part in the political follow-up of its publication. He did remain on friendly terms with TJ, whose daughter, Eirene White, remembers him as a frequent visitor at their home. He also attended a weekend conference organized by TJ in November 1938 to brief Anthony Eden about unemployment. When Eden resigned from the Government earlier that year over its foreign policy, Baldwin had advised him to turn to home affairs, and gave him a copy of *Men Without Work* to read. TJ arranged the conference 'with a view to the political and economic education of Mr Eden!', and was gratified that 'we succeeded in making him feel completely baffled by the complexities of the problem'. But by November 1938 the threat of war had put peacetime problems in the shade, and most of the conversation was on other matters.

Curiously the actuality of war in 1939 proceeded to abolish unemployment as a practical issue. But it remained very much in the mind of Beveridge and those working with him in planning for postwar society. The section of his 1942 Report entitled 'The Giant Idleness' certainly owes a direct debt to *Men Without Work*. More generally, social historians see the book as having played a part in the 'swing to the left' in Britain c. 1940 i.e. to the belief that social evils like unemployment cannot be cured piecemeal but require a consciously integrated organic state. Moreover when unemployment began to become widespread again 30 years later, scholars and others went back to the book. Reprinted in the USA in 1967 and 1985, it became a classic. In particular, its picture of demoralization has never been bettered.

What did the painter of that picture himself carry away from the experience? At the philosphical level he looked back on it ten years later after Temple's death. Temple had always 'passionately believed that moral questions were involved' in social problems. For example, the dole might be 'cheapest for society'; nevertheless 'if it meant moral degradation it was no answer'. But in the case of unemployment, Temple had also seen (what he did not always see) that 'before the moral problem could be stated, patient investigation was necessary'. Without that, we are reduced to 'general remarks about the value of human personality which cut no ice'. The implied criticism of Temple[13] shows that by 1948 Oakeshott had distanced himself at least from the naiver forms of idealism.

But at the personal level the effects went deeper: both harrowing memories and heart-warming friendships. For years he kept up with the family of a Liverpool docker, Thomas Sumner. Walter and Noel took Helena to meet the Sumners in 1937, and Noel sent them parcels of food during the war and clothes after it.[14] In the mid-1970s Walter took Robert and spent some days with Hans Singer in Crook, County Durham, revisiting scenes they had known some forty years earlier.

As soon as he got back to Winchester in January 1938 Oakeshott took up again an interest which has not yet been mentioned but which began before his secondment. It started with another of his exhibitions in Brewery, in early April 1936, this time in aid of the Winchester Cathedral Appeal Fund. He had fifty-seven items on display. Six covered 'King Arthur and the Grail Legend'. One of the six was the Malory manuscript, of which his note says that it 'may originally have been written for St Swithin's Priory early in 1486, when Prince Arthur, son of Henry VII, was born in the Prior's house, now the Deanery'.

Seventeen exhibits were 'books and documents connected with the Cathedral, College and Monasteries of Winchester'.* One of these was an illuminated miniature in the great twelfth-century Winchester Bible, a book which he had first seen in 1931. Another, which he placed alongside it, he described as 'Fragment of a Winchester Bible c. 1175, recognized by Dr E. G. Millar of the British Museum as Winchester work, probably in the same hand as the miniature exhibited' alongside. The fragment had been lent by the Pierpont Morgan Library in New York, and it became known as the Morgan Leaf. The Library sent it over in the *Queen Mary*, and he went down to Southampton to collect it. Its juxtaposition in that showcase with the miniature from the Winchester Bible was what set him off on the most absorbing quest of his whole life.

While the exhibition was open, he 'spent night after night, after the public had left, comparing the Leaf with the Bible'. He 'secured photographs of the Bible's initials, some taken with x-rays to try and find the drawings beneath the paint; a costly experiment, wholly

---

* They included the *Benedictional of St Aethelwold*. The Duke of Devonshire had agreed to lend it 'provided I came over to Chatsworth to collect it'. It is astonishing that a man in his early thirties, with no publications in the field, should have persuaded their owners to lend him such priceless manuscripts.

unfruitful.' When he went on secondment he took them with him, pasted into a huge book, and, when he could get a moment to himself, began the long study of them. 'If I didn't have my Winchester Bible photographs to look at in the evening I'd go dotty.'

During the writing up in 1937 another door was opened to him. He was at that time seeing a good deal of Charles Mitchell and his young wife Prue. Prue was a printer, who had produced for him an exquisite catalogue for the 1936 exhibition. Charles was employed in the Greenwich Maritime Museum by day, but in the evenings was working under Fritz Saxl in the Warburg Institute. Through him Oakeshott got access in 1937 to the Institute library, and later came to meet Saxl himself – a meeting crucial to his own development as an art historian.

On returning to Winchester in January 1938, he went on mulling over his photographs. By now he could distinguish five different hands among the painters, working in two styles, an earlier and a later. Among the earlier artists he identified one whom he called the 'Master of the Leaping Figures'. Outstanding among the latter was the painter of the Morgan Leaf, whom at that time he called the 'Great Byzantine Master'.

Oakeshott was also intrigued by a recent study of the twelfth-century wall-paintings (a deposition and an entombment) in the Cathedral's Holy Sepulchre Chapel. There too there were earlier paintings which had been plastered over to carry a later series. Moreover the style of the later deposition was remarkably similar to the work of the Great Byzantine Master in the Bible; and that work in turn seemed 'to be reaching out to express feelings that are almost beyond the scope of the miniaturist'. But he held back from making a firm identification. 'It would be almost impossible, in view of the very different media (in the one case a full-scale work on plaster, in the other a tiny miniature on vellum) to assert definitely that they are the work of the same artist.' All he would say is that at the least 'one artist learned from the other'. These thoughts, set out in a brief article in the *Winchester Cathedral Record* in 1939, already contained the germs of his life's work on the Winchester Bible. The quest was under way.

When the family moved back to Winchester in October 1937, they rented a house from a senior colleague. He could not let them have it for more than two years, but reckoned that Oakeshott would be a headmaster within that time, and Walter and Noel must have agreed.

In fact he had had only one term back when St Paul's came up. The situation fitted Bailey's advice to a T, and lo and behold he himself was a governor of the school and a member of the selection committee: one wonders indeed if he could have foreseen all this a year earlier.

The vacancy occurred because the sitting High Master, Dr John Bell, was moving to the Headmastership of Cheltenham. The notice was short and the governors had to act fast. On 13 May they fixed a salary of £2,500 p.a. with housing, and advertised. Oakeshott applied, with Williams and Leeson as his referees, and both of them wrote letters to Bailey, which survive.

Williams wrote in tones which were characteristically measured. He rehearsed Oakeshott's abilities and achievements, ending with mention of *Men Without Work* as 'admittedly a first-rate production' recording 'a most important piece of work'. He then summarizes.

> He is a man of most attractive character who combines in a remarkable way interest in the past and in the present. No one who meets him can fail to see his distinction of mind and character. In manner he is rather hesitative, and I used to think that this might disguise and hamper his real power, and if he desired to be a Headmaster it might stand in his way. But he is really a man of determination who finally wins confidence and, though I think there are many kinds of work for which he is qualified, I am greatly influenced by the fact that he himself desires to be a headmaster.

Leeson was perfectly fair, but altogether sharper. He started with 'Pros':

> 1 Walter would bring to any job he undertook the highest standards of duty and devotion imaginable. He is entirely selfless. Although I believe he is not a communicant member of the Church of England he is certainly a practising Christian in the widest sense of those words. 2 His horizons are unusually wide – as wide of those of any schoolmaster I have known. (Under this heading he referred to the unemployment project, without any qualifying adjectives.) 3 His health is good – better than it used to be; and I should hope, if he were appointed, that he would be able to stand the wear and tear of headmastership.

Leeson then moved to 'Cons' which he immediately qualified by adding, that 'they should be called grounds for hesitation rather than Cons':

1 He gives an impression at first sight of want of drive and vitality. He is very modest. ... Until they get to know him staff and senior boys might think him rather ineffective. 2 I am not sure how he would cope with the problems of finance, administration and discipline that a headmaster has to face, and often face without warning. ... But there has undoubtedly been an improvement since his Merchant Taylors days. ...

In conclusion, I feel that there is a great deal to be said for appointing him, but there would be an element of risk in it. It is possible that he might not be able to hold the job down; and it is also very possible that he might grow into it, and then he would make of it a brilliant success, in the best sense of those words.

The Governors of St Paul's took the risk, preferring him to the other twenty-six applicants. On 26 July 1938 at St Paul's School he was offered and accepted the High Mastership from the following January: during the autumn term the school would be run by Maurice Tyson, the Surmaster (second master). His first action on leaving the committee room was to tell the Head Porter of his appointment and ask where the chapel was as he 'would like a little time by himself'.

On 7 August, learning that Jim Stubbs, a master he had not met, was getting married two days later, he sent the couple a charming letter with a present of a silver water-jug. By the middle of September he was involved in vigorous correspondence with Tyson about plans for the school in the event – which could well be imminent – of war. Already within weeks of his appointment he had shown cause to doubt two of Leeson's reservations: he could win the loyalty of the staff, and he was ready to take decisive action.

September 1938 was the month of the Munich Crisis. Tension mounted steadily in the first half of the month. On the 15th, and again on the 23rd, Chamberlain flew to Munich to meet Hitler. On the 27th the British fleet was mobilized, but on the 29th Chamberlain flew to Munich for the third time. On the following day he signed the agreement with Hitler which abandoned Czechoslovakia and relaxed the tension for the moment.

At Winchester boys came back before term to dig trenches, and

Leeson wrote to parents telling them what the school would do in case of war. At St Paul's the admirable Tyson, entering upon his temporary inheritance, had been given no corresponding instructions. He wrote to alert Oakeshott, who replied in a long letter on 16 September: 'I agree with you that we should have something cut and dried in our minds' in case of war. He suggested the idea of moving out to a 'camp school' in the country, as run by the National Association of Boys' Clubs. Then comes a characteristic digression. 'I want to talk to you about those [plaster casts of] Roman Emperors some time ! I must confess quite privately but candidly that they give me the pip. I do hope you agree and that we can some time have them stowed away in decent retirement.' Finally he reverts to the main issue: 'I suggest that with these (and other ideas of your own, no doubt) in mind you should get in touch with Sir Frank Watney during the next few days and if he approves get a circular [to parents] in draft.' Colonel Sir Frank Watney was – and had been since 1921 – Clerk to the Mercers' Company who owned, subsidized and governed St Paul's.

On 18 September Oakeshott wrote again to Tyson, enclosing the draft of a proposed circular for Tyson to clear with Watney. 'The suggestion has been made that, if suitable accommodation could be found in some part of the country less liable to attack, the school might reopen there' – sc. after a temporary closure – 'on a restricted basis for the duration of the war. The Governors are exploring the possibility of this.' The 'suggestion' was in fact very close to what was done a year later. But it was months before the Governors got round to 'exploring' it. On 21 September Oakeshott added a further point: the letter to parents 'might give us some idea as to whether any number of them would patronize a school reestablished in the country'.

Meanwhile on 18 September Tyson had written to Watney, asking for 'some instructions, secret or otherwise'. Watney replied coolly: 'I was under the impression that intructions were given to Mr Bell [the previous High Master] that the school should be closed temporarily. If you think it necessary, there is no reason why you should not inform the boys to this effect so that they can tell their parents, but of course the great thing is not to produce an unnecessary scare.'

Tyson on 22 September wrote to Oakeshott, referring to this 'very colourless' letter: he had written again but had no reply. 'I really shall have to try to get the Governors to face [these questions] resolutely, and if you were to be there too it would give me more courage to be as persistent as I ought to be.' His own aside is equally characteristic. 'The Government tells us airily to disperse, as if we were one of the more volatile forms of Summer Shell.'

A day or so later Tyson and a colleague 'paid a nocturnal call on the Chairman'[14] and secured a promise of support in whatever line of action he decided on. On 26 September he wrote to parents: 'If a state of national emergency is declared, the School will be closed immediately, and will probably remain closed for as long as the emergency lasts.' The letter goes on to invite parents in that event to take up an offer from the LCC to 'remove children on trains to places in the neighbouring counties where they will be billeted as a temporary measure'. But the final note is more cautious than Oakeshott's draft: 'parents must not read into the scheme any indication that we are proposing to run a boarding school in new premises.'

The Munich agreement on 30 September gave time for fuller planning. The most urgent task was to prod the Governors. The best chance of doing this was through Cyril Bailey. As well as being an old friend, Bailey was one of the nine university governors put in by the constitution of 1900 to balance the thirteen Mercers, and as 'Paulinorum Paulinissimus' he carried great weight in the school also. He had himself written to Watney during the Munich crisis, saying 'we ought not to let the school either be disbanded or dispersed among other schools'. Now (mid-October) he and other university governors had 'been thinking of the urgency of making some emergency plans', and one of them had written to Mercers' Hall to ask that it should be included on the agenda for the next meeting on 18 November. On 17 October he told Oakeshott all this and proposed that 'we make a report that can be discussed' at the meeting.

Passing this on to Tyson, Oakeshott identified three possibilities (i) 'Your' [i.e. Tyson's] 'idea of a temporary amalgamation with some other school; (ii) the camp idea; and (iii) the empty institution idea' e.g. a Church Training College recently closed. He suggests that Tyson should follow up (i) and he himself the others. He ends on a hopeful note; that 'it really does look as if we'd get powerful support on the Governing Body for any reasonable plan we can evolve for "carrying on".' He also proposed an investigation of costs and the setting up of a planning committee on the staff.

Astonishingly the minutes of the Governors' meeting on 18 November contain no record of any discussion about war emergency plans. But another proposal of Bailey's on Oakeshott's behalf fared better. Hitherto at Governors' meetings the High Master was present only by specific invitation. Now it was to be presumed that he would be present, unless asked to wait or to withdraw for any item or items.

Oakeshott left Winchester at the end of that term and moved to London. He left behind in safety at Winchester his valuable books, including that 'commonplace book c. 1600' in an unknown hand, which he still had not found time to study. He was now ready for his first big command: in spite of Leeson's legitimate doubts, he was the right man in the right place at precisely the right time.

5
St Paul's
1939–1946

The school of which Oakeshott now became High Master was once described by him as 'a powerhouse of the intellect'. That was something he was used to at Winchester. But there were differences, no less significant. The chief was, as he put it in Antony Jay's 1974 film *Four High Masters'*, 'a remarkable quality of independence'. The staff, instead of being a community – a sort of extended family – all had their own lives and their own ideas, and were extremely suspicious of any interference on the part of their colleagues. Similarly with pupils: those at boarding school

> get an extraordinary degree of support from the school and rely on it much more than the Pauline. They associate their time at school with a group of buildings and a particular countryside to which they have become deeply attached at an impressionable age. At St Paul's the link is especially with individual masters and the small group with whom they worked in their last year or so.

He liked to quote the remark made by Themistocles when he told the Athenians they must evacuate Athens, leaving the city empty to the Persian invaders, and take to their ships: 'It is not walls but men that make a city.'

The walls which housed St Paul's in 1939 had been built only in 1884, but were already regarded as too cramping. Leeson's move of Merchant Taylors' to Northwood in 1933 had been a success, and by 1937 the Mercers had more or less decided to transplant St Paul's to new buildings on land they owned at Osterley. The threat of war in 1938 preempted any such move; and soon they learned that, if war came, not merely would the pupils have to leave Hammersmith but the buildings would be requisitioned.

This was dire news indeed. If St Paul's were to close now,

ostensibly for the duration, who could be sure that it would ever re-open? At all costs it must be kept going somewhere safe out of London. To the new High Master, to all his staff, and to a few non-Mercer Governors, the conclusion was compelling. Why then did the Mercers drag their feet? Forty years on Oakeshott tried in retrospect to see the situation through their eyes.

He conceded, to start with, that they had many other responsibilities. There was the Company: its Hall and its endowments. The endowments included land and buildings, in other places as well as Hammersmith. Even their interest in education was not confined to the two St Paul's Schools, one for boys and one for girls. They also had still at that time Mercers' School, 'the Company's School in a more intimate sense than St Paul's, and right in the city'.

There was a second, more personal, factor. Colonel Sir Frank Watney, who had been Clerk to the Mercers since 1921, was

> dead against the scheme [sc. of evacuation] for understandable reasons. He was an old man – too old to look ahead to the end of the war – and old men (*experto crede*) do not like being rushed. We were all pressing for improvisation, which was the only conceivable way of doing things. We got no support whatever from Sir Frank about this. . . . I was after all very new to the job, and he may well have thought that a High Master in his middle thirties with no administrative experience simply could not be trusted.

But there was more to it than individual personalities. 'Relations between the Company and the previous High Master had not been good', and they were further soured in 1935 by the appointment of a school bursar to act as the Mercers' 'watchdog on the spot'. His instructions were to authorize no expenditure without reference upwards. Even when, at the end of 1938, the school had been given somewhat grudging permission to go ahead with plans for evacuation, no extra expense was to fall on the Company.

Undeterred, Oakeshott and Tyson, with the unanimous support of the staff, set to work on the search for a new home. The ideal requirements were listed as follows:

> (i) a country district where the school could use the official billeting scheme 'to house those Paulines whose parents wish them to continue their education with us;

(ii) a nearby Public School which would be willing to give us facilities in the use of playing fields, laboratories, library etc;
(iii) one or more large houses in the same neighbourhood which the authorities should be asked to allot to us for teaching purposes.'

Such a plan 'avoids the difficulty which is inherent in every other plan that has been put forward, of making a day school into a boarding school'. St Paul's would remain, in the essential respects, a day school.

Among a large number of schools considered, three were visited, at least by Oakeshott and Tyson: Dauntsey's School near Devizes; Hurstpierpoint in Sussex; and Wellington College, near Crowthorne in Berkshire. Of the three, Wellington looked the most promising. The local billeting officer was encouraging. Bobby Longden, the Master of Wellington, an old acting friend of Oakeshott from Oxford, was welcoming. His school had boarding accommodation standing empty, which could house the few boarders at St Paul's. Even better, Wellington was just building new science labs, and the old ones could be mothballed in case they were needed. Thirdly, there was a large mansion nearby, only partly occupied, at Easthampstead Park. As a final bonus, the village of Crowthorne was within cycling distance of West London.

If the Governors approved the plan, it could be more or less self-financing: parents wishing to take part would be asked for a subscription of £1 a head for such purposes as building trestle-tables, buying in emergency rations, or transporting and storing library books. Oakeshott submitted the staff's plan on 17 February 1939, adding a rider of his own. 'We feel at St Paul's that, however much the situation which may compel us to leave these buildings temporarily may be deplored, there are great educational opportunities about such an undertaking.' The Governors 'Resolved that the arrangements be approved and that the High Master be congratulated on the action he had taken.'

The next month was spent in completing negotiations, particularly with the owners of Easthampstead Park, the seventh Marquess of Downshire and the Dowager Duchess. They were a strange pair. The bachelor Lord Downshire was a simple soul, devoted to his narrow-gauge railway in the grounds (was it coincidence that Oakeshott in his annual report to the Governors spoke warmly of the school's own model railway: 'the construction, operation and periodical reconstruction of the track affords unending occupation for a certain type of boy'?). Lord Downshire's stepmother was by contrast 'an exceedingly difficult person who changes her mind unaccountably'. She was willing to consider, when invited to do so by Oakeshott, the relative advantage of having studious Paulines as against rampaging evacuees in her home. But she warned him, when they came to discuss how much of the mansion the school could use, 'You must remember, Mr Oakeshott, that this house has only ninety-four rooms.' In the end the Mercers secured for £80 the option of a lease in the event of war at £250 p.a. for one wing of the Park for use as classrooms, but no lavatories.

On 17 March 1939 the school held a rehearsal for the evacuation by bicycle. About 200 boys whose parents had signed up for them to go to Crowthorne reported to various assembly points in West London and rode from them to Datchet. The organization worked well and was then put into cold storage. The chief administrative burden during this time fell on Tyson and his ARP Committee. But Oakeshott's attention to detail was, as always when his interest was engaged, remarkable. Thus we find Tyson writing to him on 16 April about plans for growing food at Crowthorne: 'CROPS. Your potato order seems a wise one. I have always supposed that of these crops the potato had the advantage of being easy to grow and *extremely easy to cook*. I may be unjust to the swede etc.'

As the summer wore on the Mercers began to relent somewhat in financial matters. The Bursar still refused to meet the bill for the palliasses and straw needed in billets which had the space but not the beds. But the Chairman could be charmed into authorizing £26.5s to provide camp beds for the boarders housed at Wellington, and £33.5s for the construction of latrines in the woods of Easthampstead Park. Meanwhile £50 of the parental contribution of £1 per head had been spent on timber stored at the Park, and many parents had also sent down parcels of clothes etc. against their sons' arrival. The plan was all now ready to go into action at short notice, except for the uncertainty about the number of boys coming, both those already in the school and those due to enter in September.

In the event the first group of staff with 150 boys went down on 1 September after Germany invaded Poland. War was declared on 3 September and evacuation ordered by the Government. As the days passed more boys and staff came in, and working parties were formed to get things ready for the beginning of term on 20 September. Everyone lent a hand in the digging of trenches and latrines, the first priority. Then Ivan Mavor, the Chaplain, led a party which converted the stored timber into classroom furniture and bicycle racks. Others did the carpentry, painting and plumbing needed to get the old Wellington science labs into use. A third group set about cultivating a rented field of fifteen acres for food – they cropped fifteen tons of potatoes in the first year – and subsequently for pigs and hens. The rent for the field was £15 p.a., and further rent of 25s. a week was incurred for a set of rooms in Crowthorne for school societies, while the managers of the local elementary school lent them a room for prep, on condition that St Paul's met the cost of blacking it out.

All these arrangements Oakeshott presented to the Governors on 17 November, stressing how little the whole enterprise was costing them. There was also a more controversial item, deriving from the fact that as time went on more and more boys arrived, until by 23 October there were 570 of them. Such a number could not possibly be accommodated in billets booked for 200.

The only solution was to acquire houses which the school could use as hostels. Since the Mercers would not put up any money for the purpose, the properties had to be rented by members of the staff. Fortunately some of the large houses in Crowthorne, built earlier in the century for retired planters etc., were now almost a drag on the market. Oakeshott and Alan Cook (another key member of staff, who succeeded Tyson as Surmaster at the end of the war) once knocked on the door of such a house. The peppery owner, hearing they were from St Paul's, opened by saying 'Ah, isn't that a board school?' Oakeshott, unperturbed, explained that they came on business, whereupon the owner changed his tune, remembered that his own school used to play rugger against St Paul's, and invited them in to tea. The banks were also accommodating with loans so that rents could be paid in advance. For men on a schoolmaster's salary, it was a brave step. 'Admittedly', said Oakeshott later, 'we knew there was money there in the last resort, and you might get the sack but the bills would be paid. But at the time it was a headache.'

Altogether nine such houses were acquired, and run as hostels by masters and their wives or sisters. One such house, Waverley, was not available for rent, so Oakeshott himself bought it with a bank loan. For most of the war Waverley was conducted as a hostel by Doris Page, whose husband was away on war service. She ran an extremely efficient and friendly hostel, which was home to twenty boys and also for three years to their High Master. With Waverley boys Oakeshott had an ideal relationship. He could befriend, encourage and broaden them while leaving disciplinary matters to a second resident master.

Noel meanwhile had gone back to live at Copse Stile. Her fourth child, Rose, was born in 1940 and there was no room for the family at Waverley during term-time. They came regularly every holidays, but in principle Walter commuted. There were no full weekend breaks in term-time, Saturday mornings being required for lessons, to fit in with Wellington's use of the playing-fields. On Sunday mornings there was a school service in Crowthorne parish church, which the High Master attended regularly and preached at from time to time. But after it was over he would put his bicycle on the train to Reading and then ride the last fifteen miles to Aston Tirrold. In fine weather he rode the whole way.

Weekday routine for the school was established as follows. From billets or hostels or (in the case of boarders) Wellington College they cycled the three or four miles in to Easthampstead Park. Prayers were said in the ballroom, retitled Hall, at 9.30, followed by lessons in the various fine rooms of the house. The lunch interval was an hour and three-quarters, which allowed boys to ride back to billets if their family's main meal was at midday. After lunch there were lessons on two afternoons. The other afternoons were given over to games, to the cadet force or scouts (*both* of which a boy could join, if he pressed), and to a host of other activities, some traditional, some peculiar to wartime.

Easthampstead Park contained not only Hall and classrooms but also library, masters' common room, book-room, High Master's study and school office. The office had to accommodate the High Master's secretary,[1] two clerks and the all-important Mr Priest. Priest had been bursary clerk for thirty-five years. He knew everything and everybody, and Bell's advice in handing over to Oakeshott had been 'When in doubt, leave it to Mr Priest; and when not in doubt, leave it to Mr Priest, of course'. On the night before term, when Oakeshott held a staff meeting in a blacked out scout hut, a master had asked what was happening about the Bursar. 'Ah, he went to Portugal for the summer and has decided to stay there with his family', said Oakeshott, adding apologetically 'I don't suppose we shall miss him very much' – to cheers all round. Priest was appointed to act in his place and later confirmed as Bursar. He proved a great standby.

The range of problems confronting Oakeshott at this time is illustrated in a letter he wrote to Noel in October.

> There are a good many things on one's mind just now, what with [sister] Maggie's overdraft and the Governors trying to insist that I should put a number of the servants (who've been with us twenty years or so) on half pay, and cases of chicken pox that Longden is fussing about (naturally, I suppose), and a representative of the Country Gentlemen's Association coming to make trouble about the Mansion, and parents writing to say that their boys are living in insanitary conditions (something in it sometimes) – not to speak of the failure of 140 parents to pay billeting-fees – and all this makes a highly complex situation, in the midst of which I'm expected to decide the rights and wrongs of Mr Swain's row with the photographic society, to teach people about Tacitus and to drop on boys for poaching rabbits.

But he was not complaining: 'I amaze myself by enjoying it all prodigiously.'

Clearly, diplomacy took up much of his time. The crucial relationship was with the billet-holders. Complainants could be importunate, especially if they felt the weekly allowance of fifteen shillings to be inadequate: 'But Mr Cook,' said one motherly lady, 'you can hardly expect me to lay an egg in front of a growing boy.' Oakeshott however set an example of imperturbable courtesy; and the boys – to whom the whole thing was, at least initially, an adventure – could be no less charming in their own way.

Next in importance came relations with Wellington. Oakeshott and Bobby Longden got on famously, and it was a personal blow when Longden was killed by a bomb outside his Lodge in 1940. Joint activities such as concerts led to a framework of friendships between the two staffs. The boys found their own *modus vivendi* which left space for some genial contempt: Paulines regarded Wellingtonians as conventional suburbanites, and were content to be called scruffy intellectuals in return. Oakeshott's touch in this context was sure. When the snow lay for days, he spoke to the school at prayers. 'I do feel most awfully strongly' (stern frown) 'that boys should not attack Wellingtonians with snowballs, except of course' (softening smile) 'under extreme provocation.'

Discipline was bound to be different at Crowthorne. Most obviously, dress regulations had to be relaxed. The black jacket and cap (or bowler hat for the senior boys) worn on a bus to school in London would have looked incongruous on a bicycle in a Berkshire lane, and was replaced by a sports coat with grey flannels or shorts. Oakeshott's general proviso that 'boys must avoid giving any impression of slovenliness or eccentricity' was skilfully worded and effective.

The bicycle was a new and central feature of Pauline life. Oakeshott later pretended to a Machiavellian motivation: the energy expended on it (ten miles a day for the boys; Tyson claimed to have ridden 18,000 miles altogether at Crowthorne) would preempt other less commendable activities. But 500 boys on bicycles can be quite a menace, so he and one of his head boys instituted a corps of bicycle monitors with authority over discipline in that one sphere. They taught those who could not ride, inspected the machines, punished dangerous riders and kept them all on authorized routes. There was one short cut through a farmyard whose owner objected to the trespass. Oakeshott one day, being late in, went that way and was intercepted by the farmer. Wearing corduroy shorts under his cycling cape, he was made to dismount and harangued: 'I've a good mind to report you to your High Master.' 'Oh, I'm most awfully sorry,' said the offender, and pushed his bicycle on.

It was not to be his lucky day, because the shorts incurred the disapproval of Mavor and other masters. Even some of the boys, who privately rather admired his light suits and floppy collars, thought short trousers insufficient for a High Master. He quickly took the hint about the shorts. But he persisted with the daily ride in all weathers, either to share the lot of the boys or more generally to bear his quota of wartime privations.

For school prayers he made two characteristic changes. Unique among schools, St Paul's retained in daily use many Latin prayers going back before the Reformation to the time of the Founder himself, John Colet. To these the singing of an English hymn had been added before the war. Now in September 1939 Oakeshott introduced an English reading, either from the Bible or from some other source. In 1942 he had printed for the use of the school a selection of the Latin *Preces* with an English translation opposite, together with some of the hymns. The English translations were by various hands including his own, and he also wrote a foreword. At the end of the foreword he quoted Colet's delightful words from the preface to the grammar he wrote for his boys:

> I pray God all may be to his honour, & to the erudicyon and profyt of chyldren my countre men, Londoners especyally, whom dygestynge this lytel work I had always before myn eyen, consyderynge more what was for them than to showe ony grete connynge, wyllyng to speke the thynges often before spoken in suche maner as gladli yonge begynners and tender wittes might take & conceyue.

Colet's words might have served also as a text for the collection of readings which he chose for Easthampstead and adapted for publication in 1950 under the title *The Sword of the Spirit*.

After prayers, lessons. By St Paul's tradition, work came unassailably first, and the tradition was superbly maintained during the war. That first winter twenty-three boys won awards to Oxford and Cambridge, the highest distinction available, and altogether 100 were won in the five years. The credit goes first to the boys and to the fine team of masters who taught them – specialists, with one brilliant generalist in Eynon Smith. Oakeshott's part was to maintain the tone, to find good replacements for staff who were called up, and to contribute what he could to the teaching. Among temporary staff he got was Jack Westrup, his old Balliol friend, whose post as music critic of the *Daily Telegraph* had been axed and who came as head of music for a couple of years en route for the Heather Chair of Music at Oxford.

Another important source of intellectual stimulus was a series of visiting speakers. For this also he laid his friends under contribution. Raven, Temple and C. S. Lewis came to preach, T. S. Eliot,[2] Laski and Wittkower (p. 126) to talk to select groups. Even a temporary disagreement could be made an excuse for an invitation to C. E. M. Joad (p. 120).

His own teaching showed the qualities he was known for at Winchester. Many Paulines owe him their love of English poetry, and one whole class owns a treasured copy of the Phoenix *Anthology of Twentieth Century Poetry* which he handed out at the start of a period and allowed them to keep at the end. He liked reading aloud, especially Hopkins, to whose rhythms his 'slightly drawling delivery was specially well suited'. He was drawn in more than at Winchester to the teaching of pure classics, though even in this the approach was his own. Geoffrey Woodhead, later a Cambridge classics don and Governor of the school, kept a revealing diary which included Oakeshott's first five terms. On 18 January 1939 'the new High Master appeared to take us. He seemed rather nervous and apprehensive of us, and has none of the aura of *gravitas* that John Bell had.' The next day 'the HM came in – in the same vein as yesterday. He rather talked down to us, we thought.' On 16 February 'HM so far forgot himself as to say "blast" when he sat on a pot of glue in the act of hoisting himself onto the table.'

By the following term they had settled down together, and Oakeshott he proposed to teach them about the tradition of manuscripts. Here he earned their respect as a professional, giving them a papyrus fragment of Callimachus for conjectural restoration. But his informality still caused comment. In the summer term of 1940 he took them for Divinity and Greek history, not to universal satisfaction. On 15 May 'If he goes on teaching history like that, it won't get us very far', and on 26 May 'he's not teaching it in the right way'. But on 12 June, at the time of the final surrender of the French, he 'went through the argument of [Thucydides'] Melian dialogue. Does this justify Hitler?'; and on 22 June he 'discussed whether we have right on our side in the war, and went on for twenty minutes after school'.

This diary shows two characteristics of his teaching: its breadth, and his emphasis on discussion.[3] Another boy recalls his tentative and much-imitated expression of a view: '*It seems to meee* – with the *me* drawn out almost to three syllables'. The generosity was also characteristic. A boy who broke his leg playing rugby in December 1939 remembers that 'the next morning WFO cycled from Crowthorne to visit me in hospital at Windsor and gave me his copy of Chesterton's *The Man Who Was Thursday*'. Another group of ten boys he took at his own expense by train to see the Winchester Bible, and stood them tea.

Apart from those he taught, the boys who got to know him best were a mixed bunch.[4] Some were head boys ('Captains of the School' at St Paul's), of whom the closest was Hugh Arnold, the first at Crowthorne. Arnold recalls an illuminating sequence of events in December 1939. Among the boys at the time were a number of refugees from Hitler. Most settled in to the school, some with brilliant success. One however was 'frankly tiresome and persistently "bolshy" towards prefects'. Arnold proposed that he be given the rare punishment of a 'prefects' beating'. Oakeshott concurred:

somewhat surprisingly, he could see merit in corporal punishment.*
But when Arnold pronounced sentence, the boy appealed to the High
Master. Oakeshott spent nearly half an hour talking to him, in order
to make absolutely sure he understood the reason for the punishment, and did not just suppose he had exchanged one tyranny for
another. He then sent him back, and the beating was carried out.

But Arnold had meanwhile made a mistake which ever after he
blushed to recall. During the half-hour's talk he was left waiting with
fifteen hungry prefects anxious to get home for their evening meal.
After twenty minutes he knocked on the door to see what was happening. Oakeshott said nothing to him at the time, nor indeed later.
But the next morning when High Master and Captain of the School
met outside Hall to go by custom into prayers together, he could
sense a change of atmosphere. In fact 'he became extremely cool and
remote for the best part of a week, just when I was about to take the
scholarship exam to Cambridge. He probably intended to avoid upsetting me at a critical time, but in fact it would have been much
better had he given me a quick blast and got it over with.' The boy
had correctly divined that the man was 'over-anxious to avoid confrontation'. Indeed, as the sequel shows, the man was affected more
than the boy.

> As I was literally about to set off for the train to Cambridge, he
> handed me a letter to read. In it he explained why he had been
> upset by what I had done. But he also enclosed a copy of what
> he had written to the College about me, so that I could see it had
> not affected his opinion of me.

Other boys who got close to him were scholars who responded to
the play of his mind. One such was Tony Wood,[5] whom he afterwards appointed to his staff at Winchester. Wood, who knew him
well enough to see how 'that dreamy mildness masked a will of steel',
recalls two revealing incidents. In 1941 the High Master went round
various classes explaining Wavell's North African campaigns, and
'one could trace his movements all over the school by the sketch-
maps he left on the blackboards'. Later Oakeshott was present at a
meeting of the school Essay Society when Wood read a paper on
Religion and Superstition. Wood began by making distinctions –

*Already at Tonbridge he 'realised that beating, with its final and immediate closing
of the account, had a very great deal to be said for it compared with almost all
forms of punishment'.

'mostly spurious semantics. . . . "I enjoyed the first part," said Walter, eyebrows disappearing upwards, "I thought it was very cunning." Damn, I thought, he's seen through it.'

At the other extreme from scholars and Captains of the School were boys who for one reason or another did not fit. Doris Page's son Geoffrey, who lived in Waverley too, became interested in painting. His father being away at the war, Oakeshott became 'like a father' to him (a phrase which Arnold also uses) and encouraged him to make a career in art. Greville Janner entered the school at the age of sixteen in 1944, having been evacuated to Canada during the blitz. As a natural non-conformist, he found 'the liberal bicycle-borne life at St Paul's a joy'. But he did enjoy running, and the school's provision for athletics was rudimentary: no team, no coaching, no track. He went to see Oakeshott, who suggested he got it started himself. He did. Oakeshott even came to watch – and when Janner became Southern Junior champion in the 100 yards, wrote him 'a whimsical note of shared victory'.

The same thing happened when Janner complained to him about the dreariness of the school magazine, *The Pauline*. Oakeshott suggested that he restore *The Debater*, a magazine which G. K. Chesterton had started as a boy for the same reason, but which had now lapsed. He himself wrote a characteristic foreword to the first issue of the new series, complete with a long sentence of self-parody.

> In the HIGH and FAR-off times there appeared at fitful intervals a magazine. It had the erratic and intermittent brilliance which the astronomers say is peculiar to the variable stars, that trim balance which marine architects call the quality of sailing close to the wind, perhaps a touch of that monstrous beauty which a character in *Hassan* ascribes to the hindquarters of an elephant. . . . Well, here is *The Debater* again. And delighted the authorities are to turn once again (within reason of course) a blind eye to it.

For the historian however *The Pauline* has its uses. The issue of October 1939 contains a fact-packed account of early days at Crowthorne under the well-chosen superscription of *Caelum non animum*: 'we have changed our address, not our spirit'. One judgement of interest is that 'the average Pauline gets far more open-air activity than ever before'. Oakeshott's own verdict on the evacuation was presented to the Governors in February 1940. He saw two advantages. 'Though [it] has reduced the size of the school, it has increased its cohesion to a remarkable degree, and the psychological effects have been apparently altogether favourable.' Parents had commented on the improved sense of responsibility and self-assurance of their boys. 'In organized games alone the results are almost all on the debit side, though physique is not suffering as a result.'

Among the staff Oakeshott met a certain amount of initial criticism. Men whose idea of a High Master was formed on Bell took time to grow accustomed to the young scholar who had succeeded him. The Old Pauline Mavor found him too informal, and the cynical Eynon Smith dubbed him a dreamer – the boys for a time christened him 'Johnny-head-in-air'. But it was not long before he had won them round in various ways. Eynon Smith was converted as a result of new and more spacious end-of-term report forms which Oakeshott introduced.* Reading some perspicacious comments by the High Master on boys in his own form, he confessed in the staff-room 'I've come to the conclusion that he's a very clever ... devil' – words which were high praise from him. Eynon soon became a close friend and took his meals in Waverley.

Mavor also did not take long to realize that Oakeshott was rock-solid on the traditional virtues, and their friendship too was lifelong. When Mavor was dying in a Scottish hospital in 1967, Oakeshott went to see him. He spoke of that visit at his memorial service later, in words that deserve quotation.

> To see him was almost like looking at one of those wasted bodies which the stonemasons of long ago used to carve, lying below the coffin; or perhaps like a medieval saint and ascetic, the skin like parchment clinging round the bones; but wonderfully serene. When he spoke, the old charm was there to the full. The dark eyes lit up; there was the old eagerness to talk about books, about the things he had collected, about this school, about the one more visit he would pay to the south before he withdrew to the little community where they would look after his last days. I kept trying to go, afraid one would be tiring him; but he insisted I must stay till the last moment that was possible. It was a great joy that so little before death, he was so full of life.

---

* 'End-of-term reports always fascinated me,' he wrote in 1981, partly because they threw so much light on the ideas and qualities of those who had written them'.

How much he was aware, then, of the twilight and the hurrying approach of night, I do not know. We hardly spoke of it. But if, as I think he knew, [his sun was setting], for him the moon was already rising, the stars sparkling. Something new was beginning, as things old came to an end.

Oakeshott uses the word 'charm' of Mavor, and it was a word often used of himself: 'he could charm anyone into anything', said Richenda Stubbs, who played a vital role in charge of the sanatorium. But 'charm' is too superficial a word. What we are really talking about is love, love which he gave and love which he evoked – in part because he was vulnerable. When Richenda had a daughter he wrote: 'If she's got the charm, and the enormous energy, and the hundred-and-one other enviable qualities that her mother has, she'll be an asset to the post-war world right enough.' Three years later the little girl died after a long illness, and he wrote

When there are these terrible illnesses, so terribly prolonged, there must be some sense of thankfulness that at last they come to an end – but as a poet said 'this seeing the sick endears them to us', and the very fact of their hopeless helplessness makes them the more loved. One must remember what a sweet, happy child Janet was – and must remember that sweetness, and happiness, like that is tremendously worth while, however short it is.

At St Paul's, as later at Winchester, it was Oakeshott's gentle qualities which in the first instance won people's affection and loyalty. He never allowed himself to show anger. 'It is impossible to imagine him ever giving offence to anyone,' said Arnold. He did not have a commanding personality like Bell or Leeson. But anyone who thought him soft-centred was much in error. When he wanted something badly, as he wanted to save St Paul's, his determination was steely. *The Pauline* of October 1939 wrote of his 'faith' and his 'unfailing optimism'. It was this combination of steel with velvet, together with his gift for bringing out the best – and more than the best – in staff and boys, that inspired those who knew him. He was not an organizer: 'Organization', said Cook, 'meant pushing people around, and he never enjoyed that.' The organization was provided by talented and loyal subordinates like Cook and Tyson. To them he always gave the credit. But his was the inspiration. And it did 'save' the school – the judgement is that of his successor as High Master.

The Mercers, too, were carried along. The 'exercise in the extempore', as he once called it, was an evident success. Money gradually became available for school purposes. In November 1939 Sir Frank Watney's legal assistant was appointed 'to act in the Clerk's absence until further notice'. Watney was beginning to stand back, though he did not formally resign until 1941. In May 1940 the Mercers came down symbolically to Crowthorne for Apposition (the annual prize-giving), *bringing their own wine* (Cook's italics) and inviting the staff to a luncheon. In July 1940 Sir Cecil Clementi became Master of the Company and *ex officio* Chairman of Governors. Though a good businessman, he was also a classical scholar who had edited Catullus. Moreover Oakeshott had taught and admired his son at Winchester. For a year Oakeshott had an easy and happy relationship with his Chairman of Governors such as he would not enjoy again for over a decade. Cook's judgement was that from 1940 on Oakeshott 'wound the Mercers round his little finger and got them to do whatever he wanted'. Another way of putting it would be that from henceforth they encouraged and supported him fully in his planning to strengthen the school for wartime survival and postwar growth.

The first matter that needed to be put right was the legal and financial basis of the hostels. It was done in two stages. At each of them Oakeshott worked out a proposal which he put to Clementi: Clementi accepted it and subsequently reported it to the Governors. The first scheme was for the Governors to take over the leases of all the rented hostels on terms by which, Oakeshott argued, 'there will probably be an economy'. But he then realized that most of the masters had been running them at a loss – in one case a loss of £350 for the year 1940. The second scheme was therefore much more generous: it would cost £2,650 p.a. which, said Clementi, 'there would be no difficulty in providing out of the resources of the school'.

Subsequently (in February 1942, but it is convenient to deal with it here), the Governors regularized the position of Waverley too. They recalled that Oakeshott's emoluments in Hammersmith had included a High Master's house, worth roughly £250 p.a. This sum they agreed to pay him, backdated to September 1939. Should he himself move out of Waverley, as at that time he was intending to do, he would let the school continue to use it as a hostel. For that use he was 'unwilling to accept more than £130 p.a., though the Surveyor says that a fair rent, compared with the other hostels, would be higher'.

Oakeshott next turned his attention to Colet Court. This was an independent preparatory school, just across the road from St Paul's in Hammersmith, for boys aged eight to thirteen. As a private family trust it had nothing but the name of Colet to connect it formally with St Paul's. But before the war St Paul's used to draw much of its intake from Colet Court and, while having reservations about its standards, was glad to do so. In 1939 Colet Court was split in half: about sixty day boys stayed in London, while sixty boarders were evacuated into the country. The country section had already had to move twice when an opportunity arose in 1941 to bring it to Crowthorne.

Wellington, like St Paul's, had had a drop in numbers in the period 1938–40, and decided early in 1941 to close Wellesley, one of its boarding houses. Oakeshott proposed to his Governors in May that Colet Court should be offered formal incorporation in St Paul's, coupled with accommodation at Wellesley. He gave two reasons: to safeguard his own recruitment, and to enable a more coherently planned curriculum from ages ten to eighteen. All parties agreed to the plan. In August the Colet Court boarders moved in to Wellesley House. From then on the work – and the staff – came under his aegis, and he himself went up to Hammersmith once a week to teach the boys still there.

But at the back of Oakeshott's mind there was a further reason for interest in Colet Court. The interest derived from ideas about the future which were already being mooted among schools like St Paul's. At headmaster level, he himself had been coopted to the Committee of the Headmasters' Conference in January 1941. At governor level – the level that mattered when the long-term future of the schools was under consideration – St Paul's had a more weighty involvement. On 4 April 1941 Clementi had convened and chaired a meeting at Mercers' Hall which agreed to set up the Governing Bodies Association. The focus of interest at both levels was sum-marized in a report written by Oakeshott for his Governors on 8 July.

There has for some time been a strong feeling that, if it should be possible without loss of independence, Public Schools should open their doors wider. . . . It seems to me to be of the highest importance that the increasing degree of social democracy . . . should be mirrored in the public schools.

He went on to mention various ways in which certain London schools already offered scholarships to boys from elementary schools, and to propose that St Paul's should follow the precedent of Christ's Hospital. Specifically he suggested that out of its 153 scholarships it should reserve say thirty-three at any one time (roughly five a year) for elementary schoolboys, and in addition that the Mercers should make grants to the parents of such boys towards the cost of lunches, books and uniform. He had clearly already discussed the proposal with the LCC, and was able to report that they 'would probably be prepared to grant maintenance allowances to the parents'.

The Governors, after deliberation, accepted all these proposals in principle. They decided however that, although the scheme could be published now, it should not be implemented until the return to London lest 'its operation might be impaired by the unwillingness of [London] parents to allow their sons to attend a Boarding School'. The proviso was sensible, the decision of principle remarkable – and greeted with acclamation by the LCC. It is true that the ideas were in the air, and that the scheme would not cost the Mercers much; but it represented a revitalized and extended commitment to education.

With both these matters in hand, Oakeshott turned his attention thirdly to the school's academic policy. As a first step he wanted to enlist the advice of His Majesty's Inspectors by inviting a Full Inspection. Clementi agreed – until he learned that 'the Inspectors would want to inquire into the finances of the school and therefore of the Company'. But he allowed himself to be persuaded, and 'a strong team' of HMI visited the school at the end of September 1941.

When they left, Oakeshott wrote privately to the new Master (H. A. Watney, who had succeeded Clementi in July):

> The Inspection, though it has produced a packet of criticisms – or rather because of that – has proved most useful. In some things [i.e. some criticisms of the work] I am sure they are right, in others I am fairly sure that they are wrong; for they tend naturally to be 'in the fashion' and I have an idea that in some respects it is time the fashion swung back to us rather than our catching it up.

Among welcome criticisms, they 'drew our attention to a fact of which some of us were already acutely aware, namely, that St Paul's concerned itself too little with the progress of the ordinary boy, though the school was interested enough in the work of the scholar'.

Their written report, when it came, made a related point, that even for the scholar 'there is a danger of over-concentration on examinations to the exclusion of subjects of general educational value'.

The Inspectors' summary of the school's finances is illuminating. 'The income is derived mainly from endowments and fees. The Endowment consists of the annual payment of £30,000 from Dean Colet's estate. Fees bring in £29,092. The total expenditure amounted in 1938 to £63,385, of which £30,000 is for salaries of teaching staff . . . The financial position is very strong.'

In June 1942 a remarkable meeting was called. Its nominal purpose was 'to discuss Colet Court', but besides the High Master, the Master of the Company and the Clerk, those present included the Directors of Education for the County Councils of London, Middlesex and Cambridgeshire, and Archbishop William Temple, newly translated to Canterbury. All were in firm agreement that, if the offer of scholarships to elementary schoolboys was to be implemented, the Mercers must be able to guarantee schooling from the age of eleven and so not only the school but the property of Colet Court must be acquired.

They went on to consider another likely development, that post-war secondary schools would be 'multilateral', i.e. would have not only an academic but also a non-academic side. For such purposes the Hammersmith site would be inadequate. But the school must on no account move permanently out of London: 'very grave disapproval of the Osterley site was unanimously expressed'. Next 'a riverside site' was discussed and three alternatives mentioned. One was Fulham Palace; but that, in the opinion of the Primate, was 'not in the market for educational purposes'. The other two were Ranelagh and Hurlingham.

When the Governors considered the report of this meeting, they agreed to buy the land and buildings of Colet Court for about £20,000. The rest of the report they merely 'received'. The policy gradually crystallized that, before pursuing any idea of moving to a new site, even within London, they would try improving the use of the present one. For the next three years Oakeshott bent his fertile mind to showing that 'the plan of maintaining St Paul's as an urban day school at Hammersmith does not imply a simple acceptance of the *status quo*'.

His first concern, in planning for a better school, was to deal with 'the problem of the ordinary boy (and its acute form, which may be called the *very* ordinary boy)'.[6] The solution must lie in early diagnosis followed by the provision of 'adequate facilities after the war for the boy who thinks with his hands'. With the facilities would go 'a senior scholarship syllabus to suit a boy who is going in for a practical engineering career, and who could not make much of the more academic studies'. The thinking is inchoate, but the general drift of it certainly fits the philosophy of the multilateral – or at any rate the bilateral – school.

Oakeshott's vision however extended further. Already in 1942 he was arguing that 'the great urban school of the future may have to play the same part in the life of the city as the Village Colleges[7] are playing in the life of the countryside'. The essence of the idea was 'to fuse the education of the child with the education of the adult', in the belief 'that something like this may be the modern counterpart of the humanist ideal which was the inspiration of the Founder of St Paul's'.

A year later he was looking to the model of the American Campus School, where a group of schools might work together on linked sites – in this case, St Paul's Boys' and Girls' Schools and Colet Court. The complex might hope to build certain facilities which would be beyond the reach of a single school: an exhibition room; a theatre available also for performances by outside companies; and even a planetarium which might draw audiences from all the schools in London.

In order to realize such a vision, more space would have to be acquired. Here however there was an opportunity. St Mary's Church, immediately adjacent to the Boys' School in Hammersmith, had just been destroyed. By chance Oakeshott had himself been invited by the Bishop of London to take part in a reconstruction survey of the London parishes. At the time he had said he would gladly do so except for that part of London where St Paul's had an interest. In July 1944 he wrote to the Bishop to say the school would indeed be interested in acquiring the St Mary's site if it were decided not to rebuild the church.

One other aspect of the school's life attracted his constant attention. When he went to St Paul's in 1939 he espoused the day-school ethos with all the enthusiasm of a convert. When the school moved to Crowthorne he claimed that it was having the best of both worlds, day and boarding, even though the boys had no more contact with their homes than straight boarders. As time wore on, he thought it through a little further, and came to distinguish various forms and grades of the boarding experience. He was therefore ready in 1944, as he had not been in 1939, to contemplate abandonment of the two full-time boarding houses. On the other hand he saw the advantage to some Colet Court boys of a period away from home, and envisaged residential camps for *all* boys aged ten to thirteen after the war. He also made a firm decision that on return to London he would retain the Crowthorne tradition of the extended lunch break *for all pupils*; in that way 'a day school steals a few of the advantages of a boarding school in concerning itself with the whole life of a boy rather than simply with his classroom development'.

All these ideas for change, and others which he discussed with his Governors, would of course cost money. Would the Mercers be willing to spend it? In a private letter to the Master written after the return to Hammersmith in 1945, he advanced a crafty argument. He began by stressing 'the immensely strong financial position of the school, or of the estates held in trust for it'. But

> in these days that must carry some danger with it. . . . No doubt in Colet's day it seemed unthinkable to the wealthy monasteries that their property should be confiscated, and the King could never have 'got away with it' unless it had been easy to make a case before the people that the monasteries were hoarding their wealth, not using it for the public good. For similar reasons I believe that it would be prudent to have a forward educational policy, and let it be known that we have big plans for the future. . . . Our resources lay on us the obligation to lead the way in educational experiment.

None of these ideas, except perhaps for the planetarium, was peculiar to Oakeshott. Political and educational reform were both in the air from 1941 onwards. Public Schools were motivated by three parts altruism to one of anxiety. Traditionally, their voice was uttered through the Headmasters' Conference, of which Leeson was Chairman throughout the war. Having been coopted to the Committee in January 1941, Oakeshott was put up to propose an important motion on its behalf at the AGM in December. The motion was 'That the Committee be instructed to open negotiations with the Incorporated Association of Headmasters to explore possibilities of amalgamation'. The IAHM was the parallel organization of secondary school headmasters. The two together could represent the whole field of secondary education for boys. HMC would 'lend its prestige to the fight for freeing the secondary schools which are at the moment under the thumb of unsatisfactory education committees'. IAHM could help to arrest 'the danger that the public schools may be by-passed when the future education of the country is planned'. His arguments were supported among others by Birley, now Headmaster of Charterhouse, and the motion was passed – though in the end nothing came of the negotiations.

But HMC had now another weighty ally in the newly formed Governing Bodies Association. Together GBA and HMC approached R. A. Butler as President of the Board of Education with an invitation. He responded in July 1942 by setting up the Fleming Committee 'to consider means whereby the association between the public schools and the general educational system of the country could be developed and extended'. The Fleming Report, published in July 1944, was widely approved. It was commended to the Mercers by Bailey, who had played an important part behind the scenes within GBA. Oakeshott spoke in support of the general philosophy on the grounds that the present 'social cleavage in education' does 'at least as much harm to the boy from the comparatively sheltered and well-to-do home as for [sic] the boy who does not share these apparent advantages'. But when it came to practical proposals, the Report's recommendation for public day schools stopped well short of the scheme already approved by the Mercers for St Paul's in 1941.

Oakeshott's social concern was by no means confined to the future of the public schools. When Men Without Work was published in 1938, the indefatigable Oldham set about creating a permanent basis for Christian social criticism. His methods were various. Most influential was the Christian News Letter which he edited and produced himself thoughout the war. There were also groups which met regularly, read papers and from time to time published them. Oakeshott was a founder member of one of these groups, which came to be known as 'The Moot'.[8] The membership consisted partly of those who had been concerned with the unemployment inquiry (Temple, Lindsay, Moberly, Tawney, Miss Iredale and Oakeshott) and partly of others, including T. S. Eliot, Oliver Franks and many old friends of Oakeshott, such as Charles Raven, Henry Brooke and H. A. Hodges. Oakeshott attended six meetings of the Moot, starting with the first in September 1938. At that meeting Middleton Murry read a paper out of which came, six months later, Eliot's Idea of a Christian Society.

At the same meeting there was much discussion of how best to exert a Christian influence on public opinion. Some favoured a research organization, others an Order. Oakeshott preferred an Order, whose 'members should be prepared to make some sacrifice, such as giving up social position and income'. By 1939 the divide was rather between the two *foci* of politics and philosophy. The philosophers were led by Hodges, who at the meeting in December 1941 read a paper on 'Christian Thinking Today'. Oakeshott used extracts from that paper for readings at St Paul's, but he attended no more meetings of the Moot, which continued throughout the war.

One reason for his withdrawal may be that in such matters he now had direct access to the top. In March 1940 he 'went to Lambeth for an exceedingly interesting and exclusive gathering (2 archbishops, Sir Walter Moberly, Dr Oldham, T. S. Eliot and the Wig [i.e. himself]) about educational policy in general'. Four months later, after the fall of France, he put up to Lang the idea of trying to get agreement among all the churches about 'peace aims'. Lang was as encouraging as his cautious and uninspiring nature allowed. Oakeshott thereupon drafted a document for publication – so hastily that he failed even to keep a copy for himself. Lang sent the draft round widely for lay comment, and then put it before a meeting of Church leaders. At the meeting Temple was supportive, and offered to see Halifax about it; so was Bell of Chichester. But 'some of the "old gang", including the Archbishop of Canterbury, [were] against taking any action at the moment'. The meeting 'decided that, if there *is* an attack on this country and *if* it's staved off, they'll try to get something done about it in October'. Oakeshott conceded that 'they may be right', but was disappointed: 'It would represent a sort of landmark, not because it is good, but because the united churches have never done any such thing.'

All that came of it in the end was his own letter to *The Times* in December 1940 arguing against the imposition of excessive sanctions upon a defeated Germany, lest they lead to unemployment among the victors. Nevertheless his standing in church cirles was assured. In 1941 his proposers for membership of the Athenaeum[9] were the Archbishops of Canterbury and York. Early in the following year Lang resigned and Temple succeeded. Temple attended the St Paul's meeting in June 1942, but that is the last recorded contact between him and Oakeshott. He died in 1944 at the age of sixty-three, mourned as much outside the Church as inside it.

The Christian connexion led also to one of the strangest – and in the event least happy – involvements of Oakeshott's life. In 1941 R. A. Butler became not only President of the Board of Education but also Chairman of the Conservative Reconstruction Committee. Reconstruction was the talk of the time, and Labour was threatening to hog the conversation. Butler 'was unusual among Conservative politicians of this period in believing that ideas were important in politics. In tactical terms he was a supporter of empiricism, but privately he hankered after an older Tory vision, or myth, of organic Christian hierarchy'.[10] When he came to set up sub-committees, therefore, he welcomed intellectuals, in whom any shortfall in party loyalty could be made up by a Christian commitment.

As Chairman of his Education Sub-Committee he chose Geoffrey Faber. Faber was Fellow and Estates Bursar of All Souls, as well as Chairman of the family publishing house, and a respected ex-Chairman of the Publishers' Association. He had also married a cousin of Butler's, and was not without political ambitions on his own account. His credentials were unassailable.

Faber had also known Oakeshott on and off since 1922. A letter to him written by Oakeshott in 1932 recalls 'what was (I think) actually my first evening in Oxford, when I dined with you in All Souls. I still remember with shame that I had no tail coat, and with gratitude that you pretended not to notice.' The purpose of the letter was to offer for publication a short paper on some educational topic which he had read to a society of schoolmasters.[11] He ended it with a characteristic touch. 'I feel horribly guilty even referring to your past kindness to me. What makes Christian morality so appallingly difficult is that the after-effects of kindness are so much more troublesome than those of sending people straight away about their business.'

Faber did not publish the paper but must have kept in touch; nor will he have failed to notice Oakeshott's part in *Men Without Work*. He may also have read some of Oakeshott's subsequent contributions to political debate. Most remarkable in view of what was to follow was an article in the *Spectator* of March 1939 on youth unemployment. 'The only cure' for it, Oakeshott wrote, 'is compulsion' i.e. compulsory training.

> But if self-respect is to be preserved, it must be implemented on a wider basis; if not universally, at least generally. . . . It might

be one of the chief factors in the remodelling of democracy; and if unemployed men worked together with men of all classes as servants of the State on the great reconstruction jobs that are crying out to be done, it would restore them and remake many of their lives into something worth while, both for them and for the society in which they live.

On 29 August 1939 he wrote along similar lines to *The Times* advocating militia training – in this case for the purpose of integrating refugees into British society. He explained to Noel that 'it seems very important to start any war with a really "liberal" and non-jingoistic attitude. Which I hoped was that of the letter.'

In addition to his own credentials, Oakeshott also had the support of Eliot, whom Faber had already coopted to his committee. 'Eliot', said Faber, 'was very strongly in favour of you.' Faber recommended him in turn to Butler as 'a young man (38) with a brilliant record, and a Churchman'. With Butler's approval he then wrote inviting him to a preliminary conference in January 1942. But he had to add: 'I don't know whether you are a conservative.'

Oakeshott, replying on 5 February, identified himself as 'a convinced Christian'. As to his politics, he did not pretend to Faber, nor Faber to Butler, that he was a conservative. But he had no qualms about taking on this work. He explained his stance in words which hark back to the unemployment study. We need 'such a fundamental change in social conditions that the vast majority of the people can feel that on the whole the state is run for the greatest good of the greatest number'. This is 'a difficult question for a Committee of the Conservative Party, with, I suppose, a natural hesitation about socialism to face. But I believe that it is much more likely to thrash out a satisfactory solution than a Labour Party committee would be.'

A few months later his party comments were less defensive. He wonders if 'our report might serve as a focussing point for those conservatives who look forward as well as back, as well as for the "Crippsites". Speaking as an outsider, that is the political combination I should like to see controlling reconstruction problems.'*

Such non-partisanship was in fact typical of the wartime reconstruction movement, a source of strength in the short term and weakness in the long. José Harris, its historian, has observed how

---

*In 1940, when he was already writing optimistically about reconstruction, he had been putting his faith in the combination Churchill-Bevin-Morrison.

a common language of visionary patriotism and a common sense of national unity mask[ed] an immense diversity of values and goals. . . . At the level of general principle, all that can definitely be said to have united the movement was, first, a belief that social problems needed to be considered 'as a whole'. . .; secondly a belief that social reconstruction required a more extensive use of coercive governmental powers than had traditionally been thought tolerable; and, thirdly, the belief that such coercion need not necessarily entail the abrogation of personal freedom.

Oakeshott subscribed to all three beliefs, and his experience of unemployment supplied the moral fervour.

Harris illustrates these general comments by three case studies, one being of Faber's sub-committee. Oakeshott she describes as being, after Faber himself, 'the most dynamic member of the group, a man with considerable knowledge of and pronounced opinions upon many aspects of contemporary economic and social structures'. Certainly Faber's files show Oakeshott as the member who wrote most often and in most detail with comments upon Faber's drafts and with suggestions of his own, which Faber often copied to the others.

By agreement with Butler, the sub-committee set out to produce a series of reports. The first was to be on 'The Aims of an Educational System'. Faber took it upon himself to draft that one, with special help from Eliot. Harris sums up its main thrust as follows. 'Social solidarity and the organic nature of the state imperatively required a sacramental dimension in social policy and, in particular, public support for doctrinal teaching in schools.' As much as half the report, in fact, was on religion and morals. Somewhat surprisingly it was given a quite a warm reception by party and press when published during the summer.

But the programme of work for the sub-committee required that it produce also a series of detailed reports, the first of which was to be on the fourteen to eighteen age group. It was here that Oakeshott's influence was greatest. His hand may already be seen in a passage of the First Report which provides an explicit link to the Second.

The State must not fail to resolve that, at whatever cost, mass unemployment shall never again sap the vigour of the people. . . . The educational approach to the training of character has tended to forget that character must be 'tough' as well as 'good'. . . . The problems of strengthening and stiffening character cannot be solved solely in the school. ... The educational importance of bodily training lies mainly in its intimate connexion with character-building.

Oakeshott brought with him not merely an analysis of the problem but a proposal for its solution, deriving from his recent experience at St Paul's. A year earlier he had reported enthusiastically to his Governors that on two of the three weekly half-holidays the senior boys were giving up their time to one form of National Service or another. He listed the Home Guard, the ARP Service, a corps of roof-watchers, the school farm, the collecting of waste paper and the Air Training Corps. During that intervening year a new organization had been added, the Junior Training Corps; but unlike the ATC it was confined to schools.

On 10 February 1942 Faber wrote to Butler to say that four of them had begun work as a sub-sub-committee.

> In the course of our discussions Oakeshott started an idea which seemed to the rest of us so good that I was urged to put it up to you at once. It is that the JTC [Junior Training Corps] might be expanded [outside schools] on the lines of the ATC [Air Training Corps]. The new JTC syllabus is atractive to boys – Oakeshott says 'fascinating'. Its object, he claimed, was 'to produce boys who shared the qualities of the poacher and the gangster which Wavell says are necessary to the modern soldier, as well as having some of the more domestic virtues'.

Butler raised no objection, and Oakeshott continued to lead the thinking. On 2 April the sub-committee agreed to defer consideration of the Chairman's draft of the First Report and 'to give immediate attention to Mr Oakeshott's memorandum "The Problem of Service"'. By 18 May the draft of the fourteen to eighteen report was ready under the title 'A Plan for Youth'. Faber sent it to Butler with a note that Oakeshott ' did most of the actual drafting'.

The essence of the Plan was

> the bringing together of all existing youth organizations in a Federation of Youth under the Board of Education. Local Authorities would set up (or encourage voluntary organizations or the Services to set up) clubs, youth squads or pre-service training corps or other means of developing the young in body, mind and spirit and of giving them opportunities for service to the

State. Employers would be required to release young employees for one day a week, while the unemployed would have to give up 'a specified part of their time' to some form of approved service.

This bland summary, taken from the *The Times* leader on the day of publication in September, concealed some tense discussion in the ten weeks after Butler was shown the first draft. That draft embodied the conviction of all but one member of the sub-committee, that the scheme would never work if participation were voluntary: as one of them wrote to Oakeshott in April, 'the basis of our report is compulsion'. But Butler's Consultative Committee would have none of it. On 10 June he required Faber to 're-phrase very carefully ... omitting the impression that complete compulsion is to be adopted for Youth – a policy which it would be impossible to get accepted by the present [coalition] Government'.

Oakeshott did not give in easily. He would be 'very sorry to see the proposals redrafted in such a form that the underlying assumption "youth wants orders, not cajolery" was reversed'. But Butler was adamant. 'The crux of the paper lies in para 15, where Youth Committees are to *ensure* that they are enrolled. You cannot get away from the fact that this is *compulsion*. I should be inclined to add the words "ensure so far as they can", but this may spoil your sense.' In the end the issue was resolved by a new sentence. 'We realise that the recommendations we are making must ultimately involve compulsion – but this would be neither desirable nor effective till there is an adequate provision of facilities and leaders.'

There was a second difference, at least of emphasis, between Oakeshott and Butler. Oakeshott took a low view of most local authorities. 'My own experience in an excellent education office made me realise that a petty official in charge of a department is not always above using his position to make the schools feel that the ultimate power is in his hands.' Hence his passionate determination to avoid interference by local authorities. Just as one function of the public schools was to defend freedoms which grammar schools too should one day enjoy, so now it was essential that his 'Plan for Youth' should come under the Board of Education. Butler's antennae were alerted again. 'I am a little alarmed about Oakeshott's views. ... Do not let him or anyone else underrate the world of the Local Authorities and voluntary organizations in which we live.'

When the Plan was published on 16 September 1942, everything confirmed the accuracy of Butler's political instincts. *The Times* criticized 'the appearance of regimentation', and commented that 'the use of the term "the State" invites misunderstanding in this connexion'. The *Daily Telegraph* complained of 'the form of totalitarianism without its content'. The *Spectator* observed less reasonably that 'the Committee must be animated by a considerable wistful admiration for the Hitler Youth'.

Letters to the press for the next few days were virulent, with frequent accusations of fascism etc. Hardly a voice was raised in its defence. Oakeshott, whose involvement was not yet public, entered the lists with a long letter to *The Times* on 22 September. Its tone was conciliatory, and he conceded a number of points. But on one he stood firm. 'The principle of compulsion is a dangerous one, and it is a very good sign that we should all mistrust it like the plague. But compulsion for what? If it means that children from 14 to 18 will be compulsorily kept within the orbit of the education and health services, that appears, to me at any rate, to be a tremendous gain.'

But it was too late. On 1 October the Conservative Central Council held a conference to consider the report. Butler did his best to commend it, though even he conceded the semantic point. 'I think we shall never get a better word than "community" – and I greatly prefer it to the word "state".Somehow that word smells wrong.' Faber, on the defensive from the start, gave the names of his committee, including Oakeshott 'who had written most of it'. The tone of the discussion was hostile – 'pink slop' was one of the choicer phrases – and Faber 'did not exercise his right of reply'. No vote was taken, and the report was tacitly dropped.

The press on the following day was gleeful. But it prompted Birley to write two letters, one public, one private. To *The Times* he wrote as 'a schoolmaster who would certainly not be ready to accept as they stand the two interim reports'. But he pointed out that the principle of compulsion is in fact common in education, and that any comparison with Nazi methods was at best a debating point. To Oakeshott, while not concealing his points of disagreement, he offered balm: 'the misrepresentations of the critics have been fantastic'.

But not even he, as an old friend, saw how deep the hurt had gone. The person who saw that was Doris Page, whose diary records these three successive entries.[12]

– All sorts of scathing letters in the press about the HM's report,

including Laski and Joad. The HM wrote to Joad and said as he
had said so many rude things about him he'd better come and
lecture to the school by way of apology. I said I would have been
angry but the HM said that didn't do any good and proved you
were in the wrong.
– Joad wrote to say he'd come on Monday morning! HM said
he was in need of moral support so I pointed out that the public
had already forgotten . . . and in the end he seemed more cheerful. He does so hate limelight.
– HM and I went to a concert at Wellington. On the way there
he said he felt ashamed of appearing in public places after the
awful remarks about his report. I told him not to be so absurd.

His other friends on the staff also shared his hurt but were consoled.
They had been fearing that the school might lose him to a political
career. Now they were safe.

To Faber Oakeshott wrote a note of sympathy and offered to
resign. Faber insisted that the report had been 'fully agreed' by the
sub-committee, and pressed him to stay, at least for the work on the
public schools which was to be the next stage. For a few months he
continued to write papers and to propose meetings in the hope that
something could be salvaged from the wreck of A Plan for Youth. For
example, on 26 November he wanted to see a manifesto published
proposing that the school leaving age should be raised to fifteen
immediately the war ended, and to sixteen as soon as practicable
thereafter; and that education up to eighteen should be (O blessed
ambiguity!) 'universal'. Faber said he would try it on Butler, but
Butler was not throwing good money after bad. The sub-committee
continued to meet, but no more of its work was published. Butler
turned elsewhere for advice on social policy.[13] If Oakeshott continued to attend, he ceased to contribute.

But the question remains: how did Faber's sub-committee come so
to misjudge public opinion? Certainly there appeared to be a wide
gap between the 'reformers' and the public. The reformers traced
their lineage back through the Moot and Temple's interwar committees to the Balliol idealist tradition, and beyond that to Hegel and
Plato. Among them neither the concept of compulsion nor the language of the State raised hackles.[14] And to anyone looking back on
the 1940s from the perspective of later decades, with a school leaving
age of sixteen, with peacetime conscription, and with 'the Welfare

State' finally exorcizing the sinister noun, it might seem that the chief mistake of the reformers was to presume upon a consensus that did not yet exist.

But the dynamics of such groups suggest a further factor. If the sub-committee came together already predisposed on the issue of principle, they were also inspired in detail by Oakeshott's combination of experience and fervour. To that extent he was right to take the rejection of the report as a personal humiliation. He licked his wounds in private. But he never again raised his head above the parapet of educational politics. He even resigned in mid-year 1943 from the Committee of HMC, and ceased to play a part in its affairs except when Birley briefly persuaded him back ten years later.

His last word on the fiasco of 1942 comes in a strange letter to Faber, written when he was under some stress in January 1944.

> I only entered the edge of educational politics at a time when it seemed on the cards that the whole world might tremble. . . . Well it hasn't trembled, bless its heart! I become daily more convinced that I can go on doing my job without having to face the danger of utter chaos; and as I see this more clearly, the things that I am really interested in – my teaching, detective work with the past, the children and so on – begin to put in more and more undisputed claims.

By withdrawing in 1943 Oakeshott also gave up any effective concern for social issues. True, he was an ambivalent member of the Beveridge Commission on commercial broadcasting in 1949–50; and when unemployment reappeared as a serious problem in the 1970s he showed in a newspaper article where his sympathies still lay. Moreover others continued to think of him as he had been. Carr-Saunders, retiring from the Directorship of the LSE in 1956, wanted Oakeshott to succeed him.[15] In 1966 he was invited by Archbishop Michael Ramsey to chair a proposed Commission on Church and State. He declined both invitations, courteously but firmly.

But withdrawal from these fields left him far from inactive. 'Detective work with the past' had indeed been calling him since his time at Winchester. It had two main foci, medieval illumination and Renaissance maps. The latter seized him first, and led him down unexpected paths.

Shortly after the evacuation from Dunkirk in May 1940, the USA, not yet in the war, transferred fifty destroyers to the navy of the Allies. Reflecting upon 'the shared inheritance[16] of the English-speaking peoples – an inheritance in very truth, to use the psalmist's phrase, founded upon the seas', Oakeshott decided to write 'a narrative of some English maritime and overseas enterprises during the period 1550–1616' as 'the only tribute [he] could pay to the successors of Drake and Hawkins and Raleigh and of the crews who made their enterprises possible'. He wrote most of it during the winter of 1940–1. The dedication is to Prue Mitchell, who had been killed in an air raid in 1940. Any author's profits were to be paid to the Training Ship *Arethusa* as a 'token of gratitude to an institution that is doing fine work for the Navy'. The book was published by CUP late in 1942, entitled *Founded upon the Seas*.

It hit just the right note for the times. The First Lord of the Admiralty, A. V. Alexander, wrote to say 'I enjoyed it so much that I bought several copies of it to give as Christmas presents.' It also earned a far wider range of notices than any of his other books. In Britain and the USA, in national and provincial newspapers, in general and specialist journals (including *Yachting Monthly* and *Shipbuilding and Shipping Record*), reviewers lavished a largely uncritical praise. Some of the specialists betrayed knowledge of the author, e.g. *History* noted correctly that 'Mr O. is easily tempted to wander from the sea to the land'. *Literati* saw the chance of a long article. Masefield[17] discoursed on the rigging of sailing ships. Sir John Squire devoted most of his piece to extended quotations, a procedure he justified by the verdict that 'Oakeshott's prose, though he never indulges in heroics or a forced brilliance, is extremely vivid and lively'.

Squire was right. The first thing to say about the book is indeed that it is eminently readable. Oakeshott's narrative pace rarely slackens, and his descriptive powers can compass equally the excitement of the Armada or the pathos of Raleigh's last hours. Sadly, none of his later works provided such scope for his skill in telling a story.

In a quiet way the book also enhanced his reputation as a scholar. The *TLS* noted his disclaimer of original scholarship, but observed that 'an author who had consulted the Ulm Ptolemy of 1486 in the library of Winchester College and a plan of *Nombre de Dios* made at the time of Drake's attack, which has never before been published, has hardly need to apologize on that score. . . . His interest in and knowledge of ancient maps is evidently extensive and peculiar.'

But none of the reviewers noticed one other striking feature of the book. Written on a patriotic subject in the middle of a war for national survival, it might easily have been chauvinist and (retrospectively, if not yet prospectively) triumphalist. In fact it maintains a balance that is typical of its author.

> The movement of exploration, like most of the great achievements of Western civilization, is European in character. . . . The calendars and astronomical tables which English seamen used were printed mainly in Germany or in Italy. When Raleigh tried to plant a colony in Virginia, the splendid 'prospectus' for it was printed in Frankfurt, and besides the English edition, there were editions in French, German and Latin. . . . The difference was simply that with the English the achievements of the seamen became part of the national tradition, part of the texture of English life, in a way that happened nowhere else, save perhaps among the Dutch.

The final pages of the book tell the story of Pocahontas, the daughter of an Indian chief, and her saving of the colony of Virginia. 'She too is part of the shared inheritance of the English-speaking nations. For she trod not only the wild woods of Virginia but, for a few fleeting weeks, the streets of London and the steps of Whitehall Palace; and in England she died. And on that slender thread had hung, for a single moment, the fate of Raleigh's new English nation.' It was a delicate tribute to those who had given the fifty destroyers.

Out of all this there grew the strangest event in Oakeshott's life. In the spring of 1943 the shy scholar, 'bespectacled and owlish' as he seemed to his boys, wangled his way as a civilian on to a transatlantic convoy to New York and spent two miserable weeks at sea, in pursuit of – what? Clearly his Elizabethan heroes provide a part of the answer. They exemplified a fusion of thought and action which had doubtless attracted him from his early years. His modern hero, Wavell, who had come to inspect the OTC for him in 1939, was a man of the same mould. He had been winning brilliant victories in Africa and loyally going to defeat in Greece. Brother Jack was now a brigadier. Even Charles Mitchell was teaching people how to interrogate captured U-boat commanders. Yet with all that going on in the world, there was he in Crowthorne, in a reserved occupation, among boys. He could read to them at prayers from Drake and Hakluyt, or quote that fine passage of Milton 'I cannot praise a fugitive and cloistered virtue'. They would then go off, some of the most promising, to their deaths, leaving him to write consoling letters, to take his turn at roof-watching, and to sit on Admiralty interview boards.

In February 1943 he reported to his Governors on the two attitudes the boys took to the war.

> There are those who are deeply interested by the technical developments of war and who read all that there is to be read about new weapons, new methods and the lessons of campaigns already fought; and there are those who regard all this as a necessary evil and look forward to the post-war world and its problems as the thing which should be their main concern. . . . There is much to be said for both.

At the same meeting the Governors resolved 'that the High Master be granted leave of absence for an indefinite period in connection with his war activities'.

What had happened was this. When *Founded upon the Seas* was published in late 1942 he had made an approach to the Admiralty through his former Winchester colleague Gleadowe, to see if he could join a commando raid. The Admiralty not surprisingly said no to a commando raid, but would take him on a merchant convoy if he could go anywhere at short notice. In return he would write a pamphlet on convoys for the Ministry of War Transport. He told Noel of this on 5 February. 'It really is a chance, not of course in the least from the literary point of view but much more because it is the *kind* of experience that all the lads who pass through one's hands are going to go through. I feel (and Tyson feels) that it would make me enormously the better schoolmaster.' The Governors agreed.

When Oakeshott learned that his convoy would be going to Nova Scotia, another idea occurred to him.[18] He had been asked to give a lecture to the Society of Antiquaries late in 1943 on the Winchester Bible. From Halifax he could get to New York, the home of the Morgan Leaf which had so excited him at the 1936 exhibition (p. 85). Perhaps now he could get an even longer look at it. But when he got to New York and presented himself at the Pierpont

Morgan Library it turned out that the real treasures had been evacuated to a cave in the Middle West. Had the librarian had warning, she could have brought it back for him; but movements of convoys had to be kept secret.

To make things worse, he himself was ill on both crossings and spent most of the time in his cabin. The shrewd old ship's doctor advised a thorough examination when he got back to England. 'While there is no reason to worry, there's evidently something not quite right.' Fortunately he had brought with him the *Prometheus* and the *Phaedo* in Greek, so he was not dependent on the ship's library for reading matter.

Judged against its official object, the voyage proved no less disappointing. The commodore of the merchant ships in the convoy, who knew why he was there, regarded him as 'a piece of useless rubbish' and 'placed obstacles in the way of [his] collecting useful material'. His report, when written, was naturally full of praise for the courage and determination of the crews. But his recent experience on the unemployment inquiry, and the comparisons he could now make of British with Norwegian and American ships, tempted him to severe criticism of the men's conditions of service. He called for the 'raising of standards of accommodation and wages in British ships'. In exasperation he added a final sting. 'Some British ships are among the slums of the world's merchant fleets in the amenities they provide for seamen, and there is some justification in the allegation that this represents not chance, but policy.'

The report was 'unacceptable',[19] the pamphlet never published. Its rejection was no doubt less painful than that of 'A Plan for Youth' in the previous year. But in later life Oakeshott spoke of it only rarely, and then with typical wry humour. What he chose to recall were 'the pockets full of silk stockings which the crews brought back' and 'the so-called air umbrella, which consisted of a small plane which came out one evening when we were being worried by a submarine' and whose bomb-release jammed – 'quite proper conduct, I suppose, for an umbrella'.

The trip did however have one huge consolation: the hospitality he received during his time in New York. 'I don't remember *ever* enjoying a week more than I've enjoyed this week.' The Cambridge University Press gave a cocktail party for him and another author. But it was the family, the aunts and cousins, Noel's as well as his own, who really looked after him. They took him to the new musical

Oklahoma, to the Russian Ballet, and to the 'superbly laid out' Metropolitan Museum of Art. He even coincided with a smart family wedding. The bride[20] remembers 'seeing a forlorn figure in a worn tweed suit waiting on the doorstep with a blanket roll tied up with a rope. It was Walter.' They took him in, polished him up, fed him and fêted him. From this and later visits he acquired a host of American friends, a love of American hospitality (the quality rather than the quantity), and a respect for American culture which lasted all his life.

But when he returned to St Paul's and the staff learned what he had been up to, there were criticisms from Mavor and others. They were not entirely disarmed by his comment that 'things were going so smoothly that even the sort of figurehead that I was, was quite unnecessary'. Even Cecilia thought it was 'naughty of him'. Cook, generalizing in retrospect, observed that 'you never knew where Walter was' – but then added loyally 'though he was always there when needed'.

By 1943 Oakeshott was also well on the way to completing the admittedly short text of his next book *Artists of the Winchester Bible*. He had found time for a first draft in the early months of 1939, but in the interval his closer acquaintance with Fritz Saxl and the Warburg Institute had been showing him how far he had to go before he could venture to publish in a field for which he had no training. The Institute was centred round the great collection of comparative material which Aby Warburg had formed in Germany in the period 1910–30 and which Saxl had been able to rescue and bring to England in 1938. But 'the Warburg' was not just a collection: there was also a tradition of art history, and a small band of devotees including Rudolf Wittkower and Gertrud Bing.

The tradition went back, as did that of Berenson, Clark and even Beazley, to the celebrated German scholar Wölfflin. Wölfflin was the founder of modern art history, defined as the history of artistic vision, and achieved by the careful comparison of one artist or work of art with another. Warburg had gone on to link that with other aspects of history – politics, literature, religion and philosophy. Saxl's achievements were to preserve the Institute (until it was handed over in 1944 to London University) and to spread the gospel.* His correspondence with Oakeshott, especially in the years 1941–7, shows

*'The brilliant work of Saxl and others was to show how we are to "think" Romanesque.' (WFO, 1975.)

him typically so devoted to the encouragement of a younger scholar that when he himself died prematurely in 1948 he had too little of his own work already published. He not only gave advice when asked but also constantly made suggestions: an article here, a book there, or a foreign scholar on a rare visit to England. In short, he inducted Oakeshott into the Central European tradition of art history. He also tried, though with less success, to curb some of his flights of fancy.

The year 1940 seems to have been absorbed for both of them by problems of moving out of London, made more difficult for Saxl by the fact that some of his staff had only recently escaped from Hitler and were still classed as enemy aliens. So when Oakeshott wrote in 1941, having just heard that the Downshires might be vacating the rest of Easthampstead Park, to suggest that the Institute might move in ('I can't imagine anything better from our point of view'), Saxl had to reply that the Park was in a 'protected area' and therefore out of bounds. In July Oakeshott tried again: Wellington was about to vacate a house and 'we've often got what we want from the Berkshire police'. He added the observation 'I feel you are nearer the front line of the real war, which is the war of culture against barbarism everywhere'. In the event the Institute found a home at Denham, over the boundary into Buckinghamshire but only ten miles away by bicycle. Work could start.

Having summoned up the courage to send Saxl his first draft, Oakeshott went over on 11 February 1942 'for my tutorial'. Criticism was genial but extensive. He went away realizing that the text would need to be 'entirely recast', and Saxl sent him 'a few references' to that end. But they were both agreed that in a book of that kind – as indeed in their lectures on similar subjects – the very first priority was the selection and quality of the photographs. And here Saxl could offer invaluable help in the person of his photographer Fein.

So in April 1942 Oakeshott invited Saxl and Fein to spend three days as his guests in Hereford, studying and photographing the Winchester Bible in the Cathedral Library there, to which it had been transferred for safety.

I told him of my theory of the artist whose drawings underlay the paint, and I told him about the x-rays and our failure to get a result. His brow lightened, and he said 'Run out and get an electric torch', which I did. I bought a pocket torch for 3s. 6d.

He held the leaf up, and shone the electric torch behind it; and there quite clearly was what we were looking for.

When Oakeshott received Fein's photographs a few days later, he wrote to Saxl overjoyed. 'Look at the Amos initial, the beardless prophet with the lion; look how the lines of the muscles on the lion's flank show through the paint, and the curls of the lion's mane, so utterly different from what it is in paint alone.'

But in some respects the photographs made things more complicated. By dint of spending 'hours and hours with them every evening', he realized for example that 'there are at least two artists masquerading under the name of the Master of the Leaping Figures'. And he was the more inclined to go further than the cautious Saxl had recommended. 'In some ways I can't altogether take your advice, and find my mind continually on the go trying to sort out those hands not only into groups but into artists. In a few instances I am content to leave it, master or pupil. . . . But the arrival of a good photograph of the Morgan Leaf has set me off again properly on the quest of the distinctions between that group.' In another letter he wrote 'if one can particularize further, of course, it would be amusing'. Saxl accepted Oakeshott's decision, but some reviewers of his later books were not amused.

By 12 October 1942 the revised text was ready for typing at the Warburg. Oakeshott wrote 'I hope you will like it better than the last', and wanted to come and talk about it, to 'get away from all this nonsense about Fascism with which I seem unwittingly to have become identified'. Saxl, who could not see him, wrote to say it would be two guineas for the typing. 'It seems a bit much for 20 pages, but I am sure you have been told that it takes rather longer to decipher your hand than it does normally.'

Earlier in 1942 Oakeshott had told Geoffrey Faber what he was working on. 'I see,' said Faber, 'trying to do a Beazley with a medieval book!', and offered to look at the text. At the end of October Oakeshott sent it him with the photographs. Faber replied on 17 December apologizing for the delay: 'you know how occupied I have been.' His verdict was clear. 'The drawings [i.e. photographs] are breath-taking. . . . Your essay also has interested me extremely. There can be no doubt but that we shall want to publish, and to make the publication a worthy one; that is why delay is unavoidable in the present circumstances', i.e. wartime shortage of paper.

A few days later Saxl wrote to him with a comment on *Founded upon the Seas*. 'To produce a book on the rise of English power during the war and to state everywhere so clearly the negative side as well as the positive is, I think, really an achievement. There is no other country where such deliberate self-criticism would be the natural attitude of a man of character as in England.' In reply Oakeshott made in more personal terms the point he had made to his Governors.

> The mistake seems to me to lie in thinking of it as a dilemma: *either* glorify war in the Nazi way, *or* go to the other extreme and admit of the pacifist solution. Neither of them is tolerable to me in my present job. If the children one teaches are leaving school at 18 to go straight into the RAF or whatever it might be, life would be intolerable for them supposing they were brought up to feel that in all circumstances war was wrong; that it was uninteresting; and meant the destruction of all good qualities in a man's nature. It may mean the destruction or the submergence of some; but it means too the emergence of others. . . . It may be that nevertheless I've glorified war too much (I do sometimes find it most desperately interesting). If so, I've made a bungle.

The long letter ends on a characteristic note. 'You oughtn't really to have bothered to read my book – it isn't worth the likes of you reading it. I'm under no illusions about it, and it makes me almost ill to see a copy of it about the place now.'

In 1944 de la Mare of Fabers floated the idea that the Winchester Bible book when published might be the first of a series. Oakeshott's reaction was that, if so, Saxl should be the general editor, though he himself might tackle 'an Anglo-Saxon book, simply because when we had our Winchester exhibition I did get one artist isolated in my mind'. He goes on to express a typically optimistic view of human capabilities. 'If one watches a lot of old pigeon-fanciers in a London Men's Institute, or listens to spotters talking about aeroplanes ("that new design has de Havilland written all over it") one realises that 50% of mankind are potential connoisseurs. We ought to bank on this.'

Nothing came of de la Mare's idea for some fifteen years. Long before that, in August 1945, Oakeshott's own *Artists of the Winchester Bible* saw the light of day. In sending Saxl a copy he wrote 'I doubt whether even you quite realise how much it owes to you. But even if it had never been published, the contact it gave me with the Warburg would have made it far more than worth doing.' What he meant is shown by a letter written three years earlier after one of his visits to Denham. 'It is singularly refreshing to meet a community in which there's the sense of people living the good life in terms of untarnished friendliness. Of course it comes from having someone there who's not only a scholar but also a saint. It makes one realise how far most of our communities fall short of what they ought to be.' The generosity is typical. Others have told of hearing Saxl and Wittkower 'fighting like cats'. If Oakeshott heard, he would not have noticed; and if he had noticed, he would not have told.

The introduction to the *Artists of the Winchester Bible* contains all the appropriate acknowledgements, especially to Saxl. The dedication[21]

MATRI DILECTAE

PIETATIS ERGO SERAE TAMEN

DEDICAT FILIUS

expresses his remorse that he had not thought to dedicate either of his earlier books to his beloved mother. Her health was now declining fast, and she died in the following month.

In length, the book is scarcely more than a monograph: twenty-two pages of text and forty-four of illustrations. But in that short compass it broke a remarkable amount of new ground. Its focus is the identification of six different artists, whom he names the Masters of: the Leaping Figures; the Apocrypha Drawings; the Genesis Initial; the Morgan Leaf; the Amalekite; and the Gothic Majesty. In many cases he could show that the figures were drawn by one hand and painted by another. By that and other criteria he built up a sequence for which he offered a provisional chronology.[22]

Scholars have accepted all the names and virtually all the attributions. To this extent he was justified in going beyond Saxl's caution. But that caution frequently stood him in good stead when it came to his inferences and conjectures: at any rate a higher proportion of them have stood the test of time than in his later books. A reviewer of his last book on the Bible in 1981 described this 1945 book as 'still one of the most stimulating, readable and humanistic introductions to the development of English art in the period'.

The Artists of the Winchester Bible is in fact a miniature masterpiece in itself. Reviewers, whether scholarly or popular, recognized its quality. They praised text, photographs, book production and price. The public took the same view. The August print-run of 3,000 was quickly sold out, and a second impression of 2,500 was issued in October.

Of the scholarly reviews the most interesting was that of Tristram, the doyen of English experts on medieval wall-paintings.[23] Oakeshott in his new book still hesitated, as he had in 1939, to identify the Morgan Master with the artist of the visible wall-paintings in the Holy Sepulchre chapel of the Cathedral. Tristram now used his review to dismiss the hesitation: 'the mastery of the artist is so complete that it transcends limitations of scale'. Emboldened, Oakeshott went to see him to ask what might be the prospect of removing the visible wall-paintings and exposing the earlier ones underneath. 'No,' said the old man, 'not yet. The technique is not available. But it will come one day'. It did (p. 263), though Tristram did not live to see it.

In the autumn of 1943 Oakeshott suffered another long bout of ill-health. The first diagnosis was 'flu. But it was a severe and prolonged 'flu, with its usual accompaniment of sleeplessness. He said later that he 'felt so bad that term that he couldn't go through that again'. In January he was referred to a specialist, who diagnosed asthma and advised him to move out of Waverley; so he went for a while to live in the Old Rose Inn at Wokingham. After the second visit to the specialist in February he reported to Noel: 'I am getting on fine, but there were rather more unsatisfactory symptoms of a general kind (I gather circulation and so on) than he told me before, and they're not finished yet. He won't hear of me going back to Waverley before next term, and says that even then I'll have to go relatively slow and not go up on my little jaunts to London.'

The cause of his asthma is generally supposed to have been Bo Langham's cat. Langham was a hearty man who taught boxing and lower school science and, according to Cook, 'did things like improving boys' swimming'. He lived with his sister Marjorie in Waverley and acted as house tutor. Each of them had a cat, and there seems to have been no love lost between them and Doris Page who had two children and a dog. Her children suffered badly from asthma and, though neither of them reacted to the cat, she was convinced that Oakeshott did. To protect him she waged what she called a 'cat war', which came to a head in the Lent term of 1944.

Her diary entries about it are pure farce, though as always she has penetrating comments on Oakeshott.

Jan 6: I told Bo that the cat must go away a few days before the HM is due back, to clear the air of cattery. Bo said that was absurd and anyway it was more likely to be the coke fires upsetting the HM than cat.

[In the event the cat went away only on the morning of Oakeshott's visit. He had an immediate attack of asthma, which she told him was the cat's fault. Oakeshott] was silent. He will never admit that it might be the cat as he doesn't want to hurt Bo.

Jan 23: Eynon [Smith, who was clearly no neutral,] gave me his medical book on 'Middle Age and Old Age' and I duly read out all the bits on Cat Asthma to Marjorie, but apparently with no good results.

Jan 24: I went to dinner at the Rose Inn with the HM. I was horrified to see a CAT there (!) and apparently it doesn't affect the HM!! I must keep this a dark secret.

Feb 12: Bo said 'there is some slight suggestion that the cat may be upsetting the HM'. I told Bo I had asked the HM point blank if he thought the cats were upsetting him and he made a typical HM answer that he hoped he would be so well when he returned that nothing in Waverley would upset him.'

In the Easter holidays of 1944 the Pages were away and all the Oakeshott family came to live in Waverley. On return Doris found the cat still there and, sure enough, Oakeshott had had another attack of asthma. On her insistence the cat was sent away immediately. Ten days later he had a further attack. Doris discovered that 'the HM had been in Bo's room that evening. . . . I expect the room is full of cat fluff, so I suggested to the HM that he should stay away until he felt stronger to cope with the evil influences there! Since then he has been much better.' So ended 'the tale of the Cat'.

One is left wondering what *did* cause the asthma. Was it the cat? Or Langham? Or the war waged against them both by the good Mrs Page? Whichever it was, he was in poor health for some months. Most of that time he stayed at the Old Rose Inn, where he missed the boys and their conversation, and they missed him. Nor were his spirits greatly revived by the prospect of a visit in March 1944 from the best-known Old Pauline of the time, Field-Marshal Montgomery.

Oakeshott had from time to time received messages from

Montgomery for the school. One which he kept from 1943 reads as follows: 'I am now enjoying very good hunting in Italy, and as a result of this we seem today – 9 September – to have knocked Italy out of the war.' He added 'You may like to have for the school autographed copies of my last two messages to my Army.' The letter was hand-written on Fascist Party notepaper and ends with school-boy humour: 'I find this captured Fascist notepaper is very useful!!'

Now in March 1944 Monty proposed to visit the school – 'to see a boxing match. Make what you like of that,' said Walter to Noel. 'I am instructed that there is no need for secrecy. Rather the reverse, I gather! It'll be a bit of a chirp for the boys I suppose; and of course in a way I rather enjoy that kind of a binge. And as for The Rose, where we'll be dining, well, they've almost started on the menu already.'

There were other blows. Eynon Smith, who was living in Waverley for the term, went up to London for the weekend and was killed by a flying bomb. His death 'really did knock me sideways. . . . I knew him intimately (and vice versa). All in all,' he wrote on the eve of Monty's visit,

> I feel in profound disharmony with the world in general at the moment. Bloody-minded, I call it. People get like that at the end of wars. . . . That's partly why I find the 'Monty' prospect grim. I should guess he's probably the bloodiest minded of any. Wavell won't get like that. There's an anthology of his, *Other Men's Flowers* it's called, just out.

For Oakeshott, Montgomery always suffered by comparison with Wavell.

The Master of the Mercers came down for Monty's visit and stayed in Oakeshott's room in Waverley. That too was a source of irritation. 'I deplore the idea of [his] dropping cake all over the carpet and spilling tea-leaves into the books. But that's what one gets paid a salary for, so I always assume. *What* the Master will think about the Doris régime I don't know. He may give me the sack on the spot on the grounds that I'm giving countenance to the idea that I'm living in sin.'

But shortly after Monty's visit there was compensation. The American Ambassador in London, J. G. Winant, was an old boy and former master of St Paul's School, Concord, New Hampshire. Oakeshott conceived the idea of a link between the two schools. He would inaugurate it by a presentation 'to commemorate the present period of the friendship between the United States and Great Britain, with the hope that this friendship may be no less close in the years which follow'.[24]

On 7 July 1944 Winant came down to Crowthorne to receive the present: 'a first edition (1518) of Erasmus's *Epigrams* containing all the verses that he wrote at Colet's request for St Paul's School'. Before the presentation of the book, little Rose presented him with a buttonhole, and the school sang the Battle Hymn of the Republic; speeches were made by the Captain of the School and the Ambassador; after it they sang 'I Vow to Thee, My Country'. Finally the boys put on Shaw's *The Devil's Disciple*, set in New Hampshire in 1777.

Winant was delighted. So was Oakeshott. Ten months later, on 3 May 1945, with the war in Europe now drawing to a close, he gave a dinner in Winant's honour at the Savoy. Although it was a private occasion, there were thirty-eight guests, headed by Wavell. Geoffrey Fisher, the new Archbishop of Canterbury, proposed the toast of Anglo-American Friendship. Both episodes show Oakeshott in typical vein: a deeply held principle, expressed in a personal gift, chosen and presented with meticulous but self-effacing care.

Meanwhile at Crowthorne 'the Doris régime' lasted only one more term. In July 1944 the Downshires left Easthampstead Park for Ireland, and the Mercers took a lease of the whole mansion 'for the period of hostilities in Europe and 18 months afterwards', at a rent of £750 p.a. of which the school would contribute £500. The extra space made it possible in September 1944 to open a new hostel in the building. This was needed because, although numbers in the school had declined from 1939, the supply of billets had declined much more sharply. The new hostel also had enough accommodation for the Oakeshott family, who were thus reunited at the school for the first term since the war began.

It would not be for long. The war was moving to its close, and all thoughts turned to getting back to London. For the family, Oakeshott badly wanted a place in the country where they could all be together in the holidays and the children could invite their friends. It could be financed by the sale of Waverley as soon as the school was ready to move. He started looking round in the spring of 1944, and in the summer found what he was looking for. It was the Bell House at Merstham, near Ashford in Kent.

On 5 August he wrote to Noel about 'the house of which

particulars are submitted herewith for Mrs O's kind attention'. The tone was only partly jocular, because Noel compared all other country houses to her beloved Copse Stile and few could stand the comparison. The Bell House too was an old farm house, 'far roomier, far prettier' than another they had seen earlier: in fact 'to my thinking a place of the greatest charm'. It had a garden and orchard, was well placed for walks and bicycle rides, and only eight miles from the sea. True, it was badly in need of repairs; which, with building controls in force, meant it would be a long time before they could use it. But that fitted their financial position quite well. With Noel's concurrence he opened negotiations.

Meanwhile there was the much less tractable problem of getting the school buildings in Hammersmith back from the War Office. After being famously used for the planning of Operation Overlord they were now occupied by the Austrian Control Commission. In the meantime they had suffered considerable damage in a raid in July 1944, and the sooner the repairs (estimated to cost about £20,000) could be started, the better. In October Wellington gave notice that they would be wanting to resume the use of their boarding house lent to St Paul's, preferably in the following May but in any case not later than September 1945. It was therefore necessary to exert pressure on the relevant government departments. Oakeshott went to see the Board of Education and was given to understand that they had 'secured a promise from the War Office that they would put no one else in our buildings once the present occupants went out'.

In February 1945, however, it transpired that in place of the Austrian Control Commission a Polish organization had been installed. Oakeshott wrote again to the Board of Education in what he called 'the most violent language of which I was capable'. His actual words were 'I must honestly confess to have been absolutely appalled by the prospect which [your letter] opens up'. All the arrangements for accommodation at Crowthorne were coming apart at the seams, he said. One of the masters' wives in charge of a hostel 'had a breakdown at the end of last term, and it is doubtful whether she will ever be able to come back to the job again'.

But bigger guns were needed. The Mercers enlisted the help of Lord Selborne, Minister for Economic Warfare (himself a Mercer) and Field-Marshal Montgomery. Questions were asked in the House of Commons and letters written to *The Times*. In May the Secretary of State for War gave hope that 'the premises should be released by 30

July'. By mid-July no confirmation had been received. Then suddenly at the very end of term came the good news: the school was definitely theirs from 31 August. The beginning of term was put back till 1 October – three hectic months to go!

That last summer term at Crowthorne was marked by an event which had many reverberations for Oakeshott. At the end of May 1945 he repeated his famous Merchant Taylors' production of the *Oresteia*. This time again, as with the Balliol Players, it was in the open air, in front of the mansion in Easthampstead Park. Antony Jay recalls a remark of Oakeshott's during rehearsals. Asked what on earth the parents would make of Aeschylus, he replied 'in that wonderful drawl which all of us endlessly imitated: "I don't think you need worry about that. My experience of semi-intellectuals, of which our audience will be largely composed, is that if they see something they think they ought to like, they think they like it." '

In the performance itself, Jay's Cassandra was singled out for praise by the reviewer. But he also recognized the power of the choruses: the grim, spell-binding chant of the Furies (Westrup's music, of course) and the final procession when they had been metamorphosed into a procession of metics (foreigners living in Athens), wearing their scarlet cloaks and brandishing their blazing torches. It was a memorable occasion which in retrospect came to seem like a grand finale to the six long years in exile.[25]

On leaving Berkshire Oakeshott expressed the gratitude of St Paul's by a present to the Wellington College library. This was a set of printed maps, in almost immaculate condition, of some of the Iron Duke's battles. Oakeshott had bought them in Guildford in 1939, noting with astonishment that the earliest of the maps of Waterloo had been printed only about a week after the battle.

The scene that greeted the returning exiles in September 1945 was not entirely encouraging. On top of the effects of more than one air-raid, the Poles had on their last night in the school inadvertently caused a fire which allegedly did more damage than the Luftwaffe. But enthusiasm was enormous. 'Masters and boys in cheerful co-operation set to, to scrub and clean and arrange ...' wrote Bailey. 'For the High Master difficulties were again not a matter of complaint but a welcome chance for improvisation.'

And improvisation had to begin at home, for the old High Master's house had also suffered in the bombing. Since it was not very attractive anyway, the Mercers had decided to restore it for new use as a boarding house, and to provide him with a flat nearby in Latymer Court. The flat was much too small for the family, but three of the children were away at boarding school in term-time, For holidays the Bell House was now at last nearly habitable. Meanwhile, in the summers of 1944 and 1945, the whole family went for a fortnight to North Wales, where the three older children had the time of their lives hill-walking with their father.

In January 1946, while the rest of the family went off to Aston Tirrold, Walter and Helena went down to put the finishing touches to the Bell House: in particular to ensure that it was 'even warmer than Copse Stile' for Noel. To escape there from London *en famille* at Easter 1946 was a joy. But it was when they got to Winchester that it proved its real value, as a retreat for them and as a place which they could lend to friends or invite them down to visit.

The announcement that Oakeshott was to succeed Leeson at Winchester, when it was made at the end of March 1946, came as little surprise. Work went on as usual during the final term, but inevitably it was a time of speeches and articles assessing his achievement and saying goodbye. Tyson in *The Pauline* wrote of his contacts with the world outside the school and his 'very great gift of persuasion' in dealing with those who inhabited it. 'Within the school, surely, there has never been a Head of any great school so approachable or so ready to tolerate interruption. No work of his own seemed to stand in the way whenever parent, master or boy wanted his advice or help.' Finally

> all realised that this was a High Master who led the school with the direct and unhurried confidence of a thinker whose objectives were of permanent value and whose guiding principles were remote from any form of opportunism or self-seeking. In the post-war world which boasts of its toughness it is refreshing to behold the success of one whose habit is to credit others with unsuspected talents and qualities.

Bailey, who had known him longer than anyone, wrote only that 'He was everybody's friend, with the strange additional gift of making people friends of one another'. But perhaps the most penetrating of all was a tribute by Robert Harman, boy editor of *The Debater*.

> Chesterton said of Walker [High Master in his time] that he was a public man in his private character. It might be said

of Walter Oakeshott that he was a private man in his public character. He did not boom majestically at us from a distance. Nor have we ever seen him angry over trifles. . . . He has led the school with very great success through eight of the most critical years of its history and left it more vigorous than ever.

His last public appearance at St Paul's was at Apposition (Prize Day) on 4 July 1946. The ceremony proper was preceded by a briefer one. Monty, the Guest of Honour, unveiled a plaque in the Mercers' Board Room, the room in which he had planned Operation Overlord. Oakeshott's own valedictory speech unfortunately remains veiled in the bureaucratic prose of *The Pauline,* but a few personal touches shine through. Looking back over his seven years he 'emphatically disclaimed' any credit for past achievements. It belonged to many others. He paid 'a particularly warm and graceful tribute to the ladies of the community'. As to his hopes for the future, 'it had always been, and would always be, his firm endeavour to make the great benefits of public school education increasingly widely available. He thanked the Governors for their farsightedness and generosity in supporting the scheme he had designed to that end at St Paul's.' The hope, to his sadness, was never realized. The achievement remains. Shortly before his death he described it to Jasper Gaunt as 'the most successful (if that means anything) job I ever did'.

In August 1946 he spent three weeks on a lecture tour of the British Army of Occupation in Berlin, Austria and Italy. The lectures, organized by the Army Education Corps, alternated between unemployment and medieval art. It was not exactly the holiday he needed between two demanding jobs. Neither lecturing to the troops nor the social life of the officers' mess came naturally to him. Moreover the heat as he moved south brought him out 'in red blotches all over face and hands – most disfiguring'.

However he made the most of an entirely new experience. The moral and spiritual vacuum of postwar Berlin appalled him. Italy was not much better. 'What Fascism has actually done for the poor man is worse than nothing. The two nations of rich and poor have never been so far apart as they are now. I'm turning over in my mind an article for the *Economist* about it.' But he was interested in everything he saw – people, countryside, architecture – and, if compensation were needed, it was provided by the antiquities. Torcello was 'almost the first time that mosaics have really excited me'. And the tour ended in Rome – his first visit, and the start of a love affair that was to last the rest of his life.

All this he reported in letters to Noel. She spent much of the month at the Bell House, which she came to like better. 'High on the asset side I place the fact that the piano is in a good light.' He was delighted. 'I'm glad you are coming to terms somehow with the Beller. I was afraid you never would, perhaps.' She also made visits to Winchester to try to get things ready for their move on his return.

6

Winchester as Headmaster

1946–1954

Oakeshott was one of only eight men who applied for the head-mastership of Winchester in succession to Leeson. Eric James and Robert Birley had also been approached but neither wished to be considered. The sub-committee of four Fellows was chaired by Lord Simonds as Warden, and included Sir Walter Moberly. They interviewed only Oakeshott. The distinction he had shown at Winchester before the war, coupled with his proven record of drive and vision at St Paul's, made him the outstanding candidate. In recommending him to their colleagues, the sub-committee added the gratuitous rider that, even if James or Birley had applied, they would still have preferred Oakeshott. He was appointed on 23 March 1946.

The headmastership of Winchester was to prove the most demanding job of his life: the most rewarding in some ways, the most stressful in others. On the one hand it gave scope to his strengths, above all his gift for personal inspiration. Not that he was called upon to give the kind of leadership in action which he had shown in the evacuation of St Paul's. It was rather in the things of the spirit, the Platonic trio of truth, beauty and goodness, that his own 'exaltation'[1] raised the aspirations, and enlarged the lives, of those who came under his influence. In this context his great work on the fabric of the chapel – something for which his previous posts had offered no scope – can be seen as an object lesson in aesthetic and spiritual education. On the other hand Winchester probed his weaknesses as never before or after. As Leeson had feared, 'the problems of administration and discipline' came to haunt him. There was no serious opposition to him, but there was running, and wounding, criticism. Essentially what his critics were saying is 'you are not tough enough for this job'. He agreed with them sufficiently to contemplate resignation more than once, and in the end to be thankful for release.

1 The Employee

His salary on appointment was £3,250 a year, together with allowances totalling £1,000 p.a. but no pension. The £4,250 was nothing like as substantial as it appeared, and Leeson before he left made a generous plea to the Fellows on his behalf specifically for some pension provision. He pointed out that since 1866 the remuneration of the headmaster had never been lower than £3,500 p.a. and had sometimes been higher, and that an HMC survey had recently found that 'cases in which no pension was payable were uncommon'. He suspected that Oakeshott's ' private means were limited', and had 'grave doubts whether, living in this house, with mounting costs of domestic service, and having four children of school age or under to educate, he will be able within his salary figure to make arrangements for his old age'. Leeson's plea, made without Oakeshott's knowledge, was not heard.

A scrutiny of the allowances would have revealed further problems. For example the £200 p.a. allowed for a secretary, another figure unchanged since the early years of the century, now permitted only a part-time appointment. This may well have been adequate for Leeson, but it was not enough for Oakeshott, and both he and the school suffered. A further £250 p.a. was allowed for the upkeep of various gardens. This again looked good, since the head gardener was provided with a house free of rent and rates, and the headmaster had the produce. But Oakeshott had to pay the gardeners' wages as well as other costs of maintaining the garden, and his accountant calculated in July 1947 that he was about £250 p.a. out of pocket.

An even greater source of worry and discomfort was the headmaster's house. A vast mid-Victorian barracks of a house, it had fourty-four rooms, a huge central staircase, and no central heating. Their fuel ration was entirely taken up in keeping the chill off the bath-water, nothing being available for stoves to heat the central part of the house. No decoration had been done for ten years, and only £100 p.a. was allowed to make good the backlog.

It was the cold that hurt most. Whereas the Leesons had seemed relatively impervious, the Oakeshotts felt the cold all their lives. Walter, who suffered badly from chilblains, wore mittens about the house all the winter. Noel, always frail and somewhat faddist, normally had her breakfast brought up to her in bed by Walter. Once, when she got up to join the family at breakfast in the pantry, she came down in overcoat, hat and gloves. He too would draw attention to the inconveniences of the house by bicycling down the long corridor from the kitchen to the back door.

A house of that size was designed for resident servants – fourteen of them, to be precise. In Rendall's time, when Oakeshott first remembered the house, there were still elevenr. Noel too was used to servants. She was saved, for their first year, by a cousin, Lady Betty Shirley, who came to live with them. This at least gave her company and support – for Noel was if anything less handy about the house than Walter. Much of her time was always spent in trying to find staff; and when found they were often less than ideal. 'I am very much stumped', she wrote to Walter in January 1947, 'to know what to do about Miss N. She is decidedly common in appearance, with a roving eye, and Aunt Emily thinks we couldn't possibly have her at meals if anyone else were there.' Meals were frugal, partly out of principle: cake on Sundays only, and bread often left to grow stale 'for the good of the soul'. When school visitors had to be entertained, staff wives would rally round, or Walter take them out to a meal in the town.

Many heads of similar schools had to live in similar large houses. But in most of them the running expenses of the establishment (not the cost of food) were borne by the Governors. At Winchester they all fell on the headmaster. This, by the accountant's calculation, made a total of £2,050 paid out in expenses during the year 1946–7. With tax and surtax deducted, Oakeshott was left with a net spendable income of £929. He put it to the Warden and Fellows that, if they were willing to meet his expenses themselves, and to cut his salary correspondingly, his spendable income would rise to £1,636. In 1948 they did agree to take on £1,800 p.a. worth of expenses, and reduce his salary to £2,950, of which £500 was deemed to be an allowance for hospitality. The £1,800 retained the figure of £250 for secretarial help, but included a new allowance of £50 p.a. for the office telephone.

All this raised his total emoluments from £4,250 to £4,750. His position was eased, but his anxiety about money – 'blackest of all cares', he wrote at the time[2] – remained deep. Some of his colleagues believed he was not as poor as he thought he was. But his modest capital was tied up in the Bell House at Merstham, which brought in no income because he lent it to friends for nothing. He ran no car until 1951, when he bought a prewar 'fish-van' for the children to learn to drive on. Above all he had the growing expense of the children's education in the days when there was no inter-school system of fee-reductions for staff children.

The problems of the headmaster's house were never solved in Oakeshott's time. The Warden and Fellows expressed sympathy but proved unable to act on the scale required. First there were postwar building restrictions; then they had no money; and by the time they bit on the bullet in 1953 Oakeshott was already on the point of leaving. Among the reasons he gave for doing so were the discomforts of the house and the absence of a pension.

In all these matters the decisions lay with the Warden and Fellows. The Fellows were a more powerful body than the Mercers, but by tradition they deferred to the Warden, who was often a distinguished public servant. Wardens normally held office for five years, and had the use of extensive lodgings within the school, where the Fellows held their meetings over a weekend twice a term. These arrangements, which were quite different from those at St Paul's, could be a source of strength to a headmaster. But everything depended on the relationship between him and the Warden, and Simonds and Oakeshott were dissimilar to the point of incompatibility. As Lord Chancellor, Simonds expected to get his own way, and cynics said that he had voted for Oakeshott (whom he once described as a 'pinko') because he knew he could bully him.

Another difference from St Paul's – and another key figure – was the bursar. Relations between headmasters and bursars are always precarious, for a good reason. Whereas the former's first instinct is and should be to say ' yes', the latter's is and should be to say 'no'. At Winchester the constitutional position was that the bursar was responsible solely to the governing body, whose servant he was, and not at all to the headmaster. On that point Captain Claude Merriman, RN (Retd) was clear. As far as control of expenditure went, it was fair enough. But it did not stop there. Merriman held most schoolmasters in some contempt as sophisticated incompetents, and the headmaster was no exception.

At the end of the Oakeshott's second term there occurred an event whose repercussions were felt for some years. On 1 April 1947, the last night of term, some boys gathered for a play-reading in the old Moberly Library above the Masters' Common Room opposite the headmaster's house. The boy who turned out the lights saw that an electric fire had set light to the back of an upholstered chair. He put out the fire to his satisfaction and left a note offering to pay for the damage. At 3.45 a.m. Oakeshott was woken up by the crackling of the flames: the whole building was ablaze. In the words of *The Times* report, he 'raised the alarm and then led the fire-fighting work.' His bravery did not go unremarked.

The fire brigade arrived at 4 a.m. and by 6.30 had the flames under control. During that period a crowd of staff and boys gathered. Oakeshott later recalled two remarks from that time. 'One of the staff came up to me and said "It takes a thing like this to make one realise how much this place means to one." Two minutes later I heard a remark by a brilliant young scholar: "Bad show! It's going out."' Both remarks he felt to be valid in their own way. The boy was 'enjoying pure experience, as it is enjoyed in a work of art, when it is divorced from the contaminating factors of reality'.

But the damage was real. The library on the upper floor was gutted and the roof destroyed over a length of some 150 ft., with the Masters' Common Room on the ground floor below it damaged and out of use for months. The first task was salvage. The local Fuel Officer made a special allowance of coke to enable heating to be kept on, and Oakeshott typically busied himself with the drying of the books – in that very building from which he had moved out the contents of the school library on a trolley a quarter of a century before.

The second task was to rehouse the various activities involved. The third was restoration – and it was then that the awful truth emerged, that the building had been under-insured by many thousands of pounds. The consequence was that for most of Oakeshott's term of office money was very tight and his room for manoeuvre correspondingly circumscribed.

Another by-product of the fire throws light on relations between Oakeshott and Merriman. After it, housemasters became anxious about fire precautions in their houses. One go-ahead man, Robin Ridgway, invited an officer of the local brigade to visit his house and give unofficial advice. Merriman rebuked him for taking unauthorized action in a matter which could involve the school in expenditure. When Oakeshott heard of this, he wrote an uncharacteristically strong letter of protest.

What seems to me entirely unreasonable, if I may say so, is that

Ridgway should be treated as if he had been a naughty child, when his action carried with it not the slightest obligation on anyone to spend money. . . . You will honestly make nonsense of our jobs if you claim that, before we even talk over such matters with anyone, you must be consulted.

Merriman was in fact not being quite as dictatorial as that letter makes out, since a recommendation from a local fire officer, however unofficial, is difficult to disregard. But Oakeshott's dander was up. He had another grievance which he aired in the same letter.

The very small matter of the gift of that book to the [Fellows'] Library is another illustration, quite unimportant, of how puzzling one's position sometimes is. Seeing what I realised to be an important Wykehamical item for £20 in a bookseller's catalogue, and a friend [Roger Mynors], who drew my attention to it, having offered £5 towards the cost, I produced the other £15 from my own pocket, as I had a personal interest in the book, it being concerned with one of the early headmasters. Is it really a fact that a presentation of this kind to the Library cannot be made without the authority of the Warden and Fellows? If so, there are a number of things which I presented when librarian [3] which ought not to be there. Surely the idea does not make any sense at all. . . . I must claim the right to make an occasional presentation to the Library without reference to the Warden and Fellows.

In this case it is hard to justify Merriman's actions. Certainly there was no doubt of the book's importance. It is a manuscript copy, by a scholar of the 1590s, of the Greek and Latin fair copies dictated by John Harmar, the headmaster. Oakeshott wrote a delightful article about it in *The Wykehamist* of March 1948. One of Harmar's verses 'was addressed to a parent who was rash enough to ask the headmaster why his son did not learn anything useful: *artes discere vult pecuniosas*'. Another teasingly rebukes the scholars for their untidy appearance; for 'making the night hideous with unmusical noises on musical instruments'; and for visiting 'the local, or *popina* as Harmar, with the suggestion of an execrable pun, calls it'. 'Who will dare say, in view of this,' asked Oakeshott ironically, 'that there has been no progress in 370 years?' Like Harmar, he preferred an oblique approach to matters of discipline.

At the end of every school year the Warden and Fellows expected a report of some 5,000 words from the headmaster. A surprisingly large proportion of it had to be directed to financial affairs. This was because at Winchester the headmaster was responsible for all the school's expenditure on educational activity. Whenever a new 'commoner' fee was set, a proportion of it – at that time forty per cent – was earmarked for Education Fund. Out of the Fund were met not only teaching staff salaries and departmental expenses but such matters as sanatorium, library, tuckshop and a variety of games and sports. For each of these the headmaster had to present an annual report, together with the account for audit. Oakeshott was by now neither unversed nor uninterested in financial affairs, but it was a responsibilty which in other schools was borne by the bursar and his staff.

His first annual report, written in August 1947, starts by noting an 'air of return to normal after the troubles of war' but goes straight on to 'emphasize the financial and administrative problems that lie ahead'. He mentioned the fear, acutely felt then but not realized till decades later, that if the fees were raised, the professional classes might no longer be able to afford them. He sought to preempt possible economies, specifically in music and the crafts but also more generally over staffing. 'Our staff has more "free" time than any other school I know, but masters actually work harder than in any other school I know. . . . I personally should regret more than I can say any attempts to effect big savings on the staffing side.' In this the Warden and Fellows backed him wholeheartedly: he did not need to make the point again.

They did however make one important decision: to increase the intake into the school by some eight boys a year. This meant a gradual growth in total numbers of about forty boys by 1952. Financially it was a wise move, but it led to a need for more accommodation in Chapel, and even in the end for more playing-fields.

For the rest his annual reports tend to cover the same headings each year, and it is easier to treat them topically than annalistically. Two of the topics form a related pair which had also concerned him at St Paul's: the admission of county scholars, and his own junior school.

The years 1940–50 were full of schemes and hopes for 'opening the doors' of the public schools. The Fleming Report of 1944 had recommended that boarding schools should set aside twenty-five per cent of their places in the first instance for suitable applicants from maintained schools, whose fees would be met, subject to a means test, by LEAs or central government. In January 1946 GBA and HMC had accepted the scheme, and Leeson had immediately come to an arrangement with Hampshire to fund up to five scholars a year, with the school offering a fee reduction of twenty-five per cent. For September 1946 only three applicants could be found who were deemed suitable. But hopes were still high. Oakeshott believed that the balance of economic advantage was moving from the middle classes to the wage-earner, and that in the long run the schools would not survive without a major shift in their recruitment.

In 1948 there were no suitable applicants at all. In 1949 the scheme was extended to Hertfordshire, whose Director of Education was a friend of Oakeshott, but by 1951 the number of county scholars in the school could still 'be counted on the fingers of one hand'. By the time Oakeshott came to leave Winchester he realized that, although almost all the county scholars had done very well in the school and at university, there was no real hope of an increase in numbers beyond 'the mere trickle which it still is'. The basic reason is well known. Most LEAs could not justify the spending of three times as much on the few as on the many. As to central government, discussions dragged on until in 1961 the hopes were killed stone dead by David Eccles, a Wykehamist Minister of Education in a Conservative administration. While regretting 'the existence of two systems of education in the country', he 'could see no reason to use public money to subsidize the transfer of boys from one system to another'.

Oakeshott also referred in some of his reports to the social question which underlay Eccles's remarks. 'It may be', he wrote in his first one, 'that we ought now to do more than we used to do, not only to introduce boys to everyday problems but also to make possible some actual contacts outside that of the school, if the plunge into military service is not to be a violent shock to them.' Admittedly it seemed that in general boys took 'to the change [i.e. military service] easily and naturally'. This they did because of the 'natural ease which many of them seem to acquire in their attitudes to other people[4]. ... An index of it is the extraordinary record of Wykehamists in Foreign Service appointments in the last 12 months or so.' This last observation shows a remarkable shift away from his youthful stand on social issues, or even from that of three years earlier.

Had the intake of boys from maintained schools developed as he wished, Oakeshott saw an important role for the Quirister School. William of Wykeham's foundation had included provision for sixteen quiristers to augment the singing in Chapel. For them a boarding education was to be provided free, under the care of the Quirister Master. It was clear to Oakeshott that, with an age span of eight to thirteen, the school was far too small to offer a satisfactory education, whether in work or games. His immediate thought in 1946 was to expand it to about thirty by the admission of county scholars at eleven, exactly as he had planned to do at Colet Court. By the time it had become clear that that hope was vain, another reason supervened for seeking an increase in size. In September 1948 there was some serious misbehaviour among the boys, which Oakeshott believed to stem from the fact that half the boys (eight out of sixteen) were new that term.

He therefore devised a scheme in 1949 to extend the premises as a first step towards enlarging the Quirister School. The only possible source of extra accommodation was a college house separated from it by a public passageway. The plan was to bridge the passageway and move the master who occupied the house, Austin Whitaker, with his family to new accommodation. Whitaker objected, wrote to the Warden, and told Oakeshott that he was supported by other members of the staff. Oakeshott thereupon, with quite uncharacteristic firmness, said that such decisions were for governors and headmasters and, if Whitaker persisted in opposing the scheme, he would have to consider his position on the staff. Whitaker later came to see that Oakeshott was in the right. But the Governors eventually dropped the scheme.

Nevertheless Oakeshott continued to take an especial interest in the Quiristers and to report on them every year. He got junior members of the college staff to help with their teaching and games. This revealed how bright many of them were – not surprisingly, in view of their musical ability. Within the next three years three of them had won scholarships to Winchester and two to other schools. He rightly took pride in this development, though it was not for another twenty years that the problem of small numbers was solved.

2 The Headmaster

A headmaster's really important relations are not with governors but with staff and pupils. Almost all the staff in 1946, including all the housemasters, had been colleagues of Oakeshott in his previous incarnation and warmly welcomed his appointment – though some, who did not know the St Paul's story, shared Leeson's doubts. He was of course aware of the dynamics of the Common Room, and opened his first meeting with the disarming words: 'Everybody knows Winchester is run by a small caucus of housemasters'. This endeared him to the others, but was only partly true. There was no longer, as there had been in Leeson's time, a small group of barons, powerful men who enjoyed twisting a powerful headmaster's tail. But the collective strength of the housemasters was still by tradition enormous.

To start with, the entrance of most boys to the school is in the hands of housemasters. The headmaster has a say in the election of the seventy scholars, who live in College as a separate house; and he has one nomination a year to each of the commoner houses. For the rest, each of the ten housemasters chooses 'his' boys. Each term, in those days, he received from 'his' parents the whole of the school fee. Forty-eight per cent of it he made over to headmaster or bursar; the rest he retained as a 'house fee, for maintenance and supervision by the housemaster'. From then on he had, as he still has, ultimate responsibility for them in every respect. He kept constant check on the progress of their work, and arranged for their entry to university. He cheered on his house teams, and encouraged them in other recreations according to his own scale of values. He fed them in his house with his wife and house matron. If they were ill they came under the care of a doctor he had appointed to the house. Normal discipline was in his hands, only the direst breaches being referred to the headmaster. At the end of each term, when reports were sent to parents, the final judgement was made not by the headmaster but by the housemaster. Lastly, as if to reinforce the image of the castle, the headmaster would by custom not enter the houses except when expressly invited.

All this was a significant change from St Paul's, where there had been no housemasters. Another difference was the absence at Winchester of any regular place and time, apart from the Chapel, for an assembly, i.e. where the headmaster could talk to all staff and boys together about school affairs. His contacts with boys were thus largely confined to teaching contexts and to such other conversations as he could contrive.[5] But this gave plenty of opportunity for him to exert upon many of them his own unique charm and inspiration.

The core of his teaching was now history, but he also rang the changes on English and classics. When he read Plato's *Phaedo* with the classical sixth, one boy wrote in superior tones:

> Although he does not show it
> you cannot fail to know it:
> Walter Fraser
> cannot raise a
> better crib than Jowett.

Another saw the reverse side of the coin: he 'turned the exact meaning into a cooperative discovery' and 'we almost relived as participants the death of Socrates'. For English he might read poems of Herbert or Donne, still after half a lifetime associated with his unhurried speaking voice, or put forward for consideration a draft of the *New English Bible* (p. 187).

In history one of his classes on the Industrial Revolution included drawings by him of Newcomen's steam engine, in meticulous detail, as a result of which an ex-Chairman of HMC 'can *still* explain the valve system'. Another former pupil recalls the time when a lesson on Harvey's discovery of the circulation of the blood had a boy faint in the front row. 'In all this', writes a third, 'I was less aware of being taught than of sharing the thoughts of a well-stocked mind.'

With less mature forms his approach sometimes had to be varied. A would-be 'tough' boy once came into his class riding a hobbyhorse. To his chagrin, Oakeshott was not yet there, so he lent the horse against the wall, put his hat on it, and sat down to wait. When Oakeshott did arrive and saw it, his response was 'I say! A toy horse! How absolutely splendid!' The horse was not seen again. Another lowly form had been asked to draw a map which was then being handed back after correction. Near the bottom of the form sat an unacademic earl, whose map was evidently unsatisfactory. Handing it back to him, Oakeshott said, 'in that marvellous learned drawl, "You are a bad . . . bad . . . Earl."' It was the same out of the classroom. '"You have been a little inadequate" he would say to a sinner, who would go away feeling that he had offended a man whose good opinion he was sorry to lose.'[6] To use Jowett's words, he was one of the 'very few who by some happy tact have contrived so to rebuke another as to make him their friend for life'.

The boys who came closest to him were those who studied his own field of medieval art. They were the 'special historians', the most promising of those who were hoping to read history at university. Harold Walker, the forceful head of the department, encouraged them to be individualists and often had them in his own house. Since Walker was an old friend and ally of Oakeshott, sharing with him a love of art and poetry, such boys often found themselves coming to the headmaster for one-to-one tutorials in the Winchester tradition. One such was Andrew Crawshaw, later himself a history master at Eton. He noted the 'inherent artistry' of Oakeshott's teaching, 'which gave it depth even when the subject matter was fairly elementary'. Another mentions 'his enormous courtesy in tutorials, so that one's crassest remarks were never snubbed'.

To many of these boys, the hours with him were the ones which opened their eyes, awoke their intellects and determined the course of their lives, whether as amateurs of the arts or as professional scholars and museums men. The single unforgettable experience was to be taken by him to see the Winchester Bible: its effect was comparable to that of being shown the sacred objects at the Eleusinian Mysteries. 'I felt tremendously honoured to have him turn those marvellous pages, showing me the different hands at work.' Another was taken up to see it on his final Sunday in the school while Cathedral evensong was in progress ('this is one of my favourite psalms'), and comments: 'No amount of end-of-year business – 500 reports to write, innumerable loose ends to tie up – seemed to weigh in the balance against time spent with a single not particularly important boy, in a wholly other world.'

As honorary Cathedral Librarian since 1947, Oakeshott had the opportunity to pursue his own scholarship as well as showing boys the treasures. But he took his duties seriously. In 1950 it proved necessary to move the books out while the library itself was being restored. One whole holiday Oakeshott undertook to transport them himself, with the help of Crawshaw, then aged 15. The library is on the first floor of the south transept, but the stairs to it are awkward; so, to get the books down, a hoist had been suspended on a pulley from the vault of the transept. Unfortunately the pulley had been set too far to the north, so that the hoist, when raised to the first floor level, was still some feet out of reach from the landing at the top of the library stairs. The two scholars decided to move it across by tying a length of string to one corner and pulling very gently.

But instead of coming to heel, the hoist gyrated, swinging out across the transept, and hit the elaborate tomb of Bishop Wilberforce. A fragment of the marble was heard to fall. Crawshaw clambered up and had to report that they had knocked off a piece of the episcopal forelock.

> I can see to this day the look of delight that crossed Walter's face as he remarked: 'His forelock – *how* appropriate – "Soapy Sam" – I never did like him'. Then with a note of happy complicity: 'I don't think we need tell the Dean and Chapter, do you?' At the time,[Crawshaw concludes,] I expected to be dismissed for incompetence, but instead the Headmaster give me an excellent lunch at the Minster Café. I was, of course, his slave for life.

Others were captivated for a variety of reasons. Two boys hitch-hiked to Oxford in 1948 on a whole holiday to watch the University beat Walter Hadlee's New Zealanders. On the way back they thumbed a lift again – from the headmaster. Oxford was out of bounds, and they feared the worst; but all he wanted was to hear how the match had gone. Another was interested in calligraphy, and Oakeshott made arrangements for him to go up to see Sir Sydney Cockerell's collection of modern handwriting in his house at Kew – and paid for the tickets himself. An Italian boy whose mother had written out of the blue for a headmaster's nomination was walking in Meads with her son, now in his first year, when they met Oakeshott. He pulled out his wallet and showed them the photograph of the boy which she had sent him with her first letter: he had been so intrigued by her unusual approach that he carried it as a memento. A new boy who had to spend most of his first term in the sanatorium with rheumatic fever had a visit there from the headmaster: 'I wondered if you'd like me to come and read to you'; and he came every week for half an hour to read a detective story. When the school racquets pair won the public schools championship in 1950 he gave a little dinner party for them and the staff involved. In the centre of the table was the school crest, picked out in blue and white flowers. He had made it himself – 'not very good, but I wanted to do something special'. A head boy summed it up simply: 'The boys loved him. *Why did we?* It was that smile. He was charismatic with a smile without even trying.'

Similar touches endeared him to members of staff.[7] For some it began immediately. Colin Badcock, appointed in 1949 over the telephone, arrived to meet him for the first time. 'Would you like some tea?', he said, and I thanked him. In that unheated, servantless old barracks of a house the preparation of tea seemed to cause him great problems. After a long pause he reappeared with a pot and cups and apologies. 'We generally have tea', he said, 'in the airing cupboard.' From that moment I was his man.'

Tony Wood, whom he appointed in 1948, was already a friend from St Paul's days. After some weeks in post he had not been paid. Remembering that no salary had been mentioned at his appointment, he 'had a sudden fear that dons might not be paid at all'. So he went to ask Oakeshott. 'We've got a salary scale somewhere,' he said, 'but I never can remember where the beastly thing is.' Eventually he found it in a drawer. 'Yes,' he said, looking at it, 'this was really quite a reasonable scale in 1936.' And he explained that salaries were paid once a term in arrears, unless one went to the bursar to ask for 'an advance'. By some strange logic, the headmaster came out of the incident well, the bursar badly.

Not all applicants for posts were successful. Geoff Hodges, as 'headmaster's assistant', had the task of showing them round the school and reporting back. Having found one man pious and boring, he tried to be tactful. 'Isn't he perhaps rather too good to be true?' 'Yes,' said Oakeshott with a twinkle, 'I fear he is a man of unimpeachable integrity.' Hodges relished the phrase, and revered its author.

Other staff were won in other ways. A convalescent couple were lent the Bell House in the days of rationing, and found a basket of eggs on the kitchen table awaiting their arrival. When the school timetable was changed in 1952 a master got in a muddle and missed a lesson, so went to the headmaster to apologize. 'Oh dear,' said Oakeshott, as if his was the apology, 'I'm afraid I did exactly the same thing yesterday.' A man who asked him a question about 'classical' and 'romantic' art got a letter the next day – five pages of longhand, with the right-hand margin characteristically justified – arguing that those two categories need the addition of a third, 'barbaric'. He kept the letter for decades.

To generosity of time and money he added generosity of judgement, often in disagreement with his more austere colleagues. A boy leaving from the classical sixth had lukewarm reports from most of his teachers, but the headmaster suggested he had been underestimated and would be heard of again. That boy was another who went on to be Chairman of HMC. Of a more junior boy his form-master had written 'I fear he will never be a real flier.' Oakeshott commented 'I am not so sure about that judgment, but perhaps I am too apt to see my geese as swans' – and again he was right. On the same principle he wrote to Badcock: 'I like the respect your reports show for the not-so-talented. There is meat in those eggs.' Badcock comments that 'this showed one of his most engaging characteristics, a warm and real respect for people quite unlike himself. Thicks, games-players, horse-racing enthusiasts and the plain naughty fascinated him as much as the able and aesthetically talented.'

All that was admirable headmastering. When he taught his staff it was not by telling (as Leeson had done) but by showing; and he did it in such a way as to save everybody's feelings. Only one instance is recorded of his 'telling'. To a man just appointed he wrote: 'May I advise you (doubtless you know this "wrinkle" well enough) to take a great deal of trouble with the correction of work? Boys attach great importance to knowing that their written work has been looked through in detail. . . . A good deal can be done even by being careful about one's own [hand]writing on their scripts. My most careful writing is reserved for corrections; and I am sure that is right.' All typical Oakeshott until the last sentence.

Teaching he loved; from 'education' he shrank. To teach is to talk to individuals. To write about 'education' is to swamp them in generalizations, or even, perish the thought, to lose them in statistics. But headmasters have to do it. Every year something like half of Oakeshott's annual report to the Warden and Fellows was devoted to education. As a source for his views on it they are the fullest we have. His treatment of it was of course neither systematic nor exhaustive. The context, as well as his own temperament, precluded that. For a complete picture of his views, one needs to look at two other types of source. One is the papers on educational topics which he was pressed to write for outside bodies while at Winchester. The other is far more important: the sermons he preached twice a term in Chapel. For when it came to the ultimate purposes of education, or at any rate of 'this school', he was, in the Balliol tradition, happy to express them in religious language.

The task which a Christian education can do is not to offer the answers now to the difficulties that you will have to be facing in twenty-five years' time, but rather to ensure that there are good men to face these difficulties. Our task is to show you the difference between truth and distortion; between honesty and propaganda; between inaccuracy and fact.[8] And it is to confront you now with the lives and achievements of men who have done nobly and thought greatly, so that you cannot escape the inspiration of their ideas and their achievements. Our hope is to produce not men who know all the answers before they begin, but men who have the sanity and balance to discover them; men who in dark days are yet not oppressed by darkness but have eyes also for the distant light; men who have the judgment to distinguish between what is possible and what is not; and the vision and inspiration sometimes to go for the impossible and achieve it.

Apart from the reference to propaganda, there is nothing to anchor these words in the twentieth century rather than the nineteenth. The high Victorian tradition of Tennyson's 'Ulysses' and Arnold's *Culture and Anarchy*, mediated through Balliol idealism, is audible in the stress on 'vision and inspiration' and on the example of 'men who have done nobly and thought greatly'. The names of such men recur time and again in his teaching and writing as well as his sermons: Socrates and Christ, St Benedict* and Alfred the Great, Wykeham and Raleigh, Grey and Wavell. What he said about Lord Grey of Fallodon is especially revealing.

The source of his strength was I believe that he was an amateur in politics, or rather that he had a spiritual life of his own which was more important to him than the great offices of state which he filled; a world of contemplative peace which he found especially in that study of nature, particularly of birds, which was the passion of his life. ... I do not know that he was very religious. I *do* know that he had an intense spiritual life and that, if one is trying to understand what the Greek thinker meant when he said that a king should be a philosopher, a man whose life was spent in the contemplation of reality and goodness, Grey came near to personifying that ideal, though he was not in the technical sense a philosopher at all.

I shall never forget the last glimpse I had of him, standing by the door of the Warden's Lodgings; gazing with sightless eyes

*'*The Rule* is to my mind the most important book about education ever to be written.' (WFO, 1962.)

which seemed to be groping for these buildings which were so familiar to him, like some blinded eagle. You could not mistake his greatness even then. And it was not the greatness of one whose decisions had determined the future of Europe; but the greatness of an inner life into which the statesman could withdraw and from which, in the last resort, his statesmanship derived its qualities.

Grey, like most of the others on the list, exemplified the 'mixed life'.

Oakeshott's 'aims of education', as set forth in the pulpit, were typically fleshed out in terms of good men and their lives. His sermons also often revealed more of his feelings than his other writings or speeches, perhaps because in Chapel he always spoke over the heads of the adults to the boys. A sermon might, for example, appeal to a shared classroom experience. He often quoted from Dante, to the effect that 'the job of education is to confront us with what first makes us spellbound with wonder, and then leads us on to curiosity – to find out more about it'. 'I do not despair,' he added once,

> that (in spite – if you like – of all of us who teach you) most of you have had this experience. You have come to feel that the hours in which you heard Mr A passionately denouncing the unscrupulousness of Charles I, and that other hour in which Mr B painted him in vivid terms as a martyr for his people, were both part of the real stuff of education, as indeed they were if they moved you.

The exalted tone of such utterances was appropriate to the pulpit. But he also had every year to report to the Warden and Fellows on his proximate purposes in education, and on the means of achieving them. For this, secular language sufficed – though the optimism was carried over. His thoughts on these matters are assembled here, in a sequence and a system that is not his.

Seen in a historical perspective, his views on education can be characterized as elitist and conservative. Neither of these terms is used pejoratively. He was rightly concerned with the teaching of very able boys by very able masters. Within that field he shared the view of most of the staff, that Winchester had solved most of the problems. That the problems of maintained schools mostly lay outside that field, he knew from personal experience; but within it 'anything that can be done to give some insight into our aims and methods to those who run the local educational system, is important'. Even when allowance is made for the fact that this was written for the Warden and Fellows, there is an unmistakable whiff of the complacency which was the besetting weakness of Winchester at that time. Its only academic rivals were St Paul's and the leading city grammar schools – Eton was not yet in the running academically – and they could not aspire, as day schools, to provide the *breadth*. Winchester 'wolde gladly teche' but not expect to learn.

Breadth indeed ranked second only to excellence as a proximate aim of education. Both concepts were seen in terms of subjects and prizes. All subjects were potentially equal in value: 'I am tempted to think that it does not matter what is taught provided that it is exciting, that in some sense it is true, that in some contexts it is significant, and that at some stage it can be treated critically, not just commended' (1957). Moreover 'a general education depends not simply on doing more subjects, but on the subjects being taught in a general context and with insight'(1947). Nevertheless he assumed it to be desirable for boys to pursue as many subjects as possible for as long as possible. The assumption seems ultimately to have rested upon his own enormously wide range of interests. The only *argument* he ever advanced lacked teeth even then:'we are firmly convinced that the tendency of education is towards the provision of those qualities that our more general training provides' (1948).

He was delighted in 1950 when 'the English Essay prize was won by a scientist, the Science Essay prize was won by a modern linguist, while French Speech was shared between a classicist and a historian'. And he particularly admired 'a competent entry for Latin Speech' from a boy who, though he had won a scholarship to the university in science, had also won the English Literature prize (1953).

These were of course only instances of individual versatility. More substantial evidence he quoted from the external examiner for the Higher School Certificate and (later) for GCE A level, examinations which in those days were not taken by the abler boys at Winchester. The external report on the General Paper in 1951 said that 'All candidates showed freedom in dealing with their matter. There was no uniformity of treatment, and on many questions there were really interesting generalizations. The most outstanding quality was the clear analytical approach to the subject, whether it was modern music or the purpose of suffering.'

The breadth of the school's curriculum at that time was ascribable to a number of distinctive features. Until their last year or so all boys were required to write a substantial weekly essay on a general topic. Progress up the school depended not on age but on performance in non-specialist subjects, chiefly Latin and English. Specialization was started unusually late, and even then every boy on the Modern side had to do both history and French. All specialists were required to enter for a school prize in a subject not their own. External examinations were taken in the stride or not at all, which avoided the cramping effect of prescribed syllabuses: 'Our association with the [examination] system', he wrote in 1949, 'has been a loose one, and it cannot be said to have done much harm.'

With hindsight it is evident that this happy state of affairs could not last. It was certainly not evident then. Far from considering any radical change, Oakeshott extended the weekly timetable by three periods, mainly in order to give more time to general education, especially English and history. Yet he was more aware than most of his colleagues of the defects in the curriculum, both the inherent costs and the contingent flaws, and he did not conceal them from the Governors.

The chief costs were borne by intending scientists. The bright ones started late on their specialization, and were thus at a disadvantage, compared with their contemporaries, which lasted right through to Part I of their university or medical school. Oakeshott was unrepentant about this, arguing that their greater breadth, and in particular their literary skills, would pay off in the long run. The less bright, however, or those too weak on the literary side, never got far enough up the school to start specialization at all.

There were no corresponding costs on the arts side, unless it was that they got up the school too fast and thus escaped from (or were deprived of) science too early: the senior classicists were, he realized, getting an especially narrow education (1952). But this was a contingent flaw, which he would probably have been nerved to remedy if he had been able to get the right kind of science staff.

There was also a second cost in this breadth, which few saw as clearly as he did. It made too many demands on boys of less than first-class ability. The two handicaps for such boys were (i) the heavy emphasis on Latin as a key to promotion in the main school; and (ii) the absence from the specialist menu of certain relatively undemanding subjects which in many schools were the staple diet of the modern sixth: English, Spanish, economics, geography, ancient history etc.

The problem was one he was familiar with from St Paul's, but it presented itself at Winchester in a sharper form. Every year one or two boys who were not progressing up the lower school fast enough were superannuated. The staff were collectively embarrassed by this, and cases were hushed up, like an illegitimate pregnancy in the family. Oakeshott was personally pained, as he was over an expulsion. He followed such boys' careers at the schools to which they went, and reported to the Warden and Fellows. One such boy was now (1950) 'a leading light in his school, both in work and games' and was well up to standard in the sixth form. 'This seems in some ways a striking criticism of our system. ... It looks as though the severe competition which has to be encountered here may blunt the ambition and dull the spirit of some who cannot easily maintain their places.'

Up to a point this situation arises at the bottom of any selective school, whatever its cut-off point at entry. At Winchester it was exacerbated by the competitive system of promotion, coupled with the predominance of Latin, in the lower school. The former was never tackled in Oakeshott's time, the latter only obliquely. In c. 1950 Austin Whitaker, though himself a classics teacher, challenged the position of Latin, and Oakeshott decided to hold what was for him a unique event, an open debate among the staff. The Staff Inspector for Classics was the lead speaker on one side, putting the general case for tradition and urging specifically the contribution made by Latin to the writing of English. Whitaker and some scientists challenged the notion of transference, suggesting that the best way of learning to write English was by English. This view was not self-evidently absurd, but in fact there was no hard evidence either way available at that time. The issue being left to autobiographical anecdote, the traditionalists won handsomely. Oakeshott conducted the meeting with exemplary fairness but was clearly relieved by the outcome. Nothing whatever came of the debate, whose strangest aspect was that the *real* grounds for dethroning Latin were never even mentioned.

The system of promotion in the main school, competitive and therefore irregular, had one other disadvantage. It precluded any serious scheme of work in the form subjects of English, history, divinity and Latin. As a result a boy might study the same topic three terms running with different masters, while altogether missing something vital. Here again Oakeshott hesitated to change. He had recognized in his first report of 1947 that some members of staff were 'critical of what pass[ed] for schemes of work', and noted in particular that 'we have no one who is responsible for the coordination of the English teaching as a whole'. He was nevertheless 'inclined to think that there is much to be lost, as well as possibly something to be gained, by the tying up of all such loose ends, provided always that the quality of the staff is as it should be'.

His advice to a new master, due to take over a form in the main school in 1950, was typical. 'As for the English, you do what you like in that, a very wide latitude being the rule here in most things. . . . The main opportunities in that part of the school for English are the stimulation of excitement about "the things of the spirit"; the development of the ordinary forms and manners of literary expression', together with spelling, punctuation and the 'development of an ordinary legible hand. All this applies to [the rest of] your Division [i.e. form] work as well as to the English.'

In the broadening of specialist studies Oakeshott was more inclined to reform. He had a natural sympathy with a class of boys with whom others were impatient. Masters teaching the modern sixth 'are still' (1947) 'inclined to complain that the first-rate material does not come to them and that their forms are a sort of Valhalla for the heroes and the mighty men of valour. I do not altogether agree with them. There is a mature good sense in that part of the school which compares not altogether unfavourably with the more brilliant precociousness of other' specialist forms.

In fact a part-solution was already presenting itself. The history department, under the able and energetic leadership of Harold Walker, was growing fast. The number of 'special historians' increased from twenty-four in 1945 to fifty-nine in 1949, and by 1950 boys were beginning to combine history not only with modern languages but with classics and science. Taught by a powerful team, which included Oakeshott himself, it offered the opportunity and the stimulus needed by some very able boys whose talents did not lie in mathematics and Latin, the subjects which attracted most marks in the entrance examination.

The demand for English at A level was also growing. Before he left in 1954 he brought on the staff his old friend Tom Gaunt as first head of the English department. Academically the appointment was no more than a holding operation, since Gaunt had no degree in English. Moreover a department was only as strong as the informal influence exerted by its staff. Oakeshott did not hold meetings of heads of departments.

His reports to the Warden and Fellows never mention the teaching of certain subjects: classics and divinity, which he taught; mathematics* and modern languages, which he did not and could not. Science however was a different matter. Although he had no schooling in science itself, he was fascinated by the history of science, on which he gave a course to the local WEA in 1948. He was particularly concerned about 'science for non-scientists'.[9] On this he wrote an intriguing passage in his last report. He was sure of 'the vital need for some understanding of the principles of science and technology' among boys specializing in arts subjects. 'The traditional general science course in the school for the non-scientist is exceptionally good. But it remains surprisingly difficult to interest the non-specialist in science subjects.' Within a few years people were questioning how a course could possibly be good if it did *not* generate interest. Hence the great movement of the 1960s for curriculum reform, with Nuffield Science as one of its flagships. But in the 1950s that question was not asked, and the syllabuses lay undisturbed in their graves.

There remain from the school curriculum the expressive arts. Not surprisingly – since they meant so much to him – they are often mentioned in his reports to the Warden and Fellows. First in importance, to him and to the school, was music. 'I wonder whether there is any other part of the school programme that has so permanent an effect.' The facilities were good, though naturally expensive. He himself sang regularly in the school choral society, enjoyed all school concerts, and attended the inevitable inter-house competitions. In the latter he 'noticed year after year a certain lack of zest, a fear of making mistakes, which means that the performance often fails to have the tremendous vigour and enthusiasm one sometimes encounters elsewhere'. This 'does illustrate the limitations of our tradition here as well as its qualities'. He was right: the pursuit of excellence can be inhibiting.

Of the visual arts he noted in 1952 that 'a boy has opportunities here for the appreciation of beautiful things which are hardly rivalled

* But he wrote c. 1950 that 'I resent now greatly not having learnt more mathematics'.

anywhere else', but 'it has long seemed to me that the facilities we offer for the practice of "Art" are negligible, compared with what they should be.' To his sadness he was unable to bring about any improvement. Money was tight, the school's traditions were not encouraging, and the new appointment he made proved ineffective. He had brought with him from St Paul's an art master who had done well there but could not prosper in his new surroundings without the support which Oakeshott – who was no practising artist himself – could not offer.

Among the crafts however one was very strong: woodwork. 'One of the finest school workshops in the country, it is regularly used by a third of the boys in the school, with most valuable results.' It was a personal blow to Oakeshott when James Laverty, who ran it, died in 1948, 'a man who had the integrity of character which often goes with fine craftsmanship'. That tradition he was able to preserve. For other crafts, such as pottery, modelling and screen-printing, he never managed to make a proper provision, and he much regretted it.

Drama too was much handicapped at Winchester by the absence of a hall big enough for a school play. This was doubtless one reason why he never tried his *Oresteia* there, through Leeson had wanted him to do so in 1936. But the house play had its compensation in 'giving the less gifted boy a chance'. It could also provide benefits to those outside the house. A production of *The Comedy of Errors* 'was a reinterpretation of the early phase of Shakespearian comedy to the school which I have no doubt set it in an entirely new light for them'. That in a school with no English department! Even there however money was short: 'It does not seem right that masters producing plays, or the housemasters concerned, should have to finance them entirely out of their own pockets.'

Why did Oakeshott not achieve more at Winchester in the field of the expressive arts? Part of the reason was financial. The effects of the war and of the 1947 fire were still felt, and there was a permanent fear of raising the fees too high or too often. The days of conspicuous expenditure on school facilities were still far off. Yet it is surprising that neither Oakeshott nor anyone else considered incorporating the arts into the school curriculum, if only on the basis of 'taster' courses for junior boys. Time and money would have had to be diverted from the traditional academic subjects; but other schools were doing it, and one wonders if Winchester even knew.

Of Chapel services he wrote in his last report that 'being largely compulsory, they play for better or worse a very big part indeed in the education of the ordinary boy. On the musical side alone they can not only introduce him to good music but also give him a chance as nothing else will do to take some part in its performance.' Moreover the musicians responsible 'regard the services not simply as performances but as religious acts' and consequently 'there is a sense of reality and, I think, of importance about them which is of great value.' In this his own sermons played a crucial part.

In the sphere of games he recorded dutifully the school's successes. He did not pretend to any great love of them himself except for cricket and to some extent rowing. He also had an antiquarian *tendresse* for Winchester football. When an attempt was made to codify the traditional rules, he observed that 'it is in some ways stimulating if no one knows them'. His afternoon walk took him past field-games, where he lingered just long enough to see if there was anyone interesting to talk to about other matters. A delighted boy once heard him on a football touchline absorbed in discussing with Noel and Helena whether the autumn leaves were properly described as 'russet'. In 1951, when there was pressure for an increase in playing-fields to meet the increased number of boys, he set up a staff committee to consider the question. Its eventual report he commended to the Warden and Fellows, while underlining the need to ensure that nothing was done to endanger the existence of Winchester football.

Of the Cadet Force he never wrote. But here again he did his duty by visiting generals etc. A noted egyptologist [10]remembers how once on a visit to the school museum he had heard a band playing and looked out of the window. There below him was a figure he had last seen in a classroom at Merchant Taylors': Oakeshott in his baggy civvies walking round with a 'much-decorated Inspecting Officer. He kept putting on his trilby hat, and then taking it off and fumbling it awkwardly. He looked out of his element.' His brave face was required even more on the frequent occasions when Montgomery, who had a son in the school, invited himself down to attend Chapel and presented signed photographs of himself to the school prefects.

It was quite another matter when in May 1950 Wavell died. With Temple, he was one of the two men Oakeshott most admired in his life. He had naturally not seen much of Wavell during the war, but at the end of it he gave an informal dinner party at the Athenaeum, 'for 15 or 20 of his admiring friends'. Then when he got back to Winchester in 1946 he had the idea of asking Wavell to present to his old school a map[11] showing what he regarded as his 'most important contribution' to the war. Wavell chose to give the map which he had carried round with him during the Battle of Sidi Barrani in December 1940, the first victory to be won by any Allied army since the war began.[12] But Wavell was so much more than a soldier. In a way he too lived the 'mixed life'. His wide reading even enabled him, on a visit to Winchester c. 1949, to make the crucial contribution to one of Oakeshott's scholarly discoveries (p. 203).

When Wavell died the family asked, and the Warden and Fellows agreed, that he should be buried in the cloister garth. Oakeshott took endless trouble over all the details of the ceremony, including especially the wording of the inscriptions. It was quickly agreed that the gravestone should bear the single word WAVELL, but the commemorative tablet on the wall needed prolonged discussion with Lady Wavell and Archie John. The two men were again in favour of the utmost brevity, but in the end they bowed to his widow. The planning of the committal, with the cortège and the buglers of the Black Watch, was so demanding that the headmaster quite forgot to inform the bursar. The first that poor Merriman knew of it was when the college works foreman rushed in to tell him that one of the grave-diggers had put his pick through a hot-water pipe.

The staff were given better warning. Oakeshott posted a notice in the common room two days in advance saying that he would speak to the school in Chamber Court after morning Chapel to 'explain the arrangements for the afternoon'. As a result of that wording only Hodges heard the moving panegyric of which this is an extract.

> The other day I was looking with one of his family at photographs of him. We came across one that had, alone of them all, captured that assured serenity which those who knew him well, were aware of, rather than saw, in him. 'That', I was told, 'is the Singapore photograph.' It was taken at a time when more than any other he must have felt that the foundations of the sky were falling. His own achievements seemed like to be involved with everything else in a general ruin. I can imagine what it meant to his officers to be working with a man whose serenity was expressed in the very lines of his face. . . .
>
> On the service paper for tomorrow are printed the words: 'Glory is the least of things that follow this man home'.* His

* The words conclude Kipling's poem 'Lord Roberts', written in 1914.

splendid integrity; his imaginative power; his loyalty and devotion to those with whom he served; the deep affection they had for him are not qualities that always bring glory. Nor are they qualities that make life easy. In the play *Samson Agonistes* Milton talks of the grave where Samson is buried, as a place to which young men will come,

> And from his memory inflame their breasts
> To matchless valour and adventure high.

In Lord Wavell's career, if anywhere in history, you will find that high adventure; from his achievements, from his writings, and from his death, you might draw an inspiration, which, for a Wykehamist, must be greater than for any other.

Oakeshott's own serenity and self-confidence had been as sorely tried as a headmaster's can be in the previous year. The cause was criticism from some housemasters and others who thought him lax over discipline. When he got to Winchester in 1946 he had 'acted in the belief that some relaxation was desirable. . . . Patches of indiscipline are certainly due sometimes not to lack of restrictions but to restrictions which are too severe'. His first Senior Commoner Prefect, who had been one of Leeson's prefects, thought him correct in that belief. There was general welcome, for example, for his relaxation in 1948 of the rules governing dress and activities on Sundays: from now on boys were allowed both to change into games clothes and to ride bicycles between morning and evening Chapel.

But in the year 1948–9 there began to be anxiety, particularly among housemasters, about the way things were going. As a result he decided not merely to explain the situation very fully in his report to the Warden and Fellows at the end of that school year but, exceptionally, to circulate that section of his report in draft to housemasters for comment, in case they felt he had misrepresented the facts. Since the final text contains only one small amendment from the draft, it may be taken as something close to an agreed version.

He began by rehearsing instances of actual indiscipline. Only three had been brought to his attention during the year. In each case he had followed the housemaster's advice about the appropriate punishment, which fell well short of expulsion. So far so good, it might seem – though what housemasters often want is for boys in *other* houses to be punished more severely. After describing the three, he added a fourth 'symptom that perhaps too much freedom has been given'. That was a report written by a boy in *The Wykehamist* of a lecture given to a society in the town. The report was, in Oakeshott's view, 'in thoroughly bad taste'. Nevertheless 'we have to bear in mind that responsibility is only learned by making mistakes and that one of the great values of the boarding school community is insulation, so that boys can make mistakes in it without their having serious implications outside the school.'

The housemasters had a second ground for concern in the termly meetings he held with school prefects 'for discussion of any matters which they may raise'. The practice, inherited from Leeson, was 'not to take decisions at such meetings' without further consultation with housemasters. At the meeting in summer 1949 he had discussed with prefects the draft of the school rules which had already been circulated to, and commented on by, housemasters. No material changes were made as a result of this discussion, but some housemasters were disturbed at his having discussed with prefects the matter of dress, and were worried too by the quotation of an *obiter dictum* of his that 'personally I would regret any attempt to draft rules to cover every possible offence'. All this was in the circulated draft of his annual report.

The only housemaster whose comments on it survive is Oakeshott's friend Walker. He wrote a long letter back which ends: 'One does care passionately about this place & its standards; and that you shd feel you have us all behind you & with you, and we that we have yr confidence & understanding, as you have our affection and loyalty and trust.' But Walker did take up some points. The three cases of indiscipline mentioned in the draft are not the only ones: he himself is more concerned about 'the case of drunkenness at the [? school] dance and boys acting as bar-tenders' and about 'night-walking by school prefects' – these being presumably cases which had *not* been brought to Oakeshott's attention. As to the *Wykehamist* article, 'there is something fishy about wanting to multiply mistakes as a means of education – it suggests Paul's Corinthians "let us continue in sin that grace may abound".' And he does feel there is some danger of housemasters being by-passed by school prefects 'in matters of importance'.

In the course of this letter Walker also reveals that fourteen members of staff (it is not clear whether they include housemasters) had 'confided their anxieties about discipline' to 'Budge' Firth, an ex-housemaster and chaplain, now a deeply conservative elder states-man. 'The extent of the anxiety is therefore widespread.'

Oakeshott's reply lays bare his own self-doubt. He had drafted this report

> not in any way to score off housemasters, but simply to give warning to the Warden and Fellows, in as unsensational a way as I can, that the situation might arise where I would have to go. This is the last thing that I want to do. But it is quite clear that if a real and important difference, on a matter of principle, should arise with housemasters, I would *have* to go. I'm under no illusions about that. It is simply a matter of fact.

He goes on belabouring himself.

> What Budge told me about my having very largely lost the confidence of the staff I know, alas, to be true. I still hope that it *may* not be an irrecoverable loss. . . . I'm not the sort of person Budge would like me to be, and will not ever be that sort of person. Other people are looking for something rather different – but of course I am fully aware that they are not finding it.
>
> As you may imagine, I thought hard, and got little satisfaction from it, during the holidays. I'm back on an even keel now. That does not mean, however, that I've seen my way through all the difficulties; only that I've *got* to get back on an even keel to do the job *at all*. Whether I can do it properly in the long run is a matter about which I have grave doubts. But it's no good doubting one's *day-to-day* capacity. That would just lead to immediate paralysis.

Walker replied on 8 September. 'This letter has got to go by return; the things you reveal as in yr mind absolutely shattered me; they must be got out of it at all costs.' He then makes two points.

> The first is the most difficult to get across; it's so obvious to everyone else; & yet it's clear you're absolutely unaware of it. It is how much you are loved and valued, by the whole school & staff, not only as a man but as a headmaster. People find this sort of thing embarrassing to say & they know it would embarrass you to hear it; & so when they talk to you you get all their anxieties and criticism, & this is the one thing that is left out. But it is *never* left out when they're talking about you; I think

you'd be amazed if you knew how much it entered into the discussions on the discipline question, where the anxieties were real enough, and not least with those who felt the anxieties most. Budge clearly left it out altogether and would be horrified at the impression left on yr mind. I would like to show you in confidence the letter he wrote me.

The second is that I can't for the life of me see any difference of principle, nor any reasonable chance of one arising. [What is needed is] to foresee practical difficulties & get the decisions none the less circulated in good time. All this is minor administrative stuff. I can see you smiling and saying 'All very well! But with no school office or proper secretary,* it all comes on me!' Even so, it only affects method, not principle. If you will only accept, as an act of faith, how much we are all with you & behind you.

Firth's letter of 20 August, which Walker included, has this passage.

I entirely agree with what you say about the need for supporting Walter, & about his high and precious quality. . . . My own little 'say' has been said, & now I hope not to say anything more for a long time. . . . He deserves, & perhaps *needs* the knowledge that he is believed in & loyally supported amid his many difficulties. And he is, as you say, physically not robust. . . . I feel a bit anxious about the tax on his strength of his place on the BBC Commission (p. 190f).

This correspondence was preserved by Walker in a file[13] entitled 'How we saved Walter' – from himself? It is remarkable in many ways. First perhaps is the readiness with which grown men would talk of loving Walter, something attested from all periods of his life. Second is the disproportion between cause and effect, on the part both of housemasters and headmaster. The 'insulation of the boarding school community' carries with it always this danger of getting things out of proportion. In the perspective of later times, from the 1960s onwards, the whole thing was a storm in a teacup. The disciplinary problems were minor and the threat to the authority of

---

* In Badcock's words, 'It was not so much that he was "not strong in the office" as that there really wasn't an office to be strong in.'

housemasters minimal; and it would be a most unusual headmaster who considered that in a difference, even of principle, between himself and some housemasters, it should be he that had to go.

But Oakeshott *was* a most unusual headmaster, both in his strengths and in his weaknesses. He was too near the 'tender' end of the 'tough/tender' continuum, too ready always to blame himself. And from time to time the black dog of self-doubt got the better of him. He had had a bout of it in 1944; but this of 1949 was more severe, if not quite as severe as in 1927–8. Whether on this third occasion also he sought medical help to get back on his 'even keel' is not known.

The chief criticism of him by housemasters was always of indecision.[14] As a result, many of them took to making their own decisions rather than referring to him. Subsidiary complaints were of his failure to consult and communicate. 'To a young don,' said Badcock, 'it was pure joy to serve a man who seemed not so much to be running a school with rules and roll-calls, but to be beckoning us all to the gentle slopes of Parnassus because he himself found it warm and sunny up there.' But to the housemasters it was irritating to find that he 'was thinking of higher things, and forgetting the time of lock-up, or arranging lectures that interfered with House Tea'. No wonder that Anne Ridgway described him as 'not really a housemasters' headmaster'. No wonder, too, that he in turn 'dreaded housemasters' meetings'.[15]

The question whether he and they were divided in principle is more complex. Certainly his values were the same as theirs. But they knew he was a free spirit.[16] And if he were ever to stand on a principle, it would not be a general one, even a school rule, but a specific question of how to treat an individual boy. After he had left Winchester, people remembered his 'unpredictable charm'.[17] To some, especially housemasters, the charm did not compensate for the unpredictability.

One specific issue which rumbled on after 1949 was that of censorship. It arose not just from *The Wykehamist* but from an annual publication timed to coincide with the cricket match against Eton at the end of June. Known each year by a different title, e.g. *Silly Point* but collectively as 'the Eton match ephemeral', it was the literary equivalent of an end-of-term rag concert. Its material was largely in-house jokes, especially about the staff. Some keen and sacrificial master accepted the appointment of censor, and had to gauge the varying sensibilities of his colleagues. Men who felt slighted blamed not the censor but the headmaster, who in 1951 found it necessary to justify his policy. With *The Debater* behind him, he felt sure of his ground. Having written to one complainant, he posted a copy of his letter in the common room.

The letter deals first with the issue of principle.

> In agreeing to the publication of an 'Ephemeral', I had in mind that members of the school probably said much the same sort of thing about their pastors, and masters, as we once said about ours; and that good, rather than harm, was probably done by the giving of occasional licence for the publishing of such things. Wit, and even wit with some personal venom, is to my way of thinking, one of the marks of a healthy society. But when what should be witty becomes simply cheap or malicious, or when (as I think has happened here) distress is caused by some of what is published, then that is a wholly different matter.

Next, since 'it was known that I favoured the allowing of freedom', he exculpates the censor. 'His job was done with care and without prejudice, and by virtue of this it will commend itself to some reasonable people, even though it clearly does not commend itself to all.' The letter ends:

> It may be true that mistakes have been made. It would be serious if they implied any general lack of responsibility in the attitude of the school to the staff. I leave it to you and to those who think with you, to make far stronger representations to me than you have made now, if you have any reason to suspect this.

Those who knew Oakeshott recognized that on this matter he was not likely to be shifted.

He himself was not immune from the treatment. He was teased for his use of a crib. In a list of popular songs entitled 'Dons' Discs', his was 'Beautiful Dreamer'. A clerihew of 1956 was relished as much by him as by others: 'If the headmaster / spoke a little faster, / no longer would his style / be so supremely worth while.' His sermon style was parodied, particularly his apologetic references to his own reading and other doings:

> Some of you – I daresay not very many of you – may have read in the *Analects of Confucius* that the only sure foundation of

knowledge and wisdom is the practice of honesty & the search
for truth. I remember once I happened to be in Bucharest – it
was before the war when you will remember Bucharest was a
hot-bed of suspicion and intrigue – and I was sitting in a café
there and noticed a young man talking to a friend of mine who
also happened to be there. . . .

Such things were without malice, and could be not only tolerated
but enjoyed. With boys he was secure in his relations. He also had a
personal penchant for parody. Speaking at a Skinners' Company dinner he welcomed a new headmaster of Tonbridge with an apt quotation: 'Oh Hassan, thou hast left the garden of contemplation and
entered the palace of action, and the winds of complication are blowing through thy shirt.' But a conscientious search through *Hassan*
revealed no such speech.

3 The Historic Buildings

At Winchester there was one other field in which his talents had full
scope and he could therefore make an irreplaceable contribution.
That was the fabric of the medieval buildings, especially the Chapel.
In this field he found a fulfilment which delighted his friends on the
staff – and even his critics among the housemasters were glad to see
him harmlessly occupied.

To the Warden and Fellows, many of them scholars and antiquaries, he was in this vein irresistible. He had the knowledge – or at
any rate, as he once said to a boy, 'I may not know much, but I do
know where to find it'. He had the taste and, when interested, the
attention to detail. His spell disarmed pernickety critics and turned
owners into donors. His leadership, in a word, was as inspiring as
it had been over the *British Independent* and over the evacuation
of St Paul's. Even the Bursar could be swept along. He reasonably
asked to be kept informed and not to be left with increased maintenance charges. At a deeper level, however, he gave Oakeshott 'great
trouble from time to time', objecting to 'the place being turned into a
museum'.

In all this Oakeshott had one indispensable colleague. Dr John
Harvey, FSA,[18] a distinguished scholar of medieval architecture, had
in 1947 been appointed consultant architect for the historic, i.e.
pre-nineteenth-century college buildings. Constitutionally he was

responsible to the Warden and Fellows through the Bursar. Harvey's respect for protocol – and indeed for Merriman as a person – left him sometimes caught between two fires. For he quickly found that his initial impression of Oakeshott – 'a friendly light-weight, unassuming and even diffident' – was very wide of the mark. 'Behind this quietist facade he was later to reveal a multiple personality of amazing vigour. ... He had his head full of ideas like a dandelion's full of seeds.' Oakeshott was also impetuous, and impatient of what he regarded as red tape. Nevertheless the two scholars had enough in common to work together closely for six or seven years. The pace was often frenetic – on one day they exchanged four typed letters in sequence – but according to Harvey it had to be frenetic to get anything done. Not only did the school have no money: even when you had raised it from outside, you still had to prepare plans and estimates so as to apply for a building licence. All the more remarkable was their joint achievement in those few years.

Their first and perhaps greatest triumph was the rescue, restoration and reinstatement in Chapel of part of Wykeham's original Jesse window. Painted by Thomas of Oxford, and installed in the last decade of the fourteenth century, the glass had become so badly corroded and discoloured over the centuries that in 1821 the Warden and Fellows sent it for cleaning to Messrs Betton and Evans at Shrewsbury. Finding it impossible to clean, the firm made a copy of the original and sent that back instead. The copy, generally regarded as excellent for its period, has stood as the east window of Chapel ever since.

The original glass was dispersed by Betton and Evans, but efforts from 1913 onwards had succeeded in tracing about a third of it in many different places. Two people in particular had been involved in the quest: M. J. Rendall, headmaster 1911–24 and art-lover; and Herbert Chitty, Bursar 1907–27, Keeper of the Archives 1927–49 and antiquary. In 1913 Chitty had discovered substantial sections of it, including the important figure of the Founder kneeling before the Virgin, in a private mortuary chapel at Ettington Park in Warwickshire, the family seat of the Shirleys. To his intense disappointment, the family was unwilling to sell.

In 1948, however, the Shirleys decided to move from Ettington to Ireland. When Oakeshott heard of it he set to work. He got in touch with the owner through the head of the family, Earl Ferrers, who was himself a Wykehamist and had married a cousin of Noel; and the owner was prepared to sell the glass at a market valuation. So Oakeshott, Harvey and Mansel went up to Ettington, to the now deserted chapel.

It was ivy-covered, and the ivy was clinging to windows as well as walls, but we could at once see that the glass was medieval. Inside there was a strangely desolate air; prayer-books and hymn-books which since the last family funeral had scattered themselves open over the floor; chairs and pews in disarray and disrepair; but the windows authentic fourteenth century, from the Founder's east window; the drawing of the faces alone clear (for the white glass was much less corroded than the rest) and showing that marvellous delicacy which ranks it with the finest English medieval stained glass. Harvey took out his penknife and began to scrape at the corroded surface. It seemed as if something might be done to recover the colours. But having once seen the delicacy of the drawing, we were determined that somehow this must all come back home.[19]

These developments Oakeshott reported to the Warden and Fellows in March 1949 with a recommendation that, if the glass were ever recovered, it should be placed not back in the east window but 'in some window much nearer eye level where [its] quality could be seen'. He and Harvey had perambulated the whole of the college, not just the chapel, and found only one place that fitted the size. That was Thurbern's Chantry at the west end of Chapel, where there was some inferior Victorian glass at ground level. At the meeting Warden Simonds gave a strong lead and the Fellows agreed to press ahead.

The next problem was to raise the purchase price, which was agreed after valuation at £4,500. For this, Oakeshott had the brainwave of approaching Sir Kenneth Clark* as the only man with both the interest and the capital, and asking him to give it in honour of Monty Rendall, his former headmaster. Clark wrote in his autobiography that he had 'never written a cheque with greater emotion'. In his own schooldays he had not hit it off with a philistine housemaster 'who used to send for me to say only two words: "Go hard, go

*Oakeshott's attitude to Clark was always somewhat ambivalent. In 1938, when Clark got his KCB, he chuckled over a quatrain Charles Mitchell sent him: 'Rejoice all ye immortals/ that to him that hath/ has been superadded/ the Order of the Bath.' And in 1966 he wrote to Noel that he had had some people to lunch including 'the REMARKABLE CLARK'. But the two men got on well enough together.

hard' "; but Rendall had given the young Clark the same encouragement as Oakeshott was giving to his boys some thirty years later.

Chitty's researches had traced another panel of Wykeham's glass
via Parham House[20] to the Victoria and Albert Museum: might
the Trustees of the V and A be willing to let the school have it
on permanent loan? Oakeshott's initial inquiry suggested that the
answer would be no. This he reported officially to the Warden and
Fellows at their meeting in September 1948. Personally however he
never lost hope, partly because the Director of the time was a
Wykehamist.[21] At the same meeting he made suggestions, agreed
with Harvey, about the placing of the Ettington glass, together with
some other fragments already in the school's possession. If the
Victorian glass in Thurbern's Chantry were removed, and certain
structural changes made, the recovered glass could all be accommodated. He now proposed that Harvey be asked to do the detailed
measurements and prepare the plans for placing it there.

All that was accepted, together with a proposal for an expert to
restore the original glass. This was Dennis King of Norwich, to
whom, with Harvey, Oakeshott always gave credit for the ultimate
success of the work. When the glass was laid out in King's workshop
at Norwich, and Harvey came to do his measurements, a problem
soon presented itself. The plan was to remodel the stone tracery so as
to give a central position to the Virgin and Child, 'a figure of masterly
quality (plate oo) and to arrange the other figures symmetrically
round it, thus reproducing as far as possible the original plan of
the Jesse window. But they only had seven other full figures, and
desperately needed an eighth.

Oakeshott therefore in May 1949 made a last appeal to Lord Har-
lech as Chairman of the V and A's Advisory Council. His letter began
cleverly: 'Sir Kenneth Clark was down here at the weekend discussing
our suggestions for the glass which he is presenting, and they have
now met his approval. I am going to throw myself on your mercy and
ask whether, in view of their character, you would consider letting us
have your fragment of the Jesse window.' Having explained the plan,
he added the punchline: 'your figure, by the mercy of providence,
exactly completes the scheme.' More than that, providence had so
arranged things that, while the V and A figure had been stripped of its
surrounding vine-work in the nineteenth century, 'we have a considerable number of fragments of surround, which would be used to
give your figure the right setting in the Jesse window'. The V and A

agreed to let the school have the figure on permanent loan, provided that it could be detached and returned to them for special exhibitions, and 'that the school would renounce any claim upon the three major lights from the Chapel *side* windows, which form an important museum exhibit'.

The cleaning of the glass, as Oakeshott wrote in an article of 1957,

> was a technical problem of great difficulty, and I doubt whether a more wonderful job has ever been done on the restoration of a medieval window. Harvey and I made several journeys to Norwich for consultation in King's workshop, with the glass spread out over glazed tables lit from below so that it could be handled when being discussed.

An analysis by the department of glass technology at Sheffield University revealed the cause of the trouble to be impurities in the glass 'which had oxidized in the course of centuries, so that the glass was pitted and pockmarked all over'. Some of the corrosion was 'so severe that no trace of design or colour could be seen through it'. But

> fortunately medieval glass is very thick, [so] tools were devised based on those used by lens makers, and inch by inch the corroded surface was ground away and repolished. . . . As the sepia paint with which the details are drawn is always on the inside, and the corrosion on the outside, such a process does not involve any interference with the drawing. . . . In the process some depth was lost, [and therefore some of] the richness of the blue, the green and the murrey. . . . But the glass forms once more a translucent window, and one indeed which ranks among the finest works of its period.

Throughout 1950 the glass remained in Norwich, and Oakeshott paid frequent visits to see it being cleaned and replanned. Two other events occurred to affect it. One of them gave him special pleasure. Christopher Lawson, a young archaeologist in College, who had been following the work, discovered further fragments of the Winchester glass still in St Giles's Church in Shrewsbury, where he lived. These were bought; and helped, as every little did.

There also arose in 1950 a problem which caused Oakeshott to formulate the principles guiding him in all this work of restoration. The Ettington glass lacked the head of the small but important figure of the Founder, kneeling to adore the Virgin, to whom he was dedicating his College. The question was, should this figure be completed by a modern artist? The purists said no: it would be a gross intrusion. But if the figure of the Founder were removed, the new window would have to be redesigned in a way which lost the original shape. For Oakeshott that would have meant abandoning 'the consideration which has been of paramount importance in my mind, the need for the window to be a really beautiful thing for the non-expert as well as a matter of interest for the archaeologist'. In the end a clever compromise was reached. A modern artist was used, but his head of Wykeham is simply a reversed copy of another bishop's head elsewhere in the window.

In fact there was a second guiding principle in Oakeshott's thinking, one which Harvey was aware of but not many others. That was his respect for William of Wykeham and his plans for his foundation. For Wykeham was founding more of a seminary than a school: the educational function only rose to priority at the Reformation. And to Wykeham's medieval mind the purpose of the beauty was, in the phrase of Abbot Suger often quoted by Oakeshott as by his predecessors, to elevate the earthbound mind of man to the heavenly truth.

There was another tangible link with Wykeham in the sole survivor of his original ring of bells. Having been cracked in 1945, it was taken down at Oakeshott's suggestion in 1949 with a view to being placed in Thurbern's Chantry 'as a relic'. In August 1951 he wrote to Harvey from the Continent with a typical idea for using it. He had just seen in Bourges six old bells, inverted and partly filled, being used as holy water stoups. Could not Wykeham's bell be similarly inverted, placed on a tripod and used as a stand for flowers and/or a font, ' for which purpose there would be a shallow bronze bowl that fitted inside the rim of the bell'. The letter includes a rare drawing of his, showing the bell resting upside down on a tripod, which should be 'of a dark bronze, to get a contrast with the green patina of the bell'. Nothing came of this idea.

Two months earlier the restored glass had been inserted. At the same time a commemorative inscription was being prepared for the wall facing it.[22] Oakeshott's wording, brilliantly translated by J. B. Poynton, succeeds in linking Wykeham with both the glass and the bell, and ends with an address to the visitor: SIC IGITUR DISCEDE UT HODIE NEQUE SURDUM NEQUE CAECUM TE PRAEBEAS; 'show, on leaving, that you have been neither deaf nor blind'. The brilliance of the Latin lies in the word DISCEDE. On the one hand it echoes the literary convention of the Greek epigram, e.g. 'Go tell the Spartans, passer by . . .' On the other it picks up an inscription in School addressed to the boys: AUT DISCE AUT DISCEDE: 'either learn or leave'. For Oakeshott, the beauties of Chapel, those seen and those heard, were central to the education of the boys. By the time they left the school, their eyes and ears must be alert, responsive and discriminating.

The words thus encapsulated Oakeshott's philosophy of education. That Christmas (1951) he expounded what one might call its theology in one of his most moving sermons. Ostensibly on the Gifts of the Magi, it used the parable of the talents (a favourite of headmasters) but looked back to Plato and forward to Abbot Suger. There is room here only for two extracts.

The statue, even if it is by Michelangelo himself, the painting, even if it is a Leonardo, is not beauty's self, but a sort of ghost of the real beauty. In time the stone is broken; the colours fade; the canvas or the wood perishes. I have sometimes stood in front of that painting in the Chapel of the Holy Sepulchre in Cathedral – a painting of the deposition, the taking of Christ's body down from the Cross; and below, the entombment. In a sense, this painting is nothing more than a battered ruin. If the artist who made it about the year 1200 could see it as it is, he would clear the plaster away to the rubbish heap and start again. Yet, in another sense, like any great work of art, it has something strangely permanent and enduring about it, a loveliness that time finds it hard to destroy, because it belongs to a timeless world. There is a quality of line in the drooping of the dead body wonderful enough for one's heart to miss a beat still, as one sees it: even though the surface is wrecked and much of the design hardly discernible. . . .

I dare guess that some of you may have waited, as I did in Cathedral after the *Messiah*, when the lights went out: anyone who waited till that vast congregation was gone, and saw the nave as William Wynford its designer planned it – it was lit by a few candles whose light was lost far above in the shadows of the vault; their light showed simply the massive strength of those lofty columns towering upwards and none of the trivial irrelevancies that generally distract one's eyes – anyone seeing

that would have known what Abbot Suger meant when in his lumbering hexameters he claimed that
   Mens hebes ad verum per materialia surgit,
that through such material things, through these works of men's hands, the mind can be lifted towards truth. And the first justification of our gifts is this. Is it we alone who benefit or is it God? On one of the bells up in the bell-chamber, a bell cast in 1574, are four Latin words, so simple that they would be a gift in a Lower School unseen:
   Caelestes audite sonos mortales.
Yet what *do* they mean? Do they mean, 'Ye heavenly ones, listen to these earthly sounds'? Or do they mean, 'Ye mortal men, listen to these heavenly sounds'? They could mean either. They *do* mean both. Herein lies the paradox of our offerings to God.

By mid-1951 the first fruits of Oakeshott's collaboration with Harvey were in the process of being reaped. Thurbern's Chantry had been restored, and Harvey's position had been strengthened by two appointments: in 1949 as architect (not merely consultant) for the 'historic' buildings; and then in 1950 as archivist. The latter would not have happened without another uncharacteristic broadside from Oakeshott.
Chitty had been Keeper of the Archives for decades down to his death in December 1949. In his last years he had been using Harvey as a valued assistant, and the Warden and Fellows had recognized that assistance by appointing Harvey to the post of Deputy Keeper from July 1949. But on 4 February 1950 they dropped a bombshell by appointing as Keeper not Harvey but Merriman. Oakeshott wrote to Harvey the same day: 'I had no idea this was going to be done. I was not consulted in any way about it. Without a first-class row (the Bursar being present) I could say nothing. About twice a year I feel like resigning. This is such an occasion.' He also wrote a 'highly explosive' letter to Simonds, and another to Merriman. Harvey was touched but also embarrassed. 'I have enjoyed cordial relations with Merriman ... and I would go a long way to avoid any feeling of opposition or axe-grinding.' Whatever the Warden and Fellows thought of Oakeshott's démarche, at their next meeting they appointed Harvey 'Archivist under the Warden'.
Access to the archives was indeed required for the achievement of

the overall purpose, which was nothing less than the repair and restoration of all the medieval buildings. The backlog of work was appalling. First the depression of the 1930s, then the war, then the fire, coupled with some false economies, had seen to it that only the bare minimum had been done, and sometimes not even that.

A start had been made in 1949 with some experimental cleaning of the exterior stonework of Chapel. The cleaning, achieved largely by washing with water, was successful, and Harvey was asked to prepare an estimate to cover the whole of the work necessary on the medieval buildings. In March 1950 he presented his estimate, which came to £20,000. The Warden and Fellows bit hard and approved the whole programme, to be spread out over a number of years, 'the cost being met from existing capital funds'.

Then in February 1951 Oakeshott learned that there might be a chance of getting a substantial grant from the Pilgrim Trust towards the work. He himself had become a Trustee in 1949, and knew that other ancient schools had been making successful applications. The new Secretary of the Trust was Lord Kilmaine, a Wykehamist, who was willing to discuss possibilities informally. Harvey was therefore asked by the Warden and Fellows 'to submit a programme in some detail which should form the basis of our appeal in the autumn'.

That summer it became clear that the large seventeenth-century room known as School was in urgent need of repairs to its roof and ceiling at an estimated cost of £3,000-£4,000. Oakeshott therefore drafted an urgent letter to Kilmaine to sound him out. The draft was seen by the Warden who made some amendments, and also by Merriman and Harvey. The final text, sent on 21 July 1951, incorporated Harvey's estimate of March 1950 as containing 'some instances' of what needed doing, and added the later information about the work needed on School. 'What I would like is to make two appeals; one to the Dulverton Trust, with which I hope you might be willing to help [Kilmaine was a Dulverton Trustee], and another to the Pilgrim Trust.' There followed a frenzied correspondence.

23 July. K to WFO. Oakeshott's letter had been received just as the 'extremely thin' agenda for the next Trustees' meeting was due to go out. He had added £4,000 for School, making £24,000 in all. 'Some of the items are of course not eligible, but we want to get not less than £10,000 from this Trust. I agree that Dulverton is perfectly fair game.'

24 July. WFO to K, offering to stay away from the meeting: 'I feel infernally awkward about this.'

26 July. K to WFO: 'No need for you to feel awkward.'

On 31 July the Trustees granted £15,000 for specified items on the programme, not including School. The following day their letters crossed.

1 August WFO to K, thanking him and referring to his 'masterly tactical skills'.

1 August K to WFO: 'I think we may congratulate ourselves on the conduct of our case yesterday.' But there is the problem of how to approach Dulverton, since 'the Pilgrim Trustees, by their un- expectedly generous grant, have rather skimmed the cream off the programme'. Can Oakeshott think of anything 'spectacular' for Dulverton?

3 August WFO to K: 'I have one relatively spectacular project still up my sleeve, viz. that of buying the magnificent seventeenth-century panelling [from Chapel] back from Sir George Cooper. It was bought by his father, I think for £30,000, from a dealer, and is of its kind almost unrivalled in quality. ... My ideal would be to ask Dulverton for £5,000 for School and an additional £10,000 for the panelling.

Oakeshott was so excited about the panelling that he wrote Kilmaine a second letter about it the same day. But that story must await its turn later.

In all this Oakeshott had kept in close and friendly touch with the Warden. For in January 1951 Lord Simonds had been succeeded in that office by Sir George Gater. With Gater he now had the happiest of relationships for the rest of his time as headmaster. His affection and admiration came across in the address he gave at Gater's memorial service in Chapel in 1963.

One seems to see him again, walking purposefully across Meads on a Friday afternoon, his gait slightly leaning forward as if an expression of his intention; obviously on his way to see something for himself; remembering from his last visit all the details; who stoked the boiler and where they stored the potatoes; talking with that concentrated interest in other people's business – which was also his business; with that warm laughter, that unaffectedly genial, and extraordinarily simple, dignity.

On 29 September 1951 the unexpected news of the Pilgrim Trust grant was reported to the Fellows: £15,000 'towards the restoration of the stonework, lead roofs and other parts of the fabric of the Chapel, [Fromond's] Chantry and the other ancient buildings of the College, payable in instalments as required'. It was not welcomed unreservedly. Merriman in a covering note showed the humiliation he felt: 'The introduction of new sources of revenue, coupled with variations in the original schedule of works, have resulted in the appearance of considerable confusion with regard to finance.' Harvey was put out because Oakeshott had submitted an estimate that was over a year old without waiting a few weeks for an updated one, which would have shown a rise in costs of some 20–25%. But he forgave him: 'Walter sometimes did lack thought, but *never* heart. In intention he was one of the very kindest of men I have known.' So the work was put in hand.

Oakeshott's especial interest remained in the Chapel. In 1949 he had taken the opportunity which he always took to climb some temporary scaffolding and get a look at a section of the roof. The wooden vaulting was 'of well-known importance, being an early precursor of the fan-vault; the work of that great carpenter Hugh Herlond, designer of the magnificent roof of Westminster Hall'. Its last painting in 1822 had been in dull colours, but now in 1952 there emerged some exciting evidence of an earlier colour scheme.

To carry out the cleaning programme made possible by the Pilgrim Trust grant, the whole interior had to be scaffolded during the summer holidays of that year. It was then apparent that 'in the earliest version the ribs [of the vault] had been picked out in red, or, rather, one member of the moulding on each side of the main rib had been painted red, the rib itself being left in the ground colour'. When it came to the bosses at the intersections of the ribs, 'the detail was hardly visible even from immediately below, owing to layers of cobweb and dirt', but it was clear that they were 'of good quality and the gold leaf and paint on them would need virtually no treatment other than cleaning'. In fact every possible surface in the Chapel was cleaned, and the resultant brightness, in which the gold of the bosses and the restored red of the ribbing stood out, was breathtaking.

The presence of the scaffolding made it possible to consider other improvements. Looking ahead on 18 June, Oakeshott sent Harvey a list of points he had in mind. The list shows again his attention to detail. It included 'wiring for plugs from which a big vacuum cleaner could be used'.

More controversially, it included a suggestion for improving the lighting at eye level, a problem that had been exercising him for some years. The nave was currently lit from a series of pendants hanging from the vault down to ten feet above the heads of the congregation. Each pendant was in the form of a crown with an orb above it. What he now suggested was to lower them all by three to four feet, and then to echo the colours of the vaulting by gilding the orb and painting the crown the red of the ribs. 'As you know,' he wrote to Harvey, 'I've always been anxious about Chapel being too miscellaneous in appearance.' *

The suggestion about the lighting fluttered the dovecotes. Harvey felt that anything such must come not from him but from Oakeshott. 'Experience of the past five years has shown that the College is not prepared to proceed on suggestions (at any rate suggestions of an artistic kind) from its Consultant Architect.' Oakeshott in reply pointed out that his own proposals had in the past been turned down as often as Harvey's, and then went on more generally.

> One of the valuable features of this place is that we have a governing body which has a close sentimental association with the fabric. I have no doubt that this does make them in some ways a difficult body. ... But from experience elsewhere I do nevertheless assure you that it is much better to have people who are passionately interested and interfere insufferably than people who are not interested in the least.

The role-reversal which this correspondence reveals may be explained by the fact that Bursar Merriman had died a month earlier and been succeeded by a man whom Harvey knew less well but Oakeshott could cicumvent more easily.

The Warden and Fellows met on 12 July 1952. A paper by Harvey proposed the lowering of the pendants, a process by which 'consumption of electric current can be considerably reduced', and left it to Oakeshott to suggest the painting of them at the meeting. Both points were won – and he was able to go off to France for a holiday.

Anxieties, however, remained. To Noel he wrote about 'the vault

---

*Chapel was to that extent an exception to his general principle, implicit in many a letter to Harvey, that objects which are good of their kind will normally sit happily together, whatever their period or idiom.

of Chapel, now being painted, about which I dream night and day' and again about his 'fear of getting a telegram to say that Chapel roof had burnt'. To Harvey he was more specific. On the day the scaffolding was removed from the interior of Chapel, an Old Wykehamist cleric looked up at the freshly painted vault, exclaimed 'Dreadful' and rushed out. Ever sensitive to criticism, Oakeshott wrote from Arles on 25 August 'I suspect that the whole of the operation will be considered to have "doctrinal implications" and we shall be thought [to be] moving steadily in the direction of Rome anyhow. But that doesn't seriously worry me. It is much more the question simply what will look best.' Nevertheless the account of the changes in *The Wykehamist* of 14 October 1952 has an undertone of defensiveness.[23]

Eleven days earlier a spendid service of rededication had been held in Chapel for the whole school. Harvey had urged the date of 3 October as that of the original dedication. Oakeshott had insisted that room be found at the service for all the craftsmen,* even to the exlusion of staff wives. A. T. P. Williams, now back in Winchester as Bishop, was able in his sermon to recall Chitty's delight at his discovery of the Ettington glass. The singing of the hymn 'Thy hand, O God, has guided/Thy Church from age to age' left more than one member of the congregation feeling that the Reformation had been a mere blip in the long history of the school.

The cleaned, repainted and re-glazed Chapel had one other newly recovered glory to show on that day: the seventeenth century altar rails. The story of their recovery, together with the rest of the Chapel panelling, can be briefly told. Carved in 1680–3, probably by Edward Pierce, the woodwork was evicted in 1874, so that Chapel could accommodate an increased number of boys in the school. After thirty years of wandering it was sold for £30,000 (being thought then to be the work of Grinling Gibbons) to Sir George Cooper, who skilfully adapted it for his house in Hursley Park near Winchester. His son, the second Sir George, was unwilling to part with it during his mother's life – 'it was the apple of her eye', he said – but when she died in 1951, Oakeshott began to work on him again.

Cooper immediately expressed his willingness to let the College have the panelling 'for a nominal sum'. Oakeshott explained his hope of getting 'a Trust' to make a grant for purchase and reinstatement.

*Wykeham knew, as the records of his repeated hospitality to his workmen show, that the way to get the best work was to keep in constant touch with his workers.' (WFO, 1982.)

Gater then took over the negotiations with Cooper, who in December 1951 agreed to release the altar rails immediately. Shortly afterwards, through Kilmaine's good offices, the Dulverton Trust made a grant of £6,000 for the 'purchase and removal of the panelling'. Harvey, writing to Oakeshott, ascribed the success to 'the Warden's diplomacy . . . [and] your enthusiasm'.

A little later Dulverton made a further grant of £8,000, mainly for the repair and refurbishing of School. The work was put in hand forthwith, some of it only just in time. As usual, Oakeshott mastered the history of the building, and used it as the basis of an address he gave to the Georgian Group in Winchester in June 1952. His theme there was the vagaries of public taste which cause a building to be variously preserved, modified or even destroyed by later generations. He cited the judgement of School passed by a historian of Winchester in 1895, two centuries after it was built: 'Few buildings are uglier and few better adapted to their purpose.' His comment is ironic: 'Our [Victorian] forefathers thought that a building which was not beautiful was, in virtue of that, peculiarly suited to the education of young gentlemen. We are fortunate that they held this view, if it is to it that we owe the preservation of School.'

Irrespective of its refurbishment, everyone's eyes were on School because of the problem of where to put the newly recovered Chapel panelling. The Chapel panelling was of the same (Wren) period as School, but most of School was already panelled: could it perhaps be extended to make a home for both? As early as October 1951 Oakeshott had thought of throwing out two small bays to east and west. That was universally regarded as 'a crazy notion' and quickly abandoned in favour of a variant: to build a large annexe on the south side of School, running at right angles to it and entered from it through a linking lobby. This plan ran for some months in 1952. It was supported by Professor A. E. Richardson, RA, who was called in as a consultant, and by Sir Kenneth Clark, who however insisted that the right angle must not be exact.

Powerful arguments, however, were adduced against this plan, and opinion gradually swung in favour of a new building standing on its own. That served to launch a further debate: where should such a building be? Oakeshott wrote to Harvey in June 1952 that 'passions are running so high in every direction that, at the moment, I can see no one favouring any scheme but his own, even as second best'. By January 1953 the Warden and Fellows had finally rejected the idea of an annexe to School, though they were still no nearer to agreement on an alternative location.

Oakeshott therefore, impatient for progress, set about planning the architect's brief for the new building, wherever it was to be placed. He understood better than anyone the need for a building large enough to accommodate the whole school community, but he also urged moderation. 'Personally', he had written in May 1952, 'I attach very great importance to the idea that this new building, if it is ever undertaken, should not be too large. . . . We need a building for 650, but no more. Winchester gains enormously from being a comparatively small institution.' In this and other ways, according to Harvey, 'the detailed discussions, led by him, were decisive in regard to the overall dimensions [of the new building] and the disposition of the recovered wainscotting, reredos and screen.' It was not until after his time, in 1955, that a site was finally agreed for what became known as New Hall. Kilmaine engineered a grant of £20,000 from Dulverton towards its construction and £5,000 from the Pilgrim Trust for the adaptation of the panelling. Oakeshott doubtless played his usual role behind the scenes.

Mention should be made of one other fruit of the collaboration with Harvey, which led Oakeshott in a partly new direction. It arose indirectly out of the fire of 1947. Among the documents rescued then was a collection, known as *Wiccamica*, of published works about the school and its alumni. In 1950 the Warden and Fellows agreed to rehouse the collection in a room called Chantry Room, above the fifteenth-century Fromond's Chantry in the old cloister garth. A legacy being available to meet the expense of the necessary refurbishment, they gave Oakeshott and Harvey a relatively free hand within cost limits.

There ensued the usual meticulous correspondence between the two men. It concerned, first, the work to be done, which was completed in 1951. But it soon became apparent, as they delved into the archives, that this was not the first time in the school's history that Chantry and Chantry Room had been used as the library. Together they worked out the sequence in their usual way – *inter se disputando*, as Harvey quoted.[24] In March 1952 Oakeshott presented their findings in a paper he read to the Bibliographical Society. Entitled 'Winchester College Library before 1750', it contains generous acknowledgement of his debt to Harvey.

This wide-ranging concern for the school's fabric occupied an enormous amount of Oakeshott's time and energy in the years 1948–52. Ideas, especially for the Chapel, passed through his mind thick and fast, day and night, in Winchester or on the Continent. The volume and intensity of his correspondence with Harvey during this time is almost obsessional. Nothing was too small for his attention.

> One of the special occasions that sticks in my mind [writes Harvey] is a day that he spent with me in ransacking the locked upper rooms at the west end of Hall. We sorted paintings, portraits, boxes of stained glass ancient and modern, all sorts of miscellaneous fittings, and woodwork and panelling of some five centuries. Much, worm-eaten and rotten, had to be discarded, but only after the most careful consideration which he gave to everything, piece by piece.

Harvey adds that 'this was a day in holiday time, of course'. For Oakeshott the school holidays were simply an opportunity for different work. Some, like this, could be called school work. But there were also the claims of public service and the charms of private scholarship.

4 Public Service

From public service in the strict sense Oakeshott had already largely retired hurt while at St Paul's. But if the term is extended to include unpaid obligations to public bodies, the load he took on outside Winchester was remarkable – and, to his friends on the staff, alarming.

The first call came in 1947 from a man he much admired, Henry Morris, Chief Education Officer for Cambridgeshire.[25] Morris was engaged in revising the Authority's syllabus of religious teaching in schools. To that end he convened a Conference of forty people to advise, and invited Oakeshott to be one of those representing the Authority. The forty held meetings and wrote papers. Oakeshott contributed three papers: a long general one entitled 'Religious Teaching Tomorrow'; and two shorter ones on 'Sixth Form Divinity' and 'For an Upper Sixth Which Can Do Some New Testament Greek'.

It was the second paper which appealed to the Conference most. The final syllabus, published in 1949,[26] incorporated its three main points almost word for word. First, 'doubt, questions and discussion should play as large a part in [religious teaching] as in history or biology'. Secondly, 'boys and girls must be introduced to the "historical authentication" of the Gospel. The critical discoveries of the last generation have left a far surer historical basis than was ever anticipated when the movement began.' Thirdly, it is 'essential to make clear the limitations of materialism'.*

That last point he put much more sharply in the longest of the three papers. There he stated a case which was clearly not acceptable to most of the Conference: that 'if religion is taught only by specialists [in religion], it will be a failure'. He insisted that specialists in other subjects had a vital part to play. There was a particularly important role for the Christian teacher of science in showing that 'reason can have validity [only] if it derives from something outside the closed system of nature. And that can only be God.' The Christian teacher of history must show 'how apparent material progress may be accompanied by the loss of personal happiness, if men become mechanized by the production they are supposed to control'.

Among the other members of that Conference was the revered New Testament scholar C. H. Dodd. In 1948 Dodd was appointed Director of the project for the translation of the *New English Bible* and he too asked Oakeshott's help. When the project began there were established three panels of translators and a board of ten literary advisers. Oakeshott was a member of that board from 1948 until 1960, when the translation of the New Testament was published.

The *NEB* was planned to lie alongside the Authorized Version, chiefly for private reading by those who found the Jacobean English obscure or alien. The language of the *NEB* was to be 'contemporary'. If the first aim of the translators was accuracy, the literary advisers were to ensure the use of 'plain yet not pedestrian' English, 'avoiding both archaisms and transient modernisms'.

The advisers normally met in Oxford, under the chairmanship of A. T. P. Williams. Other Oxford members included Mynors and Norrington. At its very first meeting Oakeshott was put on a sub-committee of three to advise on the representation of Hebrew poetry: should it be printed as verse and, if so, how long should the 'lines'

---

*He commented that 'Perhaps the best statement of these limitations is still to be found in Plato's *Phaedo*', in a passage quoted in *Sword of the Spirit*.

be?[27]. But most of his contribution lay in the New Testament, whose Greek text he knew well.

The procedures at meetings he recalled at a memorial service for Williams in 1968.

> Often the process by which a single verse found acceptable form would take an hour, two hours, half a day. With that extraordinary patience and sensitivity to language, he could keep the attention of his colleagues focused, as minute after silent minute passed with a sporadic suggestion here or there – rejected tacitly, because everyone knew it would not do; until at last the answer was found.

In that light it must have been a hectic meeting in March 1958, when they dealt with the whole *Epistle to the Hebrews* in twenty-one hours. Oakeshott's own part in it, he said, 'was no more than to touch the hem of the garment. But the experience was something which became part of one's life.' And the draft translations made splendid teaching material for school divinity lessons.[28]

In August 1952 he was invited to give a paper to a World Council of Churches conference at Bossey near Geneva. The subject of school religion looked innocuous, but the experience was searing. 'The idea that a school could even try to be a Christian society', he wrote to Noel, 'was utterly scouted – and I've no doubt it was a healthy experience for anyone brought up in a community where religion is established to be confronted with this attitude.'

In 1950 came two other demands upon his time. First, he took the chair of the Education Section of the British Association for the Advancement of Science at its AGM in Birmingham. For his presidential address he took as his theme 'Education and Power'. As he saw contemporary society, power was drifting out of the hands of ordinary citizens into the hands of two groups of experts: the technocrats, with their lackeys the advertisers, and the bureaucrats, with their henchmen the politicians. His concern was with the former. Such a drift would not have happened a century ago. *The Origin of Species* 'sold by the thousands, as anyone who collects the early editions will soon discover'. But since then there has been 'a cleavage'. Scientists no longer write for the general reader. And until the cleavage is healed, 'the dissociation between technical development and social control will last'. The theme ties in with his concern for non-specialist science at school, and was evidently dear to his heart. But the address is, by his standards, humdrum.

Also in 1950 Oakeshott became a member of the Central Advisory Council for Education (England). Set up in 1945, the Council brought together leading figures from all branches of the education service, to advise the Minister. From time to time its members identified (or were given) national problems to look into, and produced reports on them. Most influential of its reports were those known by the names of successive chairmen of panels: Crowther (1956), Newsom (1962) and Plowden (1967).

Coming from Winchester, Oakeshott inevitably felt himself to be something of a fringe member. He was neither assiduous in attendance (eight meetings out of thirty during his four-year term) nor loquacious in discussion.[29] Yet typically he put his finger on one important issue. In September 1951 he wrote to the Chairman 'suggesting the Council should go into the whole complex of questions bearing on "equality of opportunity", and raising the question of early leaving from grammar schools. ... The Council proposed to discuss it with Mr Oakeshott at a later meeting.'

By the time the Council got round to it a year later, they had forgotten whose idea it was. The minutes of the September 1952 meeting refers to it as 'the point raised by Mr G. N. Flemming about early leavers'. Belatedly recognizing its importance, they resolved to devote their eighth Inquiry to it. Oakeshott himself contributed a little fieldwork, which he wrote up in a longish paper of 13 March 1953.[30]

His unemployment inquiry fifteen years earlier had led him to 'a healthy suspicion, pace Dr Gallup, of the counting and statistical classification of opinion'. He had therefore given 'one of our draft questionnaires' to the headmasters of two Hampshire grammar schools, one urban, one rural. With each of them he had gone carefully through the list of boys who had left last year from the fifth form, to find out what they had done after leaving and why. The conclusion was that the reasons for early leaving were 'overwhelmingly financial'.

The Council's report, entitled 'Premature Leaving from Secondary Schools', did not dissent from that conclusion. Presented to the Minister later in 1953, it was never published. One can see why. The more convincing the theoretical analysis of the problem, the less the likelihood of solving it without large-scale inter-departmental action. Oakeshott's vision was too wide.

If CACE work was light duty, the Beveridge Commission on Broadcasting 1949–50 was more like hard labour. He knew it would be, but he knew also that cherished standards were under threat. The Commission's terms of reference were in effect to consider the conditions under which commercial broadcasting, both sound and television, should be permitted. He wrote to Harvey the day before one weekend meeting: 'How much happier I'd be if it was three days in Norwich. Disagreeing with people one likes is so much more congenial than agreeing with people in whom one has no personal interest whatever!' He did not look forward to working with Beveridge, whom he knew from the unemployment inquiry of 1936–8. According to Asa Briggs, the historian of the Commission, 'people tended to like Beveridge very much or not at all'. At one meeting he 'recalled his own war-time experiences and asked directly why he had not been allowed to broadcast more frequently'.[31] It is hard to imagine anything more rebarbative to Oakeshott.

Moreover the work-load on members of the Commission was heavy. In addition to formal meetings filling sixty-two days in eighteen months, they were encouraged to undertake a variety of tasks and visits in the UK and abroad. In January 1950 Oakeshott invited himself to meet the Director of Television at Alexandra Palace, and stayed on to a tête-à-tête dinner. He admitted to never having seen a TV programme, but the questions he asked over dinner were searching. They included:

> whether the Staff Association was 'tame' or really an independent body; whether the BBC as a whole had become inert through lack of competition; to what extent was television the 'Cinderella' of the Corporation, dominated by the Sound side; and whether we normally recruited internally or externally.[32]

His host reported all this in some alarm to the Director General. He added 'I think that I succeeded in keeping the conversation fairly general for the most part', but ended with the ominous words: 'He has said that he would like a further opportunity of talking with me as soon as I feel ready to speak'.

Even more surprisingly, Oakeshott became interested in a number of highly technical aspects of broadcasting. He took it upon himself to pursue them with the BBC's experts over dinner, and in May 1950 wrote a long briefing paper on them for the Commission. When the paper was shown to BBC staff, the comments were once again defensive: 'Mr O. is under some misapprehension. ... Mr O. is making an assumption which requires considerable qualification.'

Yet all the time Mr O. was as doughty a defender of the BBC as they could have wished. For the final Report [33] of the Commission he drafted a Note entitled 'The BBC and Education',[34] which was signed by five other members. It began:

> The BBC's most noteworthy service to education seems to me to be its share in promoting interest in music, literature, drama, popular science, and (in general) in the things of the mind. When Mrs Leavis published, in 1932, her *Fiction and the Reading Public,* the outlook was depressing and there was for example no market for good poetry. Today things are different. ... The BBC has become a 'university extension' system for the public.

The final paragraph of the Note shows how unworldly he could still be. The signatories recognized the

> danger of neglecting the larger audience in the interests of the highbrow. Tommy Handley was one of the most powerful, and certainly not one of the least valuable, influences of the epoch. His was one of the few audiences where highbrow and lowbrow met. Doubtless he was a genius. But genius is brought out by the right conditions. The war and its immediate sequel created his special opportunity. Something more can perhaps be done to create the right conditions, even in more normal times, to produce his successor.

The final Report contains a second Note[35] which he did not draft but signed along with five others. It sets out the case *against* commercial broadcasting, which had not been set out in the main text. Its absence there was a sign of the times, for the movement in favour of commercial broadcasting was rapidly becoming irresistible, and legislation permitting it was expected for 1954.

In that expectation the Headmasters' Conference planned to stage a debate on the issue at its autumn AGM in 1953 and pressed Oakeshott to open it. His participation in HMC gatherings while at Winchester had been minimal. At AGMs between 1946 and 1952 he was either absent or silent. The agenda for his own Division's meetings in London were hardly mouth-watering, e.g. for that of May 1949 the first three items were the dates of inter-school shooting and rowing competitions for 1950, and a cricket tour to Jamaica – that was what *real* headmasters went to London to talk about.

Real headmasters of course were solemn men. With Oakeshott a chuckle was never far away. And that, on a famous occasion, had been the saving of him. In 1948 the following letter landed on his desk.

To the Headmaster of Winchester   Selhurst School
                                                 Near Petworth
                                                       Sussex
                                             March 15th 1948

My dear Oakeshott,

As you are no doubt aware Selhurst is to celebrate the hundredth anniversary of its foundation on June 20th. It was founded by the Puritan leader Ebenezer Oakeshot, who I understand was one of your distinguished ancestors. We would therefore regard it as a signal honour if you would come down on the day that I have named to unveil a plaque to your forebear. This day has been set aside for our Speech Day and the Minister of Education has agreed to come and present the prizes. The plaque is a simple portrait of our Founder; above it is his family motto 'Let the Oak Shoot 'and below it the School motto 'From an Acorn to an Oak Tree'.

Owing to an epidemic the School has broken up early and I am staying with my sister, Mrs Harvey-Kelly at Castle Brae, Chesterton, Cambridge and would be obliged if you would address your reply there.

                                        Yours sincerely,
                                  H. ROCHESTER SNEATH
                                              Headmaster

His reply was

From the secretary to the Headmaster   Winchester College
                                             The College
                                              Winchester
                                         March 16th 1948

Dear Sir,

In the absence of the Headmaster, who has recently departed by air for Salt Lake City, I am answering your letter of March 15th. The Headmaster would, I know, wish me to express his regret at missing such a ceremony. Before he left, I understood him to say that he was to visit Ebenezer Okeshot's grave in Utah, where as you will doubtless recall the great man breathed his last, after that quarrel with the Pilgrim Mothers fraught with such momentous consequences for the history of the Middle West. Incidentally I have always understood that since the introduction of the breech-loading gun, the family have preferred the Greek version of the motto, as being less liable to misunderstanding. Doubtless, however, the School authorities have good reason for retaining the older form of it.

According to present plans, the Headmaster will be away for about a year. But I will certainly submit your letter to him. Meanwhile may I on his behalf express the hope that the epidemic to which reference is made in your letter may not prove to be too serious?

I have the honour to be, Sir,

Your obedient servant
ANGELA THACKLETHWYCKE
(Private Secretary)

The full story did not emerge till twenty-five years later. Humphry Berkeley, when an undergraduate at Cambridge, had invented a fictitious public school with its headmaster, and written to some fifty people, mostly heads of HMC schools, with plausible requests or invitations. Oakeshott was one of only two who saw through the hoax.

All that, in 1948, had been fun. But now, in January 1953, stern duty called. Robert Birley, as Chairman of HMC, prevailed upon him to rejoin the Committee in preparation for the debate on the BBC at the following AGM. He attended five meetings during the intervening months. But evidently he was present more in body than in spirit, if one may judge by his agenda paper which survives from one of those meetings, covered by doodles trying out different shapes for various letters of the Greek and English alphabets.

Nevertheless at the AGM in September 1953 he did his stuff. The Committee's motion was 'That the Conference regards the BBC as one of the most important instruments of education in this country and would deplore measures which might open any part of its service to commercial influences'. Proposing it, he admitted that he was

not a viewer. Hardly any members of the Beveridge Committee

were viewers, and therefore the BBC offered us television sets. I went home and reported this offer to the family, and my wife said, 'When the television set comes in at the front door, I go out at the back door.' As in most of our families, that kind of ultimatum is, as a matter of fact, a subject for negotiation, and negotiations did take place; but I found that television in Winchester would be no good unless I fixed the aerial to the top of Chapel Tower. That I was not prepared to do.

The Conference wisely declined the role of Canute, and the motion was lost.

Some of his audience still remembered the story of the TV set half a century later. But it was no mere playing to the gallery. He and Noel never did have one, even in retirement. Recreation for both of them was chiefly reading and music. To the children he enjoyed reading aloud, and went on doing so until they were young adults. On special occasions there were parlour games e.g. 'Johnny, throw a light!' which came from Noel's family. Not that the children saw much of him in term-time. Even when they were at home, public life intruded. Once when Evelyn was standing innocently in front of the study fire after Sunday morning Chapel, 'Monty' strode briskly in. 'And what do you do here young man?' he asked in his smartening-up voice. 'Oh I don't know,' drawled the young man, 'I suppose I just hang around.'

The holidays were a different matter. That was the joy of the Bell House: escape. There was gardening, some of it strenuous: he and the children were proud of having planted sixty fruit-trees in the paddock. There were bicycle expeditions to churches or the sea or Romney Marsh. After Christmas the habit had grown up of a walking holiday in Snowdonia, sometimes including Noel. As the boys grew older they might be invited to join the Winchester party of climbers there. Once as a special treat Helena went with him for one of those French trips when he was gathering material for a book.

These two favourite recreations of his, climbing and Continental tours, were too strenuous for Noel. But she had her own scholarship. Visiting Beazley and others in Oxford, buying for Trendall in the London salerooms, and reviewing for the *Journal of Hellenic Studies*, she kept in close touch with the world of Greek vases. When they left Winchester in 1954 she bequeathed her collection of slides of Greek vases to the school. She also ran a well-remembered Italian class for senior boys. That, and a part from time to time in play-readings, were the chief contact she had with boys.

5 The Scholar

Oakeshott's own scholarship, pursued in the interstices of headmastering and other commitments, was satisfying and fruitful, with one brilliant discovery. The story resumes where it had left off in 1939, in the library of Winchester Cathedral. Invited by the Dean and Chapter in 1947 to become their Honorary Librarian, he was delighted. In 1981, the only occasion after 1953 on which he spoke at HMC, he relived the memory.

> I had a key to the library, and used often, in the evenings, to go there; leave the door open, looking out over the south transept to the faint light from the choir below on the crockets of that superb screen that hems the choir stalls; while to me, out of sight, evensong was sung; lessons and prayers a dull murmur – the 'blessed murmur of the mass', Browning called it, didn't he? – the singing transporting one's dull mind into what I suppose St Paul meant by the third heaven, or perhaps Suger by the *verum*, as I pondered the questions that preoccupied me: the distinctions between those half dozen artists I now knew intimately as individuals, who'd worked 800 years before on the illuminations.

No wonder Tom Howarth as Second Master said that 'Walter is always in the Cathedral Library!' The 'transporting', the escape from the world of bursars and housemasters, was life-blood to him. And the Dean and Chapter were well rewarded. In 1945 he had given them his royalties on the *Artists of the Winchester Bible*. This enabled the Bible itself to be rebound in 1948, in four volumes instead of two, so as to make it easier to handle and exhibit. The decision to rebind set him off on another quest. Before the war he had been intrigued by a passage in a book by M. R. James, describing how 'a miniature cut from a fine XIIth century Bible was shaken out of a pile of sermons at a country house'.[36] James had thought it came from a Lambeth Bible. Oakeshott wondered. This was the moment for pursuit.

James was now dead, but a mutual friend recalled him saying that the 'pile of sermons' had been in Sir Mark Sykes's library at Sledmere in Yorkshire. Oakeshott wrote to his son Sir Richard. He replied that he remembered the initial, of which his father had been proud; but that the Army had been in the house during the war and it had disappeared without trace. A few days later he wrote again to say that by an extraordinary chance it had been found. I could see it when I liked. It was holiday, and I wired to say I was coming next day, Sunday.

I walked the few miles from the station. They received me with courtesy; invited me to lunch; but 'before we sit down', Lady Sykes said, 'you'd probably like to see the initial'; and she put it into my hands, framed with glass on both sides so that the dozen or so lines of text on the back could be read, besides the illumination itself. I recognised it immediately as by the Master of the Genesis Initial.

Subsequent comparison with the text in the Winchester Bible confirmed it as the lost initial of the book of Obadiah. With a grant of £400 from the National Art Collections Fund it was restored to its rightful home in 1947, in time to be rebound. For the actual rebinding 'we devised a plan for oak boards which were designed and worked by James Laverty'. The Obadiah initial was beautifully sewn in by Beatrice Forder, who 'had already done some fine work for me, privately, in a like style with oak boards'. All this Oakeshott recorded on her death in 1973, with his usual respect for fine craftsmanship.[37]

Almost every year thereafter saw some contribution to the Cathedral Library from him: a grant in 1949 from the Pilgrim Trust for restoring it 'to its precise seventeenth century condition'; an article about the reconstruction in 1950; a catalogue for the display of Winchester books and manuscripts in the Guildhall to celebrate the Great Exhibition of 1951; and in 1952 the identification of two books in it as belonging to King Charles II.

During that time he was preparing his own second book, widening his main field. *The Sequence of Medieval Art* published by Faber in 1950, and dedicated to Rendall, follows the pattern of the first in being short on text and long on illustrations. The text was 'planned as a general survey of English medieval painting' 650–1350, relying chiefly on the manuscripts. His sequence has five main phases, which he calls Northumbrian, Late Anglo-Saxon, Romanesque, early gothic and late gothic.

Academic reviewers were not uniformly favourable. The word 'Art' in the title implied a book of much wider scope; the text was

· carelessly edited; the notes were inadequate for scholars but excessive for amateurs. On the other hand Gervase Mathew praised the eighty-six illustrations as 'admirably chosen and reproduced; and the accuracy of the sixteen that are in colour represents a new stage in the development of colour process'. Oakeshott did indeed always devote particular attention to the choice of his plates and to the colour reproductions.

The anonymous reviewer in the *TLS* commended not only the plates but also the 'flashes of dry wit and many penetrating observations on nearly all the plates'. The wit is for the most part characteristically light. But he misses no opportunity of tilting at his favourite windmills: the 'artistic dulness of Roman civilization'; the commercial production of 'art for art's sake'; and the aesthetic prejudices of the English. Thus 'an anglo-saxon lead brooch or pin in the library of Winchester Cathedral, which is as bad as anything that ever comes out of a Christmas cracker, has to be safely locked up lest the general public, knowing that it is anglo saxon, might think they ought to admire it'. Again, Englishmen of the fifteenth century, 'like all good Englishmen with money and pretensions to taste always, thought that what they bought abroad must be better than what was made in England. This time', he concluded, 'they were right' – but he gave them no marks for it. Pretentiousness always ranked high in his demonology.

Also in 1950 Faber published for him *The Sword of the Spirit*, 'a meditative and devotional anthology'. It had as its nucleus a series of passages which he had read in prayers at St Paul's. But it 'had grown out of that, in two senses of the word, and in the form now given it is intended for personal rather than public use'. It was planned 'for those who are no longer satisfied with information, and are concerned with ideas and doubts, especially those who are to be confirmed or have recently been confirmed'. Moreover 'to make such an anthology is to realize how often it is not words (or not words alone) but music or pictures which speak most clearly the language of religious feeling.' The book was published in two editions. Of the Winchester edition* (which was reprinted in 1991) he gave a copy to each member of staff and to every boy being confirmed.

Reviewers of the time noted 'a real distinction and delicacy of mind behind these choices' and 'its range, good taste and absence of

*The Winchester edition has as its frontispiece an engraving which he had commissioned from Reynolds Stone for his Christmas card a year or two earlier.

any dogmatic bias'. The range is indeed vast. It runs in time from Aeschylus and Plato through to friends such as Eliot, H. A. Hodges and Bernard Fergusson. The most frequently cited source is the New Testament. Other favourite writers are medieval saints (Benedict, Bernard, Francis, à Kempis), English mystical poets (Herbert, Vaughan, Blake) and modern 'thinkers' (Jeans, Balfour, Whitehead).

The reviewer in *The Pauline* observed a subtler feature of the book. It is 'very carefully organized under seven main headings. These lead the reader from doubt to belief.' But that road was not presented as an easy one. In a first draft of his preface, Oakeshott had written this.

> The book could not fulfil its purpose if expressions of doubt and despair were ruled out from it. Those are few, whose minds have not been at some time assaulted by such feelings. If assurance has not come to a man by way of some doubts and sometimes by way even of despair, either he is unusually fortunate or (as far more often happens) he has never reached an adult stage at all. Indeed the greatest of such expressions come from the works of the most profoundly religious poets, George Herbert or Gerald Manley Hopkins, nd are found side by side, in the works of those same men, with the most magnificent outbursts of joy and praise. The attempt has been made here too to balance the one with the other.

Hindsight enables one to discern a second movement in the placing of extracts: the progress of a life from action to comtemplation, from restlessness to repose. Many of the earlier passages in the anthology derive from or relate to his Elizabethan explorers and to others who were equally adventurous in body and mind. Those passages had been especially suitable for reading to young Paulines in time of war: in them the *Sword of the Spirit* had its cutting edge. But there was no triumphalism there, any more than there had been in *Founded upon the Seas*: no suggestion that success is assured. Headings like 'spirit triumphant', 'leadership', 'fame' and 'popularity' are here too balanced by 'fear', 'despair' and 'betrayal'.

Indeed the most telling passage in the whole book concerns a *reversal* of the road from the active to the contemplative life. It comes from the pen of Pope Gregory the Great.* Headed 'The Pope looks back with longing to his days as a monk', it opens: 'Being upon a certain day overburdened with the trouble of worldly business, I

---

*It was Gregory who took Augustine's distinction between the Two Lives and added the third category of the mixed life – though he applied it only to bishops.

retired to a solitary place congenial to grief, where whatever it was in my affairs that was giving me discontent might plainly reveal itself.' There, in conversation with his 'very dear son Peter the Deacon', he saw what it was.

> Now, by reason of my pastoral charge, my unhappy soul must engage in the business of worldly men; and where through much ministering to others it spendeth itself on outward distractions, it cannot but return impaired to those inward and spiritual things for which it longeth. For do but look how the ship of my mind is tossed by the waves and tempest, and how I am battered in the storm. Nay, when I recollect my former life, I sigh as one who turneth back his eyes to a forsaken shore.

Oakeshott had certainly known 'the trouble of worldly business', most recently in the previous year. He was more fortunate than the Pope in that his 'shore' lay in the future. But there were three or four more years of 'waves and tempest' to ride first.

In the same years (1948–50) which saw the production of *The Sequence of Medieval Art* and *The Sword of the Spirit*, he was engaged in writing a third and more substantial book in a field he had never tackled before, that of New Testament criticism. He had long been interested in – and impressed by – the textual tradition of the gospels. In c. 1948 he wrote a substantial essay arguing that Matthew's gospel derives from the apostle James, and that thus, since Mark's derives from Peter and the fourth gospel from John, the three disciples who formed the inner ring are all represented in the gospels as we have them.* Having written the essay, he showed it to various people for comment, including C. H. Dodd. Dodd returned it with pencilled comments in the margin, such as 'a strong point' and 'I have long been disposed to think so'.

Thus encouraged, Oakeshott extended his study to the rest of the New Testament. Its conclusions may be summarized. On the 'historical authentication', as he called it: 'If the attempt to express the life of Christ in terms of history falls short, it is not because the materials are inadequate, but because the mystery of its very nature is incomprehensible.' When it comes to explaining the mystery, his Platonism shows through. 'The Fourth Gospel and the Epistle to the Hebrews are the clearest testimony to the idea that in the life of Christ two

*As in *The Artists of the Winchester Bible*, he was keen to identify individuals.

worlds had met, the transient world of experience, and the eternal world of truth.'

The book, entitled 'The Gospels and History', extended to 200 pages of typescript. It was never published, for reasons that can only be guessed. Perhaps it was too orthodox, too much in line with critical opinion of the time. Perhaps he put it away for further revision and then, when he came back to it, found his views had changed. But as a work of scholarship it is no less impressive than his published work, and it adds yet another arrow to his quiver.[38]

July 1952 brought a small 'chirp' in the form of a Doctorate of Laws, at St Andrews University. The honour attested his growing reputation as a scholar, though the citation does not specify the field. November brought a much bigger one. The story began, this time, with money. Throughout his time at Winchester money had been an anxiety. He retained the Bell House, the only property they owned, but ran no car until 1951. The Harvey correspondence for 1951 contains two typical references to money. On the one hand he had been anxious for some time about his obligations to the Roxburghe Club. As a member of this exclusive club of bibliophiles, he would have, when his turn came, to print at his own expense some bibliographical rarity and give copies to all other members: how could he ever afford it? On the other hand, we find him offering to contribute out of his own pocket up to £25 ('I am very hard up at present') to make up the cost of refurbishing Chantry Room.

Now in 1952 he was faced with the need to raise a fairly substantial sum towards the university education of the children. Helena was due for Oxford shortly, and the twins after National Service in 1954. Noel wrote to him in August: 'I've raised £80 on jewelry, and I'm going to the Bank Manager again today to see if he'll take Pendy's diamonds as security.' Walter agreed. 'Finance is a terrible worry.' If there is inflation 'all my savings in insurance (about £200 a year [put by]) will be reduced to a fraction. The Bell House is the one thing that really does stay put.' There was only one solution. He had to start selling his books. To Francis Edwards in Marylebone High Street, who specialized in maps and travel books, he took up

a suitcase filled with some of my precious acquisitions, including the commonplace book, with those manuscript maps (p. 68) – I hoped it might be worth £50. Mr Edwards, the assistant told me, was out; but if I would leave the books he would send me an offer.

To console myself I walked along to the British Museum, where I knew they had a quatercenterary exhibition celebrating the births of Hakluyt and Raleigh. And as I looked round the documents in that exhibition, suddenly a bell started ringing furiously in the back of my mind. And I said to myself: 'I've seen that hand before; and if this notebook of mine isn't in the hand of Raleigh, I'm a Dutchman.'

So he rushed back to Francis Edwards – a taxi, this time – and removed the book from sale.

Back home at Winchester with it, he put on his thinking cap. If the notebook was Raleigh's, its contents must surely be working material which he had collected while preparing his *History of the World* during his imprisonment in the Tower. Eagerly he sought out the Fellows' Library copy of the *History*. Sure enough there were some striking resemblances between the two. So on 30 September 1952 he took the notebook up to his friend A. J. Collins at the British Museum, and

in a rather faltering voice I told him what I thought it was. I saw him looking at me in the way that Keepers of the Manuscripts reserve for eminent Baconians, but he said he would look at it and write. About five days passed and I heard nothing from him. At last in desperation I wrote to him and said 'I suppose there's nothing in this.'

The ensuing correspondence[39] is delicious. Collins to Oakeshott 6 October: 'Though it is still too early for me to commit the department to a final opinion, I myself feel that there is very little doubt that it is in Raleigh's hand.' By 16 October Collins could report the result of further study with his colleague Skeat: 'We have now spent as much time on your manuscript as can properly be spared', and the identification 'seems to be proved beyond any doubt'. Oakeshott to Skeat 20 October: 'It really is most awfully good of you to take so much trouble with the notebook. I've naturally been excited by it. But it was, I thought, rather impertinent of me to bother the department with it.'

Four accounts of this discovery survive. In the latest (c. 1981) he ascribed it to 'a series of extraordinary coincidences'. Some coincidences, of course there were. But, as with the Malory, fortune favoured the prepared eye. And this one 'eventually offered still more excitement to the "discoverer" than the Malory. ... Whereas the Malory went off into other hands, this second manuscript remained mine to follow up, as I had time, and opportunity, to do so.'

He first reported the discovery in a turnover article in *The Times* of 29 November, and summarized its importance. 'Here is a relic of singular interest: the working papers for one of the famous books of the world', together with a list of books which 'we may reasonably assume to be the list of the library which he had with him in the Tower'; and a poem in his own hand. 'Raleigh can be seen at work, and it would be hard to deny him' (against Ben Jonson's slander) 'the title of a scholar in his own right.'

Oakeshott then set about working through the *History*. Among other findings he notes that 'the rhetorical passages, in which he writes of Fame, of Death, of Immortality, are wonderful – if one can take these things seriously, as I still can'. But it was other features of the commonplace book that were to prove of more lasting interest to him. The library list he eventually published as a monograph in 1968. The poem to Cynthia he generously allowed a young English master, George Seddon, to publish in the *Illustrated London News* in February 1953.[40]

Yet Oakeshott still needed money. Already in December 1952 he told Collins he had 'almost decided to sell [the commonplace book] to pay off, or at any rate reduce, my overdraft. I *hate* doing it, because it is very specially in the line I've always collected and treasured.' The British Museum was interested in buying it, but it was sold to two brother booksellers, Lionel and Philip Robinson. The purchase price was in the region of £3,000, which went some way to transform his finances.[41]

Moreover the Robinsons, being scholars themselves, generously allowed him continuing access to the manuscript, pursuing the trail wherever it led. It brought him first to *The Queen and the Poet* (1960), which he dedicated to Archie John Wavell who had 'shared the excitement of the discovery'. From there he broadened out into various related fields of Elizabethan poetry on which he was still working at the time of his death.

One other 'discovery' belongs to Oakeshott's time at Winchester, though it was not published till later. In 1948 he saw in a Sotheby's preview an object which intrigued him. It was catalogued as 'a Byzantine bronze grain measure, with four lines of inscription round the rim, 5¼ins., 7th/8th century'. He was attracted to it on two grounds. The first was aesthetic: its patina and its 'strong, solid, almost massive shape, if a vessel that size can be called massive'. The second was historical. 'Measures do not normally run to elaborate inscriptions. This was long enough to suggest that it was made for some unusual situation.' And the lettering of it reminded him of the Greek script in some manuscripts of the bible written a century or two earlier than the date suggested by Sotheby's.

So he bought it, and enjoyed it as an object. 'To handle a work of classical antiquity* is in itself a satisfying experience. Greek vases are too fragile for it to be often feasible with them. But this bronze was asking for it. It used to sit on top of my shelves, above the books – and though I was no smoker, most other people were in those days, and it made an excellently capacious and indestructible ash-tray.'

He also began to study it. The Greek inscription clearly referred to the object itself. As far as he could make out, it read: 'duly cer tified hereby as a precisely accurate measure of twenty-four soldier's ounces'. This presented a puzzle. The only ration of which a soldier could expect to get 24 ounces would be bread in some form. But why should bread be measured in a cup (there had been a handle, now broken off), i.e. by volume instead of weight? And why such a stress on accuracy?

One day he told Wavell *père* of the puzzle. Wavell, who was al- ways interested in military history, had a short list of what he called his 'sixth-form generals' i.e. the best, ancient and modern. One of them was Belisarius, the brilliant commander of the Byzantine em- peror Justinian. Wavell had been reading Justinian's military his- torian Procopius, and suggested that Oakeshott should try him too.

There in Book III of Procopius's history is recorded an intriguing incident. It occurred during the transport of Belisarius's army from Constantinople to North Africa in 533 AD for a campaign against the Vandals. Procopius, who was present, explains the background. Nor- mally, he says 'the bread which is provided for an army on foreign service is carefully baked twice over, so that it will last as long as possible and not go bad in a short time.' On this occasion a corrupt quartermaster-general tried to short-circuit the usual process and thus

---

*Ashmole said of Beazley that 'his way of handling an antiquity was a lesson, not only in manners, but in attitude to life'. The same was true of Oakeshott (Jasper Gaunt).

save flour. But the bread cooked in that way disintegrated and, when the sacks were opened, was found reduced to crumb. 'The officials whose duty it was to distribute the ration had to serve it out to the troops by quart and bushel measures.'*

Oakeshott was thrilled to read this passage. Procopius's story could account for both the puzzling features of the measure. The bread was meted out by volume because it had crumbled; and the stress on accuracy was designed to allay the justifiable suspicions of the soldiery. He eventually wrote up the discovery in an article for the *Journal of Hellenic Studies*[42] and sold the measure to the British Museum. Privately he would have liked to see it renamed the Wavell measure.

This account of his scholarly output while at Winchester is far from exhaustive. Apart from books, he published during the period 1949–54 substantial reviews of ten books on art history, and four articles on libraries: these were already his dominant interests. But there were also four other reviews, together with seven published and six unpublished articles, papers or addresses.[43] Most of these were written on request, and their breadth shows the range of affairs on which his views were sought: religion and science, history and geography, literature and architecture, education and broadcasting. Even more remarkable is the sheer quantity of his output, and the time it must have taken, given the number of drafts he always went through. No wonder that, for good or ill, he did not 'interfere' in the running of the boarding-houses.

6   The Clouds Gather

The year 1952 was one of triumph, for the school as well as for Oakeshott, in the completed work in Chapel and the prospective recovery of the panelling. It was also a year of personal tragedy, a tragedy which left him scarred for life. The scene of it was College, the house of seventy scholars presided over by the Second Master. Already in 1951 Oakeshott had had occasion to report to the Warden and Fellows his concern about the tone of College.

The occasion was the impending retirement of the Second Master, Monty Wright (see illustration), who had held the post for twenty-

* 'Not an elevating story, perhaps. But then, if you somehow manage to skip back 14 centuries, you are not likely to find yourself in Justinian's study, and him busy on the *Institutes*, but somewhere on the back stairs.' (WFO, 1977.)

seven years. Oakeshott was well aware how crucial was the appointment of his successor. His first two approaches had come to nothing. Tony Chenevix-Trench, later Head Master of Eton, accepted but then asked to be released in favour of another appointment to which he felt bound to give priority on compassionate grounds. Oakeshott's next choice was one which throws light on his own character and on the perceived requirements of the post.

Archie John, now Lord Wavell, had in 1948 astonished the old brigade (though not his father) by leaving his regiment for the School of Army Education, on the grounds that in peacetime education was the more important service. Oakeshott had long admired him and had asked him to be Rose's godfather in 1941. They had in common a love of English literature and of climbing. Whenever Wavell was free he was a welcome member of the climbing party which Graham Irving used to convene in Snowdonia over the New Year. His quality emerges in a letter which Walter wrote to Noel from the 1949 party: 'How he manages [to climb] minus a hand – for the hook was lost a few days ago by accident – goodness knows.' Now what Oakeshott was especially looking for in College was Wavell's brand of unconventional leadership, which would certainly have let a breath of fresh air in to those medieval mullions. Wavell was much flattered but unconvinced of his own capacity. In any case he was expecting to be invited to rejoin his regiment for a tour of duty against the Mau Mau in Kenya – an invitation he could not conceivably refuse.

Oakeshott's third choice was Tom Howarth. Howarth had been on the staff at Winchester for short periods both before and after the war, in which he had distinguished himself as one of Monty's liaison officers. He was more of an activist than Trench and more of an academic than Wavell. It was an excellent appointment, with one snag. Howarth was by then Chief Master of the King Edward VI Foundation, Birmingham, and was not sure when he would be free to make the move. In the event, though appointed in February 1951, he did not come until May 1952.

In his report of September 1951 Oakeshott devoted some space to his anxieties about College. His language is diplomatic. He speaks of 'a decline in the prestige of College', of the lightness of control under the present regime, and of 'the new stimulus that seems to me to be needed'. In the intervening year catastrophe struck.

There was in College at that time a sensitive boy in his second year. Alan Roseveare's father, Dick, was a friend and highly respected colleague, who had come back on to the staff after an uneasy spell of headmastering. Alan had in his first year run into some academic and social problems. Some of his behaviour was strange enough to warrant his referral to a psychiatrist, who however reported no serious cause for worry.

Nevertheless the worry remained, and Oakeshott was one of the many who were on the alert. Sunday 9 March 1952 was a 'Cathedral Sunday' when school evensong was held in the Cathedral Choir.

> I happened to notice Alan, who was in the school choir, as we stood waiting in the south transept before the service. I will never forget his radiant face – radiant not for anyone there (he was oblivious of us all) but because he was away in some seventh heaven. I said to myself that his problems were solved. I wondered, mystified, how he had discovered the answer.

Next morning he caught sight of the boy again in Chapel. This time the look on his face was close to despair. But Oakeshott had to run for a train to London, and there was no time to warn anyone else before he left. When he got back in the evening he learned that Alan could not be found. He went straight round to College.

> Monty [Wright] was there; Dick came over; and then we heard that a rope from Chapel peal was missing, and we knew what the answer must be. Dick and I went to look for him. It was a marvellously clear, starred sky. We went up on to the Chapel roof. Dick went into the tower. In a moment he was back. 'I can't go further,' he said. 'He is there.' He went down to get help. I waited under the stars and remembered the radiancy on Alan's face.

At Dick's request, Walter read some prayers in the belfry. The next morning he spoke to the school in Chapel. The members of College were devastated, and he sent them home ten days before the end of term – Monty Wright's last term as Second Master.

Neither the note that Alan left nor the inevitable investigation threw any conclusive light on the causes of the tragedy. Oakeshott's concern was to relieve everyone else of the inescapable sense of guilt: Alan's family, his contemporaries in College, the staff who taught him, and above all Monty Wright. Reporting to the Warden and Fellows that August, he made a show of tranquillity. There was 'no shred of actual evidence' that 'the strains and stresses of life in

College . . . played a part in what happened in this instance. . . . My considered view is that this was some mysterious psychological aberration which, as the doctors tell us, is particularly liable to show itself in the phase of growth through which Alan was passing.' Himself he could not forgive so lightly: if only he had not gone up to London that day. . . . Some of those closest to him believe that he was 'never the same again'.

Six months later he suffered a re-run of the 1949 contretemps with housemasters. The story comes from Keith Workman, then a recent old boy, who had been brought back to do some temporary teaching. For three weeks he lodged with the Oakeshotts and had all meals with them. During that time there was 'an act of indiscipline which certainly merited expulsion. Oakeshott, that really gentle man, agonized for what seemed like days about the right course of action, and I know that many housemasters were very critical.' As before, the affair 'reduced him almost to resignation'.

Yet the picture in 1952 was by no means all gloom. An August tour of France was rewarding, the grand rededication of Chapel in October uplifting, and the identification of the Raleigh notebook thrilling. By the end of the year it even looked as though the Warden and Fellows might be taking action to improve the headmaster's house. Their agreed aim was 'to provide a home for the Headmaster which is less extensive, more convenient and warmer than the present house'. It soon became clear that they could not afford reconstruction on the scale that was necessary, but they went on for months searching for palliatives – until they were overtaken by events.

For early in May 1953 Oakeshott reported to Gater that he had been approached over the succession to Keith Murray as Rector of Lincoln College, Oxford. Gater replied on 10 May. 'This is a very different proposition from the Exeter professorship. . . . I could not and would not say a word against it.' In June Oakeshott told Gater he had decided to let his name go forward, with the caveat that he could not leave until March 1954. Gater suggested as a possible compromise that he might go at Christmas. 'Don't lose the job by arguing out of consideration for Winchester.' He had immediately recognized the financial advantage to a pensionless Oakeshott of an appointment in which he could remain till the age of seventy.

Financially it was, as Oakeshott explained to Harvey, 'one of those Gilbertian situations where one is forced by extreme financial need to take a job at a much lower salary'. Because of it, he would get a more generous grant towards the fees of the twins at Oxford; and Lincoln would put him on the College's pension scheme. Naturally there were many other factors involved in the decision to leave Winchester. One which in retrospect carried weight was the increasing unease he had been feeling at the obligation to preach in Chapel (p. 325).

The decision seems to have been taken on both sides in June 1953, with the intention that it should be announced in October. But some leak occurred, and rumours began to circulate. It became necessary for Oakeshott to inform his housemasters at their pre-term meeting in September 1953. The news was a bombshell. At least two senior men, Hampton and Walker, tried to persuade him to withdraw, and on 15 September Walker wrote to the Warden.

> Those of us who know are reduced to consternation & misery at the thought of losing him. ... By the school he is more beloved than perhaps Headmaster [*sic*] ever has been, – more, he has touched the idealism in them, which is doing Winchester incalculable good. ...
>
>   He clearly felt it a matter of principle to keep everything secret until it was too late to question. But since the thing is known it may *not* be too late to get him to withdraw. I know you have succeeded once already (over that professorship). I think (if the immediate problem which has forced him to think of going [a clear reference to his conditions of service] can be solved on yr side) that he is shakeable in his resolve by the appeal to ideals and affection. So does Howarth; we have both been talking to him this morning. It will not be easy. But may we, under yr leadership, try?[44]

The appeal, if made, proved ineffective. The Fellows were informed at their meeting on 26 September that he would be leaving next March. They resolved to ask Howarth to act for the summer term 1954 and to appoint a new man for the September, on the improved conditions of service so long denied to Oakeshott. The Fellows of Lincoln formally elected him on 21 October, and a notice appeared in *The Times* the next day.

So time ticked by, with only a term and a half still to go. But Oakeshott was feeling ill and old – 'I'm exceedingly old for my age' he wrote to Harvey in September. At the end of November he was walking back from evensong on another 'Cathedral Sunday' when he fell in with a close friend on the staff. 'Walter,' said the friend, 'you're looking terrible.' Walter then opened his heart. He was in great distress of mind and spirit and, as often, not sleeping well. 'I'm afraid', he added ominously, 'I may do something foolish.' The friend heard him out and told him he *must* get medical advice.

On 15 November he was ordered away from Winchester for ten days. He went to a hotel in Lymington where Noel joined him two days later, preceded by a postcard devoted to a match of Winchester football: 'very good Sixes, in which for a time College led, but Houses gained on them steadily.' Returning on 25 November he found a letter from Harvey. His reply is significant. 'The more I think about it, the less conceivable it sounds to get the W and F to do anything about this just now. One or two of them are clearly afraid that I am trying to jump them into various things in a hurry.'

In December the crisis occurred which darkened his remaining days at Winchester. It should be said at this point that the documents in the case were in 1976 put under embargo for forty years by the Warden and Fellows, so that the story which follows has had to be pieced together without the explicit testimony of the two protagonists, Oakeshott and Robin Ridgway, housemaster of Beloe's or K house.[45]

On the first day of the school holidays, after the boys had gone, the house matron in K house told Ridgway that the previous afternoon she had seen two boys, one older and one younger, in what she regarded as a sexually compromising position. The elder boy had already got a place at Oxford but was due to come back for one or two more terms, not as head of house but as a school prefect. Ridgway now wrote to the boy's father, with a copy to Oakeshott, in terms which father and son took as a sacking. Ridgway had in this clearly acted *ultra vires* and was seriously at fault. Moreover Oakeshott had for some time had grave doubts about Ridgway's running of his house. Some terms earlier, the father of another boy in the house had asked for an interview with the headmaster to complain. As he left, Oakeshott assured him that 'if I feel it to be necessary, I shall not hesitate to dismiss Mr Ridgway'. Now he had a specific *casus belli*.

At this point (the second day of the holidays), he made what he later described as a 'serious mistake'. Hoping to avoid a direct confrontation, he wrote to Anne Ridgway asking her to come round to see him. Puzzled but unsuspecting, she went. He told her that he wanted Robin to leave his house immediately. As to his grounds, he avoided the specific and gave her what was surely his true reason:

'he has been running an unhappy house'. 'Throughout this interview', she recalls, 'Walter never once met my eyes.'

When Ridgway heard her account he stormed round, to find Oakeshott immovable. What passed between them is not known. Oakeshott must have made it clear that giving up his house did not entail leaving the teaching staff; but to Ridgway such a humiliation was intolerable.

A day or so later Howarth went round to see the Ridgways. His position was equivocal. The two men had been friends on the pre-war staff, and their respective wartime successes were a further bond. But Howarth was never uncritical of his colleagues. On his return to Winchester as Second Master in 1952, he had thrown a number of stones into the mill-pond. In particular he had let it be known, in one of his calculated indiscretions, that 'he would not rest until he had got X out of his division [form], Ridgway out of his house, and Z off the staff altogether.'

Accordingly he now advised Ridgway to 'go quietly', because 'the Warden knows' and by implication can be expected to support the headmaster. Ridgway's wise course would be to resign on grounds of ill-health: that would improve both his compensation and his prospect of future employment. Ridgway, however, knew that his own health, though not perfect, was certainly better than Oakeshott's, and that course too was unacceptable.

So an impasse was reached. Since it was now some days into the holidays, no one could be found to offer mediation – though the old warrior Malcolm Robertson said he 'would have liked to bang both their silly heads together'. In fact compromise was impossible. Both men were obdurate, for different reasons. Ridgway had been affronted in his professional pride and dignity. Oakeshott had that natural streak of obstinacy that can go with indecisiveness. He wrote to Noel in 1940: 'As you know I'm obstinate, and if ever I *do* make up my mind about anything it isn't too easy for anyone to unmake it.' He had also made all the mistakes of a man who dreads a move that is bound to cause pain. He had done nothing to prepare the ground, either by warning Ridgway or by consulting colleagues other than Howarth. After months, perhaps years, of shivering on the brink, he had shut his eyes and jumped.*

That explains the precipitancy of his decision, but not the speed of

*He had done the same a year or two earlier over the dismissal of the manager of the school tuck shop.

1 WFO's own drawing of a four horse chariot team made for the Balliol Players'
Hippolytus, 1926.

2 Walter and Noel on their wedding day, 1928.

3 WFO as High Master of St Paul's. Presentation portrait on his leaving in 1946, by William Dring, RA.

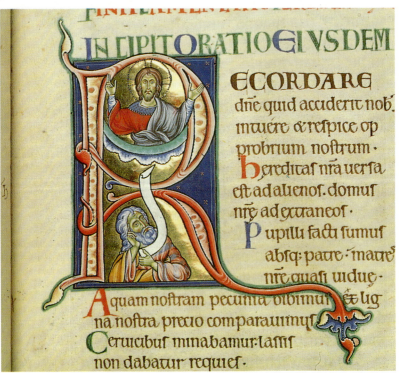

4 Two illustrated initials from the Winchester Bible: (a) the call of Jeremiah, by the Master of the Leaping Figures; (b) Jeremiah in old age, by the Master of the Morgan Leaf.

5a Bust of the Virgin Mary in mosaic made c. 705 for the old basilica of St Peter, Rome, and removed in 1609 to Orte Cathedral in Southern Italy, when the inscription and outer gold background were added.

5b Bust of the Virgin and Child in stained glass, made by Thomas of Oxford c. 1395, for William of Wykeham's east window in the chapel of Winchester College.

6 WFO as Headmaster of Winchester, 1950, in Chamber Court after Sunday Morning Chapel: (left) talking to a boy; (below) with Field-Marshal Montgomery, Monty Wright (Second Master) and Colin Peterson (senior scholar).

7 WFO in his study at Lincoln, 1960.

8 WFO, 1984; by his daughter Helena.

its implementation. Certainly Oakeshott was determined not to leave a weak link to his successor. But that aim could have been achieved without all the pain and grief. If he had given Ridgway notice to leave Beloe's at the end of the school year, he would have allowed him time to find a house of his own, and pre-empted the inevitable but entirely baseless rumour of scandal. Why did he not do so? The accepted explanation is that he was not himself. He had in fact done the 'something foolish' which he feared.

When Ridgway's long-standing friends on the staff heard the news, they rallied to his support. He was widely admired as a teacher of modern languages, and his sharp wit went down well with colleagues, if not always with boys. Having had a distinguished war, he could also call upon support outside the school. He therefore consulted his lawyer about his position. There things rested over Christmas.

On Boxing Day the Oakeshott family received the devastating news that Archie John Wavell had been killed in Kenya on Christmas Eve at the age of thirty seven. Walter himself wrote the obituary which *The Times* published on 28 December. He ended it by applying to Archie John the 'splendid phrase of Sir Walter Raleigh' which the two of them had wanted to use for the Field-Marshal's memorial tablet: 'He was one for whom the world's bright glory had not blinded the eyes of the mind.' He then went off to join the climbing group in Snowdonia – an especially poignant meeting this year.

Noel was equally upset. 'It is quite impossible', she wrote to Walter in Wales, 'not to keep thinking of Archie. I expect it is the same with you. Finally I have written these lines because it really seemed one must do something.

> Did suddenly a door blow open then?
>> Yes it blew open wide.
> Was there a blaze of light when you stepped through?
>> That was what drew me to the other side.
> Was the door slammed and have they turned the key?
>> It lies with you to say if that must be.
> Are we to grieve and shed the mourning tear?
>> If it will vivify what I held dear.
> Are we to question, wonder or surmise?
>> It was so simple, why not share my prize?*

*Noel's poem stands comparison with Christina Rossetti's 'Uphill', on which it is clearly based.

On his return to Winchester Oakeshott learned that Ridgway had decided to appeal to the Warden and Fellows. He welcomed that as taking the ultimate decision out of his hands: 'a great relief' he called it in writing to Alan Philpotts on 15 January. Philpotts, an old member of K house, was secretary of the Old Wykehamist Society and was giving Ridgway moral support. It was clear that the dispute was escalating. Oakeshott's chief concern now was to limit the damage to the community.

Though he never wavered in the view that his decision had been right, he bitterly regretted the hurt it caused, especially the divisions on the staff. Colleagues on opposite sides began to avoid each other. Many, including friends like James Mansel (chaplain and fellow-climber), believed he had behaved unjustly. Oakeshott, as a matter of principle, 'took full responsibility: never at any staff meeting or elsewhere except to the Governing Body spoke up against the man involved or gave reasons for the step taken'.[46] Part of his motivation was that, as he wrote to Philpotts, 'it is to my mind vital that supposing Robin is to come back again, the water should not have been muddied for him'. This left him only the more isolated. The strain on him was immense, and many thought him on the verge of a nervous breakdown.

At a preliminary hearing on 22 January it was evident that a decision would not be reached for some weeks. Oakeshott's doctor ordered him to take a short holiday abroad. He went for 10 days on his own to Santa Margherita in Tuscany, from where he wrote three letters to Noel. He was staying in a kind of extended guest-house run by a widow, Mrs Waldock, who also had a son in K house. By a curious coincidence Peter Waldock was the closest friend of the boy in the centre of the dispute – but then most people in the story seem to have known each other also outside Winchester. While at Santa Margherita Oakeshott did everything possible for distraction: he went for country walks, joined in Scottish reels (but avoided canasta parties) with the local expatriates, and managed to get a day in Pisa. He came back strengthened in body and refreshed in mind, but not renewed in spirit.

During January and February he went more than once to visit K house. He had placed the house for the term in the care of Kenneth Kettle, a bachelor master who had been living there with the Ridgways and knew and liked them well. Kettle recalls that 'each time we sat, with him having tears rather more than in his eyes, though not exactly streaming down his cheeks'. He adds 'I expect he was reduced (or elevated) to a mood in which he would have been grateful if the Governing Body had stood for Robin.' That judgement is plausible. Feeling guilty, not (again) for the decision but for the havoc it had created, he wanted to be punished.

In support of that interpretation is a vivid memory of his secretary Phyllis Alcock. She remembers an exchange of letters between him and Harold Cox, the sub-Rector of Lincoln. Walter wrote to say that Noel's father had died and she had come into money. As a result he no longer needed to work full-time. In the circumstances he would quite understand if Lincoln wished to reconsider their choice. Cox wrote back thanking him, but saying they were very happy with the choice they had made. What caused the correspondence, now lost, to remain in her memory was the diplomatic phrasing used by both writers: never, she said, had she read such coded language. Now it was true that Dr Moon had died in August 1953 and had left a good deal of money. But it was not evenly divided. Noel's share, as a daughter, was £6,000 – extremely useful but nothing like enough for them to live on. It seems almost certain that what he was doing was to let Lincoln off the hook if they wanted it. Had they accepted his offer, he would quite possibly have gone back to South Africa.

Eventually on 27 February the Warden and Fellows put the matter to the vote. The minutes record that they upheld Oakeshott 'by a large majority'. But the minority exacted a price. It was agreed that 'Each Fellow present at the Hearing should be free at his discretion to explain his position'. So two notices appeared in the Common Room. The Warden announced the majority decision; Lord Chancellor Simonds and two others recorded their dissent.

Oakeshott was now free to do something which mattered a good deal to him on behalf of the boy in the case. When father and son heard that Ridgway might be reinstated, they thought it wiser for the boy not to return to school. Oakeshott, however, was determined to leave no possible stain attaching to his character. In January he had him up to lunch at the Athenaeum. He had also issued an invitation in principle to come down to Winchester for a weekend to stay in the headmaster's house. When the invitation could finally be implemented in March, he insisted that they walk together side by side into Chapel.

There were other pieces to be picked up. After the decision, Ridgway had refused a renewed offer 'to return to Winchester as an Assistant Master'. On 27 March the Warden and Fellows agreed to make an ex gratia payment to him of £2,000. On 29 March a note appeared in *The Wykehamist* over the initials W. F. O. 'It has been generally known for some time that Mr Ridgway has had to give up his house in circumstances that have caused widespread regret, and have won for him considerable sympathy. It is important that it should be fully understood that no sort of personal reproach attaches itself to Mr Ridgway in this matter, a fact endorsed not only by general consent, but also by the formal resolution of the Warden and Fellows.' But from Robin and Anne Ridgway's point of view the damage had been done. He never found another teaching post, and died in 1962.

The whole sad story had a curious after-life. Nothing of it seeped into the press, but rumour abounded. Some years later an Old Wykehamist wrote a bad novel based on it. And still after a lapse of half a century it is widely believed – even by men who were on the staff at the time – that Oakeshott's appointment to Lincoln came *after* the Ridgway affair. The full story will not be known until 2016. Meanwhile the only written account available by either man is a passing reference written by Oakeshott c. 1981.[46] In it he repeats his final judgement. 'The decision, I have still no doubt, was right; the way it was done may have been wrong, but I doubt if there is ever a "right" way for such things.' And he makes no attempt to conceal the 'one serious mistake I made, partly due perhaps to the stress which the whole affair involved'. 'Such things' are so often better done by the natural butcher.

That complicated character Budge Firth did his best to smooth things over by the 'obituaries' which he wrote (unsigned, but the attribution is certain) of both men in the same number of *The Wykehamsit*. Of Ridgway he speaks warmly as a friend and colleague from pre-war days. He praises him as a teacher but says nothing of him as a housemaster. Of Oakeshott he wrote in terms which must be unique, even in this genre of literature. They carry the more weight in that Firth was a historian of the school and a biographer of Rendall.

No Headmaster of Winchester can ever have been more loved than Walter Oakeshott. The feeling towards him has been in a special degree *personal*, transcending all distinctions of age and status, and any difference of temperament and opinion. . . .

No headmaster has ever less asked for recognition, or even for any personal notice at all. . . . He has shown himself that rarest of beings, the completely unselfish man. This quality has made him, with all his infinite gentleness, in the last resort formidable, and, with all his infinite sensitivity, in the last resort invulnerable. Since his ends are entirely without self in view, nothing can deflect him from their pursuit, and since he is wholly without fear for self, he is able to bear, on behalf of all, trials and sorrows – and he has encountered both – beyond his due share. . . .

No headmaster can ever have been felt by boys to understand them more individually and more compassionately, or to be identified more deeply with themselves, with their struggles and aspirations, with their successes and disasters. Even on the rare occasions when he has chastened them, it has been, as Sir Thomas More said to his own children, 'but with a peacock's feather'.

None of these judgments would have seemed over generous. But among them was another which was over-optimistic. 'The multifarious burdens inseparable from a headmastership have temporarily overtaxed his health. This latter fact can be mentioned with propriety, since in his case suffering and travail have served, at the deepest level, to strengthen the strong and yet further to purify the pure in heart.' Pure in heart he was, but not in that sense strong. He had begun to lose faith in himself – and not only in himself.

He often recalled a question put by a bright young thing to Leeson. 'And how do you like being headmaster of Winchester, Mr Leeson?' 'Madam,' was the grave reply, 'how will you like the day of judgement?' On himself he passed the verdict in a sermon which he preached about one of his favourite books, the *Rule* of St Benedict.

> Throughout St Benedict's book there rings the phrase, like the tolling of a bell, *In tremendo iudicio facienda erit discussio*, i.e. the Abbot must answer for it. . . . The task of human leadership is to work with the magnificent best in human nature, and in so far as the abbot fails in this supreme task, he is committing the unforgivable sin.

There was much, in retrospect, to be put on the other side. He put it in another sermon, addressed to those leaving, probably at the end of his own last term.

> I am reminded of one of my favourite Elizabethan poems – I

wonder how many of you know it – the ballad from one version
of which Ophelia sings a line or two in her last scene. It is a love
ballad written by a man who is past the savage desires and the
intolerable longings of youth and is looking back gravely and
wistfully:

> I have loved her all my youth
> But now old as you see
> Love likes not the falling fruit
> From the withered tree.

But almost instantly he turns upon himself and exclaims what all of
us know and experience to be the truth.

> But true love is a durable fire
> In the mind ever burning;
> Never sick, never old, never dead
> From itself never turning.

Perhaps I may translate this to you who are leaving in terms of our
personal experience. Of course you have all had from time to time a
shower of brickbats at your heads from this place. One of the features of venerable institutions is that brickbats fall off – fly off – so
easily. Headmasters never tell secrets. But it is a fair guess that even
headmasters get a brickbat now and again. Perhaps it is a fair guess,
too, that they deserve theirs as well as you do yours.

But these are not things that matter, one slightest iota, at the end of
the day. What matters is the immense kindness that we have had,
from those who look after the school's destinies on the one hand, to
the smallest man in Junior Part [the Lower Fourth] on the other – not
forgetting those hundreds of others who serve this place in different
ways and whose lives are linked with it far more permanently than
yours or mine – those things are the 'durable fire in the mind ever
burning'. And when you think of all that I expect you feel as I do:

> time as long again
> Would be filled out, my brother, with our thanks,
> And yet we should for perpetuity
> Go hence in debt.

And when he came to look back near the end of his life, he wrote
that 'Winchester (if one may be sentimental) had become a part of my
soul as no other place is ever likely to be.'

7

Lincoln and Oxford

1954–1972

The Lincoln to which Oakeshott moved in April 1954 must have seemed, after the storms of his last two years at Winchester, close to 'heaven-haven'. His friends had hoped for a bigger college for him, but he never wavered in his belief that 'where colleges are concerned, small is beautiful'. The buildings were old enough to be interesting, and neatly concentrated, the Rector's Lodgings altogether more manageable. The salary was not princely but convenient. At one fell swoop he was free from Warden and Fellows above him and from housemasters with disciplinary anxieties below him.

Moreover the job-description seemed made to measure. His predecessor, Keith Murray, had held the college together in the postwar years by combining the office of Rector with the functions of bursar and tutor for admissions; he also, unlike the previous Rectors, presided over the Common Room. When he left to be the first Chairman of the University Grants Committee, the Fellows resolved to look for a successor who should be a scholar rather than an administrator. Having then made the preliminary decision not to elect the sub-Rector, Harold Cox, an astringent philosopher who was 'more suited to the role of critic than Head of House', they looked round further. Their first choice was Florey, the discoverer of penicillin; but he wanted to retain his Chair, which they felt to be incompatible with the duties of Rector.

At this point Vivian Green, the Chaplain and himself a future Rector, decided to 'thumb through *Who's Who*'. There he lit upon Oakeshott, who immediately looked like a scholar. A few soundings revealed a further merit in him, 'a lack of apparently headmasterly characteristics'. Cox went down to see him at Winchester. Years later Oakeshott told the story.

Harold had a profound belief (his only belief, was it?) in the importance of truth. He began by telling me that unfortunately the College's first choice had turned it down. He went on to explain that the one thing the College was looking for in a Rector, was that he should not interfere in the College's affairs.

Both men were more than satisfied, and Oakeshott's election was unanimous. 'Even Sir John Beazley,' wrote Green, 'who because of his deafness normally remained silent, humming quietly to himself in Greek, signified his assent.'

Non-interference had of course long been Oakeshott's forte. To some extent it was temperamental, born of a fear of upsetting people. To some extent it was a consequence of his 'diversity of gifts'. As Chitty once put it, 'The trouble with Walter is that he tries to do too many things.' But now it was a matter of necessity. Ever since 1931, if not earlier, he had been grossly overworking, and his health had suffered. The increasing frequency of his prolonged psychosomatic episodes tells the story: 1927–8, 1937, 1944, 1949, 1953–4. He was now only just fifty, but he had got to slow down. Lincoln was just what the doctor ordered. He never had another episode.

Noel too for a time had a new lease of life. After her first reconnaissance of the Lodgings in 1953, her verdict was that 'the rooms all seemed pleasant and sunny'. Not that her critical faculties were dormant. 'I decided all his curtains etc. were just *awful*,' she wrote to Walter, 'but I *may* even so offer for the harmless blue set, to save trouble and not for a room *you'll* use. I feel it will all be too much for me if I must get new for every room.' But she could tease. 'I do implore you to spend on cheering up pantry, upstairs passages and bedrooms, rather than painting the dining-room a slightly different shade of green. . . . I thought you could have some of your books in the *hall*. Plenty of room. Also, if desired, I can offer a site for your vast glass-fronted book-case in the drawing-room – which I think is rather a good offer!'

But in the grim January of 1954, when Walter was in Wales and she had just had a large children's party, her tone was again plaintive.

I think we must somehow organize a simpler life at Lincoln – but with a family it never can be easy. More efficient and simpler heating and hot-water arrangements would help. A few parties are essential to life, but I don't mean ever to have one like this again. I should like not to be too tired most of the time, and able to think about vases a bit.

It was really as well that she still had the children to care for. Helena had now come down from St Anne's, but the twins were just finishing their national service and were due to read Mods and Greats, Robert at Balliol and Evelyn at Corpus;* and Rose was at boarding school near Reading. There was no longer Copse Stile as a bolt-hole, the tenancy having been ended in 1951. Nevertheless there was still the Bell House for the holidays, and the lodgings at Lincoln were more like a family home than the Winchester house had been.

Not that the Lodgings ever became cosy: that was not Noel's style. She had clear ideas on how things should be done, and spent a great deal of time in a vain search for the servants (as she always called them) needed to keep up the standards. Dinner parties were formal but, since Walter could always entertain in Hall, infrequent. Her conception of the house is revealed in a story of Maurice Keen's. When he had got his First at Balliol and was telling them of his trouble in finding digs for his D.Phil., Walter suggested to Noel that they could let him have one of the empty rooms at the top of the lodgings. Noel considered the idea. 'All right,' she said, 'provided he uses the servants' staircase.' 'I tell you what,' said Walter with a twinkle supposing we took it in turns to use the front stairs: *we* could have them one day, and Maurice the next.' She conceded defeat.

She did however have her vases, and a circle of friends to go with them. The Oxford Chair of Classical Art and Archaeology is based in Lincoln. Beazley retired from it in 1956, but kept a room in the Ashmolean. He remained her friend and mentor, as she kept up with her original field of South Italian vases. Beazley's successor was Bernard Ashmole[1] who, with his wife, was an old friend of hers from Rome. Ashmole in turn was succeeded in 1961 by Martin Robertson. He too respected her work and became a friend.

For Walter also the move to Lincoln meant the resumption of old friendships. Roger Mynors was in 1954 officially away in Cambridge as Professor of Latin, but he was often back in Oxford, and in 1956 returned to take up the Corpus Chair. Hugh Keen had also come back to Oxford as Curator of the University Chest, i.e. Treasurer, and lost no time in getting Oakeshott on to sub-committees of the Chest responsible for buildings. Most fruitful for his own scholarship was a galaxy, centred on the Bodleian Library, of experts in medieval manuscripts. Three of them were already warm friends:

*The fish-van (p. 143) was put at the disposal of the twins in 1954, but died in 1955, and was not replaced.

Richard Hunt, Neil Ker and Otto Pächt. The rest quickly became so.

But the Rector's first duty was to his College. Here it soon transpired that his role was going to be even more circumscribed than at Winchester. He presided as host in Hall and as chairman at college meetings – though he rarely pressed a view of his own, except over aesthetic matters. He attended Chapel without fail, though he never preached. Otherwise he kept his distance from the Senior Common Room. Cox had made it clear that the Rector was a member of it by privilege, not by right, and he accepted this ruling with an embarrassed scrupulousness. After Hall, he would normally return to the Lodgings, leaving Cox to hold court. A junior Fellow remembers reading a magazine there in mid-afternoon when he heard a knock and saw the Rector's head appear round the door. Expecting a reproof for idleness, he was offered an apology for intrusion.

Morning coffee in the Old Smoking Room was an occasion when the Fellows liked to discuss college business. Oakeshott never went in to it unless invited. He told a senior member[2] that 'he felt unwelcome there, at such gatherings of Fellows'. When he handed over the Rectorship to Trend, the only advice he proffered was to go in to morning coffee – 'Don't make my mistake.' Trend did follow this particular recommendation, but still found the general position difficult. 'I was looking forward very much to coming back to Oxford, but the Fellows are always quarrelling, and I never know what about.'[3] It was still in 1972 a small Common Room. In 1954 it was even smaller, with only seven Fellows, and correspondingly inward-looking.

The chief thorn in Oakesott's flesh was Cox. Cynical and acerbic, he dominated the Common Room like 'a kind of bad fairy, whose corrosive scorn taught the younger Fellows high standards of negative criticism, and irreparably damaged his peers'. After an initial 'honeymoon', he took to criticizing Oakeshott to his face for indecisive handling of college business, and behind his back for 'not earning his keep'. With an effort, one may detect a note of suppressed affection in Cox's complaint: 'The trouble with Walter is that you can't find anything against him, except that he is a Christian.' Oakeshott in turn, when he came to write an appreciation of Cox for *The Times* after his death in 1974, managed to praise the 'dry sardonic wit that made listening to him an extraordinary pleasure'.*

---

*Or was it praise? 'He was surprisingly good at making statements which were true but which were nuanced so as to say also the exact opposite of what they said, which was also true.' (Michael Furmston, Fellow.)

The rest of the Fellows, almost without exception, were affectionately disposed towards their Rector – more, perhaps, than to either his predecessor or his successor. They might at times be exasperated by his vagueness in matters of business. Some of them might find him remote. All recognized his deep goodness and kindness, but only a few felt close to him. One who did not wrote thus. 'He was, I think, intensely private, shy, patrician, "other". In conversation one somehow felt he was only half attending, the other half hearing music audible only to Walter; but one had no doubt it was good music, well worth attention.'[4]

The contrast with St Paul's and Winchester is marked. In all his schools staff and pupils would readily say they loved him. The same was true of the University outside Lincoln and of the Skinners' Company. In Lincoln the word was very rarely used. Yet it seemed that his emotional nature needed this constant reassurance of love. Without its warmth the petals remained half-open.

Of the friends he had in the college, most shared his interests in literature and the arts. One of them, Donald Whitton, notes

> the importance for him of his Viennese art-historical friends, with the Welleszes standing as the paradigm of a culture where a Balliol man could feel comfortable without ever needing to feel at home. Not the least of his services to European culture is the welcome he obtained for these exiles from Middle Europe. His charm lay in the unaffected way in which he seemed to assume that you belonged and felt equally comfortable in his world.

Whitton goes on to observe that

> the courtesy also came out in self-deprecating mannerisms of speech. It was necessary to remind yourself to translate: *One does most awfully feel* meant 'I very much hope and indeed require'; *One had rather thought that* meant 'You are quite mistaken; the opposite of what you say is true'; *One wondered if perhaps* meant 'I have been thinking about this for a long time and have made up my mind'. The climax of this idiom came one day when (referring to Robert) he mentioned 'one's sort of son'.

Idiosyncrasies of speech can of course irritate as well as endear. Acts of kindness and generosity are univocal. They are attested of him by people of all kinds – new and emeritus Fellows, undergraduates and secretaries, the College boatman and the window-cleaner – and they are remembered as 'very thoughtful for so absent-minded a man'.

It was especially sad that he got to know so few undergraduates at Lincoln. In his first year or so he acted as tutor for admissions, and also did a little teaching. Thereafter he gradually withdrew except for special interests or occasions. Musical undergraduates would be invited in for an evening in the drawing room, where 'even the moderately competent were encouraged to perform'. When he organized an exhibition of Blake etchings in the library, and found a man interested, he asked him home to lunch. For another group of enthusiasts he got out some of the College's manuscripts, gave an enthralling talk on how to handle them, and demonstrated the use of ultra violet light to bring up erasures in manuscripts or Greek vases. For such men a meeting with him could still be a source of lifelong inspiration. But for most undergraduates he remained a remote figure.

> At end-of-term Collections he would not recognize most of the faces, and indeed was usually too busy trying to find the right line of his notebook and decipher his own writing to have much leisure to replace his glasses and look up at them. A Tutor would report 'Well, Rector, Mr Bloggs has frankly been slacking, and playing too much rugger, which is intolerable in one so naturally stupid'; and Walter would give a dry little cough and say 'Well, Mr Bloggs, reading between the lines, that seems a most creditable performance. Are you going anywhere interesting for the summer? Splendid. The stained-glass in the Cathedral is marvellous, do you know it?' And the blameless Moggs, coming next, would get a kick in the backside designed for Bloggs. [Whitton]

The greatest change that came over Lincoln during his Rectorship was an increase in size. The number of Fellows rose, partly through his initiative, from seven in 1954 to eighteen in 1972; the increment included the first engineering Fellow in 1964, quite a rarity in Oxford at the time. The number of undergraduate and graduate students grew almost as fast, most sharply in 1969 when the lease of the nearby Mitre Hotel, a college property, fell in. The new tenants wished to retain only the ground-floor reception rooms, and were happy to release the bedrooms. At one blow the number of undergraduate rooms was doubled. In 1953 there had been 70; by 1971 there were 183, which meant that every undergraduate could have two years in college.

The increase in numbers required an improvement in central accommodation. 1958 saw the creation of the first Middle Common Room (i.e. for graduate students) in an Oxford college, and the complete refurbishment of the grandest SCR reception room, known as the Beckington Room. Oakeshott's hand in the latter is visible in a large segmented horseshoe-shaped table, which he designed; in the liberal use of gilding for the ornamental swags; and in the design by his friend Reynolds Stone for a decorative motif on a new set of blue leather chairs.

All this expansion – including the Fellowships – required money. At the start of Oakeshott's Rectorship, the cautious policies of Murray were in force; and the alliance between Cox and George Laws, the Bursar, ensured their continuance for a while. Gradually however the arrival of younger Fellows and a change in the economic climate began to loosen things up. As the younger men saw it, Oakeshott was in favour of expansion and of a more adventurous investment policy, but was thwarted by the old guard. Eventually however Laws's prudence paid off. One of his farms, bought in the 1960s for £60,000, was sold ten years later for £800,000. Everyone could now have what they wanted.

Not that Oakeshott was just a spender. He was also, as he had been at Winchester, a fund-raiser and a giver; and when conservation required it, he rolled up his sleeves and worked himself. Thus he is remembered up a ladder in the front quad with bucket and wax, cleaning the bust of John Wesley, the College's best known former Fellow; and when it came to transferring the older and more precious books from the old to the new library, he carried many of them himself in heavy wicker baskets.

His own gifts were numerous. One of the Senior Common Rooms is still illuminated by two chandeliers given him as a leaving present from St Paul's. To the old senior library, later renamed the Oakeshott Room, he presented a set of medallions of sixteenth-century Flemish glass, so-called 'silver stain' roundels,[5] designed to decorate windows in secular buildings. He had collected them over the years with the help of his friend Dennis King of Norwich as 'the only form of medieval glass which the amateur can occasionally find'.

In raising money for the college he was ready to swallow his scruples. His skill in negotiating a grant from the Central Electricity Generating Board enabled the appointment in 1966 of a second engineering Fellow. The Board wanted some land which was part of a college farm. David Spence, the first such Fellow, recalls 'Walter, at a lunch with the Board's land agent, lamenting with a break in his voice the loss of "our nest egg".' 'At that rate', he comments, 'we had quite a few nest-eggs.' Later Oakeshott devoted much time to securing a legacy for the college from a Mrs Montgomery, the eccentric Irish-American widow of a lecturer who had died in 1936. The Fellows had inflated hopes of a legacy in millions, and Oakeshott took it upon himself to keep her sweet. Whenever she came to Oxford she would visit various properties she owned, including 'a small wood on Shotover Hill in which – so she believed – fairies lived. Oakeshott and Laws would accompany her to the wood and they would cast about for traces of the fairies. I like to think', concludes Ball, 'of the fastidious Walter suppressing his distaste for bunkum in the long-term interests of Lincoln.'

Between 1957 and 1965 the College received grants for the fabric from the Oxford Historic Buildings Trust. Oakeshott himself played a considerable part in the establishing of that Trust, which raised altogether £2.4 m. The wider story of it is told elsewhere. Here it is appropriate to record his part in the work which the Trust made possible in Lincoln.

The grant made was £25,000; the college spent a further £21,000 of its own. Most of this went on the repair and refacing of exterior masonry, all done in the best Clipsham stone. Of interior work, the chief beneficiary was the Chapel.[6] In this, as at Winchester, Oakeshott took a particular interest. First the ceiling, which had fallen into dangerous disrepair, was renovated in oak; the heraldic devices and swags were cleaned and re-gilded, and painted where necessary. The pew fronts were cleaned to reveal the original pear-wood marquetry. He personally designed new lighting for the stalls: a set of two-branched brass chandeliers on Ionic oak colonnettes. Finally in 1965 the east window was removed to Dennis King's workshop in Norwich, where the seventeenth-century glass was cleaned and re-leaded, and all mullions and traceries replaced in Clipsham stone.

Two other college projects were dear to his heart. The first was the Shuffrey lectures. When a legacy from an old member was received in 1958, Oakeshott persuaded the Fellows to devote part of the income to a series of university lectures, to be given by distinguished visitors in the Ashmolean Museum, on an artistic subject. The series was inaugurated in 1960 by the Italian architect Professor Pier Nervi, who spoke on 'Structure and Form in Architecture'. For the second in 1962 he invited Henry Moore. Moore agreed to come and meet people, provided that his old friend Kenneth Clark came too, and that instead of a lecture they discussed his works and his methods. In Oakeshott's judgment, 'the result, without the slightest breath of affectation in either party, was superb'. Moore also lent a number of his sculptures and drawings for an exhibition in the Ashmolean; there were two days of festivities in the Lodgings; and the whole programme proved a resounding success. After it Moore was offered and accepted an honorary Fellowship. A third Shuffrey lecture was given in 1965 by J. B. Ward-Perkins, former Director of the British School at Rome, after which the Shuffrey legacy was shifted to other purposes.

The second project was that which is generally regarded as his greatest contribution to the College, the acquisition at the end of his Rectorship of All Saints Church and its conversion into a magnificent library. The story is told later, but it may be noted here as the coping stone of his achievement at Lincoln. For it was Oakeshott's work on the fabric that symbolizes and embodies his deepest impact on Lincoln. The War had left a legacy of utility, even dowdiness. By contrast Oakeshott's passion for fine buildings, fine rooms and fine furnishings raised the sights of his colleagues and exerted a deep, if unconscious, influence upon all those who lived among them. In Whitton's words, 'the fact that he was an aesthete as well as a scholar meant that we did not just get pedantry (or "productivity" for that matter) proposed as a model'.* The old Platonic equation of beauty with truth and goodness had not lost its ability to inspire.

In the last resort scholarship was what the Fellows of Lincoln wanted from their new Rector. So now for the first time in his life duty and pleasure could be combined in research, writing and (given his field) European travel. Since the publication of his *Sequence of English Medieval Art* in 1950 he had been extending his range of concern both in time and space. At Winchester only the summer holidays were available for travel, but he had got to France every August from 1951 onwards, visiting and revisiting cathedrals and churches, museums and libraries. More and more he found himself interested in classical influences on European medieval art. When he was invited in 1953 to

*Ball remembers that 'he once revised something I had written, and showed me in one swift devastating lesson how to use words sparingly'.

give the Rhind Lectures for 1956 to the Edinburgh Society of Anti-quaries, he decided to take that for his subject.

The first principle of all his work was autopsy. He 'preferred to spend the time available in looking at the objects themselves rather than studying books and articles about them'. One consequence was that he had to restrict the geographical area he considered. He got to Aachen but not to Berlin or Vienna; to Toulouse but not to Madrid; to Ravenna but not to Istanbul.

Within his area – roughly that of the Carolingian Empire – he covered a surprising amount of ground. Generally he used public transport. Once he took the fish-van with two of the children, but his driving proved alarming, at least to them, and the experience was not repeated. Occasionally another relative or friend joined him, but most of the time he travelled alone. Noel never came – as a linguist she enjoyed *being* abroad but the travelling was physically too much for her – so the biographer can follow his path through the letters they exchanged.

For example at St Denis near Paris, the home of the great Abbot Suger, one can see him at work. Wanting to get a close look at an early window in the apse, he had 'succeeded in detaching [him]self from the guide and lurking in the shadows while two parties went by'. The window 'turns out to be of exceptional interest. Three or four of the roundels in it are so close to drawings in a British Museum manuscript that I almost think it may be possible, for once, to claim that the same man did the cartoons for the window. But that depends on getting a good photograph.'

At times the privacy of a letter emboldened him further. Of the sculpture at Conques he wrote this.

> What really struck me about it, seeing it in the flesh, was how *un*sophisticated, in a sort of way, it is. Many of the great XIIth century sculptures, whether one likes them or not, are obviously considerable in any company. I *don't* feel like that about Conques. It strikes me almost as being (how horrified the experts would be to hear me say this) in a sense *peasant* art.

So when it came to the point he did not say it.

The six Rhind Lectures were given in the autumn of 1956. They were published in book form by Chapman and Hall in 1960 under the title of *Classical Inspiration in Medieval Art*. The book maintains the format of the slide-lecture. Half of it consists of illustrations, in black and white. The text is ordered chronologically. It begins with a chapter on 'Classical Origins'; then follow one each on the Northumbrian, Carolingian and Ottonian Renaissances, and two on the Twelfth-Century Renaissance.

Acknowledgements in the preface begin with Saxl, to whom 'I owe, as I owe so much else, my interest in the classical tradition as it reappears in medieval art'. He acknowledges also the 'inspiration' of Beazley and the help in various ways of Ashmole, Mynors and Whitton. Finally 'many of my former pupils are responsible for ideas which I have used. . . . I wish it were possible for me to express something of what I owe to them' – a note of nostalgia for his pupils at St Paul's and Winchester.

Of all his books this received the least favourable notices. Even so well-disposed a reviewer as Joan Evans, herself also a pupil of Beazley, found many of the suggested classical influences far-fetched. She commended the book for having 'the "attack" that we admire in violinists', but complained of 'scanty footnotes, no bibliography and no index'. All had a field day pointing out mistakes. For example a ninth-century bible is described on p. 49 as the Bible of Charles the Fat, but on p. 52 as the Bible of Charles the Bald.

That was fair enough. But two American scholars adopted an altogether more savage tone. One of them, the anonymous reviewer[7] for the *TLS*, was clearly nettled by Oakeshott's occasional claim that existing research was defective: in saying so, he merely revealed his own ignorance of it. From defence she then moved to attack.

> Reliable and wide knowledge of the relevant material and literature and ability to marshal these to a purpose by the methods of critical selection, coherent reasoning and consistent documentation are the equipment anyone can be expected to acquire. Dr Oakeshott apparently felt free to dispense with such working standards.

That went well beyond the normal scholarly conventions, even in the days of anonymous reviews. Oakeshott was deeply hurt. His friends, looking back in a longer perspective, can help to redress the balance. In Charles Mitchell's view, the field was of such scope as to need a team of professionals from the Warburg Institute: failing such a team the world of scholarship should not carp but commend the courage of an amateur in tackling it. And a seasoned Professor of the History of Art, Michael Kauffmann, still after forty years recommends the book to his students ('though with a health warning') as a valuable introduction to an important subject.

The hurt remained wih Oakeshott for many years. But there was a little balm to come. It was applied by a young Cypriot in 1969. Oakeshott told the story in a letter to J. B. Owen from Famagusta.

> My ego has had an unprecedented injection of vitality. Visiting a remote monastery in the mountains, miles from anywhere, I found, inside, a maze of scaffolding, with a notice 'no visitors allowed on the scaffolding' and apparently no one there. So I went out, found a man nearby, and asked him if I might go up. He did not reply, but took me back into the church and shouted in Greek to someone evidently up in the dome, working. There was a pretty explicit 'no' in Greek from above. But being persistent, I shouted up, ANGLICE, 'I'm quite good on scaffolding and am v. much interested in wall-paintings. May I come up?' Permission was given with some muttering. When I got up there, an admirable young man introduced himself. 'And mine's Oakeshott', I said. 'What, not the man who wrote the book about classical inspiration?' he said. 'Why I've got a chapter of it in photostat up here and am working on it.'

The letter concludes with some deprecating comments whose extravagance betrays both the bitterness of the old hurt and the sweetness of the new balm.

> Of course you have experienced these simple pleasures so often (you are THE Dr Owen) that you won't understand. I am occasionally 'Oh you must be the father of Robert'. But that's the nearest I get. So this, in that remote corner, warmed me to Cyprus. (Even in the Nicosia Museum, incidentally, the person they *really* wanted to see was Noel, and I am trying to organize a visit for her to catalogue some of the vases.)

Between the giving of the Rhind Lectures in 1956 and their publication in 1960 Oakeshott had been warming a number of irons in the fire. One was recreational, in the sense that it never led to a publication, at least not of his own. In the Augusts of 1958 and 1959 (and again in 1961) he accepted an invitation to lecture on a Swan Hellenic Cruise. Judging the audience to be 'embarrassingly learned, and passionately eager for further instruction', he was determined not to talk down to them. Certainly those who were so disposed appreciated his own special contributions: a critique of (Roman) commercialization of (Greek) art; or his explanation, on the Acropolis of Athens, that the religious building there was the Erechtheum, with the Parthenon intended rather to make a political statement.

On the rarely visited island of Cythera, he was down to lecture at the museum. By courtesy of the only taxi, he got to it twenty before the passengers, to find a scene like a jumble sale, with the exhibits neither sorted nor labelled. In that time he chose eight objects worthy of attention, ranging in date from prehistoric to modern times, and spoke of each with knowledge and appreciation. It was a *tour de force*, of which very few other scholars would have been capable. But to Noel he wrote that 'none of it was labelled so that I reckoned there was quite a useful job to do taking round people who knew even less than one did oneself.'

On one cruise he got up to the Acropolis in full moon, when the authorities had been wise enough not to turn the floodlights on. 'The moonlight was so bright that the stone glowed with it: a sort of ethereal echo of the honey and pink and white which it is in daylight. It made one feel that the monuments had been built simply with the lighting of the full moon in mind.'

He also kept his eyes skinned in Greek museums for vases of the kind that Noel was currently working on, viz. protogeometric, with horned handles (p. 278). Where he found them, he sent sketches and (if Rose was with him, as sometimes) photographs. At Athens he went 'round a Museum with your *quaestiones*, and here are the answers'. Noel was delighted, and hurried off to the Ashmolean to check his finds against the published material.

A second pursuit during the years 1956–60 was the old passion for maps. In addition to the three which had first caught his fancy at Winchester, he had in about 1935 bought in Blackwell's an important cartographical book of 1532. Entitled *Novus Orbis*, the book is a collection of accounts of travels and discoveries in the New World, illustrated by maps. One of these, a map of the world, proved to be of especial interest.

In 1957 friends and admirers of Saxl put together a memorial volume in his honour. Oakeshott contributed an article entitled 'Some Classical and Medieval Ideas in Renaissance Cosmography', based on these four maps and featuring especially the one from *Novus Orbis*. The map itself is Ptolemaic, i.e. it portrays the earth as a sphere, with lines of latitude and longitude marked on it, all in a pre-Mercator projection. Round the sphere are various illustrations, probably by Holbein. Among them Oakeshott observed, at the top and bottom of the sphere, two angels *turning it by handles*. This idea, that the earth revolves on its axis, had been mooted in antiquity but was rejected by Ptolemy. In Renaissance Europe it was first given currency by Copernicus's epoch-making *De Revolutionibus Orbium* in 1543. Yet here it was in print, not in words but in Holbein's witty illustration, at least twelve years before Copernicus. This small but worthy offering Oakeshott made to the memory of his friend and mentor, the 'saint' Fritz Saxl.

Another project which had associations with Saxl was a series of books entitled the Faber Library of Illuminated Manuscripts, of which Oakeshott was general editor. Mooted in 1944, the idea had held fire for various reasons. But in the interim there had been advances in colour photography which turned the delay to advantage. The Library was launched in 1959 with six titles. Mynors and Kenneth Clark had both declined to take on a volume, but the six were a strong team, all of them personal friends: Wormald, Millar, Dodwell, Porcher, Emmy Wellesz and Mitchell. Later, other titles were added, the last being *The York Psalter* by Boase in 1962.

Some time about 1959 Oakeshott made another of his remarkable discoveries. A friend in Kent drew his attention to a forthcoming sale in a country house which contained some books likely to interest him. The sale itself was to be on the first day of term, which ruled it out for him; but he could get to the view. Among the books one especially caught his eye. It was a copy of Pierre d'Ailly's *Imago Mundi* of 1483. He knew that it was a rare book, though not till later did he learn *how* rare. He also knew what he maintained 'everybody knows', that Columbus took a copy of it with him on his great voyage. But what caught his eye were a few marginal notes in what he could now be sure was Raleigh's hand. He asked the friend to bid for him, naming a maximum price, and set off back to Oxford. But the more he thought about it in the train the more pusillanimous he seemed to be. At Charing Cross he sent off a wire 'Half as much again'. There was opposition at the bidding. But he won.

His first concern was bibliographical. He no longer had Raleigh's library list, but he knew where to find it. Sure enough, there it was: the book was Raleigh's own copy, which he had had with him in the Tower and annotated. One of the notes excited Oakeshott particularly. D'Ailly's Latin text says 'that the earth is divided into three parts, namely Asia, Africa and Europe'. Raleigh had added the discovery of a fourth part: 'Nunc et quarta pars terrae inventa est, scilicet America.' Writing up his find in the *Book Collector*, Oakeshott commented 'It is a momentary flash of Raleigh's vision of the importance of America.'

The book proved also to be of interest in Renaissance cartography. Although not published until 1483, it had been finished in 1410. That made it, by some years, 'the first geographical work in Western Europe to be deeply influenced by the *Geography* of Ptolemy, and to assimilate both his technique of map production and also some of his data of latitude and longitude'. *Imago Mundi* had filled a gap in the history of Renaissance maps.

In 1960 he commissioned a fine book in the same general field of travel and exploration. As a member of the Roxburghe Club,* it was incumbent upon him to present each member with a bibliographical rarity published at his own expense. For his own contribution he chose a series of woodcuts in the possession of Lincoln College, though for one of the series he used his own copy, 'since it happened to provide a better impression of the original'.

The woodcuts had been printed as an Appendix to a book of 1618, but he was able to show that they were originally prepared to illustrate an earlier book of 1508, entitled *A Voyage to the Orient*, and that they are the work of Hans Burgkmair, a noted German engraver. His introduction draws attention to the liveliness and at the same time the accuracy of the series, which 'has claim to be the first serious study of native life and dress made for publication in a European travel book'. The volume was superbly printed and produced for him by the Oxford University Press.[8]

But the main focus of his scholarship in the years after 1956 was the work that led to the publication in 1960 of *The Queen and the Poet*. The work sprang from the manuscript poem beginning 'Now we have present made / to Cynthia', which he had discovered on the flyleaf at the end of Raleigh's notebook. After he had sold the book in 1953, its new owners, the brothers Philip and Lionel Robinson, generously made it available to him for continuing study.[9] And their generosity did not stop there. In 1958 Philip Robinson, being himself a scholar as well as a bibliophile, and realizing that another

*'The only club I belong to, of book collectors, has a very small and snobbish membership mainly of Earls with fine libraries, but also a few "poor scholars", as the founders of schools and colleges used to call us, tagged on at the end.'

manuscript in his possession contained a poem with Raleigh connexions, drew Oakeshott's attention to it. When Oakeshott established Raleigh's authorship, Robinson allowed him first publication of it. It became no. 10 of the 'poems to Cynthia' which form the second half of *The Queen and the Poet*.

The first half of the book deals with Raleigh's stormy relationship with Elizabeth from 1580 to 1597. The second consists of text and commentary of twenty-seven poems which Oakeshott regarded as 'poems to Cynthia', i.e. from Raleigh to the Queen. Of these, he placed last the poem from the notebook, as an epilogue to the collection. The text of it he established from two sources. Chief was his 'own' autograph, first published in 1953. But he had now also a manuscript with musical setting in the library of St Michael's College, Tenbury, to which his attention had been drawn late in 1953. Collating them, he printed a text in *The Queen and the Poet* p. 205 f. In old age he wrote in shame that the transcriptions from the mss. were 'deplorably inaccurate': 'owing to a mistake for which one must obviously take responsibility, some of the proofs were not corrected.'

As to the original context of the poem, the musical setting suggests it may have been an entertainment in honour of the Queen. The tone of the poem indicates a late date, some years after the rest of the collection: it 'represented his feelings, as it were "all passion spent"'. Its presence in the commonplace book suggests that he wrote it out again after her death, when he began his *History of the World*, just as he did later with another of his poems on the night before his own execution.

Hypotheses like these account for both the strengths and the weaknesses of the book. It was not, as he points out in the preface, in his own specialist field. For that reason, he had prudently consulted the best English scholars in Oxford at the time, such as Dover Wilson, C. S. Lewis and his Lincoln colleague W. W. Robson. For that same reason, perhaps, he had felt freer to speculate. Perhaps also the tradition of scholarly writing in literature and history is more unbuttoned than in art. At any rate, *The Queen and the Poet* has the liveliness of *Founded upon the Seas*, which the Rhind Lectures do not.

Reviewers were pleased with it. It was correctly seen by *The Times* as 'a detective story, a tale of courtly rivalry and intrigue, a psychological portrait of passion and ambition . . . full of formidable conjecture'. A. L. Rowse in the *Daily Telegraph*, himself not averse from speculation, called it 'a prime contribution to our knowledge of Elizabethan literature'. A more demanding reviewer in the *TLS* had reservations. Oakeshott's ascription to Raleigh of the highly erotic poem 'Would I were changed into that golden shower', which is 'central to the story he has to tell, [is] no very strong peg on which to hang a weighty argument'. But even the *TLS* echoed the two commonest epithets of other reviewers: 'exciting' and 'fascinating'. The book remains extremely readable, and its 'overall contention has held ... that Raleigh as a courtier poet wrote for occasions, [not] as a pastime of pleasure'.[10]

Heads of Houses (i.e., colleges etc) at Oxford are free to choose what part, if any, they will play in university affairs. Oakeshott's priorities in these matters were the same, *mutatis mutandis*, as they had been at Winchester. In the university curriculum, for example, he took little interest, though he supported the young subject of engineering and the proposals for a new school of 'European Greats'. But he was still concerned about the impact of universities on school work. He applauded the ICI Transfer Scholarships, which were designed to enable sixth form arts specialists to switch to science at university. He also raised his voice in favour of a proposal to remove the Latin requirement for entrance to Oxford. His argument was that every year 40,000 children are put though the hoop of O level Latin; 15,000 of them fail, and of those who pass only a few derive any benefit beyond a paper qualification. The rest 'are led up an educational blind alley' for the benefit of Oxford and Cambridge.[11] The issue was debated for years within the University, and from time to time received the attention of a leader or letters in *The Times*. Oakeshott's most effective opponent was (Dame) Helen Gardner, to whom, when she had won a debate in Congregation in 1959, he sent 'a charming letter and a bouquet of roses'. Twelve years later the Latin requirement was finally waived for all applicants.

Of much greater interest to the new Rector of Lincoln were the old buildings of the University. As soon as he arrived in Oxford in 1954, he was recruited by the then Vice-Chancellor, Warden Smith of New College. Smith was devoted to the fabric of Oxford, with a passion which increased in impatience as both he and it grew more old and frail. As Warden of New College he was an *ex-officio* Fellow of Winchester, where he had worked with Oakeshott on the historic buildings. It was therefore natural to seek his help in Oxford.

The most imminent threat was to the Sheldonian Theatre, Wren's first great building, completed in 1669 when he was Professor of Astronomy at Oxford and still in his thirties. By 1954 it was 'not so much a romantic ruin as a shabby travesty of the building Wren had designed'. Worse, its 'decaying stone was a positive danger'. Action had to be taken, and in Smith's book it had to be the right action, viz. as far as possible the restoration of Wren's original. None of Wren's drawings had survived, but Smith asked Oakeshott if he could find any other evidence of the architect's intentions. Sure enough, the original Acquittance [i.e. accounts] Book proved to be in the Bodleian: it contained 'the fascinating account of weekly payments thoughout the scheme'.[12]

In 1954 Oakeshott wrote a paper for the Sheldonian Committee outlining his discoveries. He ends with the comment that it 'does not necessarily imply the advocacy of a return in every detail to Wren's design. Personally my mind is not yet made up on the desirability of this.' In 1956 he expanded the paper in a pair of articles for the *Oxford Magazine*, adding two hopes of his own. Specifically, he would like to see the upper room, which was 'designed as part of the University printing works', now 'restored as a museum of Oxford books, bindings and printings'. Generally, while conceding that restoration must involve 'a compromise between antiquarian accuracy and modern needs', he hoped 'that whatever changes are made, something like the spirit of Wren's original work can be recovered'. That spirit he characterized as brilliant and colourful.

By 1959 much of the exterior work was done and Oakeshott was himself Chairman of the Sheldonian Committee. 'The moral,' he now felt, 'of the startlingly successful restoration of the south front seems to be that the nearer we can get to Wren the better.' A meeting of the Committee in Lincoln in October gave him the chance to press his advantage. Circulating an *aide-mémoire* after it, he added a plea for the use of 'rather more gold than Wren was able to afford. It is known' (from the Acquittance Books) 'that drastic cuts had to be made in many of the plans as the work progressed. Gold leaf may have been one of the casualties.'

The plea for gold was typical of him, and so was the way he handled the aftermath of that *aide-mémoire*. For it turned out that Folliott Sandford, the Registrar, had also circulated a note of the meeting, which made no mention of gold. But Oakeshott had made his point, and could afford to be generous. He wrote to Sandford immediately. 'How much better your note about Saturday is than mine! Why did I not realise that there was no need whatever for me to start interfering in the processes of a great machine? Please accept my apologies'. But he got his gold.

He also had a wider role than that to play. By the 1950s there were buildings all over Oxford in need of urgent repair, and colleges began to appeal for money to do the work. Among the sources to which they turned was the Pilgrim Trust. Oakeshott was a Trustee; Lord Kilmaine, its Secretary, was also Chairman of the Oxford Society; Sir Alan Lascelles, its Chairman, was also Chairman of the Historic Buildings Council for England. It was clear to all three of them that the colleges should get together and that the University should coordinate a single appeal for all the work that needed doing. Smith readily agreed. It was much easier said than done, but in the end it was done; and 'the way in which it was done changed permanently the attitude of the colleges to each other and to the University'.

The appeal for the Oxford Historic Buildings Fund was launched in 1957, and renewed in 1962. It raised altogether £2.4 m, all of which was spent. Oakeshott took on responsibility for writing the interim Reports of the Trustees of the Fund. He produced twelve such Reports in all between 1957 and 1973, and finally edited a comprehensive illustrated record under the title *Oxford Stone Restored*.

Oakeshott's first impact upon the University was made through its buildings, and he soon found himself coopted to the relevant committees. The governance of the University in those days was effectively in the hands of two bodies, each of which had a responsibility for the fabric. The Vice-Chancellor presided over the Hebdomadal Council, a body of twenty-four members (six, including himself, *ex-officio*; the rest elected), which met every Monday in full term. It was serviced by the University's senior permanent official, the Registrar. Council had a committee responsible for Elevations and Choice of Architects and another for Building and Development: together these controlled the planning of new buildings. The University Chest, serviced by its Secretary (currently Oakeshott's old friend Hugh Keen), was responsible for financial administration though not for financial policy. One of its important committees was that for Buildings and Works, i.e. existing buildings and those new ones whose construction had been approved by Council. From 1955 onwards Oakeshott served on those three committees most of the time, and his voice became increasingly influential.

Two of these committees had a special significance for Oakeshott. The Buildings and Works Committee (BWC), like similar committees in other universities, found itself in the mid-1950s the subject of an inquiry by the University Grants Committee. The inquiry, chaired by Sir George Gater, made recommendations, one of which was that such committees should appoint a member from outside the university. For Oxford, 'who better than Gater himself? He was duly appointed in 1957 and served until 1959. In spite of his eminence he could not have been more friendly and helpful.'

So wrote Jack Lankester, the University Surveyor. But he noted with surprise that Oakeshott, who chaired the BWC during that period, 'always seemed nervous of him'. The surprise would have been less to someone who knew the details of 'the Ridgway affair' at Winchester in 1954. That affair had not ended their friendship – Oakeshott's address at Gater's memorial service in 1963 makes that clear – but it had left Oakeshott with a lasting 'regret: the worries that I caused him'. Hence his unease at the BWC.

The Committee on Elevations and Choice of Architects had from the start had happier associations for Oakeshott. Its genesis played an important part, according to him, in 'the process by which one's outlook was changed from that of a school to that of a university'. It was established in 1957 after a démarche by a young colleague of his from Lincoln, who was also Junior Proctor, David Henderson. Henderson wanted to interest Oxford in the work of modern architects, and challenged the hole-and-corner method by which appointments were traditionally made for University buildings. The result was the new committee, of which they were both members. 'Thereafter', said Oakeshott, 'architects for university buildings were chosen, not rubber-stamped.' Howard Colvin, architectural historian of the University, goes further. 'For the next 20 years [the Committee] ensured that the University's architectural patronage was exercised in a more enlightened manner.'

For example, in 1958 the Committee had to choose an architect for the new St Catherine's College. Henderson suggested Arne Jacobsen, but the suggestion found no support until Oakeshott (coming in, as was his wont, late in the discussion) urged that while sending a party to Denmark it would at least be worth looking at some of Jacobsen's work. He argued impartially that 'so much has been said about it by the Young Turks that to have sent a commission over there will in itself be a strong point in favour of whichever architect, Danish or British, is eventually chosen'. The members of the commission, which included Alan Bullock, Censor of St Catherine's, came back much impressed with Jacobsen. Oakeshott wrote in support: 'From the point of view not only of Oxford but of architecture in this country in general, the appointment of a Dane might be a very great influence for good.' In 1959 Jacobsen was appointed. His St Catherine's is widely admired.[13]

It was not long before a weightier responsibility loomed on the horizon, the Vice-Chancellorship. In those days the office was held for two years in rotation among the senior Heads of Houses. It carried influence but no power. In order to get something done the Vice-Chancellor had first to have the support of Council, a body intended to represent a wide range of opinions and ages on the staff of the University. Council could be awkward and unpredictable. Oakeshott, looking back at Smith's Vice-Chancellorship in *Oxford Stone Restored*, said that 'he was chivvied, somewhat unnecessarily perhaps (which is sometimes the Hebdomadal Council's way)'. On many issues the V-C had also to have the agreement of Heads of Houses. Of this problem too Oakeshott wrote with hindsight, having seen it from both sides. 'It was always the main pastime of Oxford colleges to see that the head of the college was well under control. He must beware lest he commit his college in any way, and he tended accordingly to be almost pathologically cautious in university matters.'

Moreover the Vice-Chancellorship entailed a very heavy administrative and diplomatic load. That load was credibly supposed to have shortened the lives of some of its recent holders, who were by definition oldish when their turn came round. The result of all this was that many Heads of Houses did not want to take it on. Most of those who did so were either politically ambitious or unusually dutiful. So it was that Oakeshott's turn came round much earlier than he expected. He had not yet been five years at Lincoln when we find him writing to Noel the following analysis of the situation (January 1959).

'John Christie [Jesus] has resigned from Council and announced that he won't be V-C. I shall try to persuade John Sparrow* [All

*Sparrow was an old friend, as bibliophile and Fellow of Winchester.

Souls] that it is his duty to do it. Apart from that and McCallum [Pembroke] who's also reported to be hesitating, there's no one apparently before me and Thomas Norrington.' (The 'apparently' shows that he was certainly no politician.) 'Let's hope to goodness that Sparrow and McCallum play up.'

At the same time as the Vice-Chancellorship, another, more attractive, post was before him, the Mastership of the Skinners' Company. Having been apprenticed to F. O. Streeten on leaving Tonbridge, he had filled the various offices in the Company's *cursus honorum*, and was now in line for the Mastership in 1960. The post was not without its responsibilities but, compared with the Vice-Chancellorship, the balance of duty and pleasure was reversed. Moreover the easy conviviality of the Company, and the disinterested friendship offered by many of its members, were proving an increasingly attractive consolation for the emotional lukewarmness of Lincoln.

By February 1959 decisions had been made. Neither Sparrow nor McCallum having 'played up', Norrington would become Vice-Chancellor in 1960. He himself 'will accept the Skinners' Mastership in 1960 and reserve the right to become V-C in 1962. A year at Skinners' Hall will really show whether one can stand "public life" any more. It's quite possible I shall be gaga or that in general being V-C would drive me round the bend. But the way is still open for 1962.'

So on the Feast of Corpus Christi in June 1960 he was installed as Master of the Skinners' Company. A story from that day shows his love of music and his ear for it. The proceedings began with a service in St Mary Aldermary sung by a small choir of boys from Tonbridge. The boys had been practising for it, paying special attention to a rather ornate 'Amen' at the end. One of the basses, Paul Thompson, had suggested in practice that he might insert, as the penultimate note, a low D; and the choirmaster had agreed. 'When I sang it at the service, I saw Oakeshott, despite his many other concerns at such a time, react slightly, and look to see which of us it was. Afterwards, over lunch, he sought me out and congratulated me. "Was that a D? Yes, I thought so."' A month later, when the new Master was presenting the prizes at Skinners' Day, Thompson went up to receive a cup. 'As he handed it over to me, Oakeshott beamed: "How's your bottom D?" What a man!'

In September 1960 Oxford turned to him for another aesthetic judgement. A septuagenarian Belgian painter, Georges van Houten, had made an offer to the University a year earlier: he would leave at least half his estate, valued at over £140,000, to the University for scientific and medical research, if it would accept his 300 odd paintings, with a small collection of oriental antiques, and promise to exhibit them from time to time. The Registrar, deputed to meet him, wrote a contemptuous report, influenced perhaps by the news that a similar offer made by van Houten to Cambridge had been turned down. Nevertheless Council agreed in principle to accept the pictures, though with no commitment to any permanent display of them.

The pictures were brought over to England in 1960 and stored in the Harrods repository at Barnes. Council asked Oakeshott to meet van Houten there and inspect his pictures. He recalled the meeting, and what he learned of van Houten's life, in a foreword he wrote to a posthumous exhibition of the paintings in the Ashmolean in 1965.

Georges van Houten came from a successful Belgian family of cocoa manufacturers but left home in 1905 to study painting in Paris. His father cut him out of his will, and for a long time he had to struggle. However his work met with some praise in Parisian salons between c. 1910 and 1930. Then he inherited from an uncle a modest fortune, which made him independent but dried up his creative urge. He ceased to exhibit and persuaded himself that 'some of his contemporaries had conspired to edge him out of his Paris reputation'. Thereafter he gradually came to feel that neither the French nor the Belgians could be trusted, nor any European nation, except (for some reason) the English. Hence his desire to find a resting place in England for his life's work.

Then in 1959 returning home one day he found his wife dead. Since their marriage in 1922 she had been the inspiration, and often the subject, of his paintings. Distraught, he 'rushed down the road to a travel agent's and told the clerk that, if he would pack the contents and despatch them to London, he could have the house'. He himself went to pieces, in body and spirit. His asthma became life-threatening, and he wandered about aimlessly for some months before settling in a hotel in Rome to wait for death.

When Oakeshott met him in October 1960, his

first impression was of a small, thin, birdlike man, fighting for breath, clothes almost dapper, but the hand shaking uncontrollably. . . . In the warehouse, in an atmosphere impregnated by

hessian and dust, were a dozen huge packing-cases. We chose
one. The first thing we saw was cotton wool wrapping in which
he thought his T'ang horse might be packed. He uncovered a
small piece. It contained the head, broken off at the neck. 'My
horse, my horse', he gasped, 'they have broken my horse'; and
he beat his head like some primitive mourner. . . . That first
encounter sums up van Houten as I knew him; frail, proud,
highly-strung, convinced that the world was against him and out
to do him down.

What the foreword does not say is that at that meeting Oakeshott
won his trust. As he put it in a later letter to Noel, 'I doubt if anyone
else would have had the patience to do anything'. In the long run,
everything worked together for good. In the short run, he had to avoid
abusing the trust. How therefore should he report back to Council? On
the pictures he could be objective: 'My own impression is that some of
[them] really may have some quality in them. It would, I think, be
possible to find half a dozen which could reasonably be on permanent
exhibition.' Of van Houten himself: 'As you know, he is subject to
violent asthma, and it will not be surprising if he dies before any
arrangement can be made. . . . May I as a next step invite him down
to Oxford and get him to meet perhaps Keen [n.b. not the Regist-
rar]?' After suggesting various legal and financial arrangements, the
report ends with a comment which reveals his residual qualms. 'On the
human side I think van Houten himself may derive a certain amount of
happiness from what is proposed, and this in itself seems to mean that
the University would not be entirely cynical about it if the matter were
pursued.'

Van Houten paid his first and only visit to Oxford on 5 November
1960. As a result of it he revised his will in such a way as to give the
University absolute discretion on its disposition of the bequest. Council now resolved to accept the gift. The pictures and other antiquities
were brought to Oxford. Apart from the exhibition of 1965, some are
on semi-permanent display on the walls of the new university offices,
where there is also a van Houten Room. A small collection of far
eastern antiquities, including the T'ang horse, is in the Ashmolean.
There the story ends for the University, but not for Oakeshott.

In 1961 he bought a flat in Rome. He had come to regard it as the
most beautiful city in the world, and the flat there was his pride
and joy for the next eight years. The idea had entered his mind at

Easter 1960. He and Noel had been staying with an American biblio-graphical scholar, Milton Waldman, who owned a flat in the via delle Mercede. On the door of the flat above was a sign bearing the ap-petizing word VENDESI. Inquiries were made and negotiations put in hand, with the result that the flat became theirs in May 1961 for some 8m. lire. The cost was met in various ways. Part came from the proceeds of the Bell House, which had been sold in 1954, not very well. He also sold some valuable books, including his Ortelius Atlas, and mortgaged half a life insurance. The rest came from Noel's in-heritance, for she – and the rest of the family – hoped she would enjoy it no less than he. Prudently, they put the property in the names of the children.

It took some months to sort out the necessary documentation: bank account, dollar premium, building permits etc. Sadly during that time Noel's back became much worse, so it was left to the children to help him get it ready for occupation in September 1961. From then on he reckoned to get there at least twice a year, though Noel came rarely. He loved the process of improving and furnishing it so that he could invite family and close friends to stay. Domestic help was readily obtainable, and he enjoyed cooking for his guests as much as he enjoyed taking them out to local restaurants. Other friends were offered free use of the flat in his absence. His pleasure was increased when in 1963 the Keens bought a flat nearby; and then in 1964 Rose and her husband, David Gaunt, came to live and work in Rome, and stayed until 1972.

Rome also brought him into renewed contact with van Houten. The safe bestowal of his pictures in Oxford had cheered the old man's spirits. He was enjoying the ambiance of Rome, old and new, and even planned to start painting again. Regularly Oakeshott would invite him in to the flat for a meal, or they would go out together to a restaurant. Once van Houten insisted on taking him to a nightclub. It was the only time he went to one in his life, and he described it to Noel as 'the dreariest evening IMAGINABLE'. More happily memorable was a dinner at Tivoli in 1963, when they went out à quatre to celebrate the Keens' acquisition of their flat.

Van Houten then dropped a bombshell. He had talked frequently of wanting to leave Oakeshott something in his will, but Oakeshott's scruples would not allow that. Now in 1963 he proposed to leave a substantial legacy to each of the four children. Such a bequest would not be at the expense of the University, which apparently might now expect something nearer to £250,000 as a result of the growth of his estate since 1959–60. Nevertheless Walter, who was by now Vice-Chancellor, discussed with Noel and with the Keens the propriety of accepting. (The children were not consulted, since it was to be a surprise to them). Only Walter saw any substantive problem. It was agreed that he should meet it by 'a statement, in confidence, to Council'.

An earlier letter of his reveals something of their own financial position.

> [van H] assumed, I'm afraid, that we are quite well off, and I am certainly not going to disabuse him; for in a sense – if we can keep the job at Lincoln till we're 70 – we *are*, comparatively speaking. Though I must say my bank balance on the wrong side looks pretty silly at the moment, it really isn't as bad as it looks; with the insurance to be paid later this year.

In fact, now that the children were effectively off their hands, with both boys in work and both girls married, they had only one big expense to look forward to, the acquisition of a retirement home.

But that problem lay ten years in the future when he took up the Vice-Chancellorship in 1962. Already in October 1961 he had, as Vice-Chancellor elect, been sworn in as pro-Vice-Chancellor to Norrington. That apparent sinecure pitched him into a deeply contentious problem which dominated 1962 and made it one of the most eventful years of his life. By half way through , he was so sure that his handling of it had lost public confidence that he thought seriously of withdrawing from the Vice-Chancellorship. By the end of it, he had taken the heat out of the problem and set it on the road to solution. The trauma of mid-summer had become the triumph of mid-winter.

The problem was how to meet the University's long-felt need for a new and larger zoology building. By 1960 plans had been prepared: a building of 94,000 sq. ft, to the design of Mr Peter Chamberlin of Chamberlin, Powell and Bon, had been approved both by the City Council, as planning authority, and by the University Grants Committee as funding body. When a new Professor of Zoology was sought for October 1961, applicants were told that 'it was proposed to make a start on the first stage of the building in 1964'.

On that basis Professor J. W. S. Pringle accepted the Linacre Chair.

But he had been in post only a few weeks when a closer look at the figures revealed a snag. In order to provide the square footage needed, the new building would have to rise higher than on the approved plan – so high as to exceed the maximum height laid down by the City for buildings in what was known as 'the Science Area'. A new site had to be found. But the only site owned by the University contiguous with the Science Area was the University Parks, regarded by many as sacrosanct.

The issue therefore began to widen. Would it not be prudent to locate the new zoology building some way away, where the University had so much land that there need be no territorial limit to the expansion of the sciences? This question, which also raised strong feelings, kept recurring throughout the year; but any alternative location was always defeated by a coalition of those (mostly scientists) who thought science was indivisible and those (mostly non-scientists) who thought it should not expand anyway. Oakeshott himself shared both those views.

The only remaining possibility was for the University to buy part of a Merton College playing field adjacent to the Science Area. But Merton was not willing to sell. It followed that an encroachment on the Parks, however distasteful, must be contemplated. At the end of 1961 Council asked its Committee on Requirements and Sites, of which Oakeshott was a member, to consider the matter. In January the Committee recommended that one acre of the Parks should be taken. On 5 February Council took a vote on the recommendation and found nine for, thirteen against. Nevertheless it agreed unanimously 'to seek the views of Congregation [on 27 February] on the basis of a resolution which indicated that Council itself was divided in its views and did not wish to express an opinion'.

To refer the matter to Congregation – the plenipotentiary body consisting of all senior members of the University – was certainly wise. It was all however a little hasty. Council on 5 February had seen no drawings of the proposed building. All that was known was that it would have to be of unusual dimensions, for what Alan Bullock in retrospect called 'a very Oxford reason'. The Science Area included the University Observatory, where a lady astronomer had been taking readings of the sun's movements. It was accepted, on grounds which owed more to chivalry than to scholarship, that nothing must interfere with her sight-lines. Consequently the new building would have to be either squat or lofty. The question was referred

by Council to the Committee on Elevations and the Choice of Architects, of which Oakeshott was as usual a member.

The Committee met on 8 February. They were clear that lofty was
preferable to squat, and agreed by four votes to two to recommend
the erection of the fourteen-storey tower block which Chamberlin
had calculated to be necessary. Council on 10 February asked Chamberlin to prepare drawings as quickly as possible, so that Congregation could have elevations as well as site plans in time for the 27th. In
the event he did well to get them published by the 20th. They showed
a building 250ft high, 100ft higher than Magdalen Tower. Oakeshott
was asked to propose the resolution in Congregation.

On the Saturday before the debate, Sandford 'drove him to all the
points of view around Oxford – Elsfield, Shotover, Wytham etc. At a
briefing for Council on the Monday I found that on the Sunday
he had done the tour again – on a bicycle.' Strictly speaking, however, Congregation was concerned only with the appropriation of the
site. Norrington being indisposed, the Chair was taken by Kenneth
Wheare, Rector of Exeter, to allow Oakeshott to propose. Leading
for the opposition was Basil Mitchell, a newish member of Council.
In the course of the general debate, Wheare asked Oakeshott to take
over the Chair so that he could speak against: 'If the Parks were to be
sacrificed, the case must be overwhelming, which this was not.' At
the end of the debate Oakeshott gave an undertaking that, if the
motion was carried, 'Congregation would have the opportunity to
consider the proposed development of the site'. With that assurance
those present resolved by 194 votes to 169 'that Council should discuss with the Curators of the Parks and the City Planning Committee
an arrangement under which an area of one acre in the Parks should
be alloted to the Science Area'.

The vote was a surprise. It appeared that the encroachment upon
the Parks had been approved, and that contention would now focus
upon the proposed building. That was certainly how it was seen by
the *Oxford Magazine* an influential but unofficial university publication. The editorial of 8 March opined that 'future generations will
regard with amazement a university which permitted a building twice
as high as Magdalen Tower to be erected in a prominent place without first being entirely satisfied about the architectural merits of the
proposed structure'. The comment was inaccurate – no building had
been 'permitted' – but all the more symptomatic of the warmth of
feeling generated by the whole issue. On a more reasoned note, the

editorial concluded that 'those proposing major changes ought to take Congregation more fully into their confidence'.

The next few months were spent by Council and its committees in polishing the development plan for re-presentation to Congregation, and by the rest of the university in lobbying. This time Council would not rush things. Plans were available to it on 1 May and a model on 4 June. As the model showed, the architect had made a great effort to distinguish his 250ft tower from the ordinary high-rise office blocks. He had broken its profile in elevation by alternate projection and recession, a design which earned it the nickname (among others) of Pringle's Pagoda.[14]Council itself remained divided about the whole proposal but had promised to put it back to Congregation. First, however, the Committee on Elevations and Choice of Architects was asked to 'examine the scheme from the aesthetic angle'.

There too opinion was divided. Mitchell, who was against the proposal, conceded that it was 'an imaginative piece of modern architecture'.[15] Oakeshott's own view of it was – and remained – hard to divine. As a member, and *a fortiori* as chairman, of a committee, he made a point of absolute loyalty to the majority decision. At the end of his life he described the design cautiously as 'unusual and in some ways unobtrusive'. (Even the historian of Oxford's architecture, Howard Colvin, was content to characterize it as 'hardly elegant in appearance'.) So the only point upon which the Committee on Elevations could agree was the same as before: better a tower than a 'slab'. Let Congregation decide.

The meeting on 21 June had before it two draft decrees:

1. That the Science Area be increased by one acre to accommodate the new Zoology building, within the blue line on the published drawing.
2. That Council be authorized to seek planning permission in accordance with the outline plans published.

Congregation was told that within Council seventeen members had voted for the first decree, none against; on the second the vote was an equal division of 11: 11. The shift of Council opinion on the first was easily accounted for by Congregation's effective approval on 27 February.

In presenting the proposals on 21 June Oakeshott was again 'chosen to lead for Council as being a sound and moderate man whom everyone liked and trusted and who could not be suspected of indifference to aesthetic considerations'. So, thirty years later, wrote Mitchell, adding that 'Walter was not at his best and I don't think his heart was in it.' Certainly Oakeshott's tone, as reported by Maurice Keen in the *Oxford Magazine*, was defensive. The best he could say was that 'aesthetically the tower would be greatly preferable to another "slab" building, and it would stand apart from the old city with its famous skyline'. Bowra, seconding him, blustered. The opposition, led by (Lord) Blake, adduced a wide variety of arguments.[16] When it came to the vote, the first proposal was lost by the surprising margin of 275: 122, which meant that the second was never put. The margin on the first may well have been affected by the existence of the second, but it certainly suggests that, if either of the votes was aberrant, it was the rushed one on 27 February. Oakeshott himself thought the decision of 21 June was wise: 'the invasion of the Parks would have been only a beginning'.

However that might be, it was apparent to all that the University had made a fool of itself. Tougher characters blamed others, Oakeshott himself. His judgement had been impugned, his advocacy rejected. If he had lost the confidence of the University, how could he proceed in three months time to become its Vice-Chancellor? Among those he consulted were Wheare, Rector of Exeter, who was next in line himself as V-C, and Sir Edgar Williams, Warden of Rhodes House, a respected University figure who had been Montgomery's chief intelligence officer in the war. Williams thought Oakeshott was being altogether too nice about it, and nerved him to carry on.[17] Wheare did the same, and Oakeshott did not resign. 'It would have been very sad if he had,' writes Blake. 'He was to be an excellent Vice-Chancellor.'[18]

He set to work as soon as he got back from Italy in September, some weeks before his official installation as V-C at the beginning of term. Norrington, on handing over, had said that 'Merton would have to be forced by a decree to give up their playing field'. Oakeshott regarded that as 'hopelessly unrealistic',[19] and set about it in his own way. A series of evening gatherings in Lincoln brought together the interested parties and explored ideas. One idea which impressed him much at the time, and proved fruitful later, was that of preserving open space near the centre of Oxford by building under ground. The idea was used ultimately for a northward extension of the Science Library, as well as of the Bodleian; and he toyed with the idea half-jokingly for a car park under the front quad in Lincoln.

The immediate problem, however, was zoology. If Oxford science was to be kept on a single site, there was now only the one hope, that Merton might be persuaded to sell its playing field. Accordingly Oakeshott went, still before term, to see Warden Mure. 'Merton was rich', he wrote later, 'and the possibility of interesting them in the finances of such a transaction was *nil*. But Mure at last agreed that ... if such was the view of the most eminent town-planner whose advice could be secured, he would put the plan to the College.' Oakeshott reported this to Council on 24 September. The gentler approach of the new V-C shows in the minute, that Council 'agreed a proposal by the Rector of Lincoln (on the suggestion of the Warden of Merton) to call an informal meeting of interested parties to consider seeking the advice of an independent planning expert'.

That meeting was held on 10 October. All present concurred in the view that the man to invite as consultant was Sir William Holford, whom Oakeshott had known and admired from Winchester days. By the end of the month he had provisionally accepted, and his appointment was announced in the press on 8 November. Things were moving smoothly in the right direction. What was needed now was to get an agreed brief to Holford on the requirements for science. This however required a further exercise in diplomacy, to smooth ruffled feathers among the scientists.

For the vote of 21 June had been interpreted by some of them as a sign that the University was wavering in its commitment to their subject, specifically to finding a site within the curtilage for its necessary expansion. Pringle took it more personally. For more than a year he had been implying that the University was failing to honour promises made to him at his appointment; which had heated the debate without making him many friends. During November Oakeshott succeeded in mollifying Pringle. In December Council made a public statement, agreed with him in advance, reaffirming the University's commitment to 'an extension of biological studies'.

But personal diplomacy could not settle the two linked questions of principle which had to be solved before Holford could be briefed: (i) how much space should be allocated for the expansion of the sciences; and (ii) whether it should be provided on a site adjacent to the existing Science Area. Already in October the Committee on Requirements and Sites had produced a long report for Council, concluding that (i) the total floor-space needed was 1m. sq. ft and (ii) the best site was the Merton playing field. That report was circulated first to the heads of the science departments and then, with their approval, to the whole University. No major objections were raised to it. Oakeshott himself agreed whole-heartedly. He was already sure that 'to divide science into two halves some distance apart would be disastrous', and now the estimate of 1m. sq. ft seemed about right: 'He did not believe that science expansion could go on at the rate it had been going on since the war – or could do so without changing the nature of the University.'

By the turn of the year 1962/3 his patient diplomacy and wide consultations had succeeded in cooling the atmosphere. It was now a matter of preparing to receive Holford's report. On Oakeshott's proposal, Council agreed that copies should be given immediately to all interested parties with a view to publication as soon as possible thereafter. It was in fact received early in May and published on the 23rd, to be voted on by Congregation on 23 June.

The Holford Report ranged widely, but the immediate focus was on science. Merton had already declared that, if Congregation voted firmly in favour, it would be willing to sell the coveted playing field. So for the meeting on 23 June Council was able to propose that 'the University should seek to acquire Merton field and should commission designs for new biological buildings on it'. The *Oxford Magazine* on 20 May was again critical of Council's 'precipitancy'. It 'has evidently had no time to reflect fully on the plan, or else it has not taken Congregation fully into its confidence'. On 6 June the magazine went further and urged that the Report should be rejected. But Congregation wanted to get on with it, and voted 235: 22 in favour.

Council was well satisfied with the outcome, but there were still two loose ends to tie up. The first was the choice of an architect for the new zoology building. Pringle and the scientists wanted to retain Chamberlin, but the Committee on Elevations etc., chaired by Oakeshott, recommended Sir Leslie Martin, and Council agreed. Martin's eventual building was warmly approved even by those loyal to Chamberlin.

The other matter was the residual feeling that more should be done to ease the transaction of business between Council and Congregation, not just to prevent a repetition of the fiasco of 1962 but to give Congregation a greater sense of participation in important decisions. To meet the feeling Council set up a Committee, under Wheare as Chairman, to 'consider the question of the communication of information to members of Congregation'. The recommendations of the Wheare Report, presented in February 1964, 'involved no dramatic change' but helped to consolidate the improved relations between the two bodies. Oakeshott's own part in it all was unobtrusive, but he welcomed the outcome.

In the long vacation of 1963 he had some weeks in the flat in Rome, which now boasted its own printed writing paper. There were various social relaxations to be enjoyed there, and he also set to work on a book about the church mosaics of the city. Refreshed, he returned to await the imminent publication of the report of the national Committee on Higher Education which had been sitting since 1961 under Lord Robbins. There was general expectation that the Robbins Report, as it came to be known, would propose far-reaching changes in the system and that Oxford and Cambridge would not 'scape whipping.

His Vice-Chancellor's Oration on 7 October therefore contained a pre-emptive defence of the Oxford system of devolved government and democratic decision-making. With recent experience in mind, he was able to argue that the colleges do not in fact, even if they could, thwart university policy.

Later, after reading the Robbins Report and reflecting upon the current criticisms of Oxford – both those made in the Report and those generated by it in the press – he became uneasy. Simpson recalls

> one evening at high table in Lincoln. The food, as ever, had been excellent; the chef had excelled himself. The undergraduates had long left the hall after their meat and two veg. Suddenly Walter said 'It must have been rather like this at Fountains, just before the dissolution of the monasteries'. A shudder went round the table. We knew he was right.

Convinced that the University could not simply do nothing, he wrote a brief memorandum for the meeting of Council on 18 November, of which the second half reads as follows.

> I do not think these attacks can be, from the nature of things, effectively answered by us, seeing that we are interested parties; nor is it easy for us to appreciate what are the real faults in our system, and what must be done if Oxford is to play a proper part in the university system of the next twenty years. The answer must be given by some independent outside body; and in

my view the time has come when we should take the initiative in asking for a Royal Commission or other independent external committee, to inquire into our affairs. ... I suggest that we might have some discussion on Monday to show whether there is any support for this idea of an external commission; and if there is, perhaps appoint a committee of not more than three or four members of Council to advise us at the earliest possible date – speed being of the essence of the matter – what form we should try to get the inquiry to take. It would then be necessary to consult the colleges and probably also Cambridge.

The recommendation here is clear, the motivation less so. The memorandum is not a summons to the barricades, nor is it a clarion call for reform. Neither of these was in his personal character or style (at least not since 1942 – see p. 121). Moreover as Vice-Chancellor he wanted to carry as many people with him as possible. Hence though the goal is clear, it is to be approached by the usual cautious route.

Both goal and approach appealed to Council. It voted 18: 2 to 'consider ways of securing the appointment of an outside commission or committee' and gave him a sub-committee of five to prosecute the idea. The other four were Wheare (Vice-Chancellor elect), Bowra, the Principal of Lady Margaret Hall and J. D. Davies, the Senior Proctor. A week later Oakeshott reported that, of five heads of houses he had consulted in strict confidence, four were in favour; and that Boys-Smith, Vice-Chancellor of Cambridge, believed only a Royal Commission would achieve anything. The sub-committee accordingly recommended that a Royal Commission should be sought. But it must be done secretly for the moment: 'It is the fact that we are taking the initiative that must be kept confidential if we are to secure the advantages of this initiative.'

Council on 2 December authorized Oakeshott and Wheare (with Boys-Smith, if willing), to see the Chancellor, Harold Macmillan, about the chances of a Royal Commission. Macmillan, when eventually contacted (he was Prime Minister as well), advised against the idea. Meanwhile time was slipping by. On 27 January 1964 Oakeshott 'suggested as an alternative that the University should persuade a small number of eminent persons not being members of the University to carry out an investigation'. A week later however he thought that 'the time for the appointment of an external committee has now passed', and that 'it would be best to set up a small internal committee to advise on what matters need to be investigated'. Council agreed, proposing Lord Franks as Chairman, with Wheare and one other as members. Again to save time, this was to be put in hand immediately and without consultation. The remit was 'to consider the recommendations and criticisms in the Robbins Report and arising out of it which particularly affect Oxford'. Council's timetable was doubtless accelerated by Robbins's chief criticism, of Oxford's 'difficulty in reaching rapid decisions'.

The key name here was Franks. Franks was Provost of Worcester, but he had previously been, in succession, Provost of Queen's, Ambassador in Washington and Chairman of Lloyds Bank. Even as head of house he had stood aside from university politics, and his reputation for impartiality was as sea-green outside Oxford as in it. But it might well be hard to persuade him. The task was given to Oakeshott. Franks in 1992 'vividly remember[ed] Walter calling on me in Worcester and in that inimitable way of his gently persuading me to say yes to his proposal that I should act as Chairman of a 3-man committee. I found that I had said yes almost without knowing that I had done so.'

The Committee reported in early March recommending the establishment of a seven-member Commission. Oakeshott, giving Council advance warning of this on 9 March, said he would like to ask Franks to chair the Commission too. Council agreed, and Franks recalled that 'with the same gentle expertise he persuaded me' to do so.[20] The following week Council accepted all the other recommendations of the committee. They included the following main term of reference for the Commission – significantly more positive than Council's for the committee: 'to inquire into and report upon the part which Oxford plays now and should play in the future in the system of Higher Education in the United Kingdom, having regard to its position as both a national and an international university.'

Support for the Commission within Oxford was near-unanimous. Even the *Oxford Magazine* on 30 April bit back its usual complaint of failure to consult, and commended Council's action as 'thoroughly welcome'. The Commission reported in March 1966. Its far-reaching recommendations were virtually all accepted, and the Franks Report is widely regarded as a turning point in the history of the University.

Oakeshott's last act as Vice-Chancellor was to give the Oration on demitting office in October 1964. To scotch any suggestion of personal achievement during his term, he drew on the analogy of fifth-century Athens, where 'a man, chosen not for his capacities but by lot, found for a short time the City in his charge. It was calculated that someone so chosen was unlikely to interfere with decisions reached by the citizen body. To become Vice-Chancellor is to be reminded of this salutary parallel.'

He also allowed himself a sentimental description of life in a college: 'a comparatively small institution, the fortunes of which together, from the question whether a Sauternes or a claret should be the alternative to port, to the question whom we will choose as undergraduates, or whom for the matter of that we choose as our Master, we jointly determine.' The context of this description was the need for a graduate college. The provision of such a college was high on the University's agenda, and he himself would be able to make some contribution to it.

To those who had known Oakeshott at Winchester and Lincoln as colleagues, and indeed as friends, there were two surprising features about his Vice-Chancellorship: how much he achieved, and how much he enjoyed it. By advance reputation he was, as Franks put it, 'not a good administrator and a bit indecisive in business affairs'. What, then, did he achieve, and how did he do it?

Of his achievements two stand out, one from each year of office. The first was to solve the problem of expansion in science. From his point of view this was the more remarkable of the two achievements. True, its success stemmed from the quiet diplomacy which came easily to him, and depended upon the magnanimity of Merton. In other ways, however, it cost him dear. He had to rise again after a public defeat by the many, and cope with confrontation among the powerful few. And this time, though at one point he nearly lost his nerve, his health stood the strain.

The second achievement, the establishment of the Franks Commission, was objectively in a different class from the first – such at least is Bullock's judgement.[21] The initiation, if not the original idea, was Oakeshott's; so was the crucial persuasion. The result, for Oxford, was momentous. But there was no altercation and no serious opposition. Subjectively, it was roses, roses all the way.

But two achievements – or indeed any number – do not add up to a policy. Did he have a policy, a vision of the University? In so far as he did, it lay more in the past than in the future. To that extent he was rightly classed as a conservative. He was in favour of new subjects and subject groupings (e.g. the combination of engineering with economics; the incorporation of art history as an option within the history school), of new ventures (e.g. a collection of oriental art), and of modern architecture, at least in principle. But fundamentally, as one of his proctors[22] put it,

> he belonged to the older world of traditional institutions and the well-tried judgment of friends and colleagues of a lifetime. His conscience compelled him to do the best he could to shore up the world he loved against what was then widely [and correctly, one might add] thought to be the future. . . . Bowra and Bullock wanted change, but weren't Oakeshott and Franks rather midwives?*

The reference to his conscience is doubly significant. Another proctor says that 'he allowed his conscience to prey upon him'. 'He wanted to do right. He wanted it very much. He wanted it . . . too much' – so Isaiah Berlin, in Aristotelian language. Williams's formulation owes more to Machiavelli: 'He was not a very bad vice-chancellor. But he was not a very good one either – because he wanted to be fair.'

This quality of fairness is attested by all those who worked with him then. Jack Lankester, his University Surveyor, recalls that 'In spite of strong reservations about some of the architectural projects which were proposed, Walter was always fair and measured in his judgments, and never used his power as V-C to impose his own views. I admired him for this.' In the words of yet another proctor, he was 'a man of total integrity, in no way a political wheeler-dealer'.

To that quality Bullock adds two others. In the arts of chairmanship he himself learned from two V-Cs: 'from Maurice (Bowra) the art of impatience, from Walter the art of patience'. Secondly, 'Walter had a natural courtesy – though he also played on it.' That courtesy was extended to everyone – one might say 'to all ranks', if he had not been totally oblivious of rank. A proctor remembers that 'he was always very punctilious about consulting those slightly anachronistic Tribunes of the People'. Senior women administrators received brooches as presents, still treasured after thirty years. All these gentle qualities contributed to his achievement. Out of the sweetness came forth strength.

He was also conscientious in a looser sense. In the chair he

---

* cf. a comment by Ball: 'We searched in vain for the radical thinker he had once been.'

conducted meetings well and was always 'efficient, if not effective'. Of course, he now had, for the first time in his life, the support of a first-class administrative team. He respected them, and they grew to respect him. It took them a little time, however, to get used to some of his boarding-school habits. For example, he would convene an informal meeting in Lincoln for 8.30 p.m., which those attending might (or might not) find to be preceded by supper, and where the secretary had to take the minutes by candlelight. The intention was generous, the result could be confusion and even indigestion.

To work with such competent people increased not only his efficiency but also his pleasure. Administration and scholarship are not as far apart as is sometimes thought. Both involve 'getting it right'; which, when properly done, satisfies the mind. Nor is power in itself distasteful, especially when the responsibility for making painful decisions can be shared. Within the University the Hebdomadal Council certainly had the power in the days before Franks – 'more than it should have done', in Bullock's view. Moreover those were peaceful days in universities, before the dissidence of the late sixties which set staff against students, or the cuts of the eighties which set don against don.

But if Council was Bullock's 'favourite committee', it was not Oakeshott's. Williams uses a vivid image to describe him in it: 'a very nice fish in a messy pool which could turn slimy'. A proctor observed him there.

> His face during controversial meetings and less obvious tugs-of-war was a study in itself. His remarks were always courteous, but from his facial expressions he seemed to be struggling with a deep distaste, if not for the matter in hand, at least for the discussion of it. What a contrast with the geniality, the unforced smiles (as they surely were), that he displayed on a social occasion or in a small congenial committee!

Such committees were where he felt most at home, and continued to serve after he came off Council.

Finally, it seemed to many that university affairs provided him with an escape from certain aspects of college life. If there were tensions in Council, at least they were not on his doorstep and at his dinner-table. When he became Vice-Chancellor, college affairs were taken over by Green and Owen (as successive Senior Tutors) and Laws, as Bursar; and it was felt in Lincoln that he 'never really took up the reins again'.

The position of Vice-Chancellor also offered Oakeshott in 1964 a rare chance to benefit both the University and a distinguished friend. The friend was Beazley, now Sir John Beazley, CH. He and his wife were becoming alarmingly frail and eccentric. Noel and Walter had been devoting an increasing amount of time to looking after them. But Noel was not strong and Walter was busy. Now Trendall came up with an idea from Australia. Its purpose was to secure on the one hand the eventual possession by the University of Beazley's working papers and photographs, and on the other hand the greater comfort of the Beazleys' last years. The University would pay him an agreed sum now, but would leave the material with him until he had no further use for it.

Oakeshott took up the idea with enthusiasm. Since Lady Beazley had always managed her husband's affairs, he wrote to her putting the plan. She replied on 19 January: 'To think that there is someone looking after Jacky's life-long work, and that the someone is you, is a great peace-giving joy.' He immediately set about the task of raising the necessary finance.

The archive turned out to include 70,000 mounted photographs and several hundred thousand small sheets of fine paper filled with notes and drawings of vases. A German expert, who came over in March 1964 at his own expense, valued them at £12,000. One way and another – chiefly from university funds – Oakeshott succeeded in raising the money. The Beazleys ended their days in relative comfort. On his death in 1970 the archive was moved to the Ashmolean museum.

Lady Beazley died in 1967. Oakeshott, always moved by death and deathbeds, wrote many years later of his last visit to her. ' "I have been reading", she said, "the story of Joseph, and I have found that forgiveness is the most important thing of all". For a few moments she was silent. I understood her to talk about her daughter; and reconciliation. It was one of the deepest religious experiences I have ever had.' He wrote also of Beazley himself at his wife's cremation. 'He could scarcely stand. There was nothing left of him, once she was dead, but that frail dignity and an unaffected politeness with which he treated the outside world – to which, for so many years, he himself had ceased to belong.'

The Oakeshotts had done a great deal for the Beazleys at the end. While Lady Beazley was still alive, Noel was constantly at their house in Holywell, helping to keep it in some order, and trying to ensure that Jacky got enough to eat. When she died, they invited him to stay in the Rector's Lodgings for some weeks. Walter became more or less his private secretary, answering letters of condolence but encouraging friends to write cards. At Jacky's funeral he chose and read the lesson, a highly Platonic passage from the Wisdom of Solomon ch. 7. He wrote the obituary for *The Times*, accurately describing him as 'the greatest Oxford scholar, in any classical field, of his generation', and a fine short notice in the *Lincoln College Record*.

Nevertheless, in spite of all they had done, Walter and Noel still felt they owed him an incalculable debt, for the joint inspiration of their lives as scholars. When they left Lincoln they found a way of paying him a last tribute. In 1958, having no retirement house of their own, they had bought as an investment a valuable Greek vase of the mid-sixth century BC. Beazley already knew the artist from another vase, and now proceeded to give him the name of the Oakeshott painter. It was 'the greatest compliment we could have been given'. In 1972 they presented their name-vase in his memory to the Ashmolean museum, where it is well displayed in the Beazley Room.[23]

The influence of a Vice-Chancellor does not cease as soon as he demits office. There is a period when, as Bullock puts it, 'the setting sun still has strength in its rays'. For Oakeshott that period enabled him to perform one further service to the University. It concerned his old love, libraries.

Among the questions the Franks Commission was looking into was 'the organization of the libraries of the University, including the relationship of the Bodleian with other university libraries'. In February 1965 Oakeshott, with the support of Mynors (now Sir Roger), wrote to Wheare as V-C proposing the establishment of a fact-finding committee on the matter, without waiting for Franks to report. His main concern was 'the possibility of determining in one central body the share of the financial cake which is to go to each of the university libraries'. He then suggested a further matter for consideration, 'the need for the University to determine priorities in library planning'. In that context he came back to his King Charles's head, the use of underground space: 'I suspect that we are simply being years out of date in resisting the idea that underground, air-conditioned workrooms can be congenial.' Finally, he set foot on more dangerous ground by proposing to add college libraries to the inquiry.[24]

Council accepted the main proposal. In March 1965 it set up a Committee on Inter-library Coordination with Robert Shackleton[25] in the chair; Oakeshott was appointed a member in July, when he finally came off Council. Reporting in November 1966, the Shackleton Committee recommended the setting-up of a permanent Libraries Board, under 'an eminent senior academic who would devote a substantial proportion of his time' to the work and be remunerated accordingly.

The Board was established in 1967. It asked for Oakeshott as Vice-Chairman, the Vice-Chancellor being nominal Chairman of important committees. The Board could not pay the £2,500 p.a. recommended in the Shackleton Report, but Oakeshott agreed to serve 'for an initial year from Jan 1968 to July 1969 at a salary of £800'. His attitude to this is reminiscent of an incident at St Paul's (p. 106). In the same spirit he had in 1963 refused to accept a mooted increase in his salary as V-C above the £1,750 p.a. which was covered by the UGC's quinquennial grant.

Oakeshott remained Vice-Chairman of the Libraries Board until his retirement from Lincoln in 1972. During that period he put in an enormous amount of administrative work on it – more than on anything else except the conversion of All Saints Church into a library for Lincoln. But it was largely wasted labour. 'The Libraries Board was, fatally, given very little real power (for example over the Bodleian Library)', and neither the Bodleian nor the various departments wished to be coordinated. In the disillusioned words of a later Vice-Chairman of the Board, 'at a mere breathing of the word "rationalization" faculties and departments form themselves up into hollow squares and prepare to defend every inch of territory with their life's blood.' As to the Bodleian, it 'constitutes some 80% of the library provision, and takes some 80% of the money. If Bodley doesn't want to play, then you might as well put away your toys.'[26] To cap it all, Shackleton himself, appointed Bodley's Librarian in 1967, turned overnight from poacher to gamekeeper, and succeeded in resisting almost all the trespasses of his creature the Libraries Board.

That Board was the only major responsibility that Oakeshott undertook for the University after his Vice-Chancellorship. Wheare asked him to take the chair of the General Board of the Faculties, the senior academic committee of the University, which indeed after Franks became more influential than Council. But he wanted to get back to writing, particularly his Roman mosaics, and asked to be excused. He did however intervene behind the scenes in various other causes dear to his heart.

First, in 1964 Oxford City Council made one of its periodical moves to solve its traffic problem by driving a road through Christ Church Meadow, an area scarcely less sacrosanct than the Parks. The University succeeded in getting a public inquiry established, and Oakeshott made a small but typical contribution to the victory it won there.

Christ Church, leading for the defence, had commissioned a pamphlet on the history of the Meadow. But by the time it was edited, there seemed no chance of getting it printed before the inquiry opened in January 1965. Its editor[27] therefore, who knew Oakeshott, went round in desperation to Lincoln. Oakeshott immediately rang up Vivian Ridler, Printer to the University, and asked him to drop everything and print it: an anonymous donor had offered £100, and he himself would raise the rest from the riparian colleges. To Ridler, 'being asked to drop everything for the most important job in the world, nay universe, was not at all an uncommon experience. But Walter was the most delightful person to work for: he never pressed too hard, and that is why we were always anxious to give him what he needed.' So the pamphlet was printed and the colleges paid up. The anonymous donor was, of course, Oakeshott himself.

Also in 1965 a chance occurred for him to further the establishment of Wolfson College. The story revolves round a house named Cherwell lying in 9.3 acres of ground north of the Parks by the river. The property belonged to St John's College but was on a long lease to the Haldane family. It had lain empty for some years when Oakeshott took up the Vice-Chancellorship in 1962. Then, however, it seemed that the Haldanes might be interested in selling it. He and the Registrar both 'saw that it must be acquired for the University. It was ideally suited for a graduate college' – something which the University badly needed.[28] Council agreed, and a first attempt was made to buy Cherwell in 1962. St John's was ready to sell the freehold if the family would surrender the lease. On reflection the Haldanes decided not to sell, but they 'promised Mr Oakeshott that we would give the University an opportunity to buy if we should think of selling'.

Two years later the University succeeded in buying an alternative site for the graduate college. This was Court Place at Iffley. The location was not ideal, being two miles from the centre of Oxford. But the house and grounds were attractive,and the need was urgent. The University therefore decided to establish Iffley College, and a nucleus of Fellows was appointed in 1965. The senior Fellow was Frank Jessup, who had been a colleague of Oakeshott in the Kent Education Office in 1930.

At their second meeting, on 3 November 1965, the Fellows of Iffley asked the Vice-Chancellor to approach Isaiah Berlin with an invitation to become their first head. It was a splendid choice. 'If there had been at that time an elective appointment for "the most brilliant man in Oxford", Berlin would surely have been elected with a huge majority.' But there were difficulties. Berlin would hardly want to move to a college limited in size; Iffley could not grow without substantial endowments; and it was expected that the big Foundations like Wolfson and Ford would not give to a college out of Oxford.

Then, at the end of November, before a definite answer had been received from Berlin, a letter came from the Haldanes with a firm offer to sell Cherwell. When Oakeshott heard of it, it seemed obvious that the site should be offered to the Fellows of Iffley if they wanted to move; so on 10 December he wrote to Jessup to alert him to this new possibility. Others shared Oakeshott's view. But there was strong opposition. Norrington and a powerful committee had master-minded the University's grand plan for such provision, which had been agreed with the UGC. They did not want it unstitched now.

Oakeshott therefore resorted to what, in an account he wrote twenty years later, he called 'indefensible methods'. He wrote again to Jessup suggesting a ruse. If the Fellows *did* want to move to the Cherwell site, they should 'discuss it with Berlin and put up to him the notion of only agreeing [to become head] provided the [Cherwell] site was made available'. In fact there is no reason to suppose that Berlin did make that condition.[29] None the less Oakeshott's comments are of autobiographical interest. It was 'the one operation over which I reckon I was wholly unscrupulous'. There may have been an element of tongue in cheek, for he added that 'the scar on my conscience isn't all that suppurating'. But it was the nearest he came in his public life to intrigue.

Whatever the exact sequence of events, everything fell rapidly into place. The University bought Cherwell and allocated it to the College; substantial endowments were promised from both Wolfson and Ford; and Berlin agreed to become the first President of Wolfson

College.[30] All this happened so fast that already on 2 July 1966 Jessup wrote to Oakeshott to thank him on behalf of 'the Fellows of Iffley-Wolfson. It is unlikely that the events of the last few weeks would have happened unless had you had written to me last December about Cherwell. . . . Without your kindly intervention we should not exist in our present form.'

Finally Oakeshott was involved in 1966–7 in another imaginative but ultimately frustrated architectural plan. As part of the redevelopment of the Science Area proposed in the Holford Report, a new home had to be found for the Pitt-Rivers Anthropological Museum. In March 1966 Council agreed to put up a new building, and to finance it by an appeal. They also accepted a recommendation from the Committee on Elevations and Choice of Architects, of which Oakeshott was still a member, that an approach should be made to a collaborative team of architects – Nervi, whose work he had much admired in Rome, with Powell and Moya in England. Architects' fees of £13,500 would be underwritten, in advance of the appeal, out of the income from the van Houten legacy.

In April 1966 Jack Thompson came out to Rome, to join Oakeshott in briefing Nervi. Thompson had long been Chairman of the Buildings and Works Committee, where, in Oakeshott's words, 'we became close friends, and I can remember no one whose administrative ability I have so much admired'. Powell and Moya came out too, and they all met Nervi and his two sons in the via Mercede flat. Walter told Noel that the interview was 'technically satisfactory in that we decided to go ahead; but awkward, in that I think the old man (who is however very polite) reckoned that we were making much too heavy weather about the details of collaboration' with the English architects.

The chief problem facing the architects was that of the limited site. The limitations were not only horizontal but vertical, since the area was residential. But the constraints served only to stimulate their imagination. The Curator of the Museum had worked out, for practical purposes, the idea of a circular building with a central dome. Nervi proposed to sink the two main floors of the building below ground (a solution congenial to Oakeshott) but to raise in its centre, to a height of 35ft above ground, 'a rotunda of fenestrated concrete. . . . The structural problem was well within the capacity of the reinforced concrete of which Nervi was a master.' So wrote Colvin, who regarded the whole design as 'a spectacular architectural concept'.[31]

The plan was approved in 1967, but sadly the cost was £3 million, and no benefactor could be found. So perished 'the last chance for the University in the twentieth century to build ... a major work of European architecture'.

Oakeshott's Vice-Chancellorship also brought him two trips abroad representing the University. In August 1964 he attended the Conference of Rectors of European Universities in Göttingen. Germany was a country he knew very little. In the 1920s he had admired the Weimar Republic, but nothing had happened since to predispose him in favour of the country.

His first comments to Noel on arrival concerned

the dowdiness of everyone all round. Immensely prosperous; but dowdy, such fashion as there is being 'novelty' in the sense of the word applied to china dogs in the catalogues. The hats worn by the air-hostesses for example are simply caricatures: a hard hemisphere with a jockey-cap peak, but all three times too small, so that it sat on the top of the head like a bad joke.

The judgement is ostensibly aesthetic but its implications are moral. His second letter, however, shows prejudice wearing off.

This has all proved far more chirpy than I had imagined. Göttingen is very charming in its way; the old university city still quite provincial and no large buildings at all, so that it remains like central Oxford ought to be, a delightful conversation piece – no one building particularly good but each saying something different from the next. And it's put itself out for us in a way that I cannot believe would be conceivable anywhere else in the world.

The Conference proceedings began with 'the most colourful procession imaginable in the fresh morning sunlight, a mile or more through the old streets to the meeting hall'. The visiting V-Cs were 'in the most sensational garments, looking as though they were Kings of Hearts or Diamonds, or a few Kings of Spades. I suppose the V-C of Cambridge and I belonged to the latter category (except that I consider myself only a knave of clubs).'

The speeches he admired less. Almost all the speakers went on far too long. 'The person who came out best was the Mayor, who seemed many cuts above what one would normally get in an English city of this size, knew what to say and when to stop saying it. ... But the chief chirp of the day was a concert in the evening by the Berlin Philharmonic Orchestra, certainly one of the best concerts I've ever heard.' The highlight was a Haydn symphony of which 'James Fergusson had a record which he played all day in Holywell. At any rate every note of it is impressed on my mind. . . . There never seemed a note which the fiddles did not bow exactly the same.'

'I'm not so sure', he concludes,

> that one hasn't been simplifying Germany far too much in one's mind and whether under a superficial identity (which consists of all the Fraus looking like clergymen's widows or potential widows; their husbands on the contrary don't look in the least like clergymen) there may not be many different Germanys. Göttingen seems to be back in the world of the *Erklärung* or whatever it is called: the brotherhood of man, the unity of knowledge, Goethe and all that. In fact they appear to be achieving (or to have achieved) what the Weimar Constitution tried.

But the historical parallel rang an alarm bell. He was all the more anxious about current signs of neo-Nazism. A German colleague embarrassed him by a casual remark that 'some fuel had been added to its uncertain flame by the work of a man called Taylor in Oxford'. He hoped 'to find out more about what the younger generation thinks of these things this evening, when I've invited 4 undergraduates to dinner! They have been helping very competently with Conference arrangements and I thought it would be a bit of a gesture of the kind that might not occur to everybody.'

In the following August, 1965, he represented Oxford at an international gathering of universities in Tokyo. He gave some lectures for the British Council and did a broadcast on Tokyo television with three other V-Cs. But he was not inspired by the gathering or by Japan itself. Hong Kong, where he also broadcast, and Manila, where he lectured, were more attractive. Not so Delhi, visited en route.

Much more interesting than all of them was Iran, where he spent some days. Archaeologist friends from the British Institute in Teheran arranged a programme of visits for him. Persepolis he thought 'the most amazing monument I've ever seen, partly by reason of its hugeness, partly because of the magnificence of its craftsmanship'. Isfahan reminded him of the Athens of the 1920s.

Even in the main street, old and new mix in the most fascinating way. I was delighted yesterday to see a young woman squatting near a grave old greybeard, who was sitting on a small carpet with a tiny table in front with paper and envelopes. She was telling him what to say in her letter, and slowly and ceremoniously he wrote it down. Meanwhile the world of the twentieth century whirled round them, the cars dashed by – and steadily they went on with their letter. I am glad to have come here.

On return to England he wrote an official report to the British Council, which had sponsored the tour. One issue predominated. People out there are

starving for English. We are doing something. But cannot we, *must* we not, do ten times as much? We are, after all, three quarters of the way through with power politics. Our two assets should be trustworthiness and *the language*. American is something. But it's not regarded as quite the same thing. English is the world language, *the* world language, *which they must have*.

He received an emollient reply.

Oakeshott's own scholarly work had to remain in abeyance while he was Vice-Chancellor, but he responded as best he could to calls from others working in his fields. In April 1963 he heard from Winchester Cathedral that the wall-paintings in the Holy Sepulchre Chapel were deteriorating at an alarming rate, and that the Chapter had asked Mrs Eve Baker to restore them. He replied immediately, that this was the moment to consider lifting off the later paintings so as to reveal the ones underneath. Ever since 1939 he had looked forward to the day when a technique was available for doing so. The technique had been developed in Italy for restoration work after the Second World War. In principle therefore the time was ripe – though he had doubts about Mrs Baker's competence for that more demanding operation.

The Chapter agreed to commission the work, and the Pilgrim Trust, on Oakeshott's recommendation, to finance it – subject to his approval of the plans in general and the choice of restorer in particular. It took sixteen months to resolve his doubts about Mrs Baker, and another twelve to agree plans and estimates. Even then the start of the work had to be put back another six months to allow for his foreign trip in 1965. Eventually in May 1966 the later paintings were successfully moved from the wall to the vault of the chapel.

The earlier paintings, now revealed, aroused great excitement. The subjects represented on them turned out, as he had suspected, to be the same as in the later ones: a deposition and an entombment. The colours were splendid: 'I am not aware', he wrote later, 'of any other wall-paintings in the South of England on which so much of the colour remains.' But the fascinating question of attribution had to be put aside for the moment.

The work on the Holy Sepulchre Chapel completed the Pilgrim Trust's programme for conserving wall-paintings. The question then arose, where should the Trust go next? The answer that suggested itself was stained glass. The chief problem here was that Dennis King's workshop in Norwich had much of the expertise but could not cope with the whole of the work. So the Trustees decided to build up a second high-class workshop. The obvious choice was York, where a team of glaziers had for many years been doing good work on the Minster. In 1966 the York Glaziers Trust was set up with substantial Pilgrim help, and with King as technical consultant.

Inevitably there were tensions. A subsidized York could undercut the other glass repair shops. The Society of Glaziers was alarmed, and Oakeshott was called upon to mediate. In 1966 he invited all parties to a meeting in the Rector's Lodgings. Noel was at her best as hostess, and Walter entertained them with 'a few pages from a late thirteenth century illuminated gradual of some quality from a chartreuse near Cambrai'. Peace was restored in the stained glass world, but it had 'required all Walter Oakeshott's tact'.[32]

One other event of the Lincoln years may be anticipated here. It completes the tally of Oakeshott's travels outside Europe and the USA. In August–September 1967 he got to South Africa for six weeks, for the first and only time since he had left it at the age of three. For many years he had been kept abreast of events there by his admiration for Patrick Duncan in his struggle against apartheid. In a sermon at Winchester c. 1950 he spoke warmly of a newspaper Duncan was editing in Johannesburg, *The African Drum*: 'on such influences it may depend whether that society is barbarous or civilized'. From journalism Duncan moved into civil disobedience, for which he was first deprived of his South African citizenship and later banned from entering the country. Back in England, his health, never strong, deteriorated. He spent weeks in various hospitals including the

Radcliffe Infirmary in Oxford, where Oakeshott used to visit him. After one such visit, in March 1967, he wrote: 'I was so excited by my few minutes with you: I could not forget it ; do not want to forget it; and never shall forget it. But I want you to get better, bless you. There *is* so much for you still to do – even tho' you've done so much already.' When Duncan died that June, Oakeshott wrote his obituary in *The Times*.

The attraction of South Africa for Oakeshott was such that at one time it seemed he might go out there to teach. Now his son Robert had done precisely that, in a pioneer multiracial school at Serowe in Botswana. Robert and Evelyn offered to pay their father's fare out, from their van Houten legacy. Evelyn would accompany him.

He described the school in a letter to Cook.

> It is a most remarkable place, run by [Patrick van Rensburg] a South African diplomat who found that he couldn't 'take' the job of 'selling' apartheid to other countries, resigned, and started this secondary school and community centre. The object is to produce good forward-looking citizens, boys and girls, who also have some experience of the simple techniques of farming, weaving, building and so on which can be practically applied in an African village on the edge of the desert without waiting for the combine-harvester to arrrive from Cincinnati.

> The original plan had been for the twins to take him round, to revisit his birthplace Lydenburg and make an expedition to the Rhodesian Highlands. Unfortunately at Serowe he first went down with shingles and then broke a rib, which anchored him for a fortnight. He did then get up to Lusaka and Salisbury and to the Victoria Falls, 'far the most wonderful natural sight I've ever seen'. But his most lasting emotion was pride in Robert's work – just the kind of venture that would have attracted him in his idealistic youth. 'I came away', he wrote to van Rensburg, 'immensely impressed, not only with the sanity of a community in which colour is neither here nor there, but with the vision of a future, greater society, extending far beyond Botswana, which one can see informing your work.'

By the time he demitted the Vice-Chancellorship in 1964, Oakeshott had already begun his next work of scholarship. It took its origin from the generous use he made of the flat in Rome, acquired in 1961. Not only did he lend the flat to friends, but he also provided them with notes on some of the places worth visiting. Of especial interest to him were the mosaics in the churches of Rome. On the one hand they spanned the very period whose art he had studied in England and France: from late antiquity to early Renaissance. On the other hand they used a different medium, one which was technically fascinating and which linked Italy with the east rather than the west.

But 'notes' with him could never be second-hand. He looked for himself, lingering but always questioning; and read enough of the background to learn that many of his questions were new. So when his notes came to the attention of the Italian experts, they pressed him to make them into a book.

He began the task in the summer of 1963. The research would be great fun. The writing would be demanding, since he now knew what kind of review he had to avoid. It would also be time-consuming, even with the flat as a base. Fortunately the College, on which his success as V-C had brought credit, gave him leave of absence for the summer term of 1965. He could therefore count on the better part of six months in Rome, with only the Japanese trip to distract him. That summer he managed to break the back of the work. Easter 1966 was for checking. The book was published in 1967 by Thames and Hudson as *The Mosaics of Rome*.

The flat was well organized for his needs and comforts. The heat of a Roman summer was if anything less tolerable to him than the cold of an English winter, but the installation of air-conditioning in 1964 made the interior habitable at all times of day. Meals he prefered to take on the terrace. They were always frugal when he was by himself, for preference as well as for economy. Breakfast was coffee and cornflakes; lunch, if he was not out on an expedition, might be a roll and pâté; for supper kedgeree, perhaps, or chicken and macaroni, or two boiled eggs in a mayonnaise made by himself, with a glass or two of wine.

His favourite place was the terrace – at least until 1966 when he installed a circular staircase leading to a new roof-garden. 'In the evening, when the sun goes down, it's delicious. One puts the light on to read, and for some reason that I don't know there are no insects.' Even during the day there is only 'an occasional wasp and an occasional and minute ant wandering aimlessly over the tiles'. He loved the evening view from it. Once there was a new moon like a thin finger nail in a sky of indescribable, plated, brilliance; because of the city's lights one sees only the planets, but they stand out as rare bright points of light. In the west one sees the dome of St Peter's, floating like a ghost. They do not cover it with flood lights but it seems to pick up enough light always to be visible.

For visiting churches etc. in Rome he walked, enjoying the exercise and the city bustle. Outside Rome he used train and bus wherever possible, though there were times when a friend's car or a taxi were needed. Expeditions in the country were undertaken partly for research, partly for pleasure. Pleasure included walking: fifteen miles a day was nothing exceptional. The best expeditions of all were with friends to Tivoli. They ended at the Sirene restaurant, overlooking the gorge, with trout *con mandorle* and a bottle of his favourite Orvieto *secco*. Research in the country was a visit either to non-Roman mosaics for comparison or to Roman ones which had been dispersed.

Whether in Rome or in the country, there were two besetting problems: access and photography. One important mosaic in a Roman convent was visible only at 11 a.m. on Sundays. Conversely the basilicas *all* had their mosaics floodlit on the mornings of the great Feasts of the Church. On those days Oakeshott could be seen scurrying frantically round Rome, covering as many of them as possible in the time.

In Santa Maria Maggiore, whose fifth-century mosaics were to him the most important group of all, access was straightforward but good photographs proved unobtainable.

One particularly wanted new colour photographs, perhaps six or eight, with perhaps twenty new details. A German [has] got permission through the intervention of the Pope for photographs to be taken, a whole new series, and I'd hoped that he'd allow me to use some of his, or at least his rejects. But he doesn't reply; and I am certain that having given permission so recently to him and having been so stingy about it, they'll not dream of giving it to me. This is a great bore.

He never did get any photographs of his own; and those taken by 'the German', Deichmann, were still unpublished in 1967.

Two letters from the summer of 1965 illustrate his adventures and his style. In both cases he was in search of fragments which had been rescued when the old basilica of St Peter's was destroyed in the seventeenth century to make way for Bernini's masterpiece. The first came from an eighth-century mosaic in the Oratory of John VII. John VII was the only Greek pope, and the craftsmen he imported for the work produced what were technically Byzantine mosaics in Rome. Of the fragments remaining the finest was now in the tiny cathedral of Orte, a hilltop town south of Florence.

I arrived at about half past three in front of the 'cathedral', which was of course closed. I asked the nearest man about it opening. He shook his head and said he supposed four. And then he pointed out that up to one side there was a door which looked as if it were where the priest or the verger might live. It led into the vestry; and from there I got into the church. It was all very spick and span. . . . I supposed that my mosaic fragment might (if still there) be behind one of the confessional boxes or something. So I peered everywhere. But there was nothing to be found.

Then two other people came into the church, both young men, one with a black beard and long black hair hanging down over his shoulders. Like John the Baptist, only *very* fat. It seemed as if he had been a 'super' in some film. His companion was a quite different kettle of fish. Same sort of age, late twenties; but very much on the spot. What was I looking for? I said, lamely, a mosaic fragment. Oh yes, he said; he knew it. It had been in the church. But now there was talk of there being a museum, where the likes of it could be put. It was locked up somewhere upstairs. Did I really want to see it? If so, we'd better go and knock up the Father and get his permission. Oh no, *of course* he and his friend would come too.

Off we went down the road, to the priest's lodgings, where the housekeeper said no, he was in the *seminario*. So we trailed off again to the local boys' school, where we found him; and my young friend told him who I was and said might we have leave to borrow the key. For about a quarter of an hour we fenced. Then it became clear that he was going to give us leave. . . . We were told to go back to a house near the church, and find Giorgio, the verger, which we did.

He took us into the vestry, unlocked a door leading up a stone stair, and took us into an upstairs store room; with four cages of singing birds in the tiny window, the floor scattered with bird-seed! Yes, it was up here somewhere; and out of a corner he lugged a huge solid oak frame, with the mosaic in it; eighth century, about 710, the head, body and hands of the Virgin, with a small stone inscription in one corner saying that it was taken from St Peter's in 1609. . . . So far as the figure is concerned as opposed to its surround, it is (I think) almost in original condition; a fragment of great quality and charm (see illustration). It was put for me under the bird-cages in the window and I knelt down to make notes.

After about half an hour, someone had a bright idea. What about a photograph? I hadn't a camera? Well that didn't matter. There was Signor X the photographer in Orte. We must all go and find him. Off we went. His shop was closed. But we tapped on the window. Out he came; short, grave, elderly, highly professional. Could he take a photo, said my new friend, fat St John the Baptist standing meanwhile in the background. Of course he could take a photograph. What of? Of course. Colour or black and white? Better try both. . . .

Back we went. A wooden table was got and placed in the right position. The first photograph was taken with the heavy frame leaning against some old junk. For the second, John the Baptist and I held it precariously balanced on the table. Steady now – very steady. Ah that would do. Hold it. FLASH. There. Yes, he'd send. I must write down the address. OAK-ES-HOTT LINC-OLN COLLEGE. Yes. And that would be 2000 lire [about £1].

So then came the distribution of largesse. Everyone protesting heartily that of course they would take nothing. But 500 l. for the verger, 1000 l. for my new friend (an absolute gem) and St John Baptist (a rogue I expect) to share. So the transaction was over, and we dispersed. Rather fun.

A month later he was on the track of another important fragment from old St Peter's. This was a roundel from the border of a huge mosaic by Giotto known as the Navicella. Giotto's original, before its destruction c. 1630, was 'one of the most famous works of Christian art'. It was now in the tiny hilltop town of Boville Ernica near Frosinone, some fifty miles SW of Rome.

The journey to Frosinone was by train, and he had to take two bites at it. The first time the train was late coming in to the terminus in Rome, and he found himself waiting on the platform among a 'large crowd, somewhat unsavoury. When it appeared, we all surged forward, and I was thoroughly jostled; yet got in all right and even found a place. But when the ticket collector came in I found my pocket had been picked. By some strange mischance, I'd been to the bank the day before and taken out 25,000 lire; all in the wallet!' To add insult to injury, he reckoned to know, from furtive glances, which the culprits were. There was nothing for it but to get out at the next stop and slink home.

Two days later his luck held: train to Frosinone, and taxi on to Boville Ernica.

My driver insisted on asking for a *Museo* as he was convinced that a mosaic *fragment* would not be in a church. We stopped and asked a couple of muleteers whose animals were tethered to a tree outside the town gate. They obviously knew nothing but directed us round the wall to a gate the other side, even narrower: made I suppose simply for pack-animals, not for anything wheeled. We scraped through. In the narrow street a ladder which stood against one side, propped up onto t'other, had to be moved. . . .

Eventually we got to the church. It was dark, but I found my mosaic almost at once. I turned to see if I could get lights put on; and discovered that the 'grape vine' had already brought along the verger of the church, immensely proud that anyone should be visiting. . . .

The work itself is wonderfully good; the head of an angel in a roundel about 2 ft in diameter, in excellent condition with apparently hardly any restorations. . . . Though this is 'a fragment only', yet it is something in its own right. One gets a sense of the *style* of Giotto, working in mosaic, which nothing else can give. A good photograph of it in colour, which I hope we may get, would be a great asset. . . .

On the way back I was delighted when we stopped by some huge stone washing tanks, where an old dame and her daughter were doing the family sheets. They were rinsing them and wringing them out; one at each end of the sheet twisting it; then when the coil was tight they had a rhythmic movement – you twist over that way, I'll over that – and their bodies leaned over like dancers in a ballet. Meanwhile my driver had borrowed the soap, washed his hands, taken a huge swig of water which I hope was clean – and was ready to start again.

Another washing place on the way back, where all the small boys with rags or hankies round their middles were bathing while their mothers and sisters did the washing. A lovely, and enviable sight. It *was* hot; but I seem to have no new bumps today, so perhaps one really does get acclimatised.

Waiting at Frosinone station for the train back to Rome he got a meal. 'It was cool, cheap and excellent. I had Fordyce's new edition of Catullus with me which I'm much enjoying. One's classical training means that he's much easier *really* to understand than the Elizabethans.'

During the same month as this last excursion, July 1965, Oakeshott decided to recast his book. In a letter to Charles Mitchell of 2 July, which accompanied four sections of his draft for comment, he had explained that 'the second half consists of a survey of the mosaics church by church'. Writing to Noel a fortnight later, he referred to a recently made will in which he had

said something about throwing away all papers except the mosaics book. I think on further reflection one ought to say *including* the mosaics book, because there's some recasting I'm trying to do now without which I don't think it ought to appear. In a way it's a comparatively easy job; but it means altering the whole shape and cutting out masses of material; and I don't see how anyone else could be expected to do that.

What he was doing was to change the structure from the topographical to the chronological. In its final shape, his seven successive periods begin with 'the antique or classical', especially Santa Maria Maggiore. Next come 'the "Byzantine" works of the sixth, seventh and eighth century', including the Virgin's head from the Oratory of John VI. Finally, after three more, the sequence ends with 'the Roman Renaissance as expressed in mosaics'. The treatment of Giotto's Navicella includes a colour plate of the roundel, which is also given the position of honour on the dust-jacket.

In the preface he identifies two questions which have been to him 'of outstanding interest': how far the mosaics are authentic, or restored; and how far they are independent of the Byzantine tradition. 'The answers to these questions obviously have to be attempted largely in terms of style and technique', style being 'a matter in which opinions are so largely subjective'. What he can claim is to 'have studied the mosaics themselves' and to have 'taken such opportunities as there have been of examining them minutely *in situ*'.

On the other hand he has 'had to be content for the most part with using sources at second hand'. And he 'cannot claim to have fully considered these mosaics in the enormous context to which they clearly belong: that of the arts as a whole in medieval Rome, or that of the religious ideas of which many of them are expressions'. In short, the book 'is not a contribution to art history [which] has its own discipline which sharply differentiates it from questions of style'. He thus disclaims any pretensions such as had invited the savage review of a decade ago.

Reviewers thus disarmed were kind. John Beckwith, who had been severe on *Classical Inspiration*, made amends by two favourable notices of *The Mosaics*.

> In a sense this book is a catalogue without the academic dryness of such works, and, although Dr O. bows right and left to his authorities, who are all impeccable, an amateur quality – the adjective is not intended pejoratively – may be detected which is to the book's advantage. It is refreshing to read a book on a subject which the author so clearly loves. Loving meant getting it right.'

And not only that: the book also 'contains a great deal of new material'.

Other reviewers went even further. One thought the publishers' blurb 'almost too modest'. All lavished praise on the production, especially the colour plates, 'many of which are notably successful for a difficult medium'. The trouble which he and his publishers had taken was well rewarded. Over the next four years *Mosaics of Rome* appeared in German[33] and French editions. It is 'still useful as a lucid and judicious account' (Kauffmann, 1994).

Oakeshott himself later described the book as 'in some ways my best book, and the only one that one may reckon "successful"'. He had also enjoyed the work for it enormously. Nevertheless in the history of his scholarship it is something of a sideline. He never intermitted his two main fields of study, those which centred upon the Winchester Bible and upon Sir Walter Raleigh.

In 1966 he was elected President of the Bibliographical Society. His presidential address in 1967 was entitled 'The Relation of Morgan MS 619 to the Winchester Bible: a bibliographical and stylistic enquiry'. The address, which was not published, harked back to that first exciting moment thirty years earlier which had set him off upon his life's longest adventure. But the main achievement of his presidency was noted by Nicolas Barker. 'At once ruthless and persuasive, he raised both its subscription and funds so as to make possible the great *Short Title Catalogue of English Books 1475–1640.*'

His presidency also spurred him to complete a substantial work of his own, the publication in 1968 of Raleigh's library list. The list is taken from the autograph commonplace book which Oakeshott had bought in 1935, identified in 1952 and sold soon after. With the help of many scholars over many years he was now able to identify most of the 500 odd books in it. 'Far the most impressive sections of the library are the geographical and cosmographical works.' By contrast there is next to no poetry. The detailed study confirmed his initial surmises. The books were those which Raleigh had with him in the Bloody Tower and used for writing the unfinished *History of the World*. As to Raleigh's authorship of the *History*, analysis of the library showed that, though 'some specialist studies were prepared by others for his use', still 'much of the work was done by Raleigh himself', including the rhetorical passages and 'the superb narrative'.

In 1971 his achievements as a scholar were recognized by the highest academic honour available outside the sciences, a Fellowship of the British Academy. A Fellowship is normally awarded on the basis of work in one subject, but Oakeshott was elected under a bye-law which admits 'persons whose qualifications do not sufficiently come with the purview of any particular Section'.

Three years later he published another of his remarkable discoveries in the Raleigh field. The story behind it he recorded privately. It began in 1966, when he saw in a Christie's catalogue a copy of the posthumous 1617 edition of Spenser's *Collected Poems*, noted as having 'Carew Raleigh's signature on the title page'. Spenser had been a close friend of Walter Raleigh; Carew was a boy of thirteen when his father died in 1618.

A copy of Spenser that had belonged to Carew Raleigh seemed as near an 'association' copy as was ever likely to come my way, and on the impulse of the moment, I went up to see it on one of the view days – before the sale.

Prima facie it was a not very attractive copy of a book that is, in itself, not very attractive. One section of it, the *Faerie Queene*, was extensively scrawled in pencil with underlinings, lines in the margin, and so on. But as I looked through it I found an entry, in pen, which made it for me at once one of the most exciting books I had ever seen.

The printed text of the *Faerie Queene* is always prefaced by a number of commendatory poems, including two by Raleigh. In this copy, Raleigh's two poems were

bracketed in pen; and outside the bracket in a fine hand and in spelling I recognized, were the words 'bothe thes of your father's making'. It was hard to look unconcerned; but this is of course one of the most important items of technical equipment on such occasions. There are almost certainly three or four others looking at those books, and only too ready to note that a particular book is evidently regarded as of particular interest by someone else. Opening this casually here and there, I saw that there were several other notes, in ink, in Lady Raleigh's hand, and, though the extensive pencil notes detracted from its likely value simply as a copy, these notes by Lady Raleigh, few though they were, gave it outstanding significance. I put it back, and spent the next half hour looking carefully at books I did not in the least want to see; then went down to ask in the office what they expected the Spenser to fetch. The answer was £25 to £30. I explained that I was anxious to secure a copy of this edition, and would be grateful if they would bid up to £60 on my behalf. On the way home I thought I had been a fool. If the book was what it appeared to be, it was of far more interest than that. So I rang up my friend Mr Clifford Maggs, came absolutely clean with him, and asked him if he would try to buy it, even if it was bid up into three figures. He went to look at it, and wrote after the sale that he had bought it for (if I remember) £70; 'but' he said 'in view of what you had said and what I saw, I was ready to go much higher than that – and if necessary we would have come to some mutual arrangement.'

Closer study of the book at home confirmed his identification of

Lady Raleigh's hand. For example Spenser's *Colin Clout* describes his friendship with Raleigh in Ireland. Being in pastoral form, it contains many 'shepherds'. Opposite one of them was written in pen 'WR: Sheppard of the Ocion'. 'This was indeed nothing new,' says Oakeshott; 'Raleigh called himself Elizabeth's "Shepherd of the Ocean"; but it was pleasant to have it there, in Lady Raleigh's hand and highly individual spelling.' A few lines further on she identifies herself by her maiden name: 'E Throckemorton his mistris'. Here then we have Raleigh's devoted widow annotating the book as a present for her son, with private information about the father he scarcely knew.

Where, then, did she get the book? Oakeshott now took a closer look at the pencil markings. These consisted not of words but of marks to draw attention to passages. A careful analysis of the passages in question, which in the case of the *Faerie Queene* amount to 10% of the whole, suggested strongly that the author of the markings was Raleigh himself. In that case they give us

> a glimpse into his mind during the last months of his life when he was in the Tower awaiting death; his reflections upon the ambition which had overmastered his career; his recollection of his [elder] son's death; his experience of darkness and despair; . . . his final conversion to the value of a life lived simply, away from the glitter of the court.

Oakeshott's published article about the book ends with the words 'It is rare for us to come into contact directly, on fresh ground, with the minds of any of the great Elizabethans. Here we seem to do so.' The evidence is not compelling. But the sceptical reader, no less than the romantic scholar, *wishes* to believe.

More important to Oakeshott than either Raleigh or Malory – let alone his other scholarly interests – was the Winchester Bible. It was a piece of enormous good fortune for him that so many other scholars interested in that same field were working in Oxford while he was at Lincoln. As well as Hunt, Ker, Mynors and Pächt, the group included the President of Magdalen, Tom Boase. Together they constituted 'a mini Research Institute' in the Bodleian – the phrase is that of a younger member, Jonathan Alexander. During the 1950s Boase, Ker and Pächt each made discoveries of major importance to the Winchester Bible. The first to be assimilated in print by Oakeshott was that of Pächt. In an article of 1961[34] he had proposed close links between the artists of the Bible and those who painted the walls of the Chapter House in the Convent of Sigena in Spain.

The remarkable quality of the Sigena paintings was first realized in 1936, when the Spanish government set about making a photographic record of all the medieval wall-paintings in Spanish churches. The photographer at Sigena, Sr J. Gudiol, was astonished by what he saw: 'a great scheme of decoration, still preserving its splendid colours, deep blues, roses and greens dominating'. Gudiol photographed all that was visible. Three months later the Civil War ruined the Convent and burnt the Chapter House. 'And so', in Oakeshott's words, 'what was perhaps the greatest series of early thirteenth-century paintings anywhere in Europe had been wrecked beyond repair.'

But the photographs enabled Pächt to make the crucial attribution. Of Oakeshott's artists, it was the Master of the Morgan Leaf whose 'work offers the closest stylistic analogy with the Sigena frescoes'. Yet there are differences – e.g. the Sigena Master is much more familiar with Byzantine practice. Had he perhaps studied the Byzantine mosaics of Sicily? Pächt left open[35] the question 'whether the step from the Master of the Morgan Leaf to the art of Sigena can be viewed as the evolution of a single personality'. To Oakeshott this offered a temptation that was irresistible. As soon as the article on Raleigh's library was off his hands, he hurried off to Spain.

The Museum of Catalan Art in Barcelona contains a room constructed to the pattern of the Sigena Chapter House. In it are exhibited what could be salvaged from the ruins: a few fragments of painting, almost all of which had lost their colour in the fire. By good fortune, the man who had cleaned and arranged them was now Director of the Museum. With his aid Oakeshott set to work on the fragments and the published photographs.

A letter to Noel of August 1969 explains his objects.

What I am trying to do is to understand something of the methods on which the paintings were done: how the production was divided up between different hands and so on; on the theory that until one can recognize the different hands here the chance of establishing a really firm identification with the Winchester Bible hands is non-existent.

The difficulties, however, were great. For example, 'one of the details of which I've got a good photo *could* be from the Creation of Adam.

But it could also represent a figure being rescued from Hell at the Harrowing of Hell.'

However Gudiol's photographs, including a number of unpublished ones, were good – so good as to permit enlargement of details. In January 1971 he had the pleasure of meeting Gudiol himself and of being driven out to Sigena, 150 miles away in the mountains. By then he had also found an excellent firm of photographers in Barcelona and, as always, was planning his text round the photographs.

The purpose of the book was 'to consider the possible identity of actual hands, at Sigena and Winchester, which Pächt deliberately postponed'. Admittedly Pächt had had 'very good reasons; comparison between full scale paintings on a wall, and miniature paintings in a book, is of itself clearly a hazardous undertaking'. But hazard never deterred Oakeshott when the chase was on.

Sigena was published by Harvey Miller in London and New York. It identified the Sigena hands with two, or possibly three, of the later artists of the Winchester Bible. Most important of them was the Master of the Morgan Leaf. In Oakeshott's view, he had not only executed some of the finest paintings at Sigena but was also responsible for planning the whole decorative scheme: his 'personality dominated Sigena'. Second was a pupil of his whom in 1945 Oakeshott had called The Master of the Gothic Majesty.

As to the latter, he now bowed to Pächt's criticism that the epithet Gothic in that title was 'not well chosen': the artist was more classicizing than Gothic. But he did not change it 'because to do so might make for further confusion'. The comment shows on the one hand how widely accepted by now were the titles Oakeshott had given the various artists thirty years earlier, and on the other how ready he was to be put right by a scholar he respected.

And *Sigena* pushes out still further. Already in *Artists of the Winchester Bible* Oakeshott had mooted the idea that the Morgan Master might have seen Byzantine mosaics at Cefalù and Palermo in Sicily. Since then the notion had been tentatively blessed not only by Pächt but also by Otto Demus in his magisterial *Mosaics of Norman Sicily* (1949). Thus emboldened, Oakeshott worked out a hypothetical biography of the Morgan Master. After an apprenticeship in England, he went to Sicily while still a young man. What he saw there, especially in the mosaics, made an enormous impression upon him, at three levels. First was the liberal use of gold leaf (something which always fascinated Oakeshott too). Second was the humanistic, naturalistic treatment of the figures. Third was the 'profound solemnity' of 'the tragic countenance'.

The lessons which the Morgan Master learned in Sicily he applied, on return to England, to his illumination,* thus instituting 'a revolutionary change' in the decoration of the Winchester Bible. From Winchester he went out to master-mind the Sigena paintings,[36] taking with him an internationally known team of artists, and his own 'tragic view of life. At Sigena, as at Winchester, are to be found examples of this same agonising over the world: in the Almighty, for example, as he is shown creating Adam – who is made to share his tragic apprehension.'

Reviewers of *Sigena* were not entirely convinced by the 'biography'. Oakeshott, said the *TLS*, 'amplifies Pächt and pushes the argument perhaps further than the Austrian scholar would wish. . . . It may be just that Dr Oakeshott's endearing enthusiasm has carried him a little too far.' The *Burlington Magazine* was similarly gentle. 'If Oakeshott takes his Winchester artists further afield than this reviewer would do, it certainly does not detract from the interest and value of his book.'

All this time Noel was working steadily away at her Greek vases. Keeping abreast of her original South Italian field, she regularly bought for Trendall in Australia. She was also in demand as a reviewer. Between 1955 and 1976 she published eight valuable reviews, chiefly in the *Journal of Hellenic Studies*. 'Over [them]', wrote Robertson, 'she took immense trouble, as over everything she put her hand to, and they are true works of scholarship.' Her scholarship had always given her the happiness that derives, as Aristotle pointed out, from doing what one excels at – though, as she told Walter with tears in her eyes on her deathbed, she was actually prouder of the songs she had composed.

About 1958 she became interested in a new field, that of ox-headed vase handles.† From its beginnings in the protogeometric period (1000 BC) this type first *spread* over a wide area from S. Italy to Cyprus, and then *persisted* over some four centuries; and the question was, why? After a long period of gestation she produced an

*WFO himself adhered to strict medieval usage whereby the term 'illumination' is confined to decoration which includes gold (de Hamel).

†These were the vases for which Walter had kept an eye out on Hellenic Cruises 1958–61.

important article on them in 1966. Her cautious conclusion provides another instance of the temperamental difference between their two approaches to art history. 'The evidence [is] conclusive [but] best expressed negatively. Potters from several different localities whose work has been assigned to proto-geometric periods, have not entirely lost the habit of occasionally adopting a very debased ox-head as a handle formation.'

Apart from her own scholarship and her care for the Beazleys – two related concerns – Noel's life at Lincoln had proved rather lonely. In term-time Walter was occupied in college or university business. For her, there was some formal entertaining, which she did well, but undergraduates were not often invited to the Lodgings. She enjoyed teaching English to the wives of foreign scholars visiting Oxford. Otherwise much of her time was spent on her own, reading (French as well as English), listening to music and writing to the children.

When Walter was at home he still took her up breakfast in bed. When he was away, as he tended increasingly to be in the vacations, she would 'start the day at 7.0 a.m. with tea and a few passages from *Sword of the Spirit*'. Her own mobility being limited and her general health uncertain, she did not often accompany him on his travels. But she went once to the flat in Rome, once or twice to her relations in France, and regularly to look after Helena and Rose when their children were being born. Imperceptibly, she and Walter had drifted apart.

In the five years between the publication of *The Mosaics of Rome* in 1967 and his retirement from the Rectorship in 1972, Oakeshott had to fit his scholarship in with the realization of his grandest and most exciting project for the College. This was the conversion of All Saints Church next door into the college library. There had been a church on the site for two and a half centuries when Richard Fleming, Bishop of Lincoln, founded the College in 1427. The church with its benefice was in his gift, and he assigned it to his new college. In 1710 Dean Aldrich of Christ Church replaced the old church by a splendid new one, but the link with the college remained close.

However it became clear in the twentieth century that there were too many churches in central Oxford for the declining population. About 1950 the Rector of All Saints, a loyal old member of the college, mooted the idea of converting it for use as a library. Oakeshott was greatly attracted by the idea, which fitted what he called 'the secular character' of the church. In 1957 he was authorized to open negotiations with the ecclesiastical authorities. Eventually in 1970 the church was declared redundant (it was never deconsecrated, and the altar-piece remains at the east end); and in the following year it was formally offered to Lincoln for use as a library.

But Oakeshott did not wait for the mills of God. In June 1968 he wrote to Robert Potter to ask him to take on the conversion. Potter was a 'period architect' with whom he had worked happily and admiringly in 1958–63 over the restoration of the Divinity School and the old Bodleian Library.[37] Together they began to prepare plans for All Saints Church.

Ideas were sought from a number of eminent architects and artists, including John Summerson, Howard Colvin, Leslie Martin and John Piper. The chief planners were a triumvirate, Oakeshott and Potter with Donald Whitton, who knew and cared a great deal about architecture. Most of the running was of course made by Potter. But Whitton, in Oakeshott's words, 'had what nowadays would be called a hot line to the spirit of Dean Aldrich in the Elysian Fields; and was able, from that impeccable source, to produce unanswerable reasons for doing now what Dean Aldrich had not done in 1700.'

Whitton's was the the crucial idea: to raise the floor by some six feet to a level which 'brought what were designed as church windows into so much better a relationship with the desks and presses of the library'. His scholarly arguments converted each of the experts in turn. And with a lower floor dug *down* eight feet (making fourteen feet in all) as a crypt, it was possible to accommodate all the books etc. without breaking up the magnificent interior of the church. Oakeshott's own contribution was to design the lectern-shaped desks based on some he had seen in the Vatican Library. The plans had been agreed by the time of his retirement in 1972.

The money however had still to be found. The College launched a special appeal and the Rector led the pursuit. He secured substantial grants from the Historic Buildings Council and from the Pilgrim and Dulverton Trusts. He travelled hundreds of miles in Britain and the USA to touch old members, both before his retirement and much more intensively after it. In these ways the College raised the £420,000 which was the final cost of the conversion.

All Saints Library was officially opened in October 1975 by Macmillan as Chancellor. A week earlier there had been a private inauguration for the College with Oakeshott as main speaker. Typically, he took the trouble to go in the night before and test the new acoustics, thus ensuring an audibility which was not achieved by all the other speakers. He spoke of his own love of libraries. 'I found long ago that what one absorbed from the atmosphere of a library – from its dignity; from its serenity; from its magnificence; from its friendliness – has had as powerful an effect on me as the books inside it.' He also insisted on the continuity of inspiration. The building 'succeeds in looking as if it has always been meant to be as it is now; not an adaptation to a new purpose, but a realization, in a new way, of the original purpose'. Macmillan picked that point up a week later.

At the end of his speech Oakeshott ventured to look forward. He abjured the confidence of a Rector of the 1820s who had written to some benefactors that with their help All Saints was now 'set to rights FOR ALL TIME' (his capitals). 'But I suspect that this will be regarded as one of Oxford's fine buildings; and that many an undergraduate and graduate will leave Oxford the better for its being so.'

That was no overstatement. Of the qualities which he had listed in a library, it is the magnificence which stands out here. The All Saints Library is the most magnificent building in Lincoln, and it is Rector Oakeshott's monument. Writing of the College in 1992, its archivist said: 'After centuries of insignificance the College is much more confident of its image and reputation. In a way the library, magnificently converted in the mid-1970s, is a symbol of that change. Lincoln now means something to people.'

Alongside this story of success there was proceeding, as if in counterpoint, another sadder one: that of his retirement from the Rectorship. It had been clear for some time that he did not need or wish to stay the full course, i.e. until 1974. In 1969 he began to prepare for an earlier move by buying a largish house in Eynsham some six miles north of Oxford and selling the flat in Rome. A combination of pressures in July 1970 made him offer to resign as from the summer of 1971.

He made the offer, and gave his reasons, in a letter to Cox of 7 July. These extracts from it show something of the tensions between the two men. Some of his reasons, he admits, 'may seem comparatively insignificant'. He began with the fact that, as a result of the plans for All Saints, 'the regular upkeep of the churchyard, as well as

of the Rector's garden, has been my responsibility, and I am beginning to dread the thought of another season of this'.

Next, 'I find that I am getting tired much more quickly than one
used to do. Soon after I came to Lincoln, you made it clear that in
your view the Rector was in a special position in regard to sabbatical
leave, and ought not to regard himself as "entitled" to the ordinary
ration.' He had had one term in fifteen years, but hesitated to ask for
another; to do so 'would mean that one got still further out of touch
with College affairs'.

'And of course', he went on, 'I must take careful account of the
note you put in about the conduct of business in College meetings,
at the end of last term, and of the possibility that it represents a
widely held view: that the College needs someone more precise in
his methods, and more assertive, to administer its affairs.' This last
criticism was indeed shared by a number of Fellows who however
would not therefore have wanted him to go. But Cox had clearly fired
it as a parting shot before handing over that month as Sub-Rector to
Green.

Oakeshott accordingly sent Green a copy of his letter to Cox.
Green replied on 8 July, pressing him to stay at least for one more
year, viz. till 1972, and in any case not to make any hasty decision.
The College could perfectly properly take over the maintenance of
the Rector's garden and the churchyard, and he was also 'pretty sure
that it would readily grant' a term's sabbatical leave. More generally
he wrote, rather as Walker had written at Winchester in 1949, 'You
may not realise the extent to which the College values your services.
The College – and I have said this to you before – is in many ways a
strange and at times quirkish body. It does not wear its heart on its
sleeve; but I'm pretty sure that it would hope you would reconsider
your decision.'

Oakeshott was touched. He wrote again on 10 July, agreeing to let
things run for a while but amplifying one point. 'I have been absurdly
tired lately. It may be nothing more than worrying about the new
house [at Eynsham], which I've been bound to do; though Noel is
interested, it is not really in her line at all, and the planning has
substantially to be done by me.'* With hindsight one can see early
warnings of the heart attack he suffered in 1973.

Eventually he agreed to stay on as Rector for another year, though

*On the Eynsham house see further below pp. 286–7.

he was grateful for the sabbatical term given him in the summer of 1971. Apart from other factors, it suited all parties to have him and Noel based for some months at Eynsham, where the conversion was done and enough furniture and books already transferred. Their absence from the Rector's Lodgings eased the substantial building works needed there as a by-product of the plan for All Saints. It thus happened that he was absent from a dramatic meeting of the Fellows on Chapter Day (6 May) 1971.

At that time there was a good deal of talk among the Oxford men's colleges of admitting women. None had yet taken the plunge. Two of the younger Fellows, Ball and Simpson, were attracted by the prospect of Lincoln leading the field, and proposed that it should be considered. To their surprise, the motion was carried. Since it involved a change in the Statutes, it required a two-thirds majority at a special meeting the following October; but everyone regarded it as close to a *fait accompli* and planned accordingly.

Oakeshott immediately confirmed his intention to resign in the summer of 1972. He was certainly not put out by the fact that the proposal had been put forward in his absence, and indeed without his knowledge. He insisted that such a decision was for the younger Fellows and not for 'old fogeys like me'. He also declared, a little less insistently, that on the principle of co-residence he was 'an agnostic rather than an opponent'.

What worried him was the effect of the decision upon the planned appeal for the All Saints conversion. He could not see an appeal being successfully directed in these circumstances to Old Members. They must be expected to be traditionalists, especially the older ones upon whom most would depend. He would be happy to take on 'a limited appeal outside the College constituency, perhaps by deciding to name the library "The Wesley Library"'. Any appeal to Old Members he would support if someone else launched it; but on balance he thought it should be postponed for a few years.

In the event, the proposal for co-residence failed by one vote to secure the necessary majority in October 1971, and did not succeed until 1976. The appeal was therefore able to go ahead as planned, and Oakeshott devoted much of his last year as Rector to it. Now that he was going, even his critics among the Fellows felt warmly disposed. When a legacy of £3,000 came in, they invited him to refurbish a pair of rooms for the use of the ever-growing Senior Common Room. It was just the kind of thing he enjoyed. His elaborate plans had to be scaled down, but it is still a fine room. Somewhat ironically, it is used now, among other purposes, for morning coffee.

8

Eynsham

1972–1987

The fifteen years of Oakeshott's life in retirement, 1972–87, were marked by two troughs and two peaks. The lesser trough was his serious heart attack in 1973, from which his health never fully recovered; the greater was Noel's death in 1976. The lesser peak was his knighthood in 1980, the greater the publication in 1981 of *The Two Winchester Bibles*, the culmination of his main work as a scholar.

Throughout that time he lived in the Old School House at Eynsham. For someone who has spent all his working life in a 'tied cottage', the provision of a retirement home is an anxiety which increases sharply as the age of sixty approaches. The Oakeshotts had never been rich. Walter's sole inheritance was £100 from an aunt; everything else he had earned himself. His capital consisted of the flat in Rome together with his movable possessions. The flat would have to go. It was put on the market at the end of 1968, but proved hard to sell.

Of course he had other resources. Whenever during his working life he had accumulated some savings – and often also when he had not – he had bought rare books and objets d'art, partly for pleasure but partly for investment. His knowledge, taste and 'eye' were such that he bought and sold well. Such sales had helped to finance the children's education, the purchase of the flat in Rome, and also his own generosity to family and friends. For he had made regular allowances to his mother while she was alive, and to his sister Maggie after her husband lost his money in the crash of 1933; and he helped with the fees of her two sons at St Paul's. To friends throughout his life he gave valuable presents, sometimes at the expense of the housekeeping.

Noel, unlike Walter, had a little money of her own. When her father died in 1953 she inherited about £6,000. This brought her in a small allowance while Walter was earning, but she fully expected to have to spend capital in their retirement in order to be sure of domestic help and comfort.

Finally there was now his pension from Lincoln. The College maintained a private fund, whose annual product was divided among its pensioners. Oakeshott had contributed for a mere eighteen years, and in 1972 could not look forward to a princely return. As it happened, however, the mortality rate among his fellow pensioners lifted his own share unexpectedly. Within a few years he was free, for the first time in his life, of financial worries.

But that happy state lay in the future. Now what they needed was a house in a place they liked at a price they could afford. The first problem was location. Noel was fundamentally a 'town' girl – she had once ruled out a possible job for him at Eton on the ground that it was 'in the provinces' – and would have liked a small house in central Oxford. Walter wanted a place large enough to accommodate his library and other treasures, and to spread himself while working. He also wanted a good-sized garden. That meant the country, and he began to prospect.

In 1968 he lit upon the old primary school in Eynsham. For a long time he did not tell Noel about it. But he wrote to Cook that it was 'terribly dilapidated but could I believe be charming'. It would also 'provide two dwelling "units", one of which we'd probably furnish (having had large houses, we've got a lot of furniture) and let'. In fact the scope which the property offered for an imaginative conversion was a positive attraction to him, as with the Bell House and the flat in Rome.

In 1969 he bought the building for a little over £2,000. Again he did not tell Noel till afterwards. From there things went from bad to worse. Noel refused to have anything to do with the conversion. Walter brought in other women friends to help. Noel, not having been consulted even about such matters as the planning of the lights, had lasting grounds for complaint. Such was the distance now between them.

The old school building had consisted of two large classrooms, one for infants and one for juniors, on either side of a central block which provided modest living quarters for the head teacher. Each classroom had its own entrance, reminding Walter of 'houses with two doors, out of one of which Noah comes, with an umbrella when it rains; out of the other Mrs Noah when it's fine'.

His 'elaborate brief' for the conversion[1] called, in the architect's words, for 'a division into roughly one quarter and three quarters, with the larger house unusually well provided with day-rooms and utilities'. A major problem was presented by the high window-sills of the classrooms. This was solved, expensively, by raising the floor two feet, on the same principle as in the All Saints Library. Even so, the classrooms were high enough to allow the creation of a first floor, running up under the eaves. With two balconies added, that also was expensive. The whole conversion, including the provision of a double garage, cost £22,260, over the years 1969 to 1971.

With the furnishings etc. added in, the total came to well over £30,000 – far and away more than he had bargained for. To meet it the flat in Rome had been sold in 1969, for about £20,000; but there were great difficulties in getting the money out of Italy, and the final instalment was not received until 1974. A loan of £5,000 came from sister Maggie, now a widow: it had been agreed that she would occupy the second 'unit'. But that still left a considerable shortfall.

So Walter sold the Borchardt measure and 'all his best' books. There were five sales at Sotheby's between December 1971 and October 1973. The measure fetched £1,250 and the four book sales £3,854.[2] Since Walter had always bought and sold books, he could treat their loss philosophically. 'Heigh-ho' he wrote in 1977 at the end of an article on the cream of his library, 'all these books have long since been dispersed. But the scattered remnants of a library are not *disjecta membra*. Each is in itself a piece of history; something one hopes that shines with a tiny added gleam, from one's ownership.'

In July 1972 Walter and Noel moved for good into the Old School House, Eynsham. In spite of its cost, the conversion was in general a great success. It had provided, in addition to the usual living rooms and three bedrooms, a big study for him and a smaller one for her. But large house though it was, it only just had room for their extensive and valuable mixture of heirlooms and acquisitions, furniture and carpets, books and pictures and other objets d'art.

At one end of the building was a flat on two floors, occupied since 1971 by Maggie. She and Noel were dissimilar in most ways, but for Walter's sake they had always managed to rub along together. He was now back in the position he had enjoyed in his youth, of having more than one woman to look after him. Maggie did not obtrude herself, but was there when wanted. In particular she shared with him the responsibility for the garden, where she was 'extremely keen, very gifted and works tirelessly'. The garden included the old asphalted school playground, of which he wrote later that 'getting it to look like anything was a business; to keep it looking like anything is even worse'.

Oakeshott had long planned what was to be the main occupation of his retirement. It was to put in place the final pieces of that larger jigsaw puzzle of which the Winchester Bible was the centre. Since his own seminal work of 1945, *The Artists of the Winchester Bible*, discoveries had been made by three other Oxford scholars. That of Pächt he had already picked off and assimilated in his *Sigena* of 1972. There remained those of Ker and Boase.

Neil Ker was one of the foremost living experts on medieval manuscripts. About 1950 he had realized that the text of the Winchester Bible must have been corrected alongside that of another large twelfth-century bible now in the Bodleian. That bible is inelegantly known to scholars by its shelf-mark there[3] as 'the Auct. bible'. But it had been given to Bodley in 1601 by the Chapter of Winchester Cathedral, so it was in Winchester that the two bibles (here A and W for short) had lain side by side. Ker showed that in some places the text of A had been amended to conform to that of W; in some places the converse; elsewhere again both A and W seemed to have been corrected to conform to a third.

Ker reported this discovery in his Lyell lectures for 1952, though he had told Oakeshott of it a year or two earlier.[4] During that same time Boase was studying the paintings in A, which he called 'perhaps the greatest repertory of Romanesque ornament' in England. On various grounds, including Ker's discovery about the texts, Boase suggested that A might be called 'the second Winchester bible'.[5]

Here were the germs of Oakeshott's last great work, *The Two Winchester Bibles* (1981). Being free now at Eynsham to devote himself to it, he had a first draft on paper as early as January 1973. But before he could take it further there was a promise to redeem to Lincoln: the completion of the appeal for the All Saints Library. During the autumn of 1972 he harvested Old Members in Britain. At the end of January 1973 he set about a trawl of North America.

Oakeshott had by now a formidable network of contacts in the USA. There were family in New York, Maine and California. There were old friends and colleagues in universities, museums and libraries on both coasts, chief among them Charles Mitchell at Bryn Mawr. To these could now be added loyal alumni, from Toronto down to

Mexico. Between them they provided bases for a variety of activities which would fill three months: the alumni for fund-raising, universities for lecturing and his own research, friends and family for occasional relaxation if not rest.

It was a strenuous programme, the more so if Noel was right to say, in a letter of 16 March, that he was overtired already when he set out. A few days later, after a weekend trip to Texas, he suffered a severe heart attack. Fortunately he was by then back at his favourite academic base, the Huntington Library at San Marino, California. He was taken immediately to the Huntington Memorial Hospital, which kept him in for a fortnight. Permission was then given for a move to the house of friends nearby, who looked after him devotedly till he was fit to come home at the end of April.

Lincoln also looked after him. On 24 March Green was able to send him a message that the appeal target had been reached, thus relieving him of anxiety about the rest of the tour. But the Fellows, regarding him as 'an essentially unworldly person', felt a further responsibility. So on the 26th they sent out Peter Atkins, a young physics don, in case he needed to be rescued. Atkins and his wife were friends of the Oakeshotts, who had lent them the flat in Rome. In the event Atkins found him in good hands. But Oakeshott was deeply touched by Lincoln's solicitude.

Noel wrote on 6 April that she might travel out to accompany him home. She could afford the fare out but not a hotel. Nevertheless she wrote to him every day, and most of her letters survive, the last batch to do so from her to him. She devotes much space to topical concerns: his health, of course, and the preparations for the imminent wedding of Evelyn, now close on forty. Other anxieties are the recurrent ones: money, her own health, and the heating system. But the sharp wit is still there. A letter of February reports receipt of an invitation from the Skinners to Ladies Day. It will be a visit to the Derby on 6 June. 'Wild horses wouldn't drag me there, but if you want to attend with some more adventurous lady, please let me know.' On 7 March Green had shown her the portrait of Walter, commissioned by the College and just completed.

NOTHING in this world could have prepared me for the sight of something so frightful. . . . The hands are *awful*. Sometimes your poor hands are blue with cold, but never that colour. The best bit of painting is the shoes, which are idealized. I know you used to polish them up most assiduously, but only an Athenian boot-boy could have produced such a shine!

Oakeshott's chief fear during his long convalescence was that he should die, or, worse, be incapacitated before he had got his *magnum opus* into publishable form. Conversely, if he could live to see it actually published, preferably by the Oxford University Press, his dearest wish would be realized. It therefore had an overriding priority once he had regained his strength. As the culmination of his life as a scholar, it was of course to be on an entirely different scale from the little monograph of twenty-two pages with which he had first announced himself. In particular it must include a good number of colour plates, and they must be as near lifesize as possible. This meant a very large and expensive book.

He had the text sufficiently polished to send it to the Press in August 1974. In July 1975 it was accepted for publication, provided that a substantial sum could be raised to subsidize the quality of production which they and he both wanted. Oakeshott set about the task with all his old single-mindedness and a renewed impatience. But neither the Press nor potential benefactors could be hurried. He therefore had time to pay various debts of honour: three in all.

First he had long promised to round off what he had done for the Oxford Historic Buildings Fund by putting together a final account of its operation. The plan was to devote most of the space to individual college and university buildings; and the material for that had already been prepared by others. Oakeshott left those accounts substantially unchanged, but added an introduction on 'The Origins of the Fund'. In it he found room to discourse upon his own two favourite concerns, good quality stone and fine craftsmanship. The same two themes run through the forty-four outstanding photographs which he chose to illustrate the text. Finally he saw the whole production through to its publication by the OUP in 1975 as *Oxford Stone Restored*.

His second debt in 1974–5 was to the Huntington Library in California for the especial care its people had given him in 1973. He offered for its *Quarterly* an article on one of its own rare books: *Love's Martyr* by Robert Chester, published in 1601. The book's title page describes it as 'allegorically showing the truth of Love, in the constant fate of the Phoenix and the Turtle'. The interest of Chester's book lies not in his own poem but in an Appendix. There Chester prints 'some new compositions' on the same subject by 'the best and choicest of our moderne writers'. The twelve poems there printed include Shakespeare's own *The Phoenix and the Turtle* and also poems by Ben Jonson, Chapman and (probably) Raleigh.

All Elizabethan allegory offers endless scope for scholarly speculation. In 1965 this whole complex of poems had been the subject of a book by Professor W. H. Matchett. Oakeshott now writes that his own 'article can be regarded as a footnote to [Matchett's] book, the main conclusions of which I find entirely convincing'. And indeed the significance of his 1975 article lies not in itself but in the obsession with which he reverted to the subject at the very end of his life.

Thirdly in 1974–5 he had a more personal debt to pay. His old Tonbridge teacher and friend Vere Hodge had died in 1970. Some years before he had given most of his estate to the school. For his working papers he had turned down an offer from an American university and left them instead to Oakeshott, appointing him literary executor. On his death Oakeshott wrote an appreciation of him for *The Times* referring to 'that small band of particular friends which give a schoolmaster's life its special rewards' – something he knew from both sides. He planned also to uproot a catalpa from Vere Hodge's garden and replant it at Eynsham at a cost of £250; but at nineteen years the tree was too old to move.

There was however a more durable project which Oakeshott was able to realize. Vere Hodge during his lifetime had written a number of occasional verses about cricket. Thirty-two of them – some previously published, some not – were now handsomely printed in a limited edition by a private press. The title *Five Overs and Two Wides* refers to the inclusion of one poem in French and one in Latin. The text was illustrated by a daughter of Oakeshott's old friend Reynolds Stone, and the book designed by her husband. Oakeshott himself wrote an introduction in which he recalled his schooldays at Tonbridge, with pen-portraits of masters. In it he manages to hint, without pitching the claim too high, that cricket may not be a religion but is more than a game, and that Vere Hodge might not be a poet but was more than a felicitous versifier. The whole production is a charming tribute from friend to friend.

In the summer of 1975 the Warden and Fellows of Winchester took a decision which caused grave alarm in the hearts of many lovers of the school, including especially Oakeshott's. They decided to consider selling the Malory manuscript. Their reasoning was as follows. First, they felt themselves under political threat. The Labour Party, which had got back into power in 1974, was threatening the charitable status of independent schools. Specifically it proposed to investigate each school's finances to see whether the endowments – which in Winchester's case were large – were being used for purposes which could reasonably be regarded as charitable. Curiously, this was a consideration which Oakeshott himself had urged on the Mercers in 1944 when he was arguing for changes at St Paul's.

The Governing Body of Winchester took this threat very seriously indeed. The Warden, Lord Sherfield, actually wrote that they were 'dealing with the most serious situation which the College had faced since the Civil War'. They therefore reviewed all their 'treasures', i.e. those assets which brought in no income. Outstanding among them was the Malory manuscript. As it happened, the Early English Text Society was in process of bringing out a facsimile edition of it; which lessened both the intangible benefit of its possession and the price obtainable by its sale. What that price might be was hard to determine in advance.

In June 1975, therefore, they decided to test the waters: 'to consider selling [it] subject to consultation with Dr Oakeshott, whom the Warden undertook to approach; and in the event of sale to invest the proceeds and use the income to provide bursaries'. Bursaries in the context meant financial assistance for the entry of bright boys from poor homes, a purpose which was, in every sense of the word, charitable.

In August Sherfield rang up Oakeshott. 'He asked if he could come and see me; there was a project they had, in which I had a right to be interested. At first I couldn't imagine what was up. Then I realized what it was likely to be. I was appalled.' Not trusting himself to speak unemotionally when they met, he prepared a note, dated 6 August, to hand to Sherfield. On the understanding that the note would be circulated to the Fellows, he would abide by their decision. 'If you decide to sell, I will certainly refuse to be associated with any protest, if any should be projected.' He goes on:

> I must confess that a sale would cause me great sadness. This is partly – mainly – because there is a presumption that your manuscript was made (I think actually for the [St Swithun's] Priory Library) at a time when Arthur, eldest son of Henry VII, was baptised in the Cathedral Church. . . . So [it] has been part

of Winchester history from the time it was written. Malory iden-tifies Camelot explicitly with Winchester.

This 'presumption' had been in Oakeshott's mind almost from the moment he identified the manuscript, and he continued to refer to it throughout his life. Sometimes he wrote of it as a certainty, some-times as a plausible hypothesis. It has not been universally accepted.

Oakeshott's note of 6 August goes on to add a second argument.

> I suspect that one day Winchester and Eton, and perhaps a few other great schools, will form the nuclei of institutions to which the ablest boys (and girls too, I suppose) will go for part of their higher education: Liberal Arts Colleges; or Graduate Schools; or whatever it may be. For such a purpose Winchester College, with its situation, its buildings, and its library seems specially favoured. If the future were to work out in that way, the Malory would remain particularly at home in Winchester; and Malory's book, with his fusion of the great French medieval romances with an English epic, is in a sense the representative of a Western European tradition to a degree that can be claimed of no other English author.

This second argument Oakeshott describes in his note as 'more down to earth'. In fact it is an imaginative vision which surpasses even the one he had set before the Governors of St Paul's thirty years earlier.

But arguments like these simply did not engage with the considera-tions that weighed on the other side. Oakeshott himself realized this after Sherfield had gone. In a retrospective account written in 1981 he put his finger on the nub of the matter. 'Of course I'm a sentimen-talist,' he wrote. 'Lord Sherfield is not a sentimentalist.' And in 1994 Sherfield was happy to accept the description: 'Where money is con-cerned, I hope I'm not.'

Oakeshott's fertile mind conceived one last idea. He put it in a letter* of 18 September to the Bursar, as secretary to the Governing Body. 'I do not think there is any chance of raising in England the sort of sum £200,000 – which I gather is being discussed. If the money were to come, it would have to come from America. I am

---

*In the same letter he mentioned the forthcoming facsimile edition. He conceded that 'with its appearance the academic interest of the manuscript has been ex-hausted. But it is an extraordinary relic like the Round Table; and its alienation from Winchester would virtually destroy that interest.'

therefore going to get in touch with friends there to explore the possibilities.'

The Fellows met on 4 October, having read Oakeshott's note of 6 August. They also considered his offer, reported by the Bursar, to approach 'friends' in America. They postponed a decision about the sale, but 'the Warden undertook to write to Dr Oakeshott, who had written to the Bursar to say that he might be able to raise the necessary money in the USA to enable the College to receive the equivalent of the expected sale price, but with the stipulation that the manuscript remained in Winchester, probably in the Cathedral Library.' Sherfield wrote on 10 October. 'We very much appreciate your readiness to take an initiative in the United States. However we should be very reluctant for you to embark on such an arduous and awkward mission, and we really prefer that you should not attempt it. There is in any case no immediate urgency. . . . The decision to go ahead was postponed.'

Oakeshott accordingly dropped the plan. But he and his friends felt slighted and steam-rollered, and the matter still rankles. Was the decision of the Governing Body as churlish as it seems? No reasons for it are recorded, but Sherfield in 1994 recalled what was in their minds. Oakeshott's plan was too vague; it had no real chance of success; and it could have dragged on inconclusively for months. Oakeshott himself, when he came to write about it in 1981, described a much more precise plan.

> I have a Californian friend, a rich woman, who chooses to spend her fortune on works of art (mainly for a museum over there). I don't know her really well, but well enough to approach her. I planned to bring her over; show her the College, the Cathedral, the manuscript and so on – and hope to persuade her. I realized of course that the matter was urgent: if the money was not forthcoming in six weeks, so be it.

Sadly, no such precise plan ever reached the Warden and Fellows. 'If we had known that', said Sherfield in 1994, 'we should certainly have thought again.' In truth, the two men were of such different temperaments that there was no meeting of minds between them. If they had been able to communicate, the outcome would almost certainly have been the same, but the hard feelings would have softened.

That outcome is briefly told. In November 1975 the Warden and Fellows resolved to explore the possibility of a sale to the British Library. Lord Eccles, who was currently Chairman of it, offered

£100,000.* Negotiations raised the offer to £150,000. On 31 January 1976 the decision was taken, with three dissentients, to sell at that figure.† Eccles later admitted that he had got a bargain, but the income from the proceeds has enabled two boys a year whose parents could not otherwise have afforded it to enter the school as Malory Scholars. As to whether it was right to sell, the issue of *principle* is still the same: the weight – and the meaning – which should be given to what Oakeshott called sentiment.

In March 1976 he wrote a long and careful article on the Malory manuscript for *The Trusty Servant*, an Old Wykehamist house journal. In it he rehearsed his theory of the manuscript's origin and its subsequent history down to his own identification of it in 1934. There is no mention of its sale, nor any nuance that could be read as a criticism of it. He was as good as his word.

The same is true of the review which he wrote later in 1976 of the Early English Text Society's facsimile of the manuscript. But in that review he adumbrated for the first time a theme which was to loom increasingly large whenever in the rest of his life he was writing or talking about the *Morte d'Arthur*. Malory, he argued, introduced into English literature a new conception of tragedy. 'There is no tragedy, only perhaps tedium, in the death of Galahad the perfect; but the tragedy in the fate of Arthur, Mordred, Gawaine, Lancelot, Guinevere, those sinning humans each so astonishingly individual, becomes almost as moving as any in literature.'

In early May 1976 Noel went into hospital. She 'had had a lot of pain for a long time and at last decided on an operation that for a younger person should have been comparatively minor but which she knew at our age might go wrong – which it did'. Peritonitis set in, 'so that things seemed desperate; then a second operation brought hope of recovery, and she seemed to be gradually climbing back to health'.

Walter went in to spend 'most of every day with her, reading to her, or talking – or just sitting with her'. He read her a lot of poetry, especially Hopkins. The three youngest children came to see her.

---

*Oakeshott and Eccles had never got on well. The antipathy was doubtless temperamental in origin but was exacerbated c. 1961, when Oakeshott, as pro-Vice-Chancellor, had resisted plans of Eccles, as Secretary of State for Education and Science, to exercise greater governmental control over universities. 'We won,' wrote Oakeshott c. 1985. 'He's never forgiven me.' Eccles's comment on this biography was 'What a job writing a whole book about W.O!'

†Critics say the Warden and Fellows let it go too cheap. They could certainly have got much more for it in the USA. but they had resolved not to let it go out of the country.

Helena could not get there, but wrote every day. Walter read Noel her letters, and 'she'd often talk about them two or three days later, in a way which showed she was living every line of them'. On 17 June he took her the proof of a long *JHS* review she had done.[6] On the 18th Rose came with her twelve-year-old son Jasper to talk about the Trojan War* and his own recent trip to Greece; and 'tho' she was desperately ill and could not talk much, it meant everything to her'. That was 'her best day'. The following day, 19 June 1976, she died.

During those six weeks, he wrote,

> we'd come to know each other far better than ever before. I realized to my shame the great qualities of uncomplaining courage, patience and heightened imagination I'd failed to recognize till almost too late. I realized above all that gentler spirit which the knocking of death on the door may summon – and which is a marvellous thing. So those last weeks will be a very precious memory. Almost the most precious of all.[7]

Those private letters reveal only the tip of the grief and remorse he felt. It was not just that they had drifted apart, or that he had failed to recognize her qualities. He had neglected her. He had become so absorbed in his projects and his friendships that he had left her out of a large part of his life. Physically she could not accompany him on his many travels. Temperamentally she could not share his unbuttoned enthusiasms. Emotionally she felt excluded by his warm friendships with both men and women. Much of this he had foreseen at the time of their marriage. All of it he now saw only too clearly.

The sense of guilt never left him. Privately, his letters are full of references to his 'selfishness'. Publicly, he expressed it in two Latin inscriptions. When *The Two Winchester Bibles* was finally published in 1981, the dedication read:

MEMORIAE CONIVGIS DILECTAE
OPVS HOC QVALECVMQVE
CVI PER TOT ANNOS TOT HORAS
ILLI DEBITAS
DEVOVI
DESIDERIO PAENE IPSE CONFECTVS
CONFECTVM TANDEM DEDICO

*As a child Noel 'used to pray every night to meet Hector in Heaven' (letter of 28 March 1927).

It is a marvellous and poignant piece of Latin, but untranslatable. There is no English equivalent for *desiderium* which means 'longing for that which one once had'; nor will 'finished' do for *confectus*. Worse, English will not really sustain the word-order, on which the distribution of lines depends.But here is an attempt to bring out the emotion with which it is charged.

> To the memory of my beloved wife
> this work, such as it is,
> to which (over so many years) so many hours
> owed to her
> I devoted,
> now with longing myself almost undone,
> done at last I dedicate.

A few years later when he came, as he increasingly did, to plan for his own death, he asked the Fellows of Lincoln for the unusual privilege of a memorial plaque in Chapel. For the inscription he chose the clause from the Lord's Prayer:

DIMITTE NOBIS DEBITA NOSTRA

The choice of text was remarkable enough. Contrary to convention it drew attention not to his successes but to his failures. But there is more to it. The Latin is not that of the Mass but of the Vulgate, the version he had read so often at morning prayers at St. Paul's. In it the word used for 'trespasses' or 'sins', *debita*, points directly to that debt which he had 'owed' but never paid to Noel.[8]

Nevertheless life somehow went on. Domestically there had to be reorganization. 'Our faithful Spanish woman necessarily had to go – and of course the house will never look the same again; she was so proud of it. I cook myself porridge for breakfast, and go round to Maggie for other meals.' Walter and Maggie had always been as close as brother and sister can be. Now, for the eleven years that he lived after Noel's death, they became as essential to each other as an old married couple. She, as the practical one in the family, kept house – her cooking was superb – and masterminded the garden. But she was much more to him than that. They shared not only a lifetime of retrospect but also a second childhood. Once again, as in their youth, they went on walks together, and picked sloes for sloe gin to keep out the winter cold.

But devoted as they were to each other, they needed separate space. When Walter put a door in the wall between his house and her flat, they normally kept it closed. For the passage of time had done nothing to bring their tastes and temperaments closer together. Though wise, she was entirely unacademic, and their social circles did not overlap. Her many friends in the neighbourhood could always find a warm welcome in her flat, with challenging but light-hearted talk, and (at the right time of day) a gin and tonic without too much tonic. Walter's friends were mostly Oxford-based and, like him, inclined to 'stick to the hock' (see p. 303). Maggie once joined him at a Ladies' Night in Lincoln, but declined further invitations to what she called 'a grand do at that college of his'. But she would sit up at night till he was safely home, and get him to tell her about it next day. Most important of all, she could laugh him out of his black moods. When he died in 1987, she 'for a little tried to live without him, liked it not, and died'.[9]

Walter's mode of working changed too after Noel's death. The door of her study he now kept permanently shut. For the rest, having the house to himself, he moved from room to room. When the work space in one room was cluttered up, he left the clutter and moved on to the next. And work was the solace. Already on 19 July he was writing to the Press that 'the Winchester Bible, like an old and intimate friend, is one of the few things about which just now I am able to think straight'. In another context he amplified the point. 'It is curious how intimate the "friendship" between a critic and the artists he has, in a sense, himself created, can be; the reason perhaps that it is imagination speaking to imagination, his to theirs.'

The immediate task was to raise the necessary subsidies. In August the Pilgrim Trust wrote to say that, if the British Academy made a grant, they would do likewise: it was 'an open and shut case'. The hope at that time was for £3,500 from the Pilgrim Trust, which, with £1,000 from the Academy, would make up half the production costs, then estimated at £9,000. On the strength of this the Press in November 1976 accepted the book unconditionally. Entitled *The Two Winchester Bibles*, it would contain 'illustrations of all the most important decorations meriting reproduction'. The plan was to publish in 1979, which by a happy coincidence was the 900th anniversary of the Cathedral's foundation.

Oakeshott made this the occasion for resigning his Pilgrim Trusteeship. He had been a Trustee for nearly thirty years. He had contributed greatly to the work of the Trust, starting with the unemployment inquiry of 1936–8, and ending with the York Glaziers' Trust. The Trust in turn had made generous grants to institutions with which he was connected; Winchester and Lincoln Colleges, Oxford University and Winchester Cathedral. He had always been sensitive about his position in the case of such grants. Now, though the application was from the Press, he would be, more personally than ever before, a beneficiary. Finally he had lost interest. 'I can't do anything', he wrote to Mitchell in September, 'without reckoning it's an offering to [Noel]. My other foolish occupations e.g. the Pilgrim Trust, have become a nonsense.' With his seventy-fifth birthday approaching, it was a good moment to go.

In the summer of 1977 the Pilgrim Trust made a grant of £2,000 for publication. This was a disappointment, the more so since production costs were now estimated at £15,000. The Press began to hesitate, and Oakeshott became anxious. A letter of 3 October thanks him for his 'gentle reminder that time is passing'. A few days later salvation appeared to be offered from an unexpected source. A large American publishing house, Harcourt Brace Jovanovic, invited the Press to join them in publishing a colour facsimile of the whole Winchester Bible.

Oakeshott himself thought the idea 'something of a nonsense'. The *text* of W, unlike that of A, was 'on the whole an uninteresting example'. Moreover neither the text nor the paintings of W had ever been finished. To the Press however it was an attractive proposition, since it enabled them to cut the number of illustrations in Oakeshott's book.

On that basis his text was agreed in January 1978. By October he had received, corrected and returned the galley-proofs. But at that moment 'the line went dead' on the proposal for a facsimile. It was too late now to revert to the original plan and to include *all* 'decorations meriting reproduction'. But some of those discarded were now indispensable. Oakeshott was especially concerned about the colour plates, which had been cut to eight. An approach in April 1979 to the Marc Fitch Foundation produced a subsidy of £500 towards the cost of two more; to this he offered to add a further £500 of his own. The Press in May agreed to provide the two more, and would 'try not to accept his £500'. Later they agreed to yet another page, making eleven all; but an internal memo of April 1980 lays down that 'he must be categorically told NOT to sneak in any further alterations'.

For all this had inevitably delayed publication. In the summer of 1979 it was put back to 1980, in April 1980 to 1981. Printing began in August 1980. At last the end was in sight. Since the book's acceptance in 1975, it had been a frustrating five years for him. His powers were declining. With every year he found the job of checking detail more arduous and less effective. His health, never robust, was precarious – he was in hospital three times in that period – and he could never be sure of living to see the final production, however glorious. With forbearance on both sides, good relations with the Press were maintained. But friends knew of his unremitting anxiety.

This concern about his own book overlapped his lifelong concern for Winchester Cathedral. From the start he had asked that half the royalties should go to the Cathedral library. In 1978 he proposed to the Press a paperback on the Bible, for sale in the Cathedral. The text would cross-refer not to the 'second' bible, as in his book, but to the wall-paintings in the Holy Sepulchre Chapel. It would fit the 900th anniversary in 1979; and he had even written a draft. The Press did not take long to say no.

Instead he wrote a long article for the *Guardian Weekend* in celebration of Cathedral, library and Bible. He was not pleased with the result. 'I don't know when I've been so upset. The whole piece was written round a marvellous sentence in Proust, in which he talks of the church at Combray and says it has a fourth dimension: the dimension of time. ... They never sent the proofs I had asked for.' They also cut his text in such a way as to nullify his usual self-effacement. It therefore records some happy personal details e.g. 'My first memory of Winchester is of a newspaper cutting shown me as a small child[10] about William Walker the Diver who, in that massive diver's suit looking like a submarine, worked for month after month to grout the foundations [of the Cathedral] with concrete.'

All this time he was continuing his own visits to the Bible, sometimes for his own purposes but increasingly often to take friends and scholars. One such visit may stand for many. In August 1979 he went down with Charles Mitchell and Jenny Sheppard, a graduate student of his, who had heard Oakeshott lecture at Bryn Mawr in 1978, and was now doing her PhD on another twelfth-century bible. She recalls the occasion, in words which echo those of his Wykehamist pupils thirty years earlier. 'We went by train from Oxford to Winchester, where I had the enormously exciting pleasure of seeing virtually the whole Winchester Bible, page by page, explained and enthused over by the great man himself. It was inspirational for me, an utterly green graduate student.' His own letter to Helena, describing the same visit, says typically: 'I managed to get my small piece of checking done quickly – and, as usual, learnt a lot from the other two.' He took to Jenny Sheppard, encouraged her work, and even proposed a collaborative article a few years later.

It was not always so, at least in prospect. A year later he wrote to Helena about another forthcoming visit with an American doctoral student. This one was 'studying a magnificent bronze candlestick in Milan Cathedral, that's the same date'. But the cathedral authorities now

> won't let anyone have the pages turned unless I'm there to do it. It's becoming a bore – and I think I'll have to write to the Dean soon, and say they must get someone who's *there*. I've promised to give them my books on illumination (as I gave the collection about mosaics to Somerville). Perhaps if I start on that it will be an excuse to abandon the duty.

He was, after all, nearly seventy-seven.

Honours came to Oakeshott rather late and few. So at least his friends judged, though he himself would never have entertained, still less expressed, the thought. Honours meant less than nothing to him, except in so far as they entailed meeting interesting people or, better still, becoming a member of a congenial fraternity. So the Honorary Fellowship to which Balliol elected him in 1974 was a source of great pleasure. He took little or no part in college affairs, but enjoyed the social occasions, especially the dinners: good food and wine (not too much of either), and interesting people with whom there was time to talk.

A highlight was the dinner given by Balliol in 1984 in honour of Macmillan's ninetieth birthday. As Vice-Chancellor, Oakeshott had been what Macmillan called his 'first prime minister', and had got to know him quite well. Now he found himself for twenty minutes before dinner alone with him and the Master's wife.

> It was an amazing experience. To hear him talk about N. Africa during the last three years of the war, I found absolutely fascinating. Then there was a little ceremony when the Porter's Lodge staff, four of them, came up to make a presentation to him of a glass bowl: one of them engraves glass as a hobby, and

M. peeering at it and feeling it [he was nearly blind] was quite delighted: it was indeed an occasion: before forty or fifty of the guests came in for champagne, prior to strolling over to Hall.

After dinner there were speeches. 'M. spoke for something like twenty minutes: amusing, creative, sentimental: a fabulous performance for his age.'

By that time he was himself Sir Walter Oakeshott, Kt. The proposal had come from the fraternity which meant more than any other to him in the last thirty years of his life, the Skinners' Company. He loved its camaraderie and believed in its mystique. There he was among friends of all ages: people interesting and influential, but in that context unassertive – for those of them who enjoyed power could wield it elsewhere. There he need harden his heart for no decisions, close his ears to no altercations; and because the company was congenial, even the business could be fun.

Top of the business agenda was the governance of Tonbridge School. As a member of the Tonbridge Committee almost continuously from 1958, he had kept in touch with the affairs of the school without ever interfering. In Committee he would remain silent until the Clerk nudged the Chairman. 'Asked for his opinion, he would disclaim expertise with some such words as "Well, of course I'm getting very out of date, but it seems to me that. . .'; but then, in his somewhat hesitant and precise manner, which reflected his natural modesty and a careful choice of words, he would deliver his advice.' It was always heard with respect, and often closed the discussion. The most memorable example of this was his speech advocating the refurbishment of the school organ in 1979. The minutes record that, when he had spoken, 'it was agreed by the Governors that by hook or by crook the organ must be fully restored, even if other expenditure had to abate'.

Another committee he enjoyed was that which managed the Lawrence Atwell Charity, a seventeenth-century Trust founded for 'setting young men on work'. The investments had done well,[11] and he enjoyed distributing 'what are still quite respectable amounts to a number of young men who are trying to get on in many different fields'. Moreover the resources of the Skinners enabled them to contemplate new projects. In 1974 he proposed a programme of research into the trade between England and Russia in the sixteenth century, in particular the part played by Sir Andrew Judde (the leading Skinner of the day and Founder of Tonbridge School) in the Muscovy Company, which had been established to find a replacement for the collapsed fur trade. The research project was accepted in principle and, though never implemented, led to one of his last publications.

But of all Skinners' committees the most congenial was the House Committee. As at Winchester and Oxford he devoted many hours, and wrote frequent letters, about the fabric of Skinners' Hall, its décor and pictures and silver and all other properties. His colleagues found 'his taste in matters aesthetic impeccable'. Experience at Lincoln had also developed his taste in food and wine – and even, more surprisingly, his eye for an investment. His particular love was hock. He often referred to the experience of being invited, when on the staff of MTS, to a Company dinner. 'Young man,' said his host, 'when you dine in Merchant Taylors' Hall, let me give you a piece of advice: STICK TO THE HOCK.'

In 1977 he gave a lunch to celebrate the apprenticeship of his two grandsons to the Company. His letter to the Clerk goes into great detail about the food and, particularly, the wine. 'Whatever the rest of us have, the Master *must* have one of his *favourite* clarets (of course for anyone else who likes it too), with perhaps a moselle, and perhaps a sweetish hock to go with the fruit.' By then the Company was becoming something of an extended family, with Evelyn and Robert already Members.

Prominent also in the affairs of the Company was Christopher Everett, whose career, guided and promoted by Oakeshott, had now brought him to the headmastership of Tonbridge itself. In 1979 he suggested, in confidence, the writing of a biography or a Festschrift for Oakeshott. The suggestion was greeted by the Skinners with enthusiasm, but 'the cause', as it came to be known, gradually changed into the attempt to get him an Honour. The citation was put together by Sandford, who had retired as Registrar of the University, and was also a former Master of the Company. The flower of Oxford lent its support.

The award was made in the Birthday Honours List for 1980: 'Knight Bachelor, for services to medieval literature'. Both parts caused comment. Some of the Skinners thought he ought to have been made a Companion of Honour. Others thought a knighthood exactly right for a lover of the *Morte d'Arthur* and a biographer of that other (Elizabethan) Sir Walter. The mention of medieval literature surprised everyone. His own characteristic comment was that the 'only service he had rendered it was NOT to edit the Malory manuscript'. He was pleased to get letters from Macmillan and Whitelaw. He was even more pleased by a little speech which the postman made when he brought the telegram. But in truth it was all a little hollow. Another Eynsham man, who used to drive him and Noel round,* saw it. 'It is such a shame it didn't come earlier', he said with an affectionate smile, 'while she was still alive: she'd have *loved* to be Lady Oakeshott.'

Nevertheless there were, as she would have said, 'chirps' to be had. The actual investiture had its comic side. He was allowed two guests, so Helena and Rose accompanied him. Rose's husband David dropped them at the Palace in his Renault 5. Walter had special permission not to kneel because of leg trouble. But he was greatly impressed by the way Prince Charles had done his homework and talked about the Winchester Bible.

Later in the year came an occasion which left an even happier impression: the annual service of the Knights Bachelor in the Norman church of St Bartholomew in the City of London. He described it in a letter to Helena.

I arrived rather early, and as I watched them come in with their wives and daughters, at first I felt that, in a ghastly way, one had become identified with the minor 'establishment', so to speak. ... The service began with a fanfare, the noisiest and most cacophonous I've ever heard. But thereafter it was really very impressive. ... After it we all adjourned to a reception at Goldsmiths' Hall: a large room with a rather surprisingly ugly air of luxury (the huge heavy chandeliers for example: it's difficult for a chandelier *not* to be beautiful, but these somehow succeeded).

In due course the Queen and the D. of Edinburgh arrived: she went round one way, he the other. I was in comparative shelter at the back; but she was being conducted round by a friend of mine, and he spotted me and beckoned me forward – and 'presented' me. I thought she was absolutely marvellous: so natural: the frock, and the pearls she was wearing, absolutely

---

*After the demise of the fish-van in 1955, he relied on hired cars. Occasionally he took the wheel himself, to the alarm of his passengers; but usually he hired a driver too.

simple; nothing showy in her manner; but talking to people as if she was really interested in what they had to say.

She asked if we'd liked the service (she'd not been there). I said 'everything except the first fanfare' – she asked who it was by: I'd forgotten, a name unknown to me; written specially for the service. So she got on to the subject of modern music, and how modern music – Benjamin Britten for example – becomes comprehensible just about when the composer dies. Only, I suppose, three minutes talk. But I was absolutely bowled over by the qualities she showed in the whole affair. People often say that she looks 'disgusted'. She seemed, this time, to be enjoying every minute of it!

The Two Winchester Bibles was finally published in the spring of 1981. It is a most sumptuous book. At 50 x 30 cms it is almost as large as the Winchester Bible itself. 'It is finely printed and cased by hand with all the traditional skill of the OUP. It contains 194 black and white illustrations and twelve colour plates printed by offset lithography, all of excellent quality.' The latter are an especial glory, being full-page. They include both sides of the Morgan Leaf and seven others from the 'first' Bible (W), with two half-pages from the 'second' (A). The Press printed 1,000 numbered copies, on sale at £140. No one could deny that they had done him proud.

Oakeshott's own Preface, after the usual gracious acknowledgements, ends on an autobiographical note. Picking up the theme of his dedication, he writes:

My wife and I were both pupils of Sir John Beazley, she a far more professional scholar than I. His is the inspiration behind this book. But if it had not been for my wife's interest and expertise in such problems in Greek art, I suppose I would never have persisted in these efforts to establish the individual relationships between the artists of the books here discussed. And I suppose I should never have begun to look carefully at medieval manuscripts had not a kindly fortune brought me up to Balliol on the same day as Roger, now Sir Roger, Mynors.

The purpose of the book is 'to find out, in detail, how the two Bibles were produced, and how the undertaking was shared out between different individual artists'. The plan of the book, and the indices etc, are such that, like the Holy Bible itself, it is not easy for the layman to find his way about it. What is said of it here, therefore, will not follow the author's sequence.

Of W itself he had not all that much to add to (and still less to subtract from) his 1945 book. Indeed the passage of time had served only to confirm its general quality. Needless to say, he leaves that to be inferred, being content to draw attention to the few points in need of correction. The only major change of emphasis lies in the dominant importance now ascribed to the Morgan Master. Studies of the wall-paintings at Sigena already suggested that he had worked (or at the least had masterminded the work) in more than one medium[12] in more than one European country. Now there were grounds for seeing his hand also in wall-paintings nearer home, in the Holy Sepulchre Chapel in Winchester Cathedral.

When the earlier paintings in that Chapel were uncovered in 1965, they were described by the great Otto Demus as 'very close to the work of the Morgan Master'.[13] Oakeshott himself had, as long ago as 1939, expressed himself similarly about the later paintings, now lifted off. In the interim he had studied the wall-paintings of Sigena. He therefore felt able in 1981 to be less tentative in the attribution of *both* sets of paintings: 'it is hard to believe in a second contemporary artist of this quality working in Winchester on the larger scale, when so many details seem to suggest his hand.'[14] In an article of the same year,[15] he fitted these two works into the biography of the Morgan Master, and added rough dates: c. 1170 for the earlier, c. 1205 for the later, with the Sigena paintings between them c. 1190.

And with every successive treatment, the Morgan Master seems to rise in Oakeshott's esteem, not just as an artist – his work is 'unique in English art of the period' – but as a man. As in 1972, what struck him especially was 'the air of tragedy which seems so often to mark his vision of [his characters], going beyond the *gravitas* which the Byzantine tradition inherited from classical antiquity'. An example is a scene portraying Saul and David. In a phrase which almost seems confessional, Oakeshott notes 'the contrast* between the simplicity of the younger man and the tragic awareness of the older'.

The 'second' Winchester Bible, A, was a more recent friend. Oakeshott's interest in it did not lie mainly in the paintings. Of the artists of W, only one worked also on A: the Amalekite Master. Most of the paintings in A are by a man who is not represented in W at all.

---

*The mind's ear can hear the short 'a' with which he always pronounced 'contrast'.

He had been named by Boase the Master of the Entangled Figures, from his favourite motif: one or more human figures pathetically caught in a tanglewood populated by monsters. Oakeshott was enormously impressed by this work, which he called 'one of the greatest inventions of Romanesque decorative art'.

But more interesting to him, because more relevant to the history of W, was the *text* of A. Textual criticism was something he had long known about and minded about.* Now he discovered with excitement that e.g. in the book of *Judith*, A preserved not only Jerome's Latin text but *also* the pre-Jerome translation know as the Old Latin. He could see that whoever commissioned A cared about the text at least as much as about the decoration. On this and other grounds he argued that A was made for – and probably also at – the Abbey of St Alban's; an argument which has not convinced all scholars.

More convincing was his identification of A with the bible famously given by King Henry II to St Hugh of Lincoln (d. 1200). The story is told in the Life of St Hugh, which Oakeshott called 'just about the best life of a medieval saint'. The King had brought his friend Hugh across from France to preside over a new abbey he had founded at Witham in Somerset. Knowing that the abbey was short of books, and learning that 'the monks of Winchester had recently completed a specially fine bible', Henry persuaded them to make him a present of it. He then gave it to Hugh, without saying where it came from. Hugh was delighted with it, not only because of its beauty but also for 'the special care with which its text had been corrected'. But one day a monk from Winchester, visiting Witham, recognized the bible. The story then came out. In spite of the visitor's protest, Hugh insisted on returning it to Winchester. The monks of St Swithun's received it back 'delighted with the book itself, but more delighted with the charm, and the abundant charity, of the sender'.

Writing in 1945, Oakeshott had tentatively suggested that the bible in question might be W, though he conceded the difficulty, that W was never finished. For some years now,[16] however, he had been clear that the bible was not W but A. Apart from other considerations, the reference to its textual accuracy clinched the matter in his eyes. In a catalogue he prepared for an exhibition in the Bodleian in 1980, he confidently referred to A as 'St Hugh's Bible'.

One general feature of *The Two Winchester Bibles* strikes a

---

*He once surprised his audience in a 'leavers' talk' at Winchester by saying 'I sometimes think textual vice is more reprehensible than sexual vice.'

biographer with especial force: Oakeshott's powers – or at any rate his enthusiasms – were still, at the time of writing*, undimmed. It has been said that his *oeuvre* represented a life-long effort to conform to a Germanic ideal of art criticism. If so, the effort was a failure. He remained himself, for good or ill. This last major work still throws off new ideas like sparks from a catherine wheel. If he was to be proved wrong, so be it: nothing venture, nothing win.

Moreover he was as ready as ever to express a personal view. Although, in the words of one reviewer, 'no other writer on medieval illumination gives more telling visual evidence for his various attributions', nevertheless on occasions he was happy to invoke 'a general feeling much less precise but to me very much more important'.[17] For in truth 'his marvellous eye', as another reviewer called it, and his fifty years' familiarity with his subject, had earned him the right to use simple epithets like 'lovely' and 'subtle'. The same goes for his humanizing touches of description. For example, in the *Micah* initial in W the prophet leaps on the back of a lion to tear open his jaws. But the picture, he says, lacks all vitality: Micah's legs are 'dangling inconclusively', while 'the lion might be on a visit to his dentist'. Elsewhere some badly painted human ears look as if they are 'fixed on from the outside like a theatrical disguise, or the acquisition of a prize-fighter'.

Reviews were few, because of the price of the book, but long and generous. Their writers, even if they did not know Oakeshott personally, knew that they were reviewing not just a book but a life. They therefore wrote with a long perspective. If they had negative comments to make, e.g.'£140 is a lot to pay', they directed them at publisher rather than author. The final verdict was expressed by Heslop in *Art History*. Oakeshott's conclusions will not stand for ever: he would not expect, or even wish, them to do so. But 'no matter who else writes in future on the subject of the Winchester Bible, the material will always be Oakeshott's. No reservation one may have . . . could or should change that.'

As soon as Oakeshott saw a copy of the published work himself, he was appalled, like any author, at the mistakes he had allowed to pass. To the meticulous Mynors he wrote two shamefaced letters. 'I shall send you a note of obvious *corrigenda* when I've bought a large envelope for them'; and later 'some [are] misprints, some just

*The first draft of the text was written by 1973, his seventieth year. It is uncertain how far subsequent drafts improved it.

blunders'. But he was cheered by the summer's reviews, and then in the autumn he received a unique boost. It was provided by his old friend Roger Powell, the bookbinder.

Three years earlier he had asked Powell (who was then eighty) to recommend someone to make a special binding for his own copy of *The Two Winchester Bibles*, 'a splendid one made for posterity so to speak'. Powell immediately offered to bind it himself as a present. It was 'something I should very much enjoy making. You may not fully realize', he wrote to Oakeshott, 'how much you have done for me, directly and indirectly over the years.' This was true. In 1948 Powell had been invited by Winchester College to bind the Malory and seventeen other manuscripts in its possession. A little later Oakeshott had seen the Books of Kells and Durrow in Dublin in a parlous condition, with 'pages in both actually loose, and there for anyone to help themselves'; and had persuaded the Pilgrim Trust to commission Powell to rebind them. As Powell himself said in a letter to the Press in 1980, 'The Winchester Bible and my first sight of it marked a development in my career for which I shall ever be grateful to WFO.'

The Press let Powell have an unbound copy; he bound it himself in black leather, with a large gold W and A on front and back repectively. He also had an assistant put gold leaf on all the colour plates which had gold in the original. Oakeshott had been disappointed with the representation of the gold in the published book. Now he was enraptured – and amazed too at 'the illuminating effect of the gold on the other colours'. It was a treasure which he showed off to all his friends, drawing special attention to the way it lay absolutely flat when opened.*

By the end of 1982 he had written the first of what might be called his follow-up pieces on the Winchester Bible. The story of this one goes back to 1954, when he had visited a famous exhibition in Paris of French illuminated mss. of the twelfth century. There the organizer of the exhibition, Jean Porcher, had drawn his attention to a manuscript of Pliny from Le Mans. Porcher told him that its illuminations were by the same hand as those of the Auct. Bible in the Bodleian; but whether they were both French works, or both English, he did not know. Oakeshott at that time had not heard of the Auct.

*Learning that his grandson Jasper had bought a copy of the book for himself, he got Powell to gild it similarly for him.. His own copy he and Powell jointly presented to the Bodleian in February 1987.

Bible, but after Boase's identification of it as the 'second' Winchester Bible, he became very interested in the Le Mans Pliny.

In 1974 he had set out to see it again in its home. But fate was unkind. 'On the way the tiny line that operates from Gatwick to Tours lost my very small suitcase, which they didn't allow me to take in the cabin, and didn't find it till I turned up for my flight home four days later – it had all my notes in it, so the journey was virtually useless.' But soon afterwards some excellent photographs of the manuscript were published, which saved him from repeating the journey. With their aid he could be sure that the Le Mans illuminator was the Entangled Figures Master himself. He could now answer Porcher's question to his own satisfaction: both were St Alban's work. The article setting this out, though completed in 1982, was held up in the *Burlington Magazine* so as to coincide with the great exhibition of Romanesque Art on the South Bank in 1984.

In 1983 he carried through the second piece of follow-up work on the Winchester Bible. In reviewing *The Two Winchester Bibles*, Alexander had suggested that, if the plan for a facsimile were finally abandoned, the whole Bible should be 'published by the Chapter on colour microfiche with a full description. On grounds of security alone this is urgent.' The suggestion was adopted and the film published by World Microfilm Publications. To accompany it, Oakeshott resurrected a ' Catalogue of the Initials' which he had written in 1973 to go with the abortive colour facsimile. It is an extremely clear and comprehensive description of them – all of them except the Morgan Leaf, which the Chapter does not own. With cross-references not to A but to the wall-paintings in the Holy Sepulchre Chapel, the publication meets, albeit much more expensively, the need for which Oakeshott had in 1979 suggested to the OUP a paperback.[18]

Finally in 1984 he wrote an article defending his view that the Auct. Bible was made in St Alban's under the auspices of Abbot Symon. The view had been attacked in a book of 1982. In reply he conceded that in certain circumstances he 'might have to think again, if still capable of doing so'. But the circumstances were unfulfilled; and he had some new arguments to buttress the old. One in particular he felt to be weighty. He had been to look again at Abbot Symon's own Bible, now in Cambridge. There he had made an exciting discovery: another important textual feature which was found also in A but rarely (perhaps not at all?) elsewhere.

The day after his return home he wrote to Jenny Sheppard. 'I was so excited by this that I could not get to sleep; came downstairs about half past three, and wrote a long letter to Roger Mynors about it, went out to the post with it (the only Saturday post goes early) and went back to bed and slept briefly.' What he asked Mynors was whether that feature is known in any other twelfth-century bible.

Sheppard herself was aware of Oakeshott's 'frenzied excitement', as she calls it, and comments justly that 'he seemed to need these wild goose-chases'.[19] The question arises, why? What was driving him? To some extent it was the knowledge that time was running out: 'the fear of declining faculties mirrored in his physical difficulties'. There was an echo during those last years of Tennyson's 'Ulysses', desperate insistence that 'some work of noble note may yet be done'. But perceptive friends saw also a tincture of a deeper fear. Was there, for example, as one of them[20] surmised, an element of self-portraiture in the grim desciption Oakeshott wrote of the Job initial in the Auct. Bible, painted by the Entangled Figures Master.

> His [the EFM's] initials have at their best an inner significance, as it might be called, of their own. ... One recurrent theme is the helplessness of man, caught in the toils of an irrational savage environment: like Milton's twilight wood, with 'calling shapes and beck'ning shadows dire'. His Job can be taken as an example of his work at its finest. Here the [presiding] genius of the tanglewood

has the head of a king, but from the neck down it is a dragon holding the head of an old man in its talons. From the dragon's tail spring the toils of the wood.

> Entangled helplessly in [them], with a snarling wolf snatching at his side, and a bird of prey setting a claw on its knee, is a youthful, naked human figure, appealing desperately, but hopelessly, to the genius of the wood: and from the fronds peer out faces grim or mocking.

Those stark words – as stark as the painter's images – were quoted by Oakeshott in 1980, from his own still 'forthcoming' *Two Winchester Bibles*, in the catalogue of the Bodleian's memorial exhibition for Richard Hunt. Like the other contributors to the exhibition, he had been invited to choose his own subject and write about it; which lends some colour to the supposition of self-portraiture. And certainly his language there is no more stark than that of those early letters to Noel. If the old man clutched by the talons of the dragon is himself in the 1970s, perhaps the young man gnawed by the wolf is himself half a century earlier. If so, the gremlins left him only 'for a season'.

Be that as it may, it is certain that his *physical* health was never the same after the 1973 heart attack. But it was not until 1979 that things began to go wrong all at once. In December of that year he went in for a prostate operation. Fortunately it was so successful that he could encourage others with praise of its 'absolutely splendid' results. 'We were all amused', said a member of the Tonbridge staff, 'though secretly comforted, by his enthusiasm and lack of inhibition.' In 1981 he had to have two toe-joints amputated. A year or so later a Skinners' Company friend,[21] facing the same operation, asked him if it was painful. 'He knitted his brow as if it was difficult to remember anything so remote in time as the operation or to apply one's mind to anything so remote in space as a toe. "No," he said, "it was very little trouble, very little trouble at all." '

But his lifelong stoicism was increasingly needed. He was hardly back home after the toe operation when he went down with a severe bout of pneumonia. In 1983 he developed pleurisy while staying with Helena in Scilly, and had to spend some days in hospital. In 1985 he fell in the January snow and broke his right arm 'rather devastatingly'. The following year he had another heart attack. 'When given *digitalis*, he wrote to Cook, 'I stopped, almost in a matter of minutes, my wheezing and gasping for breath – a miraculous sensation!'

Nor was it simply a matter of physical decline. After 1973 his letters (though not to the children) refer increasingly to the gradual loss of his mental powers. Thus in 1976 'my mind (or at any rate the apparatus in it that has the job of turning up names and words) works too slowly and too erratically – hence the need for everlasting checking which does not always get done.' But (1979) 'there is still a part of one's brain that *sort of* works: the Winchester Bible silicon chips.' In 1980 'I've got to the point where my 12th-century memory is much better than my 20th-century one.' Finally in 1985 'there are some things I still hope to clear up in my own mind (and perhaps on paper too) before I settle down to living the life of (what I am sure Aristotle would have called) a vegetable.'

Indeed the heart attack of 1973 may have affected his intellectual powers more than he realized: not just memory for detail but also the capacity to organize material. There remained however what had always been his strengths: warmth and fancy, wit and charm, and a lively curiosity. Betty Shirley once described his mind as 'like a parcel neatly tied with a beautiful bow'. Whatever was in the parcel, the bow never lost its beauty. In these last years, therefore, his writing was at its best when addressed to family and friends, and he himself was at his best and happiest when in their company.

For the gremlins could be diverted only momentarily by 'frenzied' activity. In the longer run his position was close to that of Matthew Arnold on Dover Beach, As to religious faith, he could 'only hear its melancholy long withdrawing roar down the vast edges drear and naked shingles of the world'. All that was left in the end was love: 'ah, love, let us be true to one another'. His life and work from now on is best mapped on the coordinates of family and friends.

Family – children and grandchildren – had long been Walter's pride and joy. After Noel's death, when he took over her function of writing regular letters to them, they were also his consolation. In particular, Helena and Rose each had a house and garden in a delightful place which he loved to visit. Each also had children of an age to enjoy their grandfather's company as much as he enjoyed theirs.

Helena had been at Oxford like her twin brothers. She read Classical Mods and History, but her real talents lay in the arts and crafts. In 1956 she married Humphry Wakefield, a pupil of Beazley's, and they decided to make their living as professional potters on St Mary's in the Isles of Scilly. Their house had both a character of it own and a dramatic position, inside the old Garrison walls on the Atlantic seaboard. Walter loved everything about it, and went to stay there for weeks at a time.

He soon made a circle of friends in St Mary's. They ranged from a local stonemason, who had been in the next hospital bed when he had pleurisy, to Oliver Franks who had a holiday house there. The two retired men became warm friends, with old campaigns to fight again and a new shared interest in gardening. The Wakefields kept donkeys; and one of the sights of St Mary's was the ex-Provost of Worcester and the ex-Rector of Lincoln leading a donkey-cart from one house to the other with a load of good dung.

The Gaunts, Rose and David, had gone back in 1972 to teaching at Harrow but retained a pied-à-terre in Italy: no longer the flat in Rome, but a lovely farm house in Tuscany. There, Oakeshott told Mitchell, 'they live almost as peasants (except for the blessed mod. cons.) among the foothills of Monte Amiata, on a spur of a hill in a great amphitheatre of mountains and hill-top villages.' The house was surrounded by oak and chestnut woods, olive-groves and vineyards. It also had its own rocky garden straight out of a *cinquecento* painting. There he spent many happy hours. He had always enjoyed gardening, but he found the upkeep of the Eynsham garden an increasing burden. In Tuscany he could work – or even potter – at his own pace. He went out there for most Christmases up to 1985 and sometimes at Easter too. It was the base for a new scholarly inquiry which took him to Siena, and also for a last visit to his mosaics in Rome.

The eldest of Rose's children, Jasper, was the one of all the grandchildren who shared an interest in art history. When he was up at Merton from 1982 to 1986, he looked after his grandfather 'like a saint'. Walter gave Jasper many of his books during these years, and left him many more at his death – though all the 'best' ones had been sold.

Of the twin boys only Evelyn had a family, but his children were much younger than their cousins. Moreover in 1977 he moved to Scotland and rarely came south, so that from then on his father saw less of him than of his other three children. Robert on the other hand, living in London and having no children of his own, could more easily visit Eynsham to keep an eye on things. He was also the one whose career had most nearly corresponded to his father's concerns.

Next to family came friends. The bachelor Robert had something of a link role between the two categories, as this long letter to Helena in 1980 shows. The letter also illustrates his retirement life at its most varied and satisfying.

Life still seems pretty full. Last week I went up to Robert's flat [in London] for a dinner party that he gave; all the better because it was so free and easy. Jo Grimond[22] was there; his daughter Griselda, a most vivacious and charming person like her father; the two Normans [Geraldine *née* Keen and her husband Frank]; and that was the party. We had a leg of mutton which R had cooked himself, and which Frank carved, I thought with not much skill. But it all went like a bomb. Jo would keep *any* party going.

Then on Thursday Penderel [Noel's brother] took me over to a lunch given by [a Wykehamist friend of his] for some contemporaries. His wife[23] (one of Ld Wavell's daughters) had been told that it was a strictly masculine party and she wasn't allowed – I was sorry not to see her again. But it was one of those most lovely days that we occasionally have; the house is quite exquisite: not very large but Cotswold style tho' it's not actually in the hills but in the upper Thames valley: I suppose XVIIth century with lawns and 'features' of clipped yew, one a sort of alcove on the lawn, with a 'back' of two or three plants, and pillared features (a tree each) flanking it; absurd but most agreeable.

Most people were in their shirt-sleeves but Pendy and me. Partly because as you know I'm susceptible to hot sun, partly because I realized that it would be obvious that my trousers were made for someone at least a foot larger round the tummy than I am, and whose legs were much shorter, so that the trousers have to be suspended at considerably below waist level on a pair of vivid scarlet braces which Maggie has found in her wardrobe. Fortunately I don't in the least mind appearing *different* from other people; but I thought someone might have tumbled to the notion that the suit was second hand (as it is: Oxfam*); and that *might* have been thought a bit crude.

Last night the exhibition in which I've been involved was opened, with a party in Bodley. There were too many things. . . . The room was absolutely packed, and of course one knew a good many of the people there – Roger Mynors and so on. I talked to a good many and eventually tottered off, having seen virtually nothing of the exhibition. Still I'm sure there'll be comparatively few [people] when I go again..

Next week I'm going off for four days: two nights with Geoffrey Keynes, an eminent surgeon who's also an eminent authority on Blake and has a marvellous collection of him – aged 94 or thereabouts. For the next two I'm going up to Norfolk to stay with Cecilia and her husband. Then Robert is coming down for a week.

A word may be said here in passing about Oakeshott's wardrobe.

*He had bought it for £3.50, but made the mistake of trying on only the jacket.

He had never been smartly dressed. Noel put it to him bluntly in a letter of 1940. 'Wherever you bought your clothes, I don't believe you ever *could* look conventional because you cannot make yourself look all of a piece.' The nearest he came to it was at Winchester on Sundays (see illustration). Even as Vice-Chancellor he wore 'a more or less crumpled clerical suit'. In Lincoln he could be less formal. 'His dress made it easy for people to mistake him for a gardener, or the Porter off-duty. I'm sure he enjoyed being mistaken too,' adds Whitton, correctly divining 'a mischievous streak'.

A life-long feature of Oakeshott's attire was the wide brim of his hats, trilby or panama. The reason emerges from his later description of Hardy as he had been at Max Gate in 1924. He was 'wearing a broad-brimmed panama hat with a narrow black ribbon round it – the sort of hat that no-one makes these days when one's supposed to stand any amount of sunshine'. But summer or winter, the hat became a habit. An Oxford friend[24] with an eye for detail like his own writes 'When I picture Walter, I see him hurrying along the Broad, withdrawn, with the brim of his trilby hat pulled down all round. In old age his hats had even wider brims and looked even more rakish.'

As well as Scilly and Tuscany, Oakeshott went often – sometimes more than once a year – to the USA, for a mixture of holiday, research and lecturing. The centre and focus of these visits was his old pupil and friend Charles Mitchell, who held Chairs in the History of Art in various universities there, chiefly Bryn Mawr, from 1966 to 1982.[25] The Mitchells were marvellously hospitable. 'As for Jean', he wrote after one visit, 'I can't remember ever any hostess who's been so endlessly kind, providing one with the cholesterol of the land.'

Charles also arranged lectures for him in his own and other universities. This could be strenuous. In April 1979, when Walter was seventy-five, a series at Bryn Mawr was followed by the Universities of Pennsylvania and Pittsburgh, the National Gallery in Washington and the Pierpont Morgan Library in New York. On that same visit the Mitchells introduced him to Constance Jordan, a young American scholar who was also a friend of Robert. She was to be his collaborator in his last published work, on the portrait of Queen Elizabeth I in Siena.

Apart from Mitchell, he kept no close contacts from his short time at Merchant Taylors'. With St Paul's he naturally kept many more. Staff and boys of the wartime generation were bound by unusually strong ties and he was warmly welcomed on his rare appearances at reunions. In 1974 Antony Jay made a film for the Old Pauline Club about the four living ex-High Masters, of whom Oakeshott was the senior. He much enjoyed the making of it, and comes across splendidly. In it he talks of the evacuation and of what, in his eyes, constitutes the *differentia* of St Paul's as a school. It is, alas, his only appearance in a published film.[26]

In 1982 he presented to the school library of St Paul's his own copy of *Novus Orbis* (see p. 229), specially bound by Roger Powell. The binding was designed jointly by the two of them 'as a sort of memorial to their friendship', which was also specifically commemorated in an inscription[27] on the back cover. On the front cover was a Latin text whose English equivalent is 'What does a man profit if he shall gain the whole world and lose himself?' [28]

Remarkably the binding also incorporates, on the centre of each cover, two roundels, electrotype copies of a unique medallion in the British Museum. The medallion itself, of engraved silver, shows the two hemispheres, marked with the track of Drake's voyage of circumnavigation, and was evidently made soon after Drake's return. The electrotype copies had been 'gold-washed to eliminate tarnishing as much as possible. They were given to me', says an accompanying note, 'by my deeply loved, and greatly revered friend, Ivan Mavor, for many years Librarian of St Paul's School, on his deathbed.'

The same year of 1982 saw a happy coincidence. John Thorn, a Pauline of Oakeshott's time, now himself Headmaster of Winchester, was Chairman of the Headmasters' Conference. Thorn invited him to come to the AGM and open an exhibition of art by pupils in HMC schools. Oakeshott spoke mostly of the Winchester Bible, but linked it revealingly with his own career as a teacher. 'Individuals have always been my interest: schoolboys, undergraduates, medieval artists.' Thorn wrote of that occasion in 1991 when he contributed a personal memoir of Oakeshott at St. Paul's to a reprint of *The Sword of the Spirit*.

Oakeshott's contacts during those years with Winchester College (as distinct from the Cathedral) were not as close as with his two other schools. The tensions arising from 'the Ridgway affair' had largely been forgotten, but those from the sale of the Malory manuscript had not. An official visit would therefore have been awkward. Even a gift, such as he had made to Tonbridge, St Paul's and Lincoln, ran the risk of being sold as a 'treasure'.

But what mattered to him were friends. When he came in 1982 to review for the *TLS* the volume of essays which marked the school's sexcentenary, he soon wandered off from the ostensible subject to a 'praise of famous men' remembered from his time there. The list included Cyril Robinson, 'the most stimulating teacher I ever met'; Harry Altham, 'a statesman of cricket, but surely one of the finest ever arousers of enthusiasm for literature'; and Harold Walker, 'driving force behind the Boat Club and perhaps the best housemaster I ever encountered'. It was such men as these' he concluded, 'that made Winchester what it was in the 1930s, 40s and 50s.'

All these were friends from his days as an assistant master before the war. All were now dead. But from his headmastership there were many others still happily extant. In 1984 Lincoln gave him a dinner to mark his eightieth birthday, and encouraged him to invite old friends as guests. Over half of those who came were masters and boys from those eight years at Winchester.

It was a Winchester connexion which led to some memorable talks on Malory that Oakeshott gave to sixth formers in three other schools. The headmaster of Stowe, another Wykehamist of his time,[29] asked him over in 1982 to talk about his discoveries. The success of that talk led to an invitation to do the same at Radley. This time however he was joined by Peter Way, a Radley master who had been a pupil of Neville Coghill's and read the Malory extracts in a Coghillian Middle English pronunciation. Way noted the immense trouble Oakeshott had taken over the choice of extracts and his own linking explanations.

In 1984 they went to Tonbridge together for the same double act. Writing to him afterwards, Oakeshott 'characteristically referred to his own part in it as "interruptions", when in fact it was the reverse'. As a 'personal memento', he gave Way his Roxburghe Club copy of the book presented to members by Geoffrey Keynes in 1951: a facsimile of a first edition of Donne's *An Anatomy of the World* (1611).

Oakeshott's talk on Malory was, as one would expect, concerned less with his own discovery than with the text of the *Morte d'Arthur*, and especially Malory's conception of tragedy. His manuscript notes for the talk end: 'After this, if time allows, notice the comparison with Tennyson.' That comparison he made explicitly in 'Tennyson and Malory', given in 1985 as the annual lecture of the Tennyson Society at Grimsthorpe Hall in Lincolnshire. In view of the occasion, he did his best for Tennyson, but still, as in his sermons, he would not cheat. As to Tennyson's *Morte d'Arthur* (1842), 'I learnt it when I was about ten, and it has been part of my mind's furniture ever since.' Tennyson in it 'is decorating Malory's story but not adding to it'. Nevertheless the decoration is marvellous and he 'brings it off'. By the time of *Idylls of the King* (1869), however, he has come under the malign influence of Victorian moralizing. He makes Lancelot 'almost a symbol of sinfulness'; and in his *Guinevere* 'one may reckon that Malory's story is murdered'. Only in *Elaine* ('one of my most vivid schoolboy memories') does he make amends. But even there 'Tennyson has pathos: Malory tragedy.'

For that occasion Lady Jane Willoughby, Chairman of the Tennyson Society and chatelaine of Grimsthorpe, had also invited Evelyn with his family, and Robert, for the weekend. Walter, who enjoyed grand houses, sent Helena a long description of the Hall and its grounds.

> All actually far grander, domestically, than Alnwick[30] [Castle], where I've stayed one or twice: tho' I must say there was nothing at Grimsthorpe to compare with the entry of the butler, at breakfast, saying 'Buckingham Palace on the line, Your Grace'. ... But I feel I can't *ever* go [to Alnwick] again, since I can never find my way back to the living quarters from the guests' bedrooms; and one feels such a fool getting lost in a HOUSE!

Oakeshott had, during the last ten years of his life, one last service to render to Lincoln. Mrs Montgomery died in 1976 at a very ripe old age. By her will she bequeathed to the College the greater part of her estate: some in Oxford but most in Ireland. Oakeshott was one executor; the other two were her doctor and her solicitor. In 1977 he told Cook he was having to 'go over to Dublin about once a month. ... Business relationships with the Irish are traditionally difficult; and tradition is right on target. I'm ageing rapidly.' Four years later 'we've not got probate yet. It's the most awful job I've ever had to do.' The estate was nominally worth some quarter of a million pounds, but there turned out to be so many outgoings and encumbrances that what the College eventually got was a good deal less.

Of all Oakeshott's institutions it was Tonbridge with which he maintained the most regular contact. While he was at Lincoln it was mainly a formal matter. But after his retirement in 1972, and still more after his former pupil Christopher Everett was appointed Headmaster in 1975, the links became more frequent and more personal.

He was assiduous in attendance at Governors' days and Skinners' Day. He presented books to the library, and gave talks to the senior boys, of which Everett noted that 'he had the same impact he had had when he had taught us at Winchester'. The refurbishment of the organ in 1979 was an issue especially dear to his heart. Everett remembers him coming down while the work was being done and clambering all over the interior of the organ right up to the roof level of the chapel.

A year or two later Oakeshott heard that a sixteenth-century map was coming up for sale in Florence which had associations with Sir Thomas Judde. He travelled out by second-class rail to buy the map and present it to the school. Before presenting it, however, he wrote it up, as he had done so many renaissance maps before. The article appeared in the TLS in June 1984, entitled 'A Tudor explorer and his map of Russia'.[31]

The explorer was Anthony Jenkinson, who in 1557 attempted to travel overland from Moscow to China. His attempt was made on behalf of a group of London merchants including Judde. In the event he never got beyond Bokhara. But he gathered enough information about latitudes to form the basis of a corrected map of Central Asia which he prepared for his backers. Judde had died by the time the map was printed in 1562. It was first published in 1570 as part of Ortelius's great Atlas; but its date of 1562 make it the first map to be *both* made by an Englishman *and* printed in England.

In April 1984 the General Court of the Skinners' Company resolved 'to write to Sir Walter Oakeshott as the most revered and beloved of all Members of the Court to sit for a portrait of himself for the Hall by an artist of his choice'. He chose his daughter Helena as the artist, and her charming informal portrait is reproduced in the illustrations. Typically, he insisted on paying for it himself, and 'suggested that it should be hung in the Beadle's room or that of the Comptroller'. The Court accepted the gift but held out for hanging it in one of 'the public areas of the Hall where it would be seen to advantage'; and so it now is.

As his life drew to a close, Oakeshott's thoughts turned increasingly towards leaving some account, at least of the major excitements in it. Already in 1972 he had written his first account of the Pilgrim Trust's unemployment survey. But within a few years he had forgotten and written another – and so on until the fourth version written in 1984. Other narratives covered his part in various university affairs and in the sale of the Malory manuscript. All were written from memory, even those where published material was available, and are unreliable over detail, especially dates.

In 1981 he embarked on something much more substantial and systematic. He gave it the title *Odyssey in a Cockleshell*, which he explained in an introduction.

> The stories of literary and artistic 'discoveries' told in this book show them as the result, not of methodical or prolonged search, but of almost incredible pieces of good fortune. The vessel involved in such adventures can, in my case, fairly be called a cockleshell, for it has sadly lacked most of the technical equipment it should have had, if I had done what is called, in today's jargon, my homework. In two subjects alone, twelfth-century English illumination and Roman medieval mosaics, I may have made myself a competent authority, [but] only by dint of standing on the shoulders of serious scholars.

After the introduction there are chapters on: Greek antiquities; discoveries in maps; the Queen and the poet; and the renaissance in Rome, as seen in the mosaics. In 1984 he added a further chapter entitled 'Malory, Vinaver and me'. The short and lively narratives provide a valuable quarry for a biographer. But they are followed by over-long summaries of his published books and articles, and the book did not find a publisher. He therefore put it aside and turned elsewhere.

In April 1984 he had a letter from a Pauline of his time, Michael Humphrey, now a Professor of Clinical Psychology, offering to write his life. The offer threw him into some turmoil. 'He has made my head whiz round', he wrote to Cook, 'like a car that has got out of control.' When he met Humphrey, he found him 'quite delightful', and was tempted. But the family was not enthusiastic, and in the end he decided against. One of his reasons – a familiar theme of his – he gave in a letter to Helena. 'My way of doing my jobs has always been to get other people to do them and just "be around". And though that may be, in effect, quite a good way of schoolmastering or being head of a college (or even Vice-Chancellor), *no* one could pretend that it offers material for an interesting biography.'

In truth his attitude to his own life and works was ambivalent. Way noted perceptively in his diary for 2 March 1984 after a long chat: 'I should love to write WO's biography – he has had a full life and while in no way shirking mention of achievements and personalities, speaks modestly and hides his face with a movement of the hand when seeming to flaunt his distinction.'

In July 1984 Oakeshott was awarded an Honorary Doctorate of Letters by the University of East Anglia at Norwich. The honour was triply appropriate and correspondingly relished. UEA is one of the leading English universities in the field of art history. Norwich is the home of Dennis King, glazier, who had done so much for Oakeshott and for stained glass generally.[32] And the honorary doctorate, 'for being such a devastatingly successful amateur', was presented by his friend Oliver Franks as Chancellor.

Oakeshott's last published work was a 1986 article on 'The Siena Portrait of Queen Elizabeth I'. The research for it had been spread over some years and involved happy visits to Siena. It also involved a remarkable flight to New York on 17 May 1986.The pupose was to see another portrait of the Queen in private hands there.[33] He decided to do the double flight in one day – and not by Concorde either – so as to avoid jet-lag. Being uncertain of his health, he wrote to the children telling them of the plan; but to save them worry posted the letter to reach them after his return. Unfortunately he miscalculated. The letter arrived on the morning of the flight, giving them a day of maximum anxiety. The text of the article betrays an undiminished zest for the quest, but there are signs in it that his powers were now definitely failing.[34]

A much more ambitious project had occupied him for even longer. It was to be a book entitled *Elizabeth and Essex*, building on his 1975 article on *Love's Martyr*. He became very excited about it himself, putting 'a *lot* of work into it over eight years'. 'I've an idea', he wrote in a letter c.1986 'that I've understood some of [the poems] better than they've been understood hitherto. I've no doubt that one's powers of self-criticism wane; but I do know that I've had four complete drafts, getting (I'm glad to say) shorter and shorter, so that at least it reads more easily than it did three years ago.' The book remained unpublished at his death in 1987.[35]

From about 1981 onwards, Oakeshott began to make plans for the disposal of his many fine possessions. Some of the pictures and furniture had come from the family; the rest he had bought himself. Not that he was in the strict sense a collector. He was never interested in acquiring something to complete a set or to exemplify a category. He bought sometimes for sentiment (e.g. a sideboard which 'wouldn't sell at the Beazleys' sale'), often for scholarship (especially books and maps), but most commonly because an object was finely made and good to have and to handle. Handling did not preclude use e.g. the Byzantine measure which became an ash-tray or a Ptolemaic dish of blue faience which held paper-clips etc. on his desk.

In spite of his many sales and gifts, he still had enough beautiful things left at Eynsham for every room to be worth some hours of a connoisseur's time. For their disposal by gift or bequest he chose, as he always did, with the utmost care. All members of the family should receive at least one of his greatest treasures, including any with which they had an especial link.

For example, while out shopping with Helena in Paris c. 1950, he had spotted, out of the corner of eye as they walked past, a picture in a shop window. Turning back, he looked more closely. Though heavily encrusted with paint, it was clearly good, and he bought it. When cleaned, it was revealed as an unusual panel with the Virgin and Child in high relief. Similarly in Rome in the 1960s, walking with Rose down the Via Babuino, he spotted a picture of a Virgin and Child with St John. This turned out to be a copy[36] of a lost work by Guercino. These acquisitions, each of them testifying to his remarkable 'eye', went to the appropriate daughter.

Another treasure of his was a pair of fifteenth-century Italian historiated initials (i.e. illustrated with a historical scene), set in a diptych frame. They were very precious to him, and always hidden when he left Eynsham. Once, when short of money, he proposed to send them for sale; but Maggie found out, and insisted on giving him the expected sale-price. He left them, of course, to her.

There were other things he had to do to put his affairs in order. From the summer of 1986 onwards he did his best to get round all his friends for a last visit, or at least to write them a farewell letter. In June 1987 he went for the last time to Winchester Cathedral, where he was due to meet a German PhD student working on the Sigena paintings. He got up at 5.30 a.m. so as to get there and back in the day, missed a connexion, had to walk the last half mile, hurried into the Cathedral and up the stairs to the library, and 'sat gasping for breath for about a quarter of an hour'.

Cathedral was in such a state as I've never seen it before, with the whole north transept covered with metal scaffolding floor to ceiling, and immediately outside the door of 'my chapel' a chap with a huge metal cauldron on a chain being pulled up and down filled with rubble or repair material. 'You can't get in here', he said. 'Oh yes we can', I said: and we did. But it was a bit of a sad farewell (as I guess it's likely to be) after 55 years in which it's been the real focus, in a way, of my existence. Still one must be thankful for what one's had – and not complain.

As the months wore on in 1986 and 1987, it became clear that old age and ill health were finally overtaking him. His heart had long been weak; now there was liver trouble too. The medication – when he remembered to take it – was losing its efficacy. He himself, though capable at any time of responding to the stimulus of company, was losing the long-term will to live.

In early September, sensing the onset of bronchitis, he went out alone for a long cross-country walk, on the principle of kill or cure. It did neither. But by the beginning of October the end was near. Under Maggie's care he retired to bed, and the children came to be with him. For over a week he sank slowly. When the doctor spoke cheerfully, he would have none of it: 'I'm off,' he said firmly. On the last evening the children went up as usual for a glass of wine around his bed. In the early hours of 13 October 1987, a month before his eighty-fourth birthday, he lapsed into a coma and died.

Walter Oakeshott is buried next to Noel in Eynsham parish churchyard. The night before his funeral was the night of the great hurricane of 1987, and the following day was still quite wild. The air was 'clear shining after rain', but thunder was still about. As the family stood by the graveside, there was one especially loud clap. 'There!', said Maggie mischievously, 'Sir has arrived!'

Epilogue

The story of the life is done. What has it revealed of the man? A glimpse here and there, certainly: the lift of an eyebrow, as it were, or the tail of a gown disappearing round a corner. But glimpses do not make up a portrait, and may not reach to the heart. It is time to look more deeply into two activities which lie close to the still centre of the mixed life: religion and scholarship.

Of his religious views Oakeshott offered two barely compatible accounts. In about 1963 he had a conversation about religion with his goddaughter Geraldine Keen in Rome. In the course of it he said that towards the time that he left Winchester in 1954 he had begun to feel it hypocritical, holding the beliefs he then held, to preach in the school chapel; and that this had been a main reason for his leaving.

On the other hand a Minute of the Tonbridge Governors in 1979[1] contains the following report of his intervention in a discussion whether the organ in the school chapel should be restored.

Mr Oakeshott held his fellow Governors spellbound with a moving speech, explaining *as an agnostic from his schooldays** whose scepticism had been fostered by that of the two Masters most responsible for his upbringing there, how important was the function which a school chapel had in affording to children at an impressionable age a stimulus to the imagination. Religious ceremonial had provided the creative impetus for some of the noblest artistic achievements, especially in music. The organ had made a pre-eminent contribution in extending sensibility beyond the frontiers of the tangible world, and awakening a boy's spiritual perception, whether or not endowing him with religious faith... He was supported in his view of the role which religious observance, as opposed to belief, played in education by the fact that the two Masters he had mentioned had thought it right to attend Chapel regularly although themselves agnostics.

*My italics – JCD.

The compatibility of these two summaries depends upon the shade of meaning given to the slippery term 'agnostic'. Bishops and atheists alike have been known to apply it to themselves. In both cases the usage is apologetic: at once scrupulous and deprecatory. The speaker wishes to disclaim certainty in a field where probability reigns. Oakeshott in his sermons used to quote, only to repudiate, the remark of a medieval theologian, that *fides non est aestimatio sed certitudo*: faith is not a matter of balancing probabilities but of accepting certainties.'

It will not be surprising therefore to find him varying, at different periods of his life, in his estimation of the probabilities. In his youth and old age the evidence does indeed confirm that he was an agnostic in the popular sense of the term. In 1974 he wrote to his old school friend Tom Gaunt about 'what before long now will be sixty years of friendship between us. . . . Here we are still, not so far from the end of the road, *in Christo fratres*. You understand what that means so much better than I, but I have the dim sensibility of the agnostic layman which makes me know it does mean something.'²

The implication of those words is corroborated by two sentences from the letters exchanged by him and Noel during their early years. She, tentatively: 'I wonder if you'll think it a bore that I rather like to go to church sometimes. I wouldn't dream of expecting you to come, or interfering with what you think of these things.' (February 1927.) He, disingenuously: 'I only don't pray because William Brown [his psychiatrist] said it was dangerous, and if you *thought* too hard about things that are fundamentally emotional and tried to alter them, you went off the rails.' (July 1928.)

Not that he was even then deaf to religion. In April 1929, when they were at Olympia on their Greek honeymoon, he was much struck by 'the scarlet anemones in flower. They slashed the plain with colour. And some words of one of Marlowe's plays flashed into my mind: "See, see where Christ's blood streams in the firmament".'* Moreover he continued to read – Noel saw to that – and to think. In 1937, after reading a 'modernist' commentary on St John's Gospel, he wrote to her: 'Though it may seem extraordinary, I can't help

*He recalled this incident in a sermon at Winchester c.1951, adding that 'Christianity is part of the fabric of the world, a scarlet thread woven into the texture of the very universe'. His mind was always full of biblical phrases – e.g. a letter to Noel in 1927 says of a village in the Tyrol that it had 'a fruit market that smelled like the Garden of Eden and a brass band that sounded like the Day of Judgment'.

thinking that the conservative position (i.e. that *John* was actually written by an eye-witness) is much more tenable than the liberal one.' He was impressed by the 'astonishing veracity of the textual tradition of the Gospels' compared with that of the classics, and also by the sobriety of *John* compared with a Greek or Roman biographer such as Suetonius. He ended a long paragraph with a revealing phrase: 'I feel curiously ill-assorted not to believe in the "modernist" position.'

A year later, when he applied for St Paul's, his referees were two future bishops in Williams and Leeson. On the subject of his religion, Williams was silent, Leeson careful and cautious. They were wise: it was still a private matter. But as soon as he got to St Paul's he declared himself. In particular, he preached regularly and to real effect. Cook remembers a sermon of his in September 1939 as 'one of the finest I have ever heard'; and when he left in 1946 his last head boy wrote that 'he will be remembered above all for his sermons'.[3] To remove all uncertainty, we have those words of 1942: 'I am a convinced Christian.' (p. 115.)

As to the reasons for his conversion, if that is not too cut-and-dried a term, one can but speculate. If he spoke of them, no record survives. But among them was surely the influence of Temple.* In a talk he broadcast after Temple's death,[4] Oakeshott tried to analyse 'the reasons for his authority with his generation'. First was 'the very fact that he had intellectual doubts.' Indeed he was initially rejected for ordination because he 'could give no more than a very tentative assent to the Virgin birth and the bodily resurrection of our Lord'.† Temple was thus in tune with a generation whose attitude was: 'If a man with an intellect could find his way to a belief, well. But if he must accept his belief without question, second-hand, better not believe at all.' The second reason for Temple's authority was 'the central place which the life of Christ had for him[5]. . . He showed us the Lord high and lifted up.' Temple, like Oakeshott, insisted on the historical reliability of the gospels, especially the fourth.

Then at Winchester from 1946 to 1954 – even more than at St Paul's – Christianity was at the very heart of Oakeshott's headmastership.

*Oakeshott himself (wrongly but perhaps significantly) 'opined that Temple was responsible for T. S. Eliot's conversion – or reception'. (Way's diary, 2 March 1984.)

†Asked in 1992 whether the Oakeshott of the 1930s was an agnostic, Singer replied 'Yes, of course. Like Temple.' Typical of Temple also is the equation of 'Christian' with 'fully human' (p. 71).

His refurbishment of the Chapel, like its original dedication by the Founder, was *ad maiorem dei gloriam*. Of his writings, the devotional *Sword of the Spirit* was complemented by the scholarly *Gospels and History* and his pedagogic contribution to the Cambridgeshire Syllabus. In worship his example was impeccable. He never missed Chapel, even for a voluntary service. At the 7.30 a.m. midweek Communion in Fromond's Chantry, Everett remembers him as always present, even when the two of them formed the whole congregation.

But it was through his sermons that Oakeshott made most impact upon masters and boys, and was most open about his beliefs.[6] His own theological sophistication was shown by his attraction to the *Epistle to the Hebrews*. He preached about it more than once, and as always made it interesting and acceptable by his personal presentation.

> For me the mortality of Christ is the veil that hides God, and the only approach to God. I seem to see, in the Cross, a reality that is timeless, a truth that is truer than any other I experience; a love that is absolute. . . . Yet an act of faith is still needed, and however much the Epistle may assure me that everything worth while calls for faith,[7] yet I find it as hard, I suppose, as many of you do, and am left saying 'Lord, I believe, HELP thou my unbelief'.

One or two more passages may help to account for the remarkable impact of his sermons. He had quoted T. H. Huxley's comparison of life to a game of chess, in which the player on the other side is hidden from us, and 'he who plays ill is checkmated without haste but without remorse'.

> Now this, he says, is a matter of experience. And all I can tell you is that that is not *my* experience. I know that chessboard. From me also the player on the other side is indeed hidden. But I have made the mistakes, and yet the disaster has not happened. I can explain the experience only in terms of what the gospel calls forgiveness.

In another sermon he spoke further of 'the extraordinarily baffling mystery of forgiveness. There have been times in my life when I have deserved the fate, not of Peter, but of Judas; when I have not simply denied Christ but betrayed him. And our betrayals, so mean,

so contemptible, are nevertheless somehow forgiven. Worth is somehow restored.'

Sometimes he would speak in terms that had no evident theological content. At the end of one school year he spoke of

the impermanence that is the background of all our lives. To
grow older is to become increasingly aware of this transitori-
ness. Summer chases spring faster every year; and almost before
we are aware of summer, Goldengrove (as the poet calls it) is
unleafing; the gold and the russet[8] is stripped off the trees by the
gales; and we are reminded that the springs of sorrow lie in this
same hurrying change; and that the reason why things are so
unbearably beautiful is just because they cannot stay put; that
we know them in our hearts to be doomed.

The impact was felt by those of all religious persuasions and of
none. Young Christians had their faith broadened and nourished, by
his example as well as his words. Many Wykehamists of his time
were later ordained,[9] and are aware of what they owe to him. But
scarcely less impressed was a 'dogmatic rationalist', Peter Jay. He
recalls Oakeshott as he 'stood in the pulpit, in his headmasterly
regalia, with all the stained glass, fan-vaulting and other solemnity,
and with his head thrown back*, as if quizzically examining God by
his own standards; a figure of indisputable gravity, integrity and
intelligence'. As to the content of the sermons, 'he seemed to me to be
serious, to recognize the legitimacy of doubt, to wrestle with the
problems over which others so glibly glossed.' How could he speak,
in that way, to 'all sorts and conditions'? As Jay says, he never
cheated. Moreover, as in his teaching, he never talked down. He put
the finest and the deepest of himself into his sermons, and it told.

But what in all this was his theology? Everett says 'he never seemed
to be a fully paid-up member of the Christian Church'. His main
credal themes were God in creation and the person of Christ. He
spoke of sin, but said little about the other great evangelical† themes
of redemption and grace, and nothing about the great catholic themes
of church and sacraments. Incarnation and resurrection he took, like
the young Temple, as metaphors. He was most moving when he

---

*The characteristic pose is illustrated in the Dring portrait (see illustration).

†He was highly suspicious of itinerant evangelicals, and commissioned a young
master to keep an eye on them.

spoke of the men he admired and the beautiful things he loved. Beauty and goodness pointed to God; or, if one preferred to put it the other way round, God was that which underlay beauty and goodness. In that sense he was regarded by those close to him as a mystic or, more precisely, a Platonist.

If such was his faith, what changes came over it at the end of his time at Winchester? The supernatural element in it had perhaps never been strong: but it had certainly been there, and it went. Two beliefs in particular evaporated. The first was in divine Providence. In his sunshine years he could speak as follows of the Wisdom literature of the Old Testament.

> There is no attempt [in it] to underrate the devastating force which the unbeliever's argument is given by events. Yet in spite of that, the world is seen as making sense. 'And God saw that it was good'.[10] That optimism appeals to me as a matter of experience. The idea that in these earthly things, transient though they are, there is an essential goodness and even joy, does seem to me, in experience, convincing.

But at another time, or in another mood, he could see the other side. "Between the idea and the reality falls the shadow," he quoted, and went on: 'This shadow, when its darkness overcasts our ideals, leaves us groping. And sometimes the reaction is so violent that we abandon our lights entirely; that we decide to do what St John calls walking in the darkness; that we take refuge in cynicism and proclaim that everything is vanity.'

And with Providence went forgiveness. He had once said that 'the difference between the man who is religious and the man who is not lies in his sense of two things: judgment and forgiveness.' His sense of judgment – of being judged and found wanting – was strong all his life. But without Providence to make things right, without either redemption or absolution to restore worth, where could he look for forgiveness? It could be sought only from the offended. Hence, perhaps, the enormous importance he attached to an exceptionally generous letter he received from Anne Ridgway after Robin's death, and to his reconciliation with Noel on her deathbed.

Such an analysis may suggest an answer to the next question that presents itself, namely, *why* he changed his views in these matters. His children remember the acute shock to him of Alan Roseveare's suicide in 1952, exacerbated by his feeling that, if he had not been away in London that day, the boy's life might have been saved. What sort of a world was it in which the innocent could suffer so? And everyone at Winchester could see how near he came to being broken by the prolonged agony of the Ridgway affair. What sort of a world was it in which a necessary and right action could cause such deep hurt to every single person concerned?

In looking for an answer to this question, one should also not overlook the centripetal force[11] exerted by a community in the maintenance of beliefs. This force acts especially strongly upon a leader of the community who is responsible for articulating its values. St Paul's and Winchester are explicitly Christian foundations in a way that a university is not. At Winchester every boy in the school had two divinity lessons a week, and was required to attend Chapel each weekday and twice on Sunday. Many of the staff took a conscientious part in the religious life of the school, and looked to their headmaster for spiritual leadership. This he continued to give, with all his intellect and imagination, until the end of his time.[12] But it was costing him increasingly dear, and the burden of preaching was one of the reasons he gave at the time for the move to Lincoln.

Indeed after leaving Winchester he preached only once more in his life,[13] at the centenary of his preparatory school in 1957. But in Lincoln he was a regular attender at Sunday chapel, and for many years he would go to church or chapel for friendship's sake, to keep company with Noel or with friends staying in the Lodgings. More interestingly, he joined a small private group, of heads of houses and others, who would meet regularly for lunch on Mondays, but would not eat until they had said the office of sext together. In retirement at Eynsham he hardly ever went to church at all.

If one therefore looks at his life as a whole, it seems proper to speak rather of an explicitly Christian period lasting some fifteen to twenty years. If that is so, it raises two further questions. The first is, in what ways was he, or did he seem, different during that period? Those were after all the very years during which he was at the height of his personal and public influence. One might therefore have expected him to be then also at the height of his vigour and confidence. But in fact his personal troubles in 1943–4, 1949 and 1953–4 preclude any such simple equation. With a man as private as Walter, it is all too easy to rush into a misjudgement about his inner feelings. All that can be said is that his Christian beliefs during those years enabled him to give a quality of leadership which would otherwise have been impossible. And without that possibility he would surely not have sought such headmasterships.

The second question is the complement of the first: what was there that was constant in his beliefs and convictions through all periods of his life, whether avowedly Christian or not? Some answers to this question have already emerged. First is 'Balliolismus', the particular version of Platonic idealism discussed on pp. 18-19. Within that complex of ideas, the emphasis for him gradually shifted from the active to the contemplative. The foundations, however, remained: the contrast between the transient and the lasting; and the ultimate identity of the beautiful and the good.

Next came a sense of community. For him, the community must allow more tolerance (especially more privacy) than Tonbridge had; but he needed it all the same. As well as St Paul's and Winchester, he responded positively to a wide variety of communities. They included the Warburg Institute round Saxl; the community implied by the Rule of St Benedict; the Moot, with his idea of an Order; the *collegiolum* of Lincoln, with its rituals centred in Hall and Chapel; the research group in the Bodleian; and above all the Skinners' Company, which he once described as 'my other college'. Common to all these was a group of like-minded people engaged in a shared enterprise.

But at the heart of any community, and at the heart of his beliefs, was the individual. The word itself is chilly, but he clothed it with all the warmth he could muster, especially in his Winchester sermons. For example,

> I visited an unemployed man in Deptford in 1936 who lived in one room in a house where there were probably 15 other people living. He was the most utterly desolate human being I have ever encountered. Yet he was of course listed and docketed in all the pigeon-holes and all the files. But except as a name and a number he meant nothing to anyone at all. *Your* job is to see that the names which go into the pigeon-holes are still persons. . . . Those for whom you are responsible must know that they can [each] have your whole undivided attention. . . . Anyone who has tried it knows how hard that is.

He often spoke about his fear of large 'soulless' institutions – schools, businesses, even countries – in which the individual is lost. 'An institution must be judged not by its fame or its splendour or its power, but in the quality of the lives led by the individuals within it.'

In a small institution the individual counts – and so does friendship. 'You', he once said in an end-of-term sermon, 'have made your splendid contribution to the life of the school because you give it something which is individual and personal; something which you alone can give, which the next man cannot give because he is different from you.' And the principle can be extended even to countries. 'Because this island seems to me to offer greater possibilities within its institutions of that kind of experience than any other region of the world, it is here I would choose to live. We are completely bankrupt. But we remain, mercifully, in possession of our souls.'

He ended that sermon with a look forward which said much about himself.

> Don't think I am steering you off ambition. The value of the trying may be great, even if the ends achieved turn out to be worth less than they once seemed.* But there is one thing that is good in itself; one thing that brings a return thirty, sixty, a hundred fold; the good deeds, to use the phrase of Everyman, that one may be able to do for one's friends.

That last point he reinforced, in another sermon, by a quotation from Alfred the Great. 'Every other thing in this world a man desires either because it will help him to power or to get some pleasure, save only a true friend; whom we love for love's sake and for our trust in him, though we can hope for no other return from him.'

Unlike Oakeshott's religion, his scholarship is all of a piece. Its strengths and its weaknesses are two sides of the same coin.

Two of his strengths were generally admitted, even by his critics. The first is the range of his interests even within the field of art and literature, let alone outside it. This book has recorded it in some detail, but there is a sentence of Plato's which illuminates it as a whole. It comes from the great speech of Diotima in the *Symposium*[14] which expounds Plato's aesthetic theory. 'When there is the great and wide sea of beauty spread out before us, it is unworthy of a free man to spend too long in a single creek or inlet.' The analogue in Oakeshott's day to Plato's concept of 'free' was perhaps 'educated'.

*Some of his hearers wondered if he was thinking of his own ambition to be Head-master of Winchester.

The weakness corresponding to this strength was inevitably lack of depth. But it is far from certain that, if he had restricted his field, he would have gone deeper. He went as deep as he wanted to go, i.e. he posed the questions that interested him; and did his best to answer them. Let others pose theirs. He would help if asked, but he would not interfere.

His second great strength was his sense of style. Such a sense is much more than the sum of its parts, but certain parts may perhaps be distinguished. First was the intimacy with which he knew his material at first hand. He had looked and looked and looked at what he wrote about, especially the Winchester Bible and the mosaics of Rome. Next was his eye for detail. Hence his concern for craftsmanship of all kinds.[15] He knew for example how each of his artists handled gold leaf: how much of it they put on, and in what consistency, and what they put underneath it, and what effect the different techniques achieved. Finally, he had a prodigious memory, unsupported by card-index, still less by computer. As Ashmole said of Beazley, 'his memory often seemed incredible, because it was not the mechanical memory of a prodigy but ruminative – the memory of a humanist.'

So equipped, he was able to identify Raleigh's handwriting and the individual artists of the Winchester Bible. He could associate works in different media, on different continents, on enormously different scales, with one and the same hand. And his imagination leaped easily from art to literature and back again.

But a leaping imagination has its dangers, for a scholar. He himself was well aware of them. 'In the course of an unorthodox intellectual career', he said in a sermon c. 1950,

> I have formed many theories about many things. All of them have been initially exciting. Yet there was nothing in three quarters of them; nothing whatever. I now find it necessary to put a theory into cold storage for six months till I can recollect it in tranquillity and take sober account of the insuperable objections.

His critics were not entirely mollified by such disclaimers. His pruning, they felt, was not ruthless enough: the weak shoots detracted from the strong. He moved too quickly from perceived similarity to supposed influence. His friends and supporters, on the other hand, responded to his enthusiasm, commended his courage in publication, and welcomed the stimulus of even his more fanciful theories.

'Style', said Beazley, 'I was brought up to think of as a sacred thing, as the man himself.'[16] The third distinctive feature of all Oakeshott's scholarly work was his concern for 'the man himself', whether it be the author or his characters, the artist or his figures. In art, whatever the medium – paint, stone or mosaic – it was always the human figure that commanded his attention. Doubtless he was predisposed in this direction by his training on Greek vases, where everything else, decoration or props, is subordinated to the figures.

Moreover in the figures what struck him most was their most human aspect. Thus in the Chichester Roundel, 'that most lovely of English mediaeval wall-paintings', what he observes is 'the poise of the Child, the lean of the Virgin's head, the fall of the robe'. These, he said, are 'details which in the original are the unique work of a master, and the most brilliant copyist could not hope to capture them'.[17] And for him, especially in the second half of his life, the quintessence of the humanity is to be found in tragedy. It is the tragic element in the Morgan Master's work which constantly draws him; and when he compares Malory with Tennyson (or even Caxton), and Plutarch with Shakespeare,[18] the ultimate criterion is their differing conceptions of tragedy.

But this concern of his for the individual was another coin that had a flip-side. That was a deep dislike for statistical generalizations, and indeed for anything that obliterated individual distinctions. He was therefore entirely out of sympathy with the kind of sociological approach which already in his lifetime was playing an important part in art history. His distaste extended even to anything that could be quantified.[19] 'The space we need for the ranging mind', he said at St Paul's, 'is not simply to be measured in square feet.' As a critic, he could judge a length to a quarter of an inch, or an angle to a degree, but he scorned the ruler and the protractor. As a writer, he omitted from his work much that would have helped later scholars, from the dates on his letters* to the basic numerical information about the Winchester Bible.

In attempting to characterize his scholarly work as a whole, the first word that springs to mind is 'amateur'. The term is nuanced. It can be laudatory. 'He has often been called the last of the great amateurs writing on English medieval art,' wrote Kauffmann.[20] 'If so, one can only wish that the professionals had half his insight and

*Raleigh too omitted the day of the month on his letters, but vouchsafed the month.

productivity.' Bullock, who used the same phrase of him, pointed out that Oakeshott could *afford* his approach because he did not have to make his living by it. In that sense he was in the same gentlemanly, Grand Tour, tradition as Kenneth Clark. But there were important differences. Oakeshott's idea of connoisseurship embraced pigeon-fancying and aircraft-spotting; and temperamentally he was far removed from the 'pure' aesthete. The story is told of Clark that, seeing an emaciated beggar once in Spain, he was immediately reminded of an etching by Goya. Oakeshott, in front of the Goya, would have been reminded of a beggar to whom he had given alms.

There is another term that helps to illuminate Oakeshott's cast of mind. Liam Hudson in *Contrary Imaginations*[21] drew pen-portraits of two types, the converger and the diverger. Hudson's work was based on a psychological study of sixth-formers at Charterhouse against the background of their choice of subjects for specialization. The diverger, on this analysis, is emotional, untidy, intellectually promiscuous, wielder of the grand sweep and the inspired guess: typically drawn to art and literature. The converger by contrast is cerebral, meticulous, a pursuer of exactitude in a delimited field; typically drawn to languages, mathematics and science. One has but to state the divide to see Walter and Noel on either side of it.* They themselves recognized it almost from the start, and he acknowledged it in calling her 'a much more professional scholar than I'.

Amateur and professional, diverger and converger, romantic and classical, poet and prosaist – the list can be prolonged. It may seem strange that Oakeshott himself neither painted† nor wrote poetry. Yet Jasper Gaunt is right in seeing that 'much of his work is distinguished, perhaps more than anything else, by a sense of poetry'.‡ He cites 'the language, the way the sentences are constructed, the allusions, and above all the wonder he retained for what he was studying'.

What emerges from this consideration of Oakeshott's religion and his

*Hudson tentatively suggests that a typical diverger is one who identifies with a mother, a converger with a father.

†He rarely even drew, in spite of Beazley's famous advice to his pupils: 'How do you learn to distinguish the various styles of Greek vase-painters? The answer is a single word: draw.'

‡Kauffmann noted the poetry in Oakeshott's title 'The Master of the Leaping Figures', so unlike your run-of-the-mill art critic, and suggested that it was the model for Boase's 'Entangled Figures Master'.

scholarship is that each complemented the other. Central to both was his concern for the individual, the unique person. 'Individuals have always been my interest: schoolboys, undergraduates, medieval artists.' And he did not merely notice them: he focused upon them a concentrated gaze. Night after night he pored over his Winchester Bible artists, till he got to know them as friends. Similarly many people noted in him a gift which he himself had seen in Temple[22], and perhaps imitated: that when he was talking to you, you felt you had every ounce of his attention (see illustration).

The link between the two – his kinds of religion and scholarship – has been expressed most succinctly by Iris Murdoch*. Some twenty-five years ago she wrote, of art and morals, that

> the essence of them both is love. Love is the perception of individuals. Love is the extremely difficult realization that something other than oneself is real. Love, and so art and morals, is the discovery of reality. What stuns us into a realization of our supersensible destiny is not, as Kant imagined, the formlessness of nature, but rather its unutterable particularity; and the most particular and individual of all natural things is the mind of man. That is why tragedy is the highest art, because it is the most intensely concerned with the most individual thing.

More recently she has written that 'art with which we are familiar stays with us as an intimation that love has power and the world makes sense'.[23]Here is the Platonic conviction which, except in his blackest moments, sustained Oakeshott all his life. 'At the root of his beliefs was an acceptance of the oneness of truth with beauty and with goodness' – so he wrote of Leeson in 1956. Of himself it was no less true. And for him the root was grounded in the love of individuals.

But this absorption of the scholar-lover had its other side too: what was known unkindly at Winchester as 'the glazed look', when his attention was elsewhere; and his tendency later in life to walk blankly past colleagues in the High Street. In the active world it is not popular. But to another Platonist, the French mystic Simone Weil, it is the first step along the contemplative road which leads to the knowledge of God.[24]

---

*Although she and he were living in Oxford at the same time, they never got to know each other.

Not that Oakeshott's contemplative road led smoothly on, without dust and heat. Both religion and scholarship stretched his powers to the uttermost, in body, mind and spirit. Like Jacob at Peniel, he wrestled with an unknown opponent. In that mysterious story in Genesis, the opponent is finally revealed as representing both God and man.[25] And a medieval writer like Walter Hilton would not have hesitated to press the analogy with Oakeshott's inner life. In his wrestling with God, he wrung a blessing – though it did not last. But in his wrestling with man, as a scholar, he 'prevailed': the artists of the Winchester Bible did indeed 'tell him their names'.

Oakeshott also wrestled mightily in his active life, chiefly because of the peculiar nature of his ambition. It derived its force, surely, from the poverty of his childhood. The great-hearted man, says Aristotle, would rather confer benefits than receive them. Balliol idealism sharpened the sense of obligation – 'much is required of those to whom much is given' – and added a purpose and a method. The purpose was social betterment in the broadest sense. The method was appropriate to the purpose: influence rather than power, persuasion rather than command.

The method also suited the young Oakeshott's temperament. Shy and self-effacing, indecisive and fearful of confrontation, he was not equipped for command in the usual sense. His armoury included two weapons that are common to most successful people, brains and hard work, and two that are rarer, imagination and charm. But these were wielded almost ruthlessly in pursuit of his desired aims. Harvey was one of many who noted the paradox: the 'unassuming and even diffident' manner which concealed an 'amazing energy and pertinacity'. Thus Oakeshott started out in the world, with high hopes of changing it.

As a young man he believed that strikes could be resolved by reason, unemployment ameliorated through research, and education improved through legislation; and he relished the chance of having a hand in each. When he came to look back, he regularly described the unemployment survey of 1936–8 as 'the most useful job I ever did'. But after 1942, when he burned his fingers over the Conservative Educational sub-Committee, he effectively gave up social reform. No matter: to the idealists, teaching also ranked high among careers. But after 1954 he effectively gave up teaching also, to concentrate on art;

and art was a career field about which they had grave reservations. The Beautiful, to them, was never *quite* as admirable as the Good.[26]

Not that Oakeshott's idealism lasted all his life. For example he came over the years to permit himself a greater indulgence in the pleasures of the flesh. But a man's conscience is not so easily retrained, and he never lost the sense of guilt over his use of time. His late letters constantly refer to the 'selfishness' of his life, which he contrasted especially with that of Cook the schoolmaster. His own selfishness had been at the expense not only of Noel but of society. Noel, he believed, had forgiven him; himself he could not forgive.

Thus the emphasis in his life changed gradually from the active to the contemplative. Step by step he withdrew from exposed positions and commitments into an inner citadel. There, surrounded by trusted friends and familiar objets d'art, he could look back with wry amusement at his youthful optimism and look out with resigned melancholy* upon the direction the world was taking. This trajectory of life is of course far from unique. In an earlier age it might have brought him finally to a monastery, like Sir Launcelot du Lake in the *Morte d'Arthur* or many a notable figure from the medieval world, both catholic and orthodox. He himself noted a similar trajectory close to home in Henry of Blois, Bishop of Winchester 1129–71, brother of King Stephen, statesman and soldier, traveller and patron of the arts.

> As a young man he was deeply involved in the turbulent history of the time. But for the last ten years of his life he withdrew largely from political activity and gave his attention to the affairs of his diocese and the monastery of St Swithun. ... It is hard to believe that he was not responsible for launching the project for the great bible [c. 1160].[27]

Oakeshott's own times were turbulent too. His world was constantly on the move, faster than he wished to go. He himself remained in some respects an Edwardian, one for whom there was always time for people. Witness his long hand-written letters, or the courtesies which attended his dinner-parties, such as a brief biography of a neighbour on the back of a place-card. Edwardian also perhaps was his sense of privacy: his reticence over sex and money;

*Bullock called him 'a sad conservative', i.e. one who lamented change but did not fight against it like 'tough conservatives' such as Wheare.

his dislike of the 'intrusive' telephone; his preference for home-made entertainment, such as books, parlour games and music, with the wireless permitted but not the television.

In other respects he belonged firmly in the inter-war period. He was caught up in the last fling of the idealist tradition which fed the optimism of post-war planning. His views on education were grounded in the thinking of that same period and its brief survival after 1945: literature and history untainted by Temple's 'hybrid', sociology*; corporal punishment, but if possible no public examinations.

As he grew older this world began to fall apart. Taste was being commercialized, the independence of the universities eroded, *The Times* taken over by Murdoch (fortunately *The Independent* came just in time), and the country by Thatcherism. Worst of all, because most insidious, individual judgment was being obliterated by opinion polls. He had lived to be an anachronism. In Nicolas Barker's fine phrase, he was 'a romantic in a prosaic age'.[28]

With the barbarian at the gates, the inner citadel became ever more inviting. Every year he grew remoter from acquaintances and closer to friends. But for friends the magic was as great as ever – and as hard to analyse. The key to it was a focused thoughtfulness: he was unfailingly considerate of their feelings and imaginative in ministering to their pleasure. In this he was the truly unselfish man. Yet his conscience kept telling him that he was selfish and inadequate. Not far below the surface, he was acutely vulnerable. But on the surface – and almost always among friends – was a bubbling gaiety, a constant tendency to think of humorous and witty comparisons. For Mason, it was the combination of the gaiety with the unselfishness that was irresistible.

There was also a marked strain of innocence in him. His delight at a new discovery or a shared pleasure was unconcealed, like a child's with a birthday present. Like a child, too, he trusted people and thought the best of them. He persisted in ascribing to them talents and virtues they did not possess. He was never cynical, and 'did not know how to take offence'.[28] Carnivorous critics diagnosed an immaturity in this herbivore. The young, and the young in heart, were captivated.

*For Temple see p. 71; and cf. this (from a review by WFO, 1980) 'The personal detail of these surveys humanizes the discussion in a way that seldom appears in sociological discussions of urban problems these days.'

So one may think finally of Walter as he was in his happiest times, both during his active life and in retirement: the best of company, warming his hands around the fire of friendship, sparkling with ideas and fun. But for anyone who knew him at Winchester that is not enough. It is impossible to forget the exaltation of his glory days, before the world had grown grey; the conviction he then inspired, that there is still a Holy Grail to be sought and found; and the invitation he gave to all, whatever their status or talent, to ride abroad upon what promised to be the Quest of a lifetime.

Envoi

When old age shall this generation waste,
Thou shalt remain, in midst of other woe
Than ours, a friend to man, to whom thou say'st,
'Beauty is truth, truth beauty – that is all
Ye know on earth, and all ye need to know.'

JOHN KEATS, Ode on a Grecian Urn, 1820

Notes to the Text

PROLOGUE

1 Sir Folliott Sandford, his Registrar.
2 'Shot silk' is Canon James Mansel's phrase.
3 Said to Mrs Anne Grantham (formerly Ridgway) in 1962.
4 Source: Cecilia Russell-Smith (*née* Streeten).

CHAPTER I

1 According to the *Hampstead and Highgate Express* of 8 March 1879, Dr John was hit 'by the pole of one of Mr Taylor's mineral water vans, drawn by two horses', knocked down and trampled. The driver of the van was found guilty of manslaughter.
2 28 C4 in the *London A-Z*. It is misspelled 'Oakshott' in the index but is correct on the map.
3 But an Afrikaans-speaking member, on being sent the minutes in English by mistake, resigned forthwith.
4 Most of the quotations which follow come from a paper he read to a meeting of the UU (p. 345 n. 8) at Tonbridge in 1947. Entitled 'Schools Metropolitan or Monastic', it compares the kinds of education given in boarding and day schools he had known.
5 Bishop E. L. Evans supplied this touch and much useful background.
6 The correspondence is in Balliol College Archives.
7 Somervell's father had been Bursar of Harrow.

CHAPTER 2

1 This analysis draws heavily on Peter Gordon and John White, *Philosophers as Educational Reformers*, RKP, 1979.
2 I have relied much on T. G. Usborne and M. S. Whitehouse, *The Balliol Players 1923-1932*, Blackwood, Edinburgh, 1933.
3 Beazley's technique derived ultimately from a nineteenth-century Italian scientist, Morelli.
4 Mason has written of his time at Balliol in *A Shaft of Sunlight*, André Deutsch, 1987, ch. 4.
5 Nairac was a Mauritian, and became Attorney General of the island.
6 It was doubtless in connexion with this essay that he visited Germany in

1924 or 1925. He mentioned in a sermon c.1950 how much he had been struck by the inscription on a German war memorial: just the dates '1914–1918' and the words 'GOTT MIT UNS'.

7 There are three sources for the B.I. which do not fit easily together. In 1971 WFO gave an interview, with Mason, to Brian Harrison for his *History of the University of Oxford*, vol. VIII (OUP, 1994). In it he gave most credit to McVeagh. McVeagh's account of c. 1970, now in the Lindsay Archive at Keele University, gives the credit, after himself, to Lindsay. His narrative does not mention WFO by name, only 'O's beautiful sister'. To Mason, WFO was without question the moving spirit.

McVeagh does however record that 'one of the team, who looked as if he specialized in the history of art, became a great buddy of the cockney hawkers who carried the posters and collected the tuppences', and 'with his small car penetrated many outlying districts', setting up 'as effective a distributing department as one would wish to see'. This reads like WFO. If so, he had put his experience with the Balliol Players to serious use.

8 The issues are on microfilm in the British Library at Colindale.

CHAPTER 3

1 Some records of the Bec School are in the Greater London Record Office.

2 Dr James Huck. Other memories from Dr Sidney Wells (later himself Head), Graham Crosskey (later Deputy Head to Wells) and Norman Taylor.

3 Noel contributed some 'Recollections' of her schooldays to *Isabel Fry: Portrait of a Great Teacher* by Beatrice Curtis Brown, Arthur Barker, 1960, pp. 101ff.

4 In the *Anglican Church Magazine* no. 3, pp. 326ff. It is a remarkably scholarly article, with references to individual vases in museums in Rome, Munich and Petrograd (*sic*).

5 Best known for *A High Wind in Jamaica* (1929).

6 The article is unsigned but is referred to in his letters of the month.

7 WFO was not sure of the attribution to Beerbohm; see his article in *Time and Tide*, 27 October 1951.

8 L. Thorpe. Other OMTs here quoted are Messrs Tim Brown, Douglas McKean, A. J. C. Saunders and the Ven. N. K. Nye.

9 Source: Professor Dafydd Jenkins, who has also provided much useful background information about WFO's time at MTS.

10 T. B. F. Thompson

11 By J. B. Steane, 1988.

12 Source: Kent County Archives, kindly consulted for me by W. H. Petty.

CHAPTER 4

1 Her nanny is among those recorded in Jonathan Gathorne-Hardy's *The Rise and Fall of the British Nanny*, Hodder, 1972.

2 WFO also rescued a drawing of a crucifixion by Gleadowe. G. had torn it up in a moment of depression and thrown the pieces in a dustbin. WFO retrieved it, had it framed, and kept it always on his walls.

3 Noel wrote of this and two other vases in *JHS*, 1939, 283ff.

4 WFO was especially gratified by a friendly notice in *Economic History*, 490, a periodical published by the Royal Economic Society.

5 B. B. Lloyd. Other memories of this period have been supplied by J. P. du Croz and A. G. Gray.

6 WFO himself was careful to say only that he had identified the ms, not that he had discovered it. But he took some pleasure in the fact that the identification had eluded the great M. R. James. James, too, liked to escape from the cricket during the Eton-Winchester match, to forage in the Fellows' Library.

7 His scholarly comments on the text were amplified in an article for the *Gutenberg Jahrbuch*. At the other end of the spectrum he wrote a piece about the find for *Discovery*, a 'popular Journal of Knowledge'.

8 The UU or United Ushers was an elective society of promising school-masters. A member might remain, but could not be elected, after becoming a headmaster.

9 For his work on the report Singer was awarded a prize by the Royal Statistical Society. In 1994 he was created Knight Bachelor for his sub-sequent services to development economics.

10 But Owen, who admired Lindsay more than Oakeshott did, shared Balliol idealism and even Hellenism. A 1930 article of his, 'The Social Survey of a City', ends with these words: 'Maybe we shall in this way help to make democracy in our time the living thing it was for a little while in Athens 2,500 years ago: enlightened self-rule by ordinary folk.' (*Social Science Review*, 1930, 191, a reference I owe to Dr José Harris.)

11 She wrote of this trip in her posthumous contribution to the Trendall Festschrift.

12 In view of events in 1942 (p. 118), two of his observations about the young unemployed are worth noting. First, 'what the young man desires is something which will make not small, but great demands on him'. Second, on compulsory training: 'if it is applied individually and with some adequate provision for a reasonably permanent job at the end of it, there may be a case for compulsion'.

13 In making this criticism he may also have had in mind his own part in the report of the Conservative sub-committee of 1942.

14 Colonel H. Clementi Smith, Master of the Mercers' Company, was *ex*

officio Chairman of Governors of St Paul's School during his year of office. The annual change of chairmanship inevitably hampered the making of policy.

CHAPTER 5

1 His secretary was the wife of another key figure in the whole enterprise: Mr Minshull, the school engineer.

2 Hugh Arnold was present when Eliot came to talk about poetry in the spring of 1940. In discussion he was asked his views by WFO as the youngest person present, and said he preferred poetry that was not too obscure, like Owen and Rupert Brooke. 'There was a stunned silence. I remember the great man's exact words. With a bleak smile he said "Perhaps you're right." '

3 Headmasters love classroom discussion. When one has forgotten the facts, ideas beckon. When one has skimped one's preparation, a red herring is welcome. But in WFO's case it was natural.

4 In addition to those named in the text, many others have contributed memories, including Messrs Gareth Evans and Barry Smallman, and two others who kept diaries: Keith Hamilton-Jones and Graham Hennessy. Hennessy's diary is in the school archives.

5 Wood's manuscript autobiography was unfinished at his death in 1987. A contemporary of his was John Thorn, who yielded to none in his admiration for WFO's 'first-class and richly stocked mind', but felt 'it was kept at a distance from us'. See his 'personal memoir' in the re-issue of *The Sword of the Spirit*, Friends of Winchester College, 1991.

6 All highly selective schools recognize this problem. 'Ordinary' is a term of art meaning 'below our normal entrance standard'. In extreme cases it may be used of children whose abilities are in the top 5% of the population.

7 Village Colleges were currently being developed in Cambridgeshire by Henry Morris.

8 Source for The Moot: R. Kojecky, *T. S. Eliot's Social Criticism*, Faber, 1971.

9 Four years earlier he had had an offer to propose him from Tommy Wood, his old music teacher, with whom he kept in touch. He 'told him it wasn't my mark just yet awhile'(letter to Noel).

10 The quotation, and a good deal else hereabouts, comes from a magisterial study by Dr José Harris entitled 'The Debate on State Welfare' in ed. Harold L. Smith, *War and Social Change*, Manchester UP, 1986, 238ff. Her account draws heavily, as mine does, upon the Conservative Party Archives in the Bodleian.

11 Doubtless the society was the UU; but nothing else is known of the paper.

12 I am much indebted to her son Geoffrey for permission to quote from her diaries.

13 Faber himself felt let down by Butler, and abandoned his political ambitions.

14 cf. José Harris's article, 'Enterprise and the Welfare State' in *Transactions of the Royal Historical Society, 1990,* p. 138 on swallowing 'centralized state power'. Not for the last time a liberal-minded educational reformer made the mistake of supposing that a worthy end justified compulsory means.

15 By chance, Walter's second cousin Michael Oakeshott then held the Chair of Philosophy there.

16 'Shared Inheritance' was his original title for the book.

17 Masefield's daughters had been at school with Noel, and she had been to stay with them as a girl. Masefield was much taken with her and used to give her first editions of his books.

18 In later life, when his interests were centred more narrowly on the Winchester Bible, he persuaded himself that the *purpose* of his crossing the Atlantic was to see the Morgan Leaf. His correspondence with Noel in 1942-3 shows that this cannot have been so. He gave the lecture to the Society of Antiquaries in November 1943 and became a Fellow in 1946.

19 WFO's epithet. The text of the report is extant, in family possession.

20 Mrs Jean Wyatt.

21 He had originally planned to dedicate it jointly to Noel and to Alan Blakeway. Blakeway was a brilliant ancient historian, whose place he had taken on the staff at Winchester and whose death in 1936 distressed him greatly.

22 Within that short compass he also put forward, albeit tentatively, what is now the accepted solution to 'the conundrum of the Morgan Leaf'. Previously it was thought to have been removed from another related bible. WFO gave reasons for supposing that it had been made for the Winchester Bible itself.

23 In *The Sunday Times*, 16 September 1945.

24 The letter is among the Winant papers in the Franklin D. Roosevelt Library, New York.

25 A few shots of the performance can be seen on a film made by the school technicians at Crowthorne.

CHAPTER 6

1 I owe this word to Kenneth Kettle, who took it from Henry James's *The Ambassadors* to pinpoint the respect in which WFO stood out among the headmasters of Winchester he had known.

2 In the article for *Blackwood's Magazine*.

3 In 1935 he had presented to the Fellows' Library two documents of 1396 relating to William of Wykeham's acquisition of an estate as part of the school's endowments.

4 cf. Betjeman's poem 'The Wykehamist at Home': 'By cheerful unbending in soccer and social clubs *We* can get on with the masses'.

5 Memories hereinafter supplied by former pupils: in addition to those named in the text, Michael Archer, Denis Blake, Raymond Bonham-Carter, James Cornford, Roger Ellis, Michael Haslett, Murray Lawrence, Paul Lucas, John Mallet, Andrea Pampanini, John Todd.

6 Colin Badcock in *The Wykehamist*, June 1988.

7 In addition to those identified in the text, I have quoted from Podge Brodhurst, Michael Burchnall, John Gammell and Erik Sthyr.

8 The phrasing may be an echo of WFO's 1950 article in *Time and Tide*, entitled 'Journalism and Truth'. It was written in praise of Christopher Buckley, the distinguished war correspondent who had just been killed in Korea. Buckley was a long-standing friend of Cecilia and WFO, and had married her in 1947.

9 This was a main theme of his British Association Address in 1950 and of an article on Arnold of Rugby in 1953.

10 Dr Eiddon Edwards FBA.

11 cf. p. 136.

12 cf. p. 102, 354 n. 7.

13 The file was very kindly put at my disposal by Walker's literary executor, Dr Andrew Crawshaw.

14 Confirmed by G. C. W. Dicker, the only surviving housemaster of the time.

15 So Hodges.

16 The phrase is Everett's.

17 From an unsigned obituary of his successor Desmond Lee.

18 Harvey is also an indispensable source for this section. He has kept all his correspondence with WFO in immaculate order, generously made it available, and answered numberless follow-up questions.

19 WFO 1957 in *The Trusty Servant*, an Old Wykehamist journal.

20 When the original east window was dispersed in 1821, six of the figures found their way to Parham House in Sussex. One had since been acquired by the V and A, the other five by an American Professor Kienbusch. He generously bequeathed them to the school on his death, and they are now in Fromond's Chantry.

21 Sir Leigh Ashton. Ashton's still influential predecessor, Sir Eric Maclagan, was another Wykehamist.

22 The inscription, begun in 1949, was virtually finished in 1953, but not finally executed until 1956.

23 The *Wykehamist* article must derive from Oakeshott but is unsigned.

24 Harvey is quoting from Villard de Honnecourt's album about his collaboration with Pierre de Corbie c.1240.

25 For an earlier meeting with Morris see p. 109.

26 *The Cambridgeshire Syllabus of Religious Teaching for Schools*, CUP, 1949, 107f.

27 Source: Oxford University Press archives.

28 Harvey and other friends of WFO found it hard to understand how he could ever have taken part in the project. Doubtless he could not resist a combined appeal from Williams, who was Chairman of the whole Project and of the Literary Panel, and Dodd, who was Director of the Project and Chairman of the NT panel.

29 CACE papers in PRO ED 146.

30 WFO's paper is numbered PSL 30.

31 A. Briggs, *History of Broadcasting in the UK*, vol. IV, OUP 1970, 301ff.

32 These and following papers in BBC Written Archives.

33 *Report of the Broadcasting Committee 1949*, Cmd 8116, HMSO, Jan 1951.

34 op cit 237f.

35 op cit 213ff.

36 M. R. James, *The Wanderings and Homes of Manuscripts*, SPCK, 1928.

37 Beatrice Forder did expert work for WFO over many years. On her death in 1973 he wrote an appreciation in the *Winchester Cathedral Record*.

38 An Appendix argues for the authenticity of the so-called Western text of Luke-Acts. The draft of the book is now in the Getty Center.

39 Correspondence in the British Library Manuscripts Department.

40 Seddon was Alan Roseveare's form-master, and had shared WFO's dismay, and sense of guilt, at the boy's suicide (p. 206). To invite him to edit the poem was one of WFO's finest acts of generosity.

41 Both the date of sale and the sale price are uncertain. WFO himself did not record the date; the price he recalled, in a letter of 1971, as 'about £2,500.' A. N. L. Munby in *Phillipps Studies*, 5, 1960, p. 90, gave £3,000 without date; but his own ms notes in his interleaved copy of the Phillipps catalogue give £3,500 and 1955. Perhaps the payment was spread over three years for tax purposes: WFO certainly needed cash in 1952–3. In March 1953 he sold a further £400 worth of books at Sotheby's, of which the most valuable was a first edition of W. Gilbert *De Magnete*, 1600.

42 The article was probably drafted c. 1949–50, though not published till 1963. As Vice-Chancellor 1962–4, WFO had no time to do more than polish.

43 This is a conservative estimate: almost certainly there is plenty more to be discovered. Moreover many of the reviews are substantial pieces of work, running to well over 3,000 words.

44 Lady Gater gave WFO the letter after her husband's death.

45 In my attempt to put the matter fairly, I have had generous help from the following people, who have read through my drafts, made suggestions, and corrected errors of fact, though they must not be taken as accepting my version of events: Mrs Anne Grantham (formerly Ridgway), Kenneth Kettle and Sir Jeremy Morse. Morse was Ridgway's first head of house and Oakeshott's first head of school. As Warden, he has access to the embargoed file. I never discussed the affair with either Oakeshott or Ridgway.

46 From 'Odyssey in a Cockleshell' (see p. 321).

CHAPTER 7

1 Ashmole said that WFO was instrumental in overcoming his reluctance to stand for election to Beazley's chair (*Autobiography*, ed. D. Kurtz, Oxbow Books, 1994, 133f.)

2 Sir Edward Abraham.

3 Source: Professor Brian Simpson.

4 Sir Christopher Ball.

5 The roundels are nos. 1616–31 in Wm Cole, *A Catalogue of Netherlandish and N.European Roundels in Britain*, OUP, 1993.

6 See his article in *Lincoln College Record*, 1956/7.

7 The author of the anonymous review (*TLS*, 21 October 1960, 684) is said to have been Marion Lawrence of New York. The other was J. E. Gaehde in *Speculum* 26, 1961, 678ff.

8 The Press charged him just under £400 (not the full cost) for 125 copies.

9 Eventually in 1972 the Robinson brothers presented it to the British Museum, where it is now on permanent exhibition as Add. ms. 57555.

10 Keen in *PBA*, 1944, 433.

11 This position was not incompatible with support for Latin at Winchester. Winchester taught Latin for its own sake, not Oxford's.

12 Somewhat similarly, WFO is credited with having discovered, in Lincoln College Library, 'a print of the original plans for the Holywell Music Room', which enabled a 'restoration to its original form.' (*PBA*, 1977, 481; from an appreciation of Sir Jack Westrup). I have not been able to find any further details of this discovery.

13 See e.g. *History of the University of Oxford* vol. VIII, 513.

14 The design is reproduced in Howard Colvin, *Unbuilt Oxford*, Yale UP, 1983, 185.

15 This and subsequent comments from a letter of January 1993.

16 A witty if partisan account of the debate and its background is provided in [H. R. Trevor-Roper], *The Letters of Mercurius Oxoniensis*, 1970, ch. 11.

17 These and later points from an interview, October 1992.

18 Letter, January 1994.

19 From a ms account left by WFO on the back of a letter from Holford.

20 Letter of June 1992.

21 This and later points from letters and interview, 1992.

22 Source for this and p. 254: (Professor) Brian Mc Guinness. Other proc-
    tors quoted are Drs J. D. Davies, J. B. McLeod and J. H. Sanders.

23 The name-vase was published in *Burlington Magazine*, 1975, 382.

24 He had something of a librarian's instinct in the matter of sub-units. At
    St Paul's he had wanted to unify all the separate subject libraries.

25 WFO also joined Shackleton in signing written evidence to the Franks
    Commission, but the style does not suggest his own authorship
    (*Evidence*, vol. XI).

26 The verdict is supported, more diplomatically, in the *History of the
    University of Oxford*, vol. VIII, 482.

27 Dr T. F. R. G. Braun of Merton.

28 At that time the focus was upon the social needs of senior members who
    were not Fellows of a college. As time went by, the needs of graduate
    students came to weigh heavily too.

29 What swayed Council was rather Berlin's success in securing offers of
    endowment conditional upon a move to Cherwell (Minutes of 30 May
    1966). I am very grateful to Sir Isaiah himself, and to Michael Brock and
    Henry Hardy, all of whom read my draft hereabouts, for help in sorting
    the matter out.

30 Wolfson gave the buildings, Ford the endowment; hence the name.

31 The design was known in Oxford as the 'Mexican hat'. There is a
    photograph of WFO with Nervi and Moya looking at the model in the
    History of the University of Oxford, vol. VIII, plate 19, 13.

32 Quoted from the citation for WFO's Hon. D.Litt. at UEA in 1984. The
    background is set out in the *Annual Report* of the Pilgrim Trust for
    1966, 7ff. After retiring from the Pilgrim Trust, WFO served on the York
    Glaziers Trust from 1978 to 1982.

33 The German translation is so faulty that a German reviewer advised
    serious scholars to use the English original.

34 *Burlington Magazine*, 1961, 161ff: 'A Cycle of English Frescoes in
    Spain'.

35 In a late fragment of autobiography, WFO gave more information.
    'Otto Pächt, who knew my book [*Artists of the Winchester Bible*],
    wrote excitedly to tell me that, looking through photographs of Spanish
    antiquities, he'd found a series of paintings "by your Morgan Master". I
    didn't believe him. But he had.' WFO gives no date for P's letter; but
    unless his memory is at fault, it shows Pächt going much further in
    private than he went in print.

36 An appendix to *Sigena* was worked up into an article for Pächt's

seventieth birthday Festschrift. It studies the lettering of the inscriptions which identify the figures at Sigena, and suggests that they too are the work of the Morgan Master.

37 Potter wrote the chapter about that work which WFO incorporated into *Oxford Stone Restored*, 1975.

CHAPTER 8

1 The conversion was written up by the architect, John Cresswell Turner, in *Architectural Review*, May 1972, 319f.
2 The book sales included £850 for the book with the Burgkmair engravings (p. 231) and £750 for a first edition of Spenser's *Colin Clout* (p. 275).
3 The full shelf-mark is Auct. E. Infra 1 and 2.
4 The Lyell lectures were not published until 1960, under the title *English Manuscripts of the Century after the Norman Conquest*, OUP. Ker's papers, including corespondence with WFO, are in the Bodleian.
5 Boase's original study is in his *English Art 1100–1216*, OUP, 1953, 179f.
6 The review was published in *JHS*, 1976, 251f. After her death he also polished her last review for publication in *JHS*, 1977, 223f.
7 The text here is a conflation of his letters to Cook, Dancy and Mitchell. He also wrote a ms account of her last illness and their conversations during it. He showed it to Jasper, with the comment that he hoped to write it out neatly, but doubted that he would be able to. Presumably he destroyed it later.
8 In her memory the family endowed the Noel Moon travel scholarship for undergraduates reading archaeology at St Anne's.
9 The attempt to portray Maggie owes a great deal to her friend Mrs Helen Peacocke of Eynsham.
10 He was not yet nine when Walker's work was completed.
11 He served from 1974 to 1980, during which time the income increased from £16,000 to £80,000 p.a.
12 WFO even thought the MM might have been responsible, 'if only at the level of design', for some of the mosaics of the Cappella Palatina in Palermo (*2WB* 75).
13 *Romanesque Mural Paintings*, Thames and Hudson, 1968, 509, 511. Demus regarded them as an early work, representing 'the moment when an artist first made the step from miniature to mural paintings'.
14 In *Sigena*, 1972, he had taken the opposite view: the earlier painting was 'almost certainly not' by the MM (*2WB* 136). He did have *moments* of scepticism.
15 *Winchester Cathedral Record*, 1981; cp *2WB*, 78.
16 See his letter in *TLS* of 1 December 1972.
17 'General feeling' *2WB*, 82 n. 2.
18 WFO's catalogue, which is also recorded on a tape, was used by Claire

Donovan for *The Winchester Bible* (The British Library for Winchester Cathedral, 1993). The photographs in her book give a better representation of the (gold) illumination than WFO's own 2WB, and are used in the illustration section. Donovan also argues in it that the Morgan Leaf was not merely made for the WB but actually incorporated into it for many centuries, and so her book contains photographs of it, though not of the wall-paintings of the Holy Sepulchre Chapel.

19 Their collaborative article (p. 301) had proved to be one such, though it had led to a paper of her own in *English Manuscript Studies* 2, Blackwell, 1990; where see p.251 n.3 for a tribute to him.

20 Dr B. C. Barker-Benfield.

21 The Hon. L. H. L. Cohen.

22 Grimond had taken a great interest in Job Ownership, a company formed by Robert.

23 Lady Pamela Humphrys, of Marston Meysey Grange.

24 Jack Lankester.

25 WFO had tried hard to get Mitchell elected to the corresponding Chair in Oxford in 1965–6. When the attempt failed he wrote 'In some ways your appointment was the thing I've wanted to happen here more than anything else. Odd that one should be harder knocked by this than by losing a job oneself.'

26 'Four High Masters' is obtainable from Antony Jay Productions Ltd.

27 The inscription, in his usual elegant and untranslatable Latin, reads PRETIOSUM HUNC LIBRUM POSTERIS AMICI DUO LIGAVIT RP LEGAVIT WO AMICITIAE TESTAMEN PRETIOSISSIMAE

28 This is not the usual Latin of Mk. 8. 36. The variations from the standard text, especially 'himself' for 'his own soul', invite speculation.

29 Christopher Turner.

30 Alnwick is the seat of the Duke of Northumberland, then a fellow member of the Roxburghe Club.

31 The map is now displayed in the school library, together with a copy of the *TLS* article.

32 King was himself given an honorary degree by UEA ten years later.

33 The New York portrait is known as the Plimpton partrait after its owners. In Roy Strong's catalogue it is no. 43, the Siena one being no. 45 (*Portraits of Q. Elizabeth I*, 1963).

34 The judgement is that of Professor Anson Jordan of Columbia University. Having joined him in part of the quest, she allowed him, for friendship's sake, to cite her as co-author.

35 Professor W. H. Matchett kindly read the draft with great care in 1988, but could not recommend publication.

36 Some thought it was an authentic Guercino. Jasper Gaunt says that 'Walter was very fond of it, but in some ways frightened of the consequences'

of that identification, and 'preferred to let it remain a mystery'. The corresponding hope may have prompted whoever stole it from Rose's house in 1993.

EPILOGUE

1 Minute 17 of a meeting on 19 January 1979, written by Myles Glover, Clerk to the Skinners' Company and a devoted friend and admirer of WFO. His text, which is much abbreviated here, does not claim to be a verbatim report: rather to give the sense of what was said. Others present confirm its general accuracy, and recall that, while speaking, WFO kept his eyes shut and finger-tips together. The two masters must be Vere Hodge and Somervell.

2 Gaunt had been ordained in 1954. He is the author of some popular hymns.

3 None of his St Paul's sermons survives, but the description of them in *The Pauline* of December 1946, 49 would apply equally to Winchester. Some of them may have been given in both places.

4 The broadcast took the form of a review of F. L. Iremonger, *William Temple*, OUP, 1948.

5 There is an echo here of Charles Raven's theology.

6 Six ms notebooks of sermons are extant in the Winchester College archives, and four more in the Getty Center. None is dated, even by the year, and in any case there are up to four versions of each.

7 In one draft of this sermon he illustrates this kind of faith by the evacuation from Dunkirk and the early victories in the Western Desert. It may well have been given first at St Paul's.

8 cf. the story on p. 163.

9 Out of a classical sixth of some twenty-eight boys in 1950–1, six were later ordained.

10 Contrast his comments in 1928 on the *Pantocrator* at Daphni (p. 46) and in 1972 on the Creation at Sigena (p. 278).

11 This is what Peter Berger calls the 'plausibility structure' (P. L. Berger and T. Luckman, *The Social Structure of Reality*, Penguin, 1967).

12 As late as October 1953 he supported the chaplains in resisting a proposal from some of the staff to drop the daily saying of the Apostles' Creed from morning Chapel. The reason he gave was a political one: he did not want an upheaval while he himself was 'under sentence', i.e. bound for Lincoln. But if there was to be any change, 'we do not want some vague, amorphous, constantly changing service in praise of Nature and man's achievements'.

13 But he delivered some magnificent Funeral Orations, e.g. on Mavor, Gater and Williams.

14 210 d.

15 Hence perhaps also his otherwise surprising lack of interest in the composition: the placing and the spacing of the components.

16 *Attic Black Figure Vases*, OUP, 1956, x.

17 From his review of Tristram's *English Medieval Wall Paintings*.

18 The paper comparing Plutarch with Shakespeare is in the Getty Center. It was written in 1953 for an unspecified context, perhaps the school Essay Society.

19 cf. his avoidance of the vintage in ordering good wine (p. 303).

20 *Burlington Magazine*, 1987, 808.

21 *Contrary Imaginations*, Methuen, 1966.

22 'Even to the child I was then, Temple [at Repton] showed the unmistakeable mark of greatness. In talking to him I felt I was the one person he wished to talk with.' (Sir James Darling, *Richly Rewarding*, Melbourne, 1978, 36.)

23 *Metaphysics as a Guide to Morals*, 1992, 81. The earlier quotation comes from a review in the *TES* of a book of hers which neither of us can now identify. The same themes are also found in *The Sovereignty of Good*, 1970, *passim*, e.g. 'Goodness and beauty are not to be contrasted, but are largely part of the same structure.'

24 *L'Attente de Dieu*, 1950, ET *Waiting upon God*. 1951. Murdoch, in her borrowing from Weil, keeps the word 'attention'.

25 Gen. 32. 28 (RSV) : 'You have striven with God and man, and have prevailed.'

26 At the very end of his *Prolegomena to Ethics*, T. H. Green agonized over the question whether a man is justified in indulging a talent for music when there are pressing social needs to be met. His answer is 'only if he has talent to serve mankind – to contribute to the perfection of the human soul – more as a musician than in any other way.'

27 *2WB*, 8.

28 Nicolas Barker in the *Independent*, 14 October 1987.

Published Writings of Walter Oakeshott

1927 'Boys and Books', *Times Educational Supplement*, 29 January, 51 (unsigned).

1929 'Hosios Loukas', *The Times*, 21 May, 17 (unsigned).

1934 'A Malory Manuscript: the Discovery at Winchester', *The Times*, 27 August, 11ff.

1934 'The Text of Malory', *Times Literary Supplement*, 27 September, 650.

1935 'The Manuscript of the Morte Darthur', *Discovery*, 16, February, 45f.

1935 'Caxton and Malory's Morte Darthur', *Gutenberg Jahrbuch*, 113f.

1936 'Arthuriana at Winchester', *Wessex*, vol. III, no. 3, 1 May, 74ff.

1936 *Commerce and Society: a Short History of Trade and Its Effects on Civilization*, Oxford: Clarendon Press.

1936 *Catalogue for an Exhibition in Winchester College Library*, Winchester College.

1936 'Transference and the Special Areas', *The Times*, 17 and 18 November, 17f and 15f (unsigned).

1938 (With H. Singer *et al.*), *Men without Work: a Report Made to the Pilgrim Trust*, Cambridge: University Press.

1939 'Youth without Work', *Spectator*, 3 March, 34f.

1939 'Refugees in this Country', *The Times*, 29 August, 11 (letter).

1939 'The Winchester XII-Century Bible and the Paintings of the Holy Sepulchre Chapel', *Winchester Cathedral Record* 8, 14ff.

1940 'Unemployment', BBC Home Service, 15 March (talk for sixth forms).

1940 'War and Peace Aims: Reparations', *The Times*, 18 December, 5 (letter).

1941 Preface to *Preces: Hymns and Prayers for St Paul's School*, C. T. Hunt, Crowthorne, xiii–xiv.

1942 *Founded upon the Seas: a Narrative of some English Maritime and Overseas Enterprises during the Period 1550–1616*, Cambridge: University Press.

1942 'The Plan for Youth', *The Times*, 22 September, 5 (letter).

1943 'Mr W. H. Priest', *The Pauline*, 410, April 1f.

1943 'The General Management of St Paul's School', *The Pauline*, 410, April, 1ff.

1944 'The Winchester Bible', *Winchester Cathedral Record*, 13, 6ff.

1945 'The Future of St Paul's', *The Times*, 20 April, 5 (letter).

1945 *The Artists of the Winchester Bible*, London: Faber and Faber.

1945 'Epilogue', *The Pauline*, 420, December, 100ff.

1947 'Mars or Minerva', *Blackwood's Magazine*, May, 378ff.

1948 'A Miniature Romantically Restored to Winchester Cathedral', *Illustrated London News*, 24 January, 109.

1948 'An Elizabethan Headmaster', *The Wykehamist*, 934, 10 March, 299f.

1948 'A Recovered Treasure', *Winchester Cathedral Record*, 17, 4f.

1948 Review of F. A. Iremonger, *William Temple*, OUP, BBC Third Programme, 6 August.

1949 Review of C. J. P. Cave, *Medieval Roof Bosses in Medieval Churches*, Cambridge, *The Listener*, 17 March, 454.

1949 'Chapel: the Original Glass', *The Wykehamist*, 955, 30 November, 54f.

1949 Review of Joan Evans, *English Art 1307-1461*, Oxford, *New Statesman*, vol. 38, 17 December.

1950 *The Sequence of English Medieval Art 650 1450*, London: Faber and Faber.

1950 *The Sword of the Spirit*, London: Faber and Faber, printed in two editions, and reprinted, with a foreword by J. L. Thorn, 1991.

1950 Review of Christopher Dawson, *Religion and the Rise of Western Culture*, Sheed and Ward, *The Spectator*, 7 April. 470.

1950 Review of E. W. Tristram, *English Medieval Wall-Paintings*, OUP for Pilgrim Trust, *The Spectator*, 12 June, 768f.

1950 Review of H. Butterfield, *The Origins of Modern Science 1300–1800*, London, 1949, *Science Progress* 38 , 405f.

1950 'Journalism and Truth', *Time and Tide*, 9 September, 897.

1950 'Education and Power', *The Advancement of Science*, vol. VII, no. 26, September, 204ff.

1950 Review of Joan Evans, *Cluniac Art of the Romanesque Period*, CUP, 1949, *The Spectator*, 22 December, 740.

1951 'The BBC and Education', *Report of the Broadcasting Committee* 1949, HMSO, Cmnd 8116, January, 237f.

1951 'Trade Routes', *Oxford Junior Encyclopaedia,* vol. IV, OUP, 456f.

1951 'History, the Legends and the Realities', *Time and Tide*, 27 October, 1031f.

1951 'The Reconstruction of the Library', *Winchester Cathedral Record*, 20, 12f.

1952 'The Future of Broadcasting', *The Times*, 1 April, 7 (letter).

1952 Review of F. C. Wormald, *English Drawings of the Tenth and Eleventh Centuries*, Faber, and D. Talbot Rice *English Art, 871–1100*, OUP, *Times Literary Supplement*, 26 September, 621ff (unsigned).

1952 'Sir Frederick Kenyon', *The Wykehamist*, 989, 14 October, 152.

1952 'An Unknown Raleigh Manuscript. The Working Papers for the History of the World', *The Times*, 29 November, 7.

1953 Review of Sir Francis Oppenheimer, *The Legend of the Sainte Ampoule* and *Frankish Themes and Problems*, Faber, 1952, *Times Literary Supplement*, 1 May, 286 (unsigned).

1953 'Arnold of Rugby and his Legacy', *The Daily Telegraph*, 7 October, 6.

1953 *Proceedings of Annual General Meeting 1953*, Headmasters' Conference, 32ff.

1953 'The Altar Bible and the Prayer Book of Charles II', *Winchester Cathedral Record*, 22, 7f.

1953 'Earl Wavell', *The Times*, 28 December, 9 (unsigned).

1954 Review of Philip Edward, *Sir Walter Raleigh*, Longmans, 1953, *Cambridge Review*, 30 January, 252f.

1954 'Winchester College Library before 1750', *The Library*, 9, no. 1, March, 1ff.

1954 Review of T. S. R. Boase, *English Art 1100–1216*, OUP, *English Historical Review*, 11 July, 436ff.

1954 Review of J. D. E. Firth, *Rendall of Winchester*, *The Wykehamist*, 1013, 12 October, 501f.

1955 Review of C. R. Dodwell, *The Canterbury School of Illumination 1066–1200*, Cambridge, 1954, *The Library*, 10, no. 4, December, 288ff.

1955 Review of M. Rickert, *Painting in Britain in the Middle Ages*, London, 1954, *Antiquaries Journal*, 35, 245f.

1956 'Spencer Leeson', *The Wykehamist*, 1029, 24 February, 501f.

1956 Review of ed. A. Malraux, *Manuscripts à Peintures du xiime au xvime Siècle*, Paris, 1955, *The Book Collector*, 5, no. 2 (Summer), 180ff.

1956 'Sir John Beazley' and 'Egon Wellesz', *Lincoln College Record*, 1955–6, 2ff.

1956 'Foster Stearns', *Lincoln College Record*, 1955, 17.

1957 'Some Classical and Medieval Ideas in Renaissance Cosmography', *Essays in Memory of Fritz Saxl*, ed. D. J. Gordon, London, 245ff.

1957 'The College Chapel', *Lincoln College Record*, 1956–7, 8ff.

1957 'The Sheldonian Theatre Restoration', *Oxford Magazine*, 75, 304ff, 308ff.

1957 'Chapel Glass', *The Trusty Servant*, May, 4f.

1957 'Notes on the Way', *Time and Tide*, 22 June, 771f, and 29 June, 803f.

1957 Review of A. D. Lindsay, *Selected Addresses*, privately printed, *Balliol College Record*, 30f.

1958 'Cyril Bailey', *The Pauline*, 456, March, 34f, reprinted in *Balliol College Record*, 28ff.

1958 'Compulsory Latin', *The Times*, 6 June, 7 (letter).

1959 Review of eds. F. Wormald and C. E. Wright, *The English Library before 1700: Studies in Its History*, London, 1958, *The Book Collector*, 8, no. 1 (Spring), 76ff.

1959 *Classical Inspiration in Medieval Art*, London: Chapman and Hall (and New York: Geographical Society, 1960).

1960 *The Queen and the Poet*, London: Faber and Faber.

1960 *Some Woodcuts by Hans Burgkmair, printed as an Appendix to the fourth part of Le Relazioni Universali di G. Botero, 1618*, OUP for Roxburghe Club.

1960 'Cyril Bailey', *Proceedings of the British Academy*, 46, 295ff.

1960 'The Case for Change' [Latin as an entrance requirement], *American Oxonian*, 47, 5ff.

1961 Review of O. Pächt, C. R. Dodwell and F. Wormald, *The St Alban's Psalter*, London, 1960, *Burlington Magazine*, 103, no. 695, February, 73.

1962 'Renaissance Maps of the World and Their Presuppositions', *Bulletin of the John Rylands Library*, 44, no. 2, March, 380ff.

1962 Preface to *Henry Moore*, exhibition catalogue of drawings and sculpture, with notes by the artist, Oxford, Ashmolean Museum.

1963 'The Finding of the Manuscript', *Essays on Malory*, ed. J. A. W. Bennett, Oxford: Clarendon Press, 1ff.

1963 'The Borchardt Measure', *Journal of Hellenic Studies*, 83, 154ff.

1963 'Sir George Gater', *The Wykehamist*, 1112, 1 April, 122.

1964 'Professor William Jackson', *The Times*, 20 October, 15.

1965 Introduction to A. Wilton, *Georges van Houten*, Oxford, Ashmolean Museum.

1965 'Wilfrid Blossom', *Lincoln College Record*, 1964–5, 9f.

1966 'Glass Roundels in the Upper Library', *Lincoln College Record*, 1965–6, 7f.

1967 'Bodley's Librarian', *Bodleian Library Record*, 7, no. 6, February, 7f.

1967 'Isobel Henderson', *Lincoln College Record*, 1966–7, 26.

1967 'Patrick Duncan', *The Times*, 5 June, 10.

1967 Review of *The Brunt Report on the Ashmolean*, *Oxford Magzine*, November, 88.

1967 *The Mosaics of Rome from the Third to the Fourteenth Centuries*, London: Thames and Hudson (also Greenwich: New York Geographical Society, Austrian, German and French editions, *Die Mosaiken von Rom*, Vienna-Munich [Schroll], 1968, and Leipzig [Seeman], 1968; *Les Mosaiques Chrétiens des Eglises de Rome, 3me-14me Siècle*, Paris, 1972.

1968 'Bishop A. T. P. Williams', *The Wykehamist*, 1167, 20 March, 202.

1968 'Dick Roseveare', *The Wykehamist*, 1170, 18 June, 234f.

1968 'Sir Walter Ralegh's Library', *The Library*, 23, no. 4, December, 285ff.

1970 'Sir John Beazley', *The Times*, 7 May, 15 (unsigned).

1970 'H. S. Vere-Hodge', *The Times*, 29 October, 12.

1970 'Sir John Beazley', *Lincoln College Record*, 1969–70, 18f.

1971 'Carew Ralegh's Copy of Spenser', *The Library*, 26, no. 1, March, 1ff.

1971 'Spencer Stotesbury Gwatkin Leeson', in *Dictionary of National Biography 1951–1960*, eds. E. T. Williams and H. M. Palmer (Oxford: Clarendon Press), 618ff.

1972 *Sigena. Romanesque Paintings in Spain and the Winchester Bible Artists*, London – New York: Harvey Miller.

1972 'The Sigena Paintings and the Second Style of Rubrication in the Winchester Bible', *Kunsthistorische Forschungen. . . . Otto Pächt*, eds. A. Rosenauer and G. Weber (Salzburg), 90ff.

1972 'St Hugh's Bible', *Times Literary Supplement*, 1 December, 1461 (letter).

1972 'George Cruse Laws', *Lincoln College Record*, 1971–2, 32f.

1973 'Beatrice Forder', *Winchester Cathedral Record*, 42, 5.

1973 'The Spanish Fresco Mystery', BBC Radio 3, 15 October.

1974 'Ebenezer Oakshot', in H. Berkeley, *The Life and Death of Rochester Sneath* (London), 78f.

1974 Film, *Four High Masters*, Antony Jay Productions.

1974 'H. H. Cox', *The Times*, 9 July, 17.

1974 'Sir Walter Moberly', *Lincoln College Record*, 1973–4, 22ff.

1974 'Egon Wellesz', *Lincoln College Record*, 1973–4, 25ff.

1975 Review of C. M. Kauffmann, *Romanesque Manuscripts 1066-1150*, Harvey Miller, *Times Literary Supplement*, 22 August, 949 (unsigned).

1975 'Egon Wellesz', *Proceedings of the British Academy*, LXI, 567ff.

1975 'Introduction' to H. S. Vere-Hodge, *Five Overs and Two Wides*, privately printed (with illustrations by Phillida Gili), xi-xvii.

1975 'Love's Martyr', *Huntington Library Quarterly*, 39, no. 1, November, 29ff.

1975 'The Opening of the Library', *Lincoln College Record*, 1974–5, 8ff.

1976 'The Malory Manuscript', *The Trusty Servant*, June, 2ff.

1976 (With others) *Oxford Stone Restored*, Oxford: Clarendon Press.

1977 'The Matter of Malory', *Times Literary Supplement*, 18 February, 193 (article reviewing *The Winchester Malory*, facsimile edited by N. R. Ker, Oxford, 1976; and *Sir Thomas Malory, The Morte D'Arthur*, edited by P. Needham, Morgan Library, 1976).

1977 The Delight of Bringing History to Book', *The Times Saturday Review*, 19 February, 9 (reprinted in *Amphora*, 29, no. 3, 8ff.)

1977 'Mrs Gertrude Montgomery', *Lincoln College Record*, 1976–7, 23ff.

1979 'E. Vinaver', *Lincoln College Record*, 1978–9, 26.

1979 'The Winchester Mystery', *The Guardian*, 14 July, 9.

1980 'St Alban's and Winchester Contributions to St Hugh's Bible', in *Manuscripts at Oxford: R. W. Hunt Memorial Exhibition*, eds. A. C. de la Mare and B. C. Barker Benfield, Oxford, Bodleian Library, 33ff.

1980 Review of M. Biddle *et al.*, *Winchester in the Early Middle Ages: an Edition and Description of the Winton Domesday*, Oxford, 1976, *Antiquaries Journal*, 60, 393ff.

1980 'In the Shadow of the Slump', *The Guardian*, 29 September.

1980 'E. Sexton', *Lincoln College Record*, 1979–80, 35f.

1981 *The Two Winchester Bibles*, Oxford: Clarendon Press.

1981 'The Paintings of the Holy Sepulchre Chapel', *Winchester Cathedral Record*, 50, 10ff.

1981 'A £1000 Million Defence against Research Cuts', *The Guardian*, 3 August, 7.

1981 (with H. W. Singer), 'Temple and Unemployment', *The Times*, 15 October, 15 (letter).

1982 Review of R. Custance *et al.*, *Winchester College: Sixth Centenary Essays*, OUP, *Times Literary Supplement*, 20 August, 907.

1983 'Robert Birley', *Balliol College Annual Record*, 16ff,

1983 Untitled piece in ed. David Astor, *Robert Birley, 1903–82*, OUP, 7ff.

1984 'Introduction and Catalogue of the Initials' to go with microfilm of *The Winchester Bible*, World Microfilm Publications, London.

1984 'Some New Figures by the Entangled Figures Master', *Burlington Magazine*, vol. 126, no. 973, April, 230ff.

1984 'Eightieth Birthday Speech', *Lincoln College Record*, 1983–4, 9ff.

1986 'Henry Moore', *Lincoln College Record*, 1985–6, 36f.

1986 (With A. Jordan), 'The Siena Portrait of Queen Elizabeth I', *Apollo*, 124, no. 296, October, 306ff.

Index